The Essential Guide to
Back Garden Self-Sufficiency

CW00952245

The Essential Guide to
Back Garden
Self-Sufficiency

Edited by Carleen Madigan

TIMBER PRESS
London

Art direction and book design by Dan O. Williams
Text production by Dan O. Williams and Jennifer Jepson Smith

Cover design and illustration © James Nunn
Additional back cover illustrations by Bethany Caskey: top row left;
Beverly Duncan: bottom row right; Douglas Paisley: bottom row left;
© Elayne Sears: top row centre and right, bottom row centre.
Interior illustration credits appear on page 337

Indexed by Nancy D. Wood

This edition published in 2010 © Timber Press, Inc.
Second printing 2013

2 The Quadrant
135 Salusbury Road
London NW6 6RJ
www.timberpress.co.uk

Most of the text in this book is excerpted from previously published
books by Storey Publishing. For a complete list of titles and author
credits, see page 338.

To convert measurements to metric and other UK household
equivalents, please see the table on page 336.

Printed in the United States by Versa Press

Cataloguing-in-Publication Data is available from the British Library.

Nine bean rows will I have there,
a hive for the honey bee;
And live alone in the bee-loud glade.

W.B. Yeats, "The Lake Isle of Innisfree"

Back Garden Fruit and Nuts
85

Poultry for Eggs and Meat
221

The Vegetable Patch
17

contents

Meat and Dairy 257

Home-grown Grains 179

Food from the Wild 325

Easy, Fragrant Herbs 149

Welcome!

In the early 1980s, my family lived in a small house on what I now realize was a half-acre garden situated on a quiet, tree-lined street. I was just a small child then, but I still remember the vegetable patch my parents planted each year, tucked away in the far corner of our property. There must have been tomatoes and lettuce and leeks, along with the other usual vegetable garden suspects, but I paid more attention to the raspberries that scrambled along the back fence. They were sun-warmed and sweet, and whenever I snatched a handful of ripe berries and hid from my sister in the evergreens at the bottom of the garden, I felt that I had the makings of my own kingdom, or a stronghold of self-sufficiency.

In the spring, my mother and I walked the abandoned railway tracks, collecting wild asparagus. My father caught trout and smoked them, and the lingering aroma of the steel smoker inhabited the garage for the rest of the year. With some neighbours, my mother started a community support group that collected imperfect vegetables and fruit from local farmers, bottled them, and donated the goods to feed the needy in our town. She bottled produce for us, too, and a whole room in our house was filled with sparkling jars of cherries, peaches, tomatoes, and green beans. And, of course, there were her home-baked pitta bread, cereal, soups, casseroles, and pies. There was always something cooking in the kitchen.

A whole room in our house was filled with sparkling jars of cherries, peaches, tomatoes, and green beans.

John Seymour's classic *The Complete Book of Self-Sufficiency* was published in 1976. He advocated living as close to nature as possible and his book soon became an inspiration for disillusioned city dwellers seeking a more wholesome existence in the countryside. At about the same time the BBC comedy series 'The Good Life' showed (albeit in sometimes far-fetched form) that you don't need to live in the country to keep chickens and pigs and grow your own vegetables. And this is where *The Essential Guide to Back Garden Self-Sufficiency* comes in. The skills of baking bread, making cheese or preserves, and growing a few herbs can be enjoyed by everyone wherever they live.

Today, these traditional skills of making things from scratch are being rediscovered by a whole new generation of readers who want to learn what it takes to provide their own food and

> It's about loving the process of creating something delicious and the joy of sharing my creations with people I care about.

enjoy the pleasure of the home-made life. They aren't farmers, but they have a little bit of garden or allotment (or perhaps dreaming of one) and a whole lot of passion. Maybe you're one of those people.

If so, *The Essential Guide to Back Garden Self-Sufficiency* is for you. It's an introduction to the best information about food production. I hope it'll inspire you and give you a starting point, a foothold to learn a few practical skills. Whether it's bottling tomatoes from your own garden or making fresh goat's cheese from an animal you milked yourself, this book will show you the way forward. Maybe you don't have a garden or a goat, and you'll be bottling tomatoes from a nearby farm and making cheese with milk from a local dairy. It's a good start. It's also a way to pass along to your own children skills for self-sufficiency and to create in their minds the memory of time spent doing something practical and fun with family and friends.

It's amazing to me that I can still remember so much of my food life from when I was a child. Something from those days must have stuck with me, because I've become a person who gardens, forages, bakes, makes cheese, and preserves fruits and vegetables, much like my parents did. Through the summer, I harvest fresh vegetables from my garden (though most of my produce comes from a local farm), forage for wild mushrooms, freeze blueberries and cherries, and bottle apple purée, tomatoes, and peaches. On weekends during the winter, there's almost always a pot of soup on the stove and a loaf of bread or a tray of biscuits in the oven. And as long as my local dairy farmers are milking their herd of grass-fed cows, I'll be making my own mozzarella and cottage cheese.

But for me, it's not about *food production,* which sounds like an industrial term better suited to a factory farm than to my tiny kitchen. It's about loving the process of creating something delicious and the joy of sharing my creations with people I care about.

I hope that, after reading this book, you'll discover these joys for yourself!

Carleen Madigan

About Back Garden Self-Sufficiency

Whether you're starting off with an acre or two or just a ground floor flat with a small patio, there's something you can do to provide some of your own food.

Who knew, for instance, that an ordinary back garden can be planted to wheat, which you can harvest and grind for flour? Or that you can grow as many as 15 pounds of tomatoes from just one self-watering container on the back patio? Or that you can keep as many as a dozen chickens on a quarter-acre plot and still have space for vegetables, fruit trees, herbs, and even pigs? How exciting is that!

But before you pile the kids into the old minivan and head out in search of dairy goats and hazelnut trees, take some time to consider the logistics of what you're about to embark on.

Step into the Garden

The first step is simply to step outside. Take a look around and evaluate your property. How much space do you have to work with? Does your garden get enough sun to support a veg patch? (Most vegetables and fruits need six to eight hours a day in order to thrive.) How much rain does your region normally receive, and at what times during the year? Will you need to irrigate frequently? Do you live in a place that is prone to heavy frosts during the winter, or will you be able to grow a few hardy greens through the colder months?

If you're thinking about keeping animals, there's a lot to mull over, but you can start with the space they'll require. Chickens and rabbits can be kept in fairly small quarters. Pigs need a sur- prisingly small amount of space, too (see page 286). You really shouldn't think about keeping larger animals like goats, sheep, and cows, though, unless you've got at least a quarter acre to devote to pasture.

Consider Your Preferences

What kinds of food do you eat the most? Cour- gettes are one of the easiest and most productive vegetable gar- den plants you can grow, but if you don't really like courgettes there's no sense in planting them. A good plan is to make a list of the foods you and your family eat on a daily basis and start with that. You can always add a few fun things, too, but better to have your plot stuffed with carrots and tomatoes you know you'll eat than exotic pep- pers you've never tried before.

Another preference to consider is how much work you really want to do. For example, perennial fruit trees are a lot less labour intensive than most vegetables. Although the idea of making your own cheese from fresh milk may be wildly appealing to you, the thought of being tied to milking a cow or goat twice a day, every day for 10 months solid (never mind feeding and watering it twice a day for all 12 months), may not be. Even keeping chickens can become overwhelming if you don't have a full-time job. So start simple and start small.

Make Friends with the Neighbours

Before you begin, it makes sense to check in with your local authority to make sure you won't be breaching any bye laws. For instance, each town has its own regulations about what kinds of animals you can keep in your garden. Some towns and villages have bye laws designed to help keep up appearances, and might not like it if you suddenly decide to plant a wheat field or install a chicken coop in your front garden.

Hopefully, your shimmering rows of wholesome golden grain won't do more than raise an eyebrow among the neighbours but don't count on it. If they've had

You can grow as many as 15 pounds of tomatoes from just one self-watering container on the back patio.

only two hours of sleep because your rooster has been crowing through the night, they may be a little on the twitchy side and less than sympathetic to the goals of your self-sustaining mini-farm. It might be worth a quick meeting with the neighbours if you're hoping to keep animals that will be crowing, bleating, mooing, and emitting odours not normally found in a suburban neighbourhood. Even something as simple as the considerate placement of a compost pile (e.g., not over the fence from Mr. Wilson's barbecue) will be appreciated.

Preserve Your Harvest

Reading through *The Essential Guide to Back Garden Self-Sufficiency*, you'll see that each chapter includes not only information on growing plants and raising animals, but also tips on how to use and preserve the food you've produced. After all, in most areas of the country, there are only so many growing months in the year. Preserving food — which includes bottling, freezing, drying, and clamping root crops — makes it possible for you to eat from your own back garden all year round. And even if you don't currently have a garden or animals, you can try out many of the techniques in this book, using vegetables, fruit, meat, and milk from local farms.

What to Grow, Meal by Meal

One way to start working out what to grow is to think about what you actually eat. Try noting down what you eat during an average day and break each meal into its components. You might be surprised at how much of it you can grow yourself! For example, if your family eats a lot of pasta sauce, you'll want to start your vegetable garden with plenty of tomatoes, onions, peppers, and garlic. Your herb garden should have oregano, thyme, rosemary, and perhaps a bay tree (which can be brought indoors during severe winters). When harvest time rolls around, you can make a few batches of napoletana and bottle or freeze it for the winter.

How Much Food Can You Produce?

The following illustrations show some of the possibilities for the amount of food that can be produced in an average garden. A quarter of an acre, planned out well and cultivated intensively, can produce most of the food for a small family. Adding another quarter acre of paddock enables the family to keep a couple of milking goats or raise steers for beef. These are just examples of what can be done in this amount of space, allowing for a fair amount of diversity. You may decide to forgo the fruit trees and vegetables and just fill the land with oats. Or you might want simply a flock of chickens and nothing else.

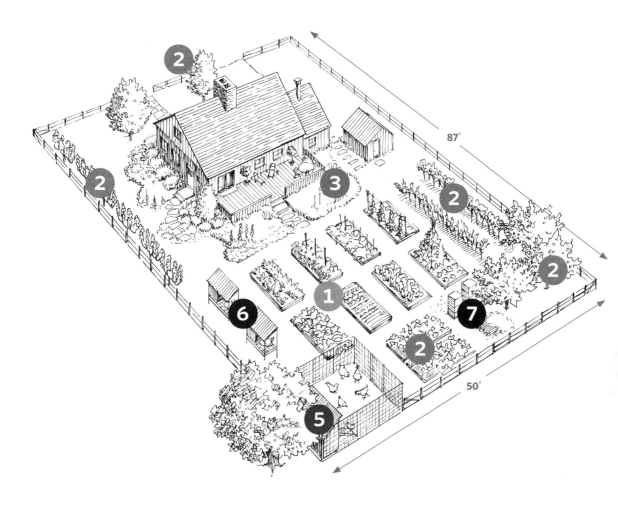

1 Vegetables	8 beds, each 4×8 feet
2 Fruits and nuts	various fruit trees, grapevines and berry canes, strawberry beds, and espaliered fruit along the fence line
3 Herbs	tea herbs like bergamot, anise, lavender, and catmint
4 Grains	not enough space to produce a reasonable quantity
5 Poultry	6 chickens
6 Meat or dairy animals	rabbits; not enough space to keep large animals
7 Wild foods	2 beehives

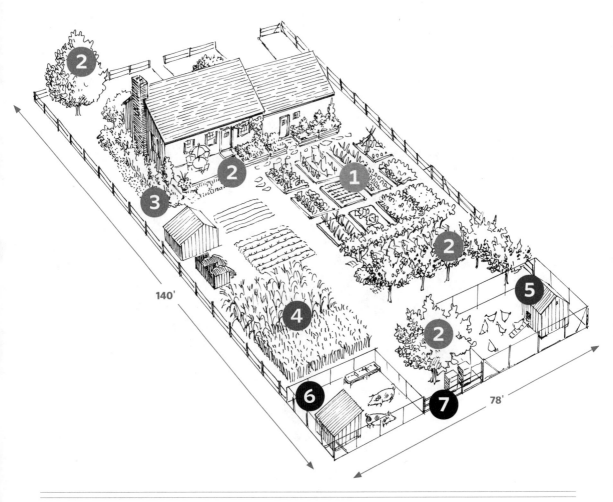

①	**Vegetables**	12 beds, each 4×8 feet
②	**Fruits and nuts**	various fruit trees, grapevines and berry canes, strawberry beds, and a kiwi arbour
③	**Herbs**	culinary herbs like thyme, tarragon, chives, and sage
④	**Grains**	25×50-foot patch of a single grain, like wheat or oats
⑤	**Poultry**	12 chickens
⑥	**Meat or dairy animals**	2 pigs, rabbits; not enough space to keep large animals
⑦	**Wild foods**	2 beehives

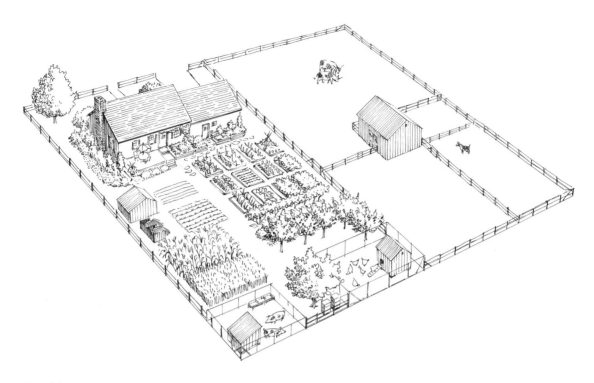

By adding a quarter acre of paddock, you'd be able to keep two or three goats for milk or a beef steer to raise through the summer.

Estimating Harvest

It's difficult to say exactly how much food you'll be able to produce from your garden, since so much depends on the kinds of vegetables, fruits, and animals you select, what the weather is like, how long your growing season is, and how intensively you're planting. But to give you a general idea of just how much it's possible to produce, given the quarter-acre layout on page 14, here are some approximate numbers:

- 50 pounds of wheat
- 280 pounds of pork
- 120 cartons of eggs
- 100 pounds of honey

- 25 to 75 pounds of nuts
- 600 pounds of fruit
- 2,000+ pounds of vegetables

purple
coneflower

sugar snap
peas

acorn squash

CHAPTER 1

The Vegetable Patch

Your first vegetable patch doesn't have to be an attempt to recreate the Eden Project. Tim Smit had a little more budget to play with than most of us—not to mention a few more staff—and gardening can be as simple or as complicated (feel free to substitute "inexpensive or costly" there) as you want to make it. The simplest version, assuming you have no land and very little money? Buy a bag of compost and two tomato plants, slice two Xs into the bag, and plant the tomatoes directly into the compost. Done! An instant garden that can be set out in any sunny spot.

The next steps up from there, of course, are planting containers (self-watering containers — see page 28 — are an especially good method) or digging in with a fully blown veg patch. As you gain experience, you might eventually want to try growing most or all of your own vegetables. It's surprising just how many pounds of food can be produced from a small plot, with

the right planning and careful attention paid to soil preparation, watering, weeding, and succession planting. Crop yields will vary quite a lot, depending on which cultivars you choose to plant (cherry tomatoes or plum tomatoes?), weather conditions, and soil fertility, but it's possible to get at least a general idea of how much you can produce (see page 15). Keep in mind, though, that this kind of undertaking is a lot of work. Start off small, maybe with just a few plants, so you don't get overloaded and become disappointed when things don't work out.

Chances are, if you're gardening for quantity, you'll want to preserve some of your harvest for the off-season. Even just a couple of tomato plants may produce more than you can eat off the vine. There are several ways to "put food by," including clamping root vegetables, freezing, drying, and bottling (see pages 56, 78, 79, and 80), to ensure that you have plenty of food to last once the growing season is over.

Starting Off On The Right Foot

Starting a vegetable garden is exciting, but it can be a little intimidating, too. Every gardener dreams of a bumper harvest, but it's hard to know how to manage the details of planting and caring for so many different crops. Here are some basic principles to keep in mind.

- **Keep it simple and start small.** Don't try to grow everything! Plant just a few easy-to-grow crops.

- **Start composting.** Once you've used compost, you'll realize you can never have too much!

- **Mulch.** To control weeds and retain soil moisture, cover garden beds with a thick layer of organic mulch.

- **Visit your garden often.** Pull weeds as soon as you see them, add mulch where it's thin, water plants that are dry, redirect wayward stems, look for signs of pests and diseases, and check for produce that's ready to harvest.

- **Take notes.** Start a journal to record spring weather, what and when you planted and transplanted, when certain pests emerged, and how much you harvested.

- **Grow what you can't buy.** Concentrate on crops that you can't find at your supermarket and ones that offer unusual colour or taste.

- **Plant crops you love.** If you adore tomatoes or peppers, grow several cultivars. Try to avoid growing the same selections offered in the high street.

- **Try crops your neighbours swear by.** It helps to know what crops are easy to grow in your area — and when they're easiest to grow. Ask your neighbours, along with experts at garden centres, garden clubs, or the local allotment.

- **Be adventurous.** Experimentation is one of the most enjoyable aspects of having a garden. Try growing some unusual edibles just for fun — purple-fleshed potatoes, white pumpkins, blue carrots, or kohlrabi, to name just a few examples.

Easy Veg Picks

While the list of easiest crops varies depending on your local conditions, there are a few super-simple standouts. Radishes and green beans top most gardeners' "no-fail" lists. Other easy crops include potatoes, summer squash, courgettes, garlic, leaf lettuce, peas, Swiss chard, and kale. Tomatoes are a bit more difficult but not by much. The newer compact hybrid tomatoes developed for patio culture are especially easy.

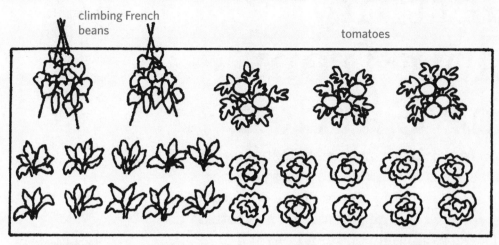

climbing French beans

tomatoes

early root crops and courgettes

early lettuce

10'

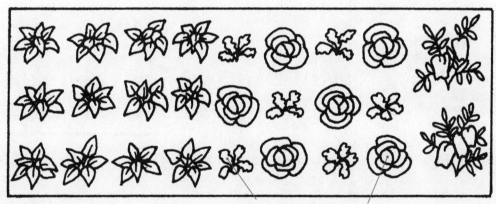

spinach

broccoli/salad greens

peppers

10'

Carefully managed, even a small plot will produce quite a bit of food and will leave you time to learn about and enjoy caring for a vegetable garden. If you have lots of space and want to try a larger garden, make it no more than 10 feet by 20 feet. Keep in mind that the ideal size for your garden depends on the crops you want to plant, too. Crops like French beans, lettuce, spinach, peppers, and carrots are perfect for a small garden, since the plants are small enough to allow you to fit a variety of crops into the available space. However, if pumpkins and squash are high up on your planting list, you'll need to prepare a bigger garden, as just one of these plants can cover half of the bed pictured above.

Getting More from the Garden

If you're hoping to make the most of a small space, you should do some advance planning. Learning about site preparation, intensive gardening practices, crop rotation, and succession planting can help you increase yields considerably.

Start your vegetable garden with a plan, just as if you were designing a flower bed. Lay it out on paper, using tracing pads or graph paper. You'll have a choice of several grid sizes; four squares to the inch is most practical for laying out a garden to scale.

Tracing paper allows you to overlay this year's garden plan on last year's (and even that of two years ago) to plan crop rotations easily. Note each vegetable variety in the layout and, after you plant, the date of planting. It's important to ensure proper spacing so you can calculate how much seed to purchase.

To get maximum sun, plant the tallest crops on the garden's north side so they won't shade shorter ones, or run your rows north and south. Plant vegetable families together so you can plan the rotation of crops in subsequent years.

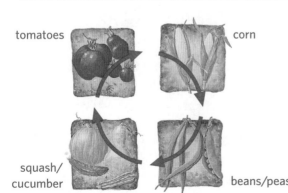

tomatoes

corn

squash/
cucumber

beans/peas

A Sun-Blocker Rotation

Trellised tomatoes, beans, peas, and cucumbers, along with corn, can grow 8 to 10 feet tall. To avoid these taller plantings casting shade on other crops, keep these in one rotation on the northeastern side of the garden.

Garden Planning Chart

Vegetable	Seeds or Plants for a 50 Row	Distance between Rows	Amount per Person	Spacing between Plants
Beans, dry	4 oz. seeds	18"	20-30' of row	6-8"
Beans, shell	4 oz. seeds	18"	30' of row	8-10"
Beans, green	4 oz. seeds	18"	30' of row	2-4"
Beetroot	½ oz. seeds	12"	10-15' of row	2-4"
Broccoli	25 plants	24"	5 plants	12-24"
Brussels sprouts	25 plants	24"	5 plants	12-24"
Cabbage	25 plants	24"	10 plants	12-18"
Carrots	⅛ oz. seeds	12"	10' of row	1-3"
Cauliflower	25 plants	24"	5 plants	14-24"
Corn	1 oz. seeds	24"	25' of row	9-15"
Cucumbers	¼ oz. seeds	48"	10-15' of row	12"
Eggplant/aubergine	25 plants	24"	5 plants	18-36"
Endive	⅛ oz. seeds	18"	10' of row	8-12"
Kale	⅛ oz. seeds	18"	12' of row	18-24"
Kohlrabi	⅛ oz. seeds	18"	10' of row	3-6"
Leeks	⅛ oz. seeds	6"	10-20' of row	6"
Lettuce, head	⅛ oz. seeds	15"	5-10' of row	10-15"
Lettuce, leaf	⅛ oz. seeds	12"	5-10' of row	10-12"
Melons	12 plants	48"	3 plants	12"
Onion sets	1 lb. sets	12"	10-20' of row	2-4"
Parsnips	¼ oz. seeds	18"	5-10' of row	3-6"
Peas	8 oz. seeds	24"	50-100' of row	1-3"
Peppers	33 plants	18"	5 plants	12-24"
Potatoes	33 plants	30"	50' of row	9-12"
Pumpkins	¼ oz. seeds	60"	1 hill	36-60"
Radishes	½ oz. seeds	12"	5' of row	1-2"
Salsify	½ oz. seeds	18"	5' of row	2-4"
Spinach	½ oz. seeds	15"	20' of row	2-6"
Squash	¼ oz. seeds	60"	1 hill	24-48"
Swiss chard	¼ oz. seeds	18"	5' of row	3-6"
Tomatoes	12-15 plants	30"	5 plants	12-24"
Turnips	¼ oz. seeds	15"	10' of row	2-6"
Watermelon	30 plants	72"	2 or 3 hills	72-96"
Zucchini/courgette	¼ oz. seeds	60"	1 hill	24-48"

Raised Beds: Easier Gardening, Healthier Crops

A raised bed is a mound of loose, well-prepared soil, 6 to 8 inches high. The beds can be permanent, with edgings of stone, blocks, timbers, or railway sleepers, or they can be remade each time the garden is planted.

Raised beds are particularly helpful if you are working with heavy soils that drain poorly. In the long run, easy maintenance and the use of hand tools make this method extremely appropriate for the home garden.

What are some other benefits? First, no one actually steps into the raised beds, so the soil always stays porous and loose and never compacts. This loose soil provides good drainage, enabling water, air, and fertilizer to penetrate easily to the roots of your plants.

If you make permanent raised beds, the garden path next to a raised bed is never used for growing vegetables. Because it is constantly being walked on and packed down, it stays dry, clean, and relatively weed-free.

Because the beds are isolated by the paths between them, you can rotate the varieties of vegetables you plant in each bed each year. This allows you to keep one particular family of vegetables from consuming all the same kind of soil nutrients. It also discourages insect pests and pathogens from remaining in the garden soil over the winter and infecting the next season's crop.

Finally, the raised-bed gardening system makes a beautiful garden that is always orderly and organized because it is so easy to maintain. You can reach into every corner to cultivate the beds and to pull young weeds as they appear. Succession planting will keep the garden constantly filled with vegetables and pleasing to the eye.

Raised beds can be supported with boards (as shown above) or other materials, or they can simply be raked into mounds (as shown on the facing page).

1. To make a raised bed, mark the area with stakes and string. Sixteen inches is a good width, but some gardeners prefer beds 3 to 4 feet wide. Make your bed any convenient length. Walkways can be up to 20 inches wide.

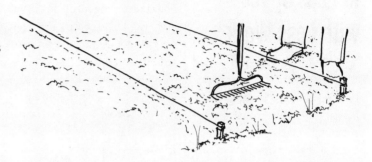

2. Using a rake, pull the soil from the walkway to the top of the bed. Stand in one walkway and draw soil toward you from the opposite walkway. Do the same on the other side.

3. Enrich the bed with compost, manure, or other organic materials. Then level the top of the bed with the back of the rake. The sides should slope at a 45-degree angle. A lip of soil around the top edge of a new bed helps reduce erosion.

Grow More in Less Space with Less Work

Wide, deep, raised-bed planting has many practical advantages in addition to offering a better growing environment. Because of the high ratio of bed space to walking space, you can grow substantially more vegetables in substantially less space. Switching from "gardener-centred" to "plant-centred" spacing results in dramatic savings. Raised beds are also less work, because they're easier to weed, water, and fertilize. And after the first year, weeding is almost a thing of the past.

Paths are narrower in a bed-based garden because they are used just for walking, not for wide cultivating machines. There are also fewer paths, because they do not occur between every row. In a traditional garden, the recommended spacing between rows is determined more by the needs of the cultivator than by the needs of the cultivar. In beds, most vegetables can be grown much closer together, resulting in a further saving of space.

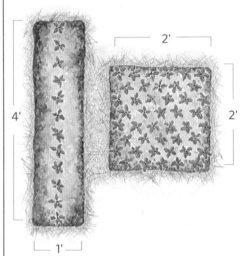

Each of these beds takes up 4 square feet of garden space. But planted in a row, beetroot yield only about a dozen plants in this amount of space, whereas a staggered, wide-bed planting scheme yields more than three times that many.

Successful Crop-Rotation Practices

Plant	Follow with	Do not follow with
Beans	cauliflower, carrots, broccoli, cabbage, corn	onions, garlic
Beetroot	spinach	—
Carrots	lettuce, tomatoes	dill
Cole crops	beans, onions	tomatoes
Cucumbers	peas, radishes	potatoes
Kale	beans, peas	brassicas
Lettuce	carrots, cucumbers, radishes	—
Onions	radishes, lettuce	beans
Peas	carrots, beans, corn	—
Potatoes	beans, cabbage, corn, turnips	tomatoes, squash, pumpkins
Radishes	beans	brassicas
Tomatoes	carrots, onions	brassicas

Succession Planting

1. Harvest your early crop and then turn over the soil, incorporating any remaining plant material. Add a little fertilizer, such as well-rotted manure, to the row.

2. Level off the soil, pulling your garden rake straight down the row.

3. Sprinkle the seeds in the row and then pat down the soil by hand. Bury the seeds with about four times their diameter of soil, then pat it down again.

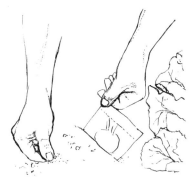

4. Water the seeds and watch how quickly they come up during the warm summer months. Weed frequently to eliminate competition for the young plants.

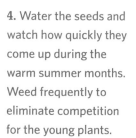

Stagger Plantings for Better Control

Even in the smallest garden, an important technique for keeping the work manageable is to plant in dribs and drabs: Plant a little lettuce seed now and a little more two weeks later. Though you'll want to plant some crops all at one time — like peppers or tomatoes — planting small batches of many crops is a good garden habit to cultivate. Whatever size garden you tend, you'll find that staggering the planting spreads out the harvest, and much of the attention that plants need in between, too. Instead of having a 20-foot-long row of lettuce or beetroot to thin on a given day, you'll have only a foot or two of seedlings to thin. Cover with plastic soil that's not yet planted to help it warm up, or cover it with grass clippings to keep it moist and suppress weeds. Or let the weeds germinate as a short-term cover crop and then slice them off before you plant your seeds.

Making a Garden Plan

A garden plan doesn't have to be complex. In fact, it probably shouldn't be, or it won't get done in the first place. These drawings show a kitchen garden, first in early summer and then later when the fast-growing crops are replaced by succession plantings. Each plant is identified by a number.

Key to Plants

1. Beetroot
2. French beans
3. Carrots and radishes
4. Oregano
5. Carrots
6. Pak choi
7. Lettuce
8. Chives
9. Summer squash
10. Swiss chard
11. Broccoli
12. Onions
13. Savoy cabbage
14. Peppers
15. Parsley
16. Spinach
17. Rocket
18. Red orach
19. Cucumbers
20. Dill
21. Tomatoes
22. Basil
23. Marigolds
24. Potatoes
25. Peas
26. New Zealand spinach

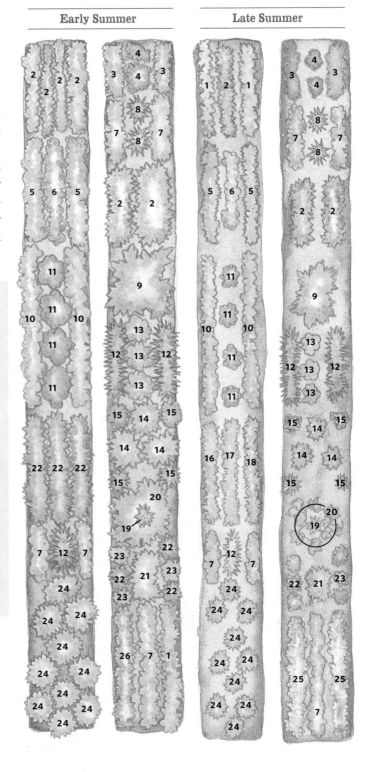

Early Summer   Late Summer

Mid-May

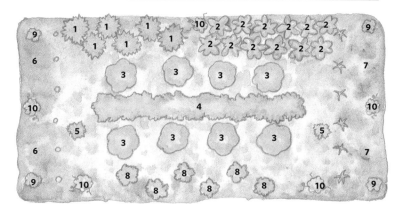

Mid-July

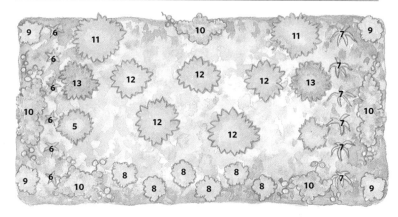

Early September

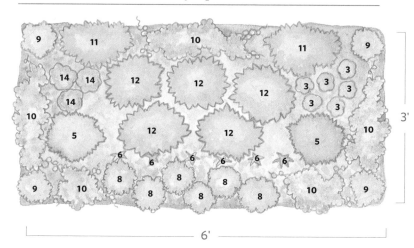

6'

3'

A Small Garden, Through the Seasons

Whether your garden is large or small, a garden plan is important to its success. With succession planting, it can provide a steady supply of great-tasting vegetables from spring through late autumn, with a few ornamental herbs and flowers adding good looks, too. The plans shown here are just a starting point; you can adapt them to grow the vegetables you and your family like most.

Key to Plants

1. Spinach
2. Beetroot
3. Lettuce
4. Radishes
5. Celery
6. Garlic
7. Leeks
8. Parsley
9. Marigolds
10. Nasturtiums
11. Tomatoes
12. Peppers
13. Basil
14. Kale

A New Way to Grow Vegetables

Many vegetable gardeners grow food for their families in the good soil of their own back gardens. But what if you don't have a back garden? How can you keep the kitchen stocked with ripe tomatoes or fresh greens if all you've got is a patio, deck, or balcony?

What about a collection of containers? Gardeners have, after all, been growing flowers, herbs, and ornamental plants that way for ages. If you can grow pansies or petunias in a pot, why not peppers, peas, or pak choi? In some ways, gardening in containers is easier than gardening in the earth — the garden plots are small and simple to manage, plants are less likely to be bothered by diseases or pests, and there are almost no weeds. That's the good news.

Compared to an earth garden, though, a traditional container garden requires frequent watering. Because vegetables tend to be larger plants that grow quickly, they need a lot of water and they need it all the time. The constant watering also creates another problem: All that water coursing through the container takes with it some of the soil's water-soluble nutrients. As a result, container gardens need to be fertilized regularly.

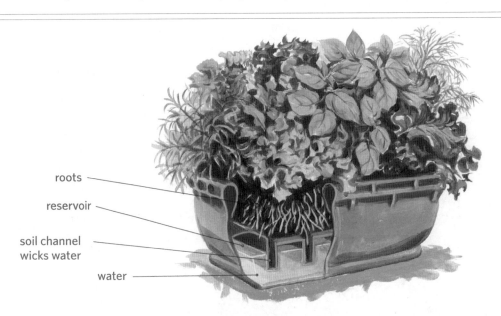

roots

reservoir

soil channel wicks water

water

Self-watering containers draw water up from below, which prevents the loss of nutrients traditional pots experience. The reservoir also supplies plants with consistent moisture; as long as the reservoir is kept full, the plants will have as much water as they need.

One solution is the self-watering container, which is different from a traditional one in that it doesn't have a hole in the bottom. Instead, it has a reservoir for water and a wicking system to make that water available to plants on demand. The result is a constant supply of water for plants and no nutrient leaching. An additional benefit for cold-climate gardeners is that, because the soil in containers warms up quickly in the spring, heat-loving plants get off to an earlier start and grow more rapidly in self-watering containers than they do in the ground.

What to Grow?

Now, what to grow? And what size container to grow it in? Much of this will depend on the varieties of plants you choose. For instance, you can grow miniature cherry tomatoes in a window box or hanging basket, but you'll need a large self-watering container with lots of soil capacity to grow a full-size beefsteak tomatoes. Another consideration is how many containers you'll be gardening in this season. If you're starting with just one, you'll be better off with a container with lots of soil space, so that you have room to grow as many different kinds of plants as you choose.

Best of the Bunch

Conventional gardening wisdom tells us that although you *can* grow vegetables in containers, they won't grow nearly as well as they would if they were in the ground. This conventional wisdom is not always true. In fact, many vegetables actually grow *better* in self-watering containers than they do in the ground. Often these are vegetables that, in addition to thriving on the consistent moisture a self-watering container offers, grow better in the warmer soil of a container or enjoy the lack of competition from weeds and other plants.

- basil
- broccoli
- Brussels sprouts
- French beans
- cabbage
- cauliflower
- Swiss chard
- aubergine
- lettuces
- onions

- pak choi
- peppers
- tomatoes

What would a garden be without flowers? Well, if you're planting a food garden, you'll probably want flowers you can eat! Edible flowers bring a spot of colour and spice to the menu, in addition to dressing up the garden.

Calendula (*Calendula officinalis*)
This large, daisylike flower adds a boost of colour to any container combination. It also provides tasty petals for a garnish in salads or with cooked vegetables.

Cornflower (*Centaurea cyanus*)
Also known as bachelor's button, and sometimes listed in catalogues under its botanical name, cornflowers are often used as a garnish in salads and desserts. Butterflies and many pollinating insects are attracted to them. Deadhead regularly to keep the plant producing.

Dianthus (*Dianthus barbatus*)
Sometimes known as sweet William, sometimes as "pinks" (though its flowers come in many other colours, too), dianthus provides colourful and spicy petals whose scent and taste are somewhat clovelike.

Marigold (*Tagetes tenuifolia*)
Not all marigolds are meant to be eaten. The ones you want in your dinner are called gem marigolds or signet marigolds. The other varieties are edible but aren't particularly tasty.

Nasturtium (*Tropaeolum majus*)
Like any other edible flower, the fragrant blossoms of nasturtium can be added to salads or used as a garnish. That's easy enough. They also make a tasty appetizer when stuffed with cream cheese (this is also a good way to eat squash and courgette blossoms, by the way). Most vegetable gardeners know that the leaves are a special, spicy addition to mesclun mixes, especially when harvested on the small side.

But wait! There's more. The seeds are edible. Don't rush out and start opening seed packets for dinner, though. What you're after are fresh, green nasturtium seeds, harvested right from the plant. Wait until the blooms have faded, then harvest the fruit that remains behind. The fruit is made up of three compartments, each of which contains a seed; separate the compartments as you harvest them.

To pickle the seeds, bring them to a boil in vinegar with salt, peppercorns, and a bay leaf and then store them (after cooling) in a clean jar in the refrigerator. Use the pickled seeds in place of capers.

Sunflower (*Helianthus annuus*)
This is edible at several stages. The immature buds are edible steamed or sautéed. If you eat the buds, though, you don't get the flowers, the petals of which add a tangy taste to salads, soups, and cooked summer vegetables. If you eat the flowers, you don't get the seeds, which are a well-known and well-liked snack.

Harvest buds before the flowers start to open. Harvest petals by pulling them from the flowers. If you don't want to share the seeds with birds and squirrels, cover the flowers with paper bags until the seeds are plump and move a bit when you wiggle them.

Violas (*Viola* spp.)
This is a catchall name for a large number of related flowers: pansies, horned violets, tufted pansies, and heartsease. There's not a flower in the garden that is more likely to put a smile on your face.

Cool- and Warm-Season Vegetables

Vegetables need a certain range of temperatures in order to grow well. Peas and spinach thrive in the cool days of early spring. Tomatoes and peppers, on the other hand, resent cool temperatures and simply won't grow until summer days begin to heat up.

The number of cool season days differs from year to year but these are typically spring and autumn days in most of the British Isles.

Cool-Season Vegetables

The cool season is that time of year when night temperatures stay above about 25°F (-4°C) and below 60°F (16°C).

The length of time cool weather lingers differs every year, but these are typically spring and autumn days in most of the British Isles.

Many cool-season crops are planted in staggered sowings to ensure a constant supply of vegetables. A safe general rule is to plant seeds every 10 to 14 days. This rule doesn't always work, however, because conditions in the garden change dramatically over the course of a spring or autumn season. As temperatures warm or cool and moisture concentrations change, the growth rates of the plants increase or decrease.

To time your staggered crops more exactly, sow the second plantings of root crops and greens, such as radishes and spinach, when the first seedlings show their first set of true leaves. For crops such as peas, make successive plantings when the seedlings are as tall as your index finger.

Cool-Season Crops

arugula/rocket	cabbage	kale	peas
beetroot	cauliflower	kohlrabi	radicchio
broad beans	Chinese cabbage	lamb's lettuce	radishes
broccoli	collards	lettuce	red mustard
broccoli raab	endive	parsley	spinach
Brussels sprouts	Florence fennel	parsnips	turnips

Warm-Season Vegetables

Planting the warm-season vegetable garden marks the end of the long transition between winter and summer and from indoor to outdoor gardening. The soil is warm enough to foster the growth of tender seeds, and the corn, tomato, and pepper plants explode with life.

Some of the plants of the warm-season garden are holdovers from spring. Carrots, potatoes, and Swiss chard can all stand cool weather, but unlike other cool-season plants, they can also tolerate or even thrive in the warm days of summer. Other warm-season crops, such as tomatoes, corn, and green beans, evolved in the semitropical regions of the world, where cool nights alternate with warm days for most of the year. This is still the best environment for their cultivated relatives; the best crops are grown where the summer nights are at least 15 degrees fahrenheit cooler than the days.

Keeping so many plants with such different likes and dis-

likes happy in one garden is a bit of a challenge, but it doesn't have to be a daunting one. Even though these plants are a varied group, they still have much in common. All of them thrive in evenly moist soil rich in organic matter and bathed in sunshine. There are some subtleties to master, but they make the resulting accomplishments that much sweeter.

Planting Phenology

Phenology is the science of using indicator plants to determine when certain weather conditions will prevail and certain insect pests will be active. Here's how you might use phenology to guide your plantings:

- Plant Swiss chard, spinach, and beetroot when the daffodils bloom.

- Sow French beans and runner beans when apple trees drop their petals.

- Transplant tomatoes, squash, and courgettes when the peonies flower.

- Transplant just before it rains, so the new transplants get well watered. Watch for swallows swooping close to the ground over fields. The insects they eat fly closer to the ground before it rains.

Warm-Season Crops

aubergine	cucumbers	runner beans
artichokes	French beans	squash
asparagus	marrow	strawberries
carrots	melons	sweet potatoes
celeriac	okra	Swiss chard
celery	peppers	tomatoes
corn	potatoes	watermelons
courgettes	pumpkins	

Extending the Season

Season extenders help you get more from the growing season in two ways: by protecting tender crops from the ravages of a late-spring frost and by helping the soil heat up quickly for warm-season crops.

Plant Protectors: Extending Your Growing Season

In some respects, the term "extenders" is a misnomer. As well as adding a few weeks to the start or end of a season, extenders actually modify the climate. They protect from not just frost but also wind, pests, rain, and snow. Low-cost, old-fashioned season extenders that remain popular and effective include cold frames, recycled plastic milk or water bottles with their bottoms removed, hay bales, newspaper, blankets, cloches, fleece, and even grocery bags with their edges turned down and weighted with soil. All work well in certain situations. We'll examine a few in some detail.

Crop Covers

Crop covers are extenders that protect your plants. There are two main kinds: fleeces and cloches.

Fleeces are soft, white "garden blankets" made of lightweight, permeable material. They require no supports and are available in numerous weights, sizes, and thicknesses. The lighter they are, the more light transmission they allow, but the lighter ones also offer less frost protection. The thicker they are, the more frost protection they provide. But the thicker covers also generate more heat — something to watch for when the sun intensifies.

Use fleeces immediately after transplanting tomatoes, aubergines, melons, cucumbers, peppers, strawberries, and other heat-loving plants. Remove them when blossoms are ready for pollination or temperatures

Fleece offers protection from frost and some pests.

exceed 85°F (29°C). In the autumn, keep covers on longer to maintain soil heat on cool evenings.

Plastic cloches are often perforated or slit to let rain or moisture through. They protect plants from pests, but they do not keep out all insects. The cloches are laid in the form of a tunnel supported by wire hoops and covered with plastic. Most offer only a few degrees of frost protection, significantly less than the thicker fleece covers. They also tend to generate more heat than fleeces, making them well suited for heat-loving plants such as cucumbers, aubergines, and melons.

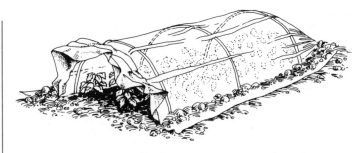

Plastic cloches supported by hoops generate more heat than fleeces do. They're best used for heat-loving crops like melons and aubergines.

Install plastic cloches as soon as the soil can be worked in the spring. They can increase vegetable germination and yields by as much as three weeks and 50 percent, especially in regions that experience a long, cold spring.

Mulches, Cool and Warm

Cool mulches control weeds by blocking visible light from reaching the soil. Many differ from warming mulches in that they reflect most of the sun's energy instead of absorb-

Starting a Hot Bed

The old-fashioned hot bed is a wonderful invention that can keep fresh lettuce on the table just about all winter long and offer perfect conditions for melons, peppers and aubergines during the summer. To build a hot bed, simply remove all the soil to a depth of 2 feet inside a cold frame. Line the earthen sides with 1- to 2-inch-thick panels of polystyrene insulation. Add a wooden frame around the insulation to brace it, if desired. Add an 18-inch layer of fresh

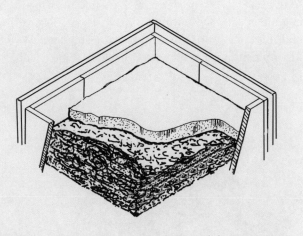

horse manure and firm well. Spread 6 inches of sand on top of the manure. Use a soil thermometer to track the temperature of the sand. As the manure composts, it will heat the sand to over 100°F (38°C). Place flats and pots of plants in the hot bed when the sand temperature drops below 90°F (32°C). The manure will heat the bed for many weeks. When the manure is composted, the hot bed can be used as a cold frame.

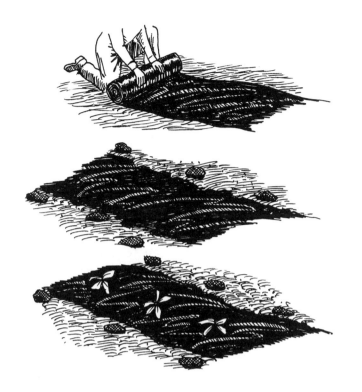

Black polyethylene mulch helps the soil warm up in spring. Seedlings can be planted directly into the plastic sheet.

ing it. Cooling mulches include straw, pine needles, and black-and-white newspaper. As they inhibit weeds, they allow water to penetrate readily. The mulch then acts as a water conservator, allowing moisture to percolate down through the soil but inhibiting evaporation. Temperatures beneath a cooling mulch can be several degrees lower than the ambient air temperature.

There are three types of warm mulches. Black polythene mulch is made of 1.25-mm black plastic sheeting. It has been used for decades, but it has some disadvantages. It is not biodegradable and is often difficult to remove from the garden. Black landscape fabric works similarly. It does not warm the soil as efficiently as black polythene, but the difference is slight. Unlike black polythene, landscape fabric allows water to seep into the soil. There is an additional dark-coloured plastic that allows a good deal of energy from the sun to warm the soil directly. It then helps retain the accumulated warmth. It is the most effective soil-warming mulch to date, but it is not biodegradable.

Mini greenhouses

Mini greenhouses are simple devices to protect individual small plants from frost. One option is the plastic milk container. Simply cut the bottom from a large container and set it over the plant. Leave off the cap for ventilation. Seedlings can be protected by setting smaller bottles over individual plants.

The best device for frost protection is the Wall-O-Water, which consists of several plastic cylinders joined together into the shape of a tepee. When you

Mini greenhouse

Wall-O-Water tepee

The cold frame is a boon to gardeners who wish to grow cool-season crops such as lettuce into the winter.

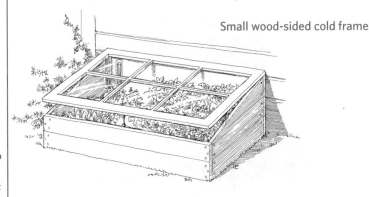

Small wood-sided cold frame

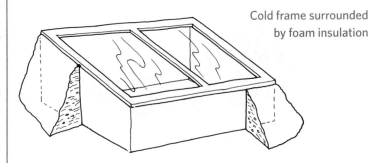

Cold frame surrounded by foam insulation

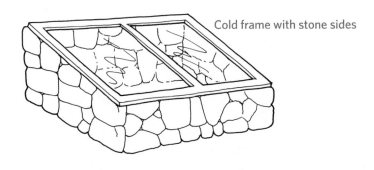

Cold frame with stone sides

place it around the plant, fill the cylinders with water. In tests among plastic milk or water bottles, cloches, and Wall-O-Water tepees, the tepees were most effective in providing frost protection.

Mini greenhouses give plants a head start on growth. However, if plants are not weaned from them by blossom time, yields will be smaller than those gathered from plants grown without the caps.

Cold Frames

The cold frame is a small, easily built structure used to lengthen the growing season. Traditional cold frames are most often made of reclaimed wood such as window frames and scaffolding planks. The headboard is about 18 inches high and the footboard is about 12 inches tall. Sloping boards connect the two and serve as support structures for the glazing. The entire structure is then set so the footboard faces south.

The cold frame becomes a small greenhouse, letting solar energy pass through to warm the soil, then trapping the heat that radiates back. This contraption is a boon to gardeners who wish to grow cool-season crops such as lettuce into the winter. For maximum heat retention, line the floor with black plastic. A thermometer in the frame helps you gauge when it's warm enough in spring to plant or becoming so hot that you need to provide ventilatation.

You can also purchase precut cold frames made with tubular polycarbonate sheets and aluminium joiners. This kind of glazing is almost as clear as glass.

Planting Dates in Relation to Frost

Hardy

Plant as soon as ground can be prepared:

asparagus	lettuce
beetroot	onions
broccoli	parsnip
cabbage	peas
carrots	radishes
chard	spinach
garlic	turnips
kale	

Semi-Hardy

Plant one to two weeks before average date of last frost:

cauliflower	potatoes

Tender

Plant on or just after average date of last frost:

green beans	sweet corn
runner beans	tomatoes

Very Tender

Plant two weeks after average date of last frost:

aubergines	melons
cucumbers	peppers
courgettes	peppers
courgettes	pumpkins
lima beans	squash

UK Weather Averages 1971–2000

MONTH	MAX TEMP [°C]	MIN TEMP [°C]	DAYS OF AIR FROST	SUNSHINE [hours]	RAINFALL [mm]	DAYS OF RAINFALL <=1mm
January	6.1	0.7	12.0	44.6	120.5	15.7
February	6.3	0.6	11.0	65.0	86.8	12.3
March	8.5	1.9	7.9	97.0	95.9	14.3
April	10.8	3.1	5.0	141.3	69.6	11.3
May	14.4	5.7	1.4	184.6	66.2	10.9
June	16.9	8.4	0.1	169.4	72.6	11.0
July	19.2	10.6	0.0	174.3	69.6	10.5
August	18.9	10.5	0.0	166.5	84.6	11.4
Sept	16.1	8.5	0.3	123.6	100.4	12.5
Oct	12.5	6.0	1.7	91.6	117.0	14.3
Nov	8.8	3.0	6.3	58.7	118.0	14.9
Dec	6.9	1.5	9.8	38.4	124.8	15.3
Year	12.1	5.1	55.6	1354.9	1126.1	154.4

Growing from Seed

If you're trying to get the most vegetables for the least amount of money, starting plants from seed is the way to go. It takes more advance preparation but is well worth the extra effort.

Starting Your Own Plants from Seeds

You'll need seeds, of course, but you'll also need a few more supplies to be successful at starting plants from seeds.

Containers

Basically, anything that can hold a seed compost, allow drainage holes, and is the right size will do. Seed-sowing trays should be 3 to 3½ inches deep and can be any size, depending on how many seeds you intend to germinate. Generally the ones you buy are made of plastic or fibre.

Peat pots are good for seeds that resent transplanting and for larger seeds. These pots are usually 2½ to 3 inches across and are combined germinating-growing-transplanting units.

Peat pellets are made of compressed peat. When placed in water, they expand into units similar in function to peat pots. They are best for larger, reliably germinating seeds and seeds that resent transplanting.

Plugs are cone- or cylinder-shaped transplants. You can buy plug trays, which have up to 200 plug holes. One seed is sown into each plug hole.

You can also use things from around the kitchen, such as coffee tins, paper cups, aluminium baking trays, milk or juice containers, and plastic food-storage containers. Before using them, wash them in soap and water and rinse them in a bleach solution (1 ounce bleach per 2 gallons water). This will eliminate diseases that might kill your seedlings.

Containers must have excellent drainage. If you make your own, be sure to punch out some drainage holes in the bottom.

Growing Mediums

There is no one perfect germinating medium, but here is a look at some of the available choices.

Baled or bagged peat moss comes from decomposed aquatic plants. It is much less widely used as gardeners become aware

Whether seed-starting containers are store-bought or recycled, they must be clean and have drainage holes in the bottom.

of the damage its use brings to wildlife habitats and our climate. Some sowing and growing mixtures still contain peat so check the labelling and choose alternatives.

Sphagnum moss is relatively sterile, lightweight, and able to absorb 10 to 20 times its weight in water. It is generally milled (shredded) for use as a seed-sowing medium.

Vermiculite is expanded mica. It holds tremendous amounts of water for long periods of time and contains a high percentage of magnesium and potassium, two elements necessary for good root growth. Although it is not usually used alone for seed germination, it is an excellent addition to a mix.

Perlite is a volcanic ash that stays cool and is therefore good in mixes used for germinating seeds that prefer lower temperatures. However, it will float to the surface when the seedbed is watered. Use the finest grade for seed germinating.

Soil from the garden should not be used to germinate seeds, unless it is first sterilized to kill weed seeds and fungi. To sterilize it, bake it in a shallow pan at 180°F (82°C) for 30 minutes. Be prepared for an unpleasant odor.

Mixtures are similar to the compost you make in your compost heap. Manufactured mixtures are checked for large large particles and balanced in terms of acidity and nutrient levels. Buy seed compost rather than multipurpose compost for sowing seed.

Double-Dig Your Garden

At about the same time that you are starting seeds, you might also start thinking about one of the best treatments for your garden: double digging.

1. Dig a trench about a foot wide and as deep as your shovel. Place soil on a tarpaulin or in a wheelbarrow.

2. Drive the tines of a garden fork as deep as you can into the bottom of the trench. Rock the handle back and forth to loosen the subsoil. Spread a little compost over the loosened soil.

3. Dig another trench alongside the first, turning the removed soil into the first trench. Continue to the far end of the bed, and fill the last trench with the soil from the first trench.

Five Easy Steps to Sowing Seeds Indoors

1. Fill a seed tray to within ¼ inch of the top with potting mixture and level the surface with a piece of wood.

2. If you are going to plant the seeds in rows, use the edge of the wood to make ¼-inch troughs in the soil. Otherwise, spread the seeds over the soil, evenly and not too thickly, then press them in with the flat side of the wood.

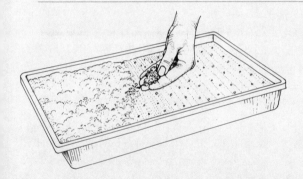

3. Cover them, remembering that they should be buried to a depth of about four times their own diameter. Try to make sure that you spread an equal amount of soil over the whole area.

4. Use a flat piece of wood to firm the soil a second time. Newly planted seeds should be watered liberally but gently — preferably with a fine spray.

5. Last, the seed trays or pots should be put in plastic bags or covered with plastic to seal in moisture. You should not have to do more watering until the seedlings emerge (at which point, the plastic should be removed).

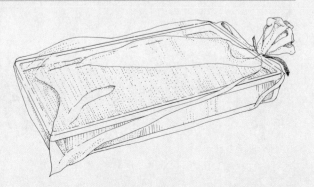

Suspend standard fluorescent lights 8 to 12 inches above seed trays.

The first sprouts you will see are seed leaves, which are food-storage cells. Once the first true leaves develop, start fertilizing. Use a soluble plant food at one-quarter the label strength when seedlings are small. Increase to half strength as the plants mature. When bottom-watering young seedlings, mix the fertilizer into the water; later, the seedlings can be fertilized from above.

Helping Your Seeds Germinate and Grow

Provide your seeds with the following environmental conditions:

- **Light** Place them near a sunny window with a southern exposure or under cool-white fluorescent bulbs. If they are by a windowsill, turn newly sprouted seedlings regularly so they will grow straight and evenly.

- **Warmth** Most seeds germinate and grow best in a spot where the temperature remains 70 to 75°F (21 to 24°C). Most seedlings prefer normal room temperatures of 60 to 70°F (16 to 21°C).

- **Moisture and humidity** Keep the seed compost moist but never soaking wet. Slip your seed trays into plastic bags or cover them with glass until the seeds germinate. Remove the cover as soon as the seeds sprout. Check the new seedlings every day to see if the medium is lighter in colour, indicating it is drying out. Water from the bottom until the seedlings are fairly large to avoid the disturbance of overhead watering.

When to Transplant

Seedlings started in trays should be transplanted to a larger container before going into the garden, or at least be thinned so they won't become crowded, leggy, or weak. Seedlings started in individual pots do not need transplanting.

Transplant or thin when the seedlings have developed four true leaves. If thinning, leave at least 1 inch between seedlings. Larger seedlings need more space. When transplanting, water the seedlings thoroughly first. If they're going into peat pots or peat pellets, wet the peat as well. Premoisten any mediums the seedlings are going into. Fill a container with the medium and then open a hole in the center deep and wide enough to fit a seedling's roots.

Pricking Out Seedlings

1. Using a spoon handle or fork, gently lift the seedling from the tray. Separate it carefully so as not to break any more roots than necessary. Always handle a seedling by its leaves, never by the stem.

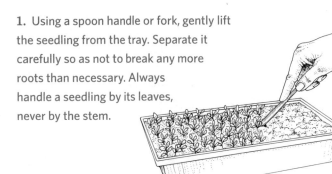

2. Lower the seedling into the new hole, placing it slightly deeper than it was growing in the seed tray, and press gently on the medium.

Transplants may droop or wilt, but they will recover if given the proper care. Some plants benefit from pinching while in the transplant stage. Simply reach into the centre of the plant and nip out the growing tip.

Special Seed Treatments

Many seeds require special handling to ensure that they will sprout. Check the package or ask your nursery whether your selections require any of the following techniques.

Scarification. Nick the outer shell with a file or knife to make it easier for the plant to start growing.

Soaking. Pour hot water over the seed and let it cool overnight before sowing.

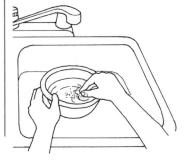

Stratification. Plants often need a re-creation of natural cycles for seeds to grow. Place the seed in a sealed container or plastic bag with four to five times its volume of moist vermiculite. Place the container in a warm spot for warm stratification or in the refrigerator for cold stratification (in the freezer if 32°F [0°C] is required). After the first month or so, examine the seed every few weeks. When small, white primary roots appear, sow the seed in soil or potting mixture immediately.

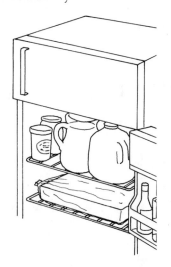

Getting Plants Ready for the Garden

Hardening off is a process that acclimatizes plants to new environments. It gradually toughens their tissues so they can adjust to a more challenging environment. One to two weeks before transplanting to the garden, place the young plants outdoors on a patio or step, first on a cloudy day,

Harden off plants by putting them outdoors in a sheltered spot for a week or two before they go into the garden.

- If the soil is dry on planting day, use a sprinkler on the rows after planting.

- Keep the soil slightly moist until the seedlings come up. Once the seeds germinate, don't let them dry out.

- Watering is usually unnecessary early in the spring, when most garden soils have quite a bit of moisture in them.

- After a rain or watering, a clay-type soil may become so hard that young seedlings can't burst through. Here's how to beat crusty soil: Drag a garden rake carefully over the seedbed with just enough force to break up the crust. The tines should penetrate the soil only about ¼ inch. You may have to water hard-packed seedbeds before loosening the soil.

then on sunny days. Mild breezes will help strengthen their stems. If a frost is expected, bring them indoors and place them back outside the next day.

Sowing Seeds Outdoors

To start an outdoor seedbed, create a loose bed 6 to 8 inches deep. Use a rotavator to make it easy and fast. Excellent seedbeds can be readied with hand tools, also.

1. Use a string to establish the edge of the row. It tells you where your first path will be. Stay right there in the path to plant, as well as to perform your other garden chores.

   Use a rake to mark the exact width of beds, making them at least 15 to 16 inches. Drag your rake down the bed, keeping the edge of the rake close to the string. Rake only the areas where you're going to broadcast seeds. Smooth the soil with the back of the rake until the seedbed is smooth and level. Remove large stones, clumps of soil, and large pieces of organic matter.

2. Sprinkle or broadcast the seeds over the bed as you would with grass seed.

3. Firm them in for good germination, using the back of a regular hoe. To germinate well, seeds should come in good contact with warm, moist soil on all sides.

4. Now comes the important step — covering the seeds with just the right amount of soil. Small seeds like carrots and most annuals usually need about ¼ to ½ inch of soil to cover them. Larger seeds such as peas and beans need about 1 inch. A rule of thumb for seeds is to cover them with enough moist soil to equal four times their own diameter.

The easy way to cover seeds is to use a rake and pull soil from 1 to 2 feet beyond the row up onto the seedbed. The important thing is to lift up the soil onto the bed and not to rake into the seedbed. Once you have little mounds of soil sitting on the entire seedbed, smooth them out gently with the back of the rake, being careful not to disturb the seeds. Once the bed has been planted, the strings and stakes can be removed.

Four Easy Steps to Sowing Seeds Outdoors

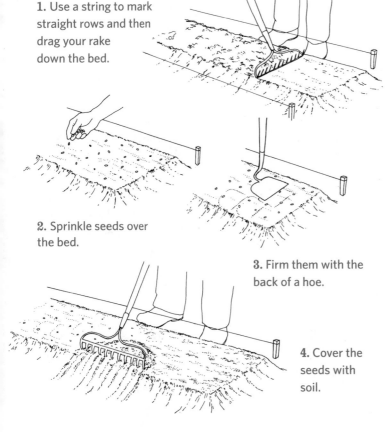

1. Use a string to mark straight rows and then drag your rake down the bed.

2. Sprinkle seeds over the bed.

3. Firm them with the back of a hoe.

4. Cover the seeds with soil.

High-Yield Gardening

People who have acres and acres of corn don't worry too much about a few straggly stalks here and there. But those who have only a 20-foot-square garden must use that small space wisely. Many factors — from spacing to weeding — have a profound effect on garden yields.

Proper Spacing

Certain plants, such as root crops (carrots, radishes, beetroot), are less sensitive to close spacing than others. Leaf crops, such as spinach, celery, and lettuce, can also grow closely together. Fruit-bearing upright plants, such as peppers and tomatoes, give highest yields when their foliage is almost overlapping. If they are spaced so the foliage of mature plants is separated by 3 to 4 inches, the total yield declines but the size of the individual fruits increases. Vining crops, such as melons, cucumbers, and pumpkins, need more space and more light.

Light

Fruits such as melons and storage parts such as potato tubers are reservoirs that hold accumulated energy gathered from sunlight by the plants' leaves. These plants should be in a spot where sunlight falls on the entire plant. Leaf crops such as lettuce and Swiss chard, on the other hand, do not need as much light.

Watering

To produce the best crops, plants should have uninterrupted growth — which translates to an even, constant supply of water. Under most conditions, this means about an inch per week; however, this may depend on the stage of growth. Ripening strawberries that receive slightly less than an inch of water per week produce smaller but sweeter fruits. A little less water while fruits are ripening will reduce the yield but increase the quality. Potatoes and onions need much less water just before harvest. This helps the crop last longer after you harvest it.

Weeds

It comes as no surprise that an unweeded garden produces smaller yields. What *is* a surprise is just how much a difference weeding makes. Studies show that regularly weeded fields produce six times as many tomatoes as do unweeded ones. Potato yields increase threefold; onions, more than tenfold; carrots, more than fifteenfold. But the timing of cultivation is critical. Do not weed after a rain of less than half an inch or you will lose soil moisture. Weed during dry times or after a heavy rain. Vegetables are most susceptible to competition from weeds from the seedling stage through the time fruits begin to enlarge and mature.

◄ If seeds fail to germinate, fill gaps in the row with additional seeds.

Pinch out suckers on tomato plants so more energy goes into main stems. ▶

▲ Hoe out weeds regularly so crops don't have to compete.

Tips for Setting Out Plants in the Garden

- Double-check planting dates before you start moving plants to the garden. Most annuals and vegetables must wait until the danger of frost is past; some can go out earlier. Tomatoes, courgettes, and cucumbers must wait until the ground has completely warmed up.

- Prepare garden soil with organic materials to get the most from your plants.

- Water both the ground and the transplants to cut down on transplanting shock. Do your transplanting on a cloudy day or late in the afternoon, so the heat of the sun won't cause excess wilting.

- Dig a hole about twice the size of the root-ball. Set the transplant into the hole deeply enough so the root-ball will be covered by ¼ inch of soil. Press the soil firmly about its roots.

- If seedlings are growing in peat pots, plant them as they are. Peel back peat pots slightly so the walls will not confine roots, and cover them completely with soil.

- Use a knife or a trowel to cut out transplants growing in seed trays that are not compartmentalized.

- Transplants in individual pots can be turned upside down and tapped out.

- Water immediately after transplanting and again every day for a week, until the plants are established. If some of them wilt, misting or shading them will help them revive quickly.

Dig a hole about twice the size of the root-ball.

Gently put the plant in place and press soil about its roots.

Growing Plants Vertically

If your garden feels crowded, take advantage of vertical space. It is healthier for climbing plants to climb upward into the air and sunlight than to sprawl on the damp earth.

Stakes

The simplest of all plant supports are stakes or poles. Drive them into the soil near the base of a plant and the climbers instinctively latch on to them. Tie tall or heavy plants to the stakes to support them. Then prune the excess growth at the top. Garden centres offer a variety of wooden, bamboo, and manufactured stakes, or you can make your own from scrap timber, pieces of metal or PVC pipe, or other rigid materials.

Tepee Trellises

Tepees make excellent supports for beans, peas, and tomatoes, and for heavily fruited crops such as melons and squash. To build one, you will need three to six poles — thin ones for flowers or lightweight plants, stouter ones for heavily fruited crops. Cut the poles 10 to 12 feet long so you can sink them 1 to 2 feet into the ground. Use twine, raffia, or strips of rawhide or cloth to lash the poles together near the top. Pull the poles into a tight bundle, wrap the twine around the bundle a few times, and tie it snugly. Prop the bundles over

Try Vertical Growing to Expand Your Gardens

- Produces fruit that is cleaner and less susceptible to damage from rotting, insects, and slugs.

- Allows more air and sunlight to reach the plants.

- Makes cultivating and harvesting easier.

- Requires less space.

- Yields generally larger crops.

- Creates a shady garden spot.

- Provides a framework for plant coverings.

- Allows more efficient watering.

- Makes monitoring and managing pests easier.

- Allows for earliest, cleanest, and longest-lasting harvests.

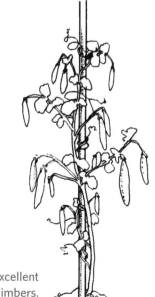

Simple stakes offer excellent support for twining climbers.

Constructing a Tepee Trellis

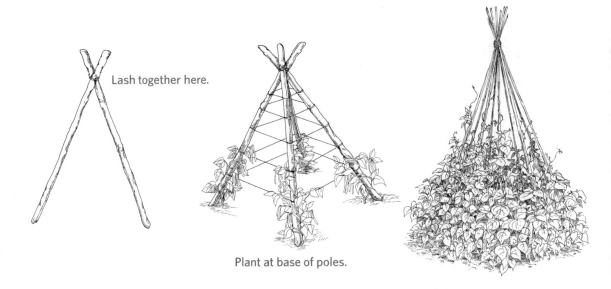

Lash together here.

Plant at base of poles.

Making tepee trellises is easy. Use three to six or more poles to make a tepee. Sink them at least 1 foot into the ground and lash them together at the top. Not only does this create a sturdy and attractive structure for climbing plants to scramble up, but it also provides a cool and shady nook underneath in which children can snooze, read, or hold tea parties. Leave one section between the poles unplanted for easy access.

the planting area, positioning the bottom ends so each pole will support one or two vines. Thicker poles are heavy enough to be freestanding.

Fence Trellises

Drive a post at each end of a row and place other posts in between where needed. String with twine, wire, netting, or wire mesh and you have a fence-type trellis. Fences over 20 feet long should have an extra post installed every 10 to 12 feet. By attaching cross arms to the end posts and running wires between them, you can convert the simple fence trellis into a double fence or clothesline trellis that can support two or four lines instead of just one.

Cages

Another simple and efficient method to contain sprawlers is a cage. Cages can be nailed together from scrap 1 × 2 timber

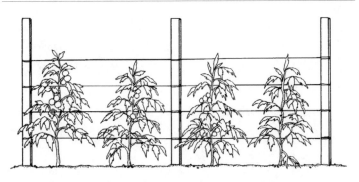

Fence trellises provide sturdy support for tomato vines.

or made with sturdy wire mesh. Bend the mesh into shape and arrange it over transplants such as tomatoes and cucumbers. Round or square cages, 2 to 3 feet in diameter and 3 to 4 feet high, will both contain and support a variety of climbers.

A-Frames

Construct an A-frame trellis of lightweight timber — 1 × 2s or 2 × 4s. Wire-mesh fencing, garden netting, or vertically or horizontally strung wire or twine will serve as the plant support. You can design an A-frame in any dimensions, but it must be of manageable size if it is to be portable. Both sides of this versatile trellis are used, and it can be made sturdy enough to support heavy crops such as squash and pumpkins.

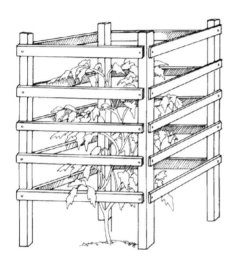

Cages are another favourite technique for supporting tomatoes.

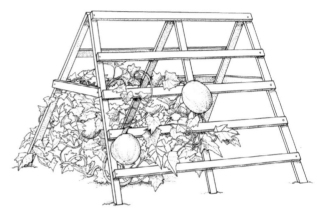

Use A-frame trellises for vines with heavy fruits, such as melons, squash, and pumpkins.

Harvesting Vegetables

As a home gardener, you have an advantage over the commercial vegetable grower in that you do not have to harvest crops before they are ripe. You can pick your vegetables just as they reach their prime.

In general, bring things in from the garden just before you are going to eat them or prepare them for storage. With every minute that passes from the time the produce is picked, the vegetables lose quality and food value. Never leave fresh vegetables sitting around for a long time. Keep them in a refrigerator or a cool, dark cellar. This will slow down the deterioration process.

Some vegetables can be picked before they are completely mature. Young onions, beetroot, carrots, cabbages, and the leaves from lettuce plants that have not formed heads are all delicious. Most of the early crops in your garden will mature quite suddenly, so there is an all-too-short period of time to harvest them. Later varieties are not apt to mature quite so quickly.

If you want your plants to continue to bear vegetables, keep them harvested. Pick everything as soon as it is ready, even if you know it is impossible for you to use it all. Throw any surplus on the compost pile. Or better still, make plans to share with friends, neighbours, and anyone in need. Giving away fresh vegetables is one of the friendliest gestures of all.

The crops you harvest later in the season are the easiest and best ones to store. If you have a root cellar, it will have cooled off by this time. Potatoes, cabbages, and turnips should be ready just in time to go into the root cellar. Eat your first plantings of beetroot and carrots throughout the summer months and plan to use later plantings for bottling and freezing.

Big, big vegetables have passed the point of being ripe, tender, and flavourful. Many gardeners like to grow vegetables commonly called "table size." This means harvesting beetroot, for example, when they are slightly larger than a lemon. Carrots shouldn't be much bigger around than your thumb.

The more you harvest, the more you grow. If you don't pick your lettuce, it will go to seed. Chard and other heat-tolerant greens can be cut continuously all summer long.

Won't They Freeze?

Some edibles can *survive* a bit of frost, but others actually relish it. Spinach, kale, and a few lettuce varieties ('Winter Density', 'Rouge d'Hiver', and 'Arctic King') have evolved a cold-weather strategy that allows them to survive even subzero temperatures with ease. As colder temperatures signal the coming of winter, these plants begin to produce compounds (including sucrose) that act as antifreeze; they prevent the formation of ice crystals within a plant's cells. By the time really cold weather arrives, spinach, lamb's lettuce, and kale are ready to survive whatever Mother Nature serves up. As an unintended culinary bonus, these "chilled-out" salad greens are sweeter than they were before the frost hit them.

Seed Saving

Saving seeds is a good way to wind up the gardening season. By allowing a few plants to reach their full maturity, you won't have to buy seeds the following spring.

Harvesting and Cleaning Seeds

Timing is important when harvesting seed. Observe your plants carefully and note the time and method of their seed dispersal. You'll soon get a good sense of when to collect seeds from each plant.

Methods for collecting seed vary, determined in part by the type of plant you are working with. Some seeds can be removed from their pods by hand. With others, the entire plant must be cut down and threshed (beaten or flailed). Many seeds can simply be shaken free of their pods into a container.

Storing Seeds

Most seeds can be stored for at least a year and still germinate, as long as the storage conditions are right. Temperature is critical. Try to keep seeds consistently cold, or at least cool; fluctuating tempera-

---

Harvesting and Cleaning Seeds

1. When seeds are thoroughly dry and seem about to scatter, cut off the seed heads with secateurs.

2. Lay them out on a light-coloured surface in a warm, dry place for a week or so, or place them upside down in a bag and tie the bag shut until the seeds have released themselves. Leave a few small air holes in the bag.

3. When the seed heads are dry, separate out the individual seeds and remove any plant

debris or chaff, especially green leaves and stems. The debris may be big enough to pick out by hand, or you can sift it. For small seeds, use a kitchen sieve.

4. When the seeds are clean, spread them out indoors to continue drying for a week or so before being stored. (Seeds with beards or tufts should not be given this extra drying time.) Pick out and discard seeds that are lighter than the rest. These have usually lost viability.

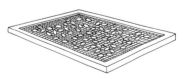

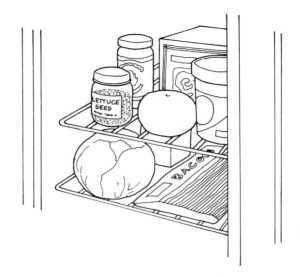

tures can be fatal. The refrigerator, or any other place that stays just above freezing, is ideal for storing most seeds. They can also be stored in the freezer, but they must be completely ripe and very dry.

Moisture may be an even more important factor. Since seeds begin to germinate when they absorb water, moisture is the death of seeds in storage. Always dry seeds thoroughly before placing them in storage containers. Make sure the containers themselves have no trace of moisture inside and that no moisture can enter them.

The refrigerator, or any other place that stays just above freezing, is ideal for storing most seeds.

Don't forget to label everything throughout the seed-collecting process. You don't want to confuse your cherry tomatoes with your beefsteaks. Mark each batch of seeds with the variety name and date collected, and any other information you want to include.

Store seeds in a variety of small containers: screw-top glass jars, such as baby-food jars; paper or glassine envelopes, labeled and sealed inside glass jars; plastic or metal film containers; prescription medicine containers; and tins with metal lids. The container shouldn't be airtight (this would prevent gas exchange), but it should be closed securely to keep out moisture and pests.

Characteristics of Common Vegetables Saved for Seed

Crop	Plant Type	Seed Viability* (Years)	How Pollinated	Need Isolation If You Are Collecting and Saving Seed
Beans	Annual	3	Self	Limited
Beetroot	Biennial	4	Wind	Yes
Broccoli	Annual	5	Insects	Yes
Brussels sprouts	Biennial	5	Insects	Yes
Cabbage	Biennial	5	Insects	Yes
Carrots	Biennial	3	Insects	Yes
Cauliflower	Biennial	5	Insects	Yes
Celery	Biennial	5	Insects	Yes
Chinese cabbage	Annual	5	Insects	Yes
Corn	Annual	2	Wind	Yes
Cucumbers	Annual	5	Insects	Yes
Eggplants/aubergines	Annual	5	Self	Limited
Kale	Biennial	5	Insects	Yes
Kohlrabi	Biennial	5	Insects	Yes
Leeks	Biennial	3	Insects	Yes
Lettuce	Annual	5	Self	Limited
Melons (all)	Annual	5	Insects	Yes
New Zealand spinach	Annual	5	Wind	Yes
Okra	Annual	2	Self	Limited
Onions	Biennial	1–2	Insects	Yes
Parsley	Biennial	1–2	Insects	Yes
Parsnips	Biennial	1–2	Insects	Yes
Peas	Annual	3	Self	Limited
Peppers	Annual	2	Self	Limited
Potatoes	Annual	NA	Self	No
Pumpkins	Annual	5	Insects	Yes
Radishes	Annual	5	Insects	Yes
Soybeans	Annual	3	Self	Limited
Spinach	Annual	5	Wind	Yes
Squash	Annual	4	Insects	Yes
Swede	Biennial	5	Insects	Yes
Swiss chard	Biennial	4	Wind	Yes
Tomatoes	Annual	4	Self	Limited
Turnips	Annual	5	Insects	Yes

* Ideal storage techniques can significantly prolong seed viability.

Vegetables A to Z

Now for the best part of all — choosing your plants! Have fun, grow well, and eat heartily.

Asparagus

Asparagus is a perennial that can be grown from seed but is usually started with one-year-old crowns planted in late spring. From first planting to harvest, asparagus takes about three years to mature. You can also purchase two-year-old crowns or roots. These are more expensive, but they save you a year of waiting.

Planting. Set out asparagus crowns in spring. Asparagus grows in most types of soil, but it does best in soil with good drainage so improve heavy clay with grit or horticultural sand.

- Dig a trench 12 to 18 inches deep and add 6 to 7 inches of aged manure or compost or a little peat moss.

- Sprinkle on a dusting of 10-10-10 fertilizer, add 1 to 2 inches of soil dug from beside the trench, and mix everything together.

- Create mounds at the bottom of the trench about 12 inches apart.

- Set each crown, roots down, on top of a mound and drape its roots down around the mound. Place the crowns at least 4 inches below the soil surface (step 1).

- Fill up the trench to cover the crowns with a couple of inches of soil. The soil level will be a little below the rest of the garden. When the shoots grow up, fill in the trench with a little more soil to give the stalks support (step 2).

Harvesting Asparagus

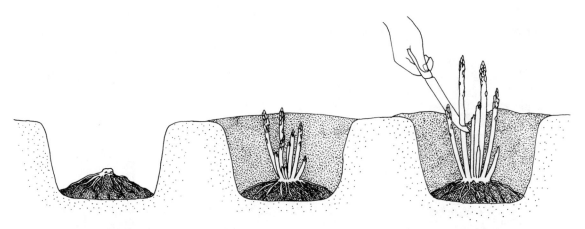

1. Set one-year-old asparagus crowns in a deep trench on a mound of enriched soil.

2. Fill the trench with soil as stalks develop.

3. Cut spears with a knife, just below soil level.

Care. In the first year, mulch small spears after they emerge. Let plants grow through the summer and autumn without cutting shoots or ferns. Let tops die down in late autumn. Simply put, let them be.

In spring of the second year, cut and clear out old ferns. Remove mulch and apply a balanced fertilizer such as blood, fish and bone. Don't harvest, just mulch, weed, and wait.

In the third year, cut away the old ferns, pull back mulch, and fertilize. When spears reach 6 to 8 inches or as thick as your finger, harvest. If they're thin, let them grow to ferns.

Harvest. Carefully cut spears a hair below the soil surface (step 3) with a knife. As they get older and stronger, you'll be able to harvest for five to eight weeks each spring before letting the remaining stalks grow ferns. After the last harvest each spring, pull weeds, fertilize, and mulch.

Beans

Beans are warm-weather vegetables. Plant seeds directly into soil when the danger of frost is past and the soil is warm. They will grow in any soil (except very wet ones) and don't require much fertilizer. Beans can be divided into three types:

Green beans. These include the many varieties of French and runner bean. Harvest them when pods are young and tender.

Shell beans. Broad beans and lima beans are the best examples. To harvest, open the pods or shells and collect the beans.

Dry beans. These beans come from plants that have completed their growth and have produced hard, dry seeds inside pods. When mature, they are packed with protein. To harvest, separate the beans from their hulls and store.

Growing Dry Beans for Storage

Dried beans are very high in protein, making it well worth devoting space in the garden to them. There are also hundreds of bean types to try, from canellino to borlotto and flageolet. Plan an average of 10 to 20 plants per person when planting in the spring. Keep in mind that cold, wet weather fosters disease and that most dried beans, whether bush or semi-climbing, require a long growing season (as long as 100 days).

To direct-sow beans, layer grass mulch 4 to 6 inches deep on the bed in autumn. This will decompose to about 2 inches by spring, will keep the soil warm 6 inches deep, and won't pull nitrogen out of the soil, enabling

Dry beans are easy to grow and are packed with protein.

you to plant earlier in the spring. Plant beans 1 inch deep and allow 2 to 6 inches between plants and 12 to 30 inches between rows, depending on which variety you're planting.

Some gardeners recommend soaking seeds before planting, but research indicates that presoaked seeds absorb water too quickly, causing the outer coats to spill out essential nutrients, which encourages damping-off seed rot. Yields can increase by 50 to 100 percent if you inoculate with *Rhizobium* bacteria (simply roll seeds in the powder).

Because beans are nitrogen fixers (and inoculating them enhances this characteristic), they require little fertilizer throughout the growing season. Regular watering is important, as is trellising or other support for climbing varieties.

Harvest. Many beans can be harvested young and eaten green or left to mature and harvested as dried beans. For the latter, wait until a plant's leaves have fallen in autumn to pick dry pods or to pull the entire plant. Harvest before the first frost. Some dried beans, however, should be picked as soon as any split pods are spotted because beans often drop from the shells as they dry. Cure them for several weeks in a well-ventilated, sheltered space, piling them on screens or slatted shelves to allow plenty of air to circulate and prevent rotting. Beans are dry and ready to thresh when they don't dent when bitten.

Here are four methods of threshing:

- Thrash the plants back and forth inside a clean galvanized metal dustbin.
- Place the plants in a large burlap sack and flail.
- Put plants in a cone-shaped bag, tie the bottom, and walk or jump on the bag.
- Put the beans into a bag with a hole in the bottom; tie the bottom closed. Hang the bag from a tree and beat well, then place a container below and untie the hole. With the help of a good wind, the chaff will blow away and the beans will fall into the container.

Storage. Remove all bad beans (those with holes or insect damage). Place beans on shallow trays and heat at 170 to 180°F (77 to 82°C) for 10 to 15 minutes. Cool thoroughly, and store fully dried beans in airtight jars in a cool, dry place.

A Primer on Preserving

There are many methods of storing and preserving foods. Common storage, or "root cellaring," is the simplest method. If you live in an area with a cool or cold climate, you can store many vegetables for several months in a cold cellar or any space with the appropriate atmosphere. This method requires no preparation and can be used for onions, carrots, beetroot, potatoes, squash, pumpkins, cabbage, and fruits such as apples. Dried seeds, such as beans and split peas, and grains require only darkness and a cool, dry spot protected from the three Ms — *mould, moisture,* and *mice.*

Other methods are freezing, bottling, pickling, fermenting, drying, and making jams and jellies. Freezing is the easiest and can be used for almost any fruit or vegetable. Fewer nutrients are lost compared with other methods, but it does involve the most expensive equipment and the continuing use of electricity. Bottling by boiling-water bath is the tried-and-tested method to preserve high-acid foods like fruits and pickled vegetables; pressure bottling is necessary for other vegetables, such as beans, peas, corn, and beets, which are "low acid." Low-acid foods can also be preserved by freezing, drying, fermenting, or pickling. Choosing a preserving technique will depend on the equipment you have available or can afford to buy. Equipment such as jars, freezer containers, and a pressure cooker should be purchased well in advance of the season while they are still plentiful. It can be downright discouraging in August to be faced with baskets of tomatoes rotting away because the shops have run out of Kilner jar lids. And though you may be able to acquire supplies by shopping online, your produce will lose its peak quality while you wait for the items to be delivered.

Unless they are kept cold and moist, vegetables will lose taste and nutrients within a few hours once picked. If you buy or pick vegetables in bulk and then find that you are unable to process them

Beetroot

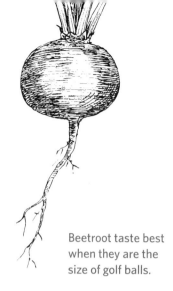

Beetroot taste best when they are the size of golf balls.

Beetroot should be planted in spring about two weeks before the last frost, sowing them in succession every two weeks until July. Make a large planting about 90 days before the first winter frost.

Sow about 2 inches apart in square-foot blocks, about ½ inch deep. Seedlings sprout in two weeks if soil temperature is below 50°F (10°C), or in one week at 75°F (24°C). Thin the beetroot to 3 to 4 inches apart, then mulch with clean straw to retain moisture and retard weed growth. Keep steady moisture levels to avoid fibrous roots. Beetroot like a pH of 6.5 to 8.0. Sweeten the soil with about a pound of lime for each square yard of bed before planting.

Golf-ball-sized beetroot are the tastiest (unless they're long-right away, wash them quickly in cold water, drain them, put them in large plastic bags, and keep them in the refrigerator. Do not cut or peel them, as this hastens the loss of nutrients. Stored in this manner, they should be good for one or two days, and in the case of root crops and cabbage considerably longer. But for good quality, preserve vegetables as soon after picking as possible.

Most fruits will keep for a while, but if they are ripe, they should be kept cold until you can use them. Raspberries and other soft fruits that deteriorate rapidly must be handled gently and briefly and preserved immediately.

Food preserving actually starts in early January with the arrival of seed catalogues. Study them carefully. Many new hybrids are designated as especially good for bottling or freezing. You may want to choose a few new varieties each year. Sometimes you will hit on a family favourite, or at least increase your knowledge for next year. But be realistic. Take into account your family's likes and dislikes. It is easy to get carried away by the glossy pictures. If your family will not eat a certain vegetable, you will have wasted your time and garden space by planting it. Save your garden plan from year to year. If you also record the varieties and how well each did, you will be spared from making the same mistakes and be at least partially assured of repeated successes.

Some good vegetable combinations that you might want to grow and preserve together are tiny peas and onions, corn and limas (succotash), tomatoes and celery, and courgette and aubergine. For bread-and-butter pickles, you will need onions and cucumbers; for relishes, red and green peppers and onions are needed together. Sweet red peppers are mature green peppers; in order to have red and green at the same time, allow all the peppers on a few of your plants to mature to the red stage while picking green peppers as needed from other plants.

season types). Winter storage beetroot can be pulled when a frost threatens in early winter, preferably after a dry spell. In mild-winter areas, store the roots right in the ground under 8 to 12 inches of straw. Otherwise, pull them out and allow them to cure in the sun for a few hours. Trim the foliage, leaving half of the stem above the crowns, and pack the beets in moist sand.

Broccoli

Broccoli is grown as an over-wintered crop in the UK so should be sown in spring and planted out in summer for cropping the following spring. The centre head must be cut out before it blossoms, even if it's on the small side. When the head is young, its individual buds are packed very tightly. As long as the buds stay tight, let the head grow. When they loosen up and spread out, they are about to produce yellow flowers. After you cut the centre head, smaller heads or side shoots will form; though small, they can be eaten, so keep them picked.

Cut the centre head of broccoli before it flowers.

Encourage bigger Brussels sprouts by removing all leaves.

Brussels Sprouts

Sow in March/April for planting out in May/June and harvesting through the winter. The sprouts form where a leaf grows out of the thick stalk, starting at the bottom. To encourage early sprouts to grow big, break off the lowest branches and continue up 6 to 8 inches, until the point at which tiny sprouts begin to form. These are ready for picking five to seven days

To encourage early sprouts to grow big, break off all the branches as soon as you see tiny sprouts begin to form.

1. Remove outer leaves from firm, mature heads of cabbage. Wash and drain. Remove core and shred cabbage with a knife or shredder.

2. Carefully weigh 5 pounds to ensure correct cabbage-to-salt proportions.

3. Measure 3 tablespoons kosher salt and sprinkle over 5 pounds prepared cabbage. Mix well with spoon or hands. Allow 15 to 20 minutes for cabbage to wilt slightly.

4. Pack cabbage into a 1-gallon jar. Press firmly with hands or a wooden spoon until juice is drawn out to cover shredded cabbage.

5. Put a heavy-duty plastic bag on cabbage and fill with water until it sits firmly, allowing no air to reach the cabbage. Ferment for five to six weeks. Gas bubbles indicate that fermentation is occurring. Temperatures between 68 and 72°F (20 and 22°C) are ideal for fermentation.

later. As you harvest, snap off more branches higher up.

Cabbage

It is possible to have continual cabbages throughout the year. Set out summer cabbages in wide rows in late winter or early spring. Sow spring cabbages in midsummer, some in the garden and some in seed trays in partial shade outdoors; plant them out in autumn for harvesting the following spring. Sow winter cabbages in April/May, plant out in July and crop through the winter.

If cabbage heads start to crack, they are probably growing too fast in the centre (often caused by heavy-handed fertilizing). If you see a cracked head, hold it and twist the whole plant halfway around, like turning a tap. This breaks off some of

Stagger cabbage plants in wide rows.

Curing with Brine

Salting, an ancient method of preserving, was based on the discovery that large amounts of salt will inhibit spoilage. However, using a great deal of salt means that the food is not fit to eat until it has been desalted and freshened by being soaked in several changes of water, resulting in the loss of many nutrients.

When small amounts of salt are used, however, fermentation occurs. The bacteria change the sugars of the vegetables to lactic acid, and the acid (with the salt) prevents other spoilage organisms from growing. This lactic-acid fermentation is the method used in making sauerkraut and other "sour" vegetables. Since the salting is so mild, the consumption of both vegetable and juice can be enjoyed, and nearly all the nutrients are preserved.

The Chinese may have been the first to preserve food by the fermentation process. The present-day *yen tsai* — meaning "vegetables preserved in brine" — is prepared with mixtures of various vegetables that have been available since ancient times. Turnips, radishes, cabbages, and other vegetables are used in these preparations, and salt is added if available.

Some of the vegetables that can be fermented in the home with success are cabbages, Chinese cabbage, turnips, swedes, lettuce, green tomatoes, and snap beans. Cucumbers are also fermented when brined the long way for pickles.

When properly prepared, all of these foods will be crisp but tender. They are pleasantly acid and salty in flavour, and they are good in salads (except for sauerkraut) or served whole on the relish tray, without freshening. They are also good cooked with meat.

Chinese cabbage

the roots and slows the inner top growth of the plant. Give the plant another quarter turn in a few days if the cracking continues.

Carrots

Carrots need a stone-free, well-worked, fertile soil that drains well. The plant's taproot must meet no resistance in the soil if it is to grow straight.

Carrots produce best in a raised bed of tilled soil at least 8 inches deep. They like compost but no manure unless it's well rotted. For potassium, work wood ashes into the top 4 inches. Start sowing carrots two weeks before the last spring frost. Make successive plantings every three weeks until July. Space ¾-inch-deep furrows about 4 inches apart. When sowing the seeds, try to place them ½ inch apart — not an easy task. Because carrots are slow to germinate, gardeners often mix radish seeds with carrot seeds to mark the rows.

Well-shaped carrots need stone-free, well-worked soil.

Add a ½-inch layer of sifted compost to the bottom of each furrow, place seeds sparingly on top, then cover with ¼ inch of sand. To help germination, cover the bed with burlap sacks, soak them, and keep the bed moist until the carrots sprout. Remove burlap, then water daily until seedlings are well established.

Because they grow slowly, seedlings can't compete with weeds. Hand-weed until the plants are 2 inches tall. Thin to 3-inch spacing, then mulch with chopped leaves, pine needles, and compost.

Cauliflower

Cauliflower is less tolerant of hot weather than its relatives are, so set out your plants very early in spring or plan on an autumn crop. Heads that mature in high heat are apt to have a bitter taste or bolt very quickly.

For your first crop, set out some plants three to four weeks before the last spring frost. Pinch off a couple of the lower leaves.

When heads are 4 to 5 inches across, blanch them by preventing sunlight from reaching the heads. This keeps the heads creamy white and sweet tasting. Blanch by tying the plant's leaves around its head. Blanching normally takes four to eight days, but it may take a little longer in the autumn.

Begin harvesting when heads are completely white. Depending on the variety, the heads will be 6 to 12 inches across. Be sure to cut the heads before the tight flower buds start to open. Unlike broccoli, cauliflower does not produce side shoots so one head per plant is the limit.

Blanch cauliflower by tying leaves over the head.

Collards

This perennial is one of the oldest members of the cabbage family. Although collards went out of fashion, the seed is widely available again and being cold-hardy they make useful winter greens, providing large rosettes of blue-green leaves.

Use one of two planting methods: (1) in spring, sow seed or set out plants to stand 10 to 15 inches apart; or (2) in summer, sow seed thinly and let seedlings grow until large enough for greens, then harvest seedlings to give 10 to 15 inches of spacing.

Collards require little fertilizing. Successive plantings are not necessary for a continuous supply. Harvest seedlings or entire plants, or gradually pick the lower leaves.

Pick lower leaves of collards to prolong harvest.

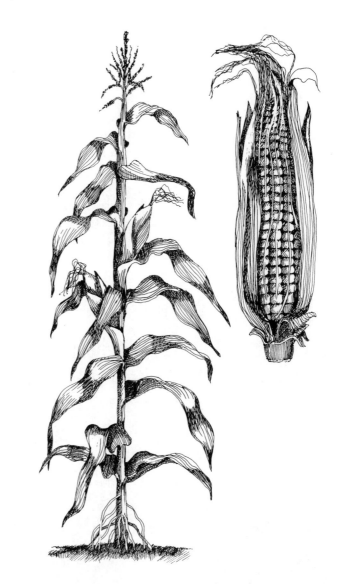

Sweet corn is ready to pick when the juice in the kernels is milky, not watery.

Corn

Corn is a member of the grass family. To support its heavy appetite, corn needs a ready supply of food. Enrich the soil well in advance of planting. If possible, plow under a 1-inch layer of manure the preceding autumn or grow a green-manure crop. Turn this crop under in spring before planting corn.

If you want fresh corn week after week, plant early and mid-season varieties the same day. The result will be five to six weeks of steady eating. Or you can stagger planting dates by sowing a block of corn every 10 to 14 days for about a month. Corn does best in a full day of sun. Because of its height, plant it on the north side of a garden, where it won't shade other sun-loving plants.

For sturdy corn, plant seeds 10 inches apart in a furrow or trench, then hill the plants as they grow. Plant sweet corn in blocks of at least four rows to ensure good pollination. If you're planting popcorn, keep it at least 100 feet away from other corn.

Thin the seedlings to 8 to 12 inches apart. Leave the tillers (those extra-long stalks growing from the base) on the plants. When the plants are small, keep weeds under control so corn doesn't have to compete for nutrients. Watering is most effective at the time of tasseling and when kernels are forming. Soak the soil at least 4 inches deep. For spectacular corn, side-dress twice during the growing

season with liquid plant food such as diluted fish emulsion or comfrey tea.

Sweet corn is at its best for only a few days, 18 to 20 days after the silks have been polli-nated. Its juice is milky. Test by puncturing a kernel with your fingernail to see if it squirts out. If you're too early, the juice will be watery; too late, and the ker-nels are doughy. Look for dark green husks, brown but not brit-tle stalks, and well-filled ears.

Cucumbers

Outdoor cucumbers belong to the squash family and should be sown after all risk of frost has passed. They are gener-ally grown in mounds and send out vines. Cucumbers do well on trellises and resent trans-planting, so it's best to sow them in the ground. Since trellised plants dry out more quickly, watch their water supply.

Side-dress with a 5-10-10

Cucumbers thrive when trained up a trellis, but they must be watered frequently.

Curing cucumbers and other vegetables in a brine "strong enough to float an egg" is a great way to use up a bumper summer harvest. A 10 percent brine (see step 2) will float a fresh egg, and in it we cure many vegetables that are then used for sour, spiced, and sweet pickles: cucumbers, green tomatoes, green beans, onions, and cauliflower.

1. Prepare vegetables by washing, trimming, and removing stems and blossom ends. Use whole, immature cucumbers — from tiny gherkins up to 7 inches. Wipe rather than wash, unless very dirty. Beans should be blanched in boiling water or steamed for 5 minutes. Small green tomatoes and onions can be left whole. Cut cauliflower into florets.

2. Weigh vegetables and pack into a clean container. Cover with a cold brine of 1 pound of pickling salt to 1 gallon of water. A gallon of brine will be needed for each 2 gallons of vegetables.

3. Cover the vegetables with a plate an inch or two smaller in diameter than the container. Weight it down to keep the vegetables under the brine.

4. The following day, add more salt at the rate of ½ pound for each 5 pounds of vegetables. This addition is necessary to keep the brine strong enough despite the liquid drawn from the vegetables by the salt. Place the salt in a mound on top of the cover rather than directly into the brine, so it will not sink to the bottom.

5. At the end of the first week, and for four or five succeeding weeks, add ⅛ pound salt for each 5 pounds of vegetables. To help remember when and how much salt to add, tape a timetable to the container, marking off each time the salt is added.

6. Remove any scum that forms; be sure to keep every pickle completely submerged in the brine. Add more 10 percent brine if necessary.

7. Fermentation will continue for four to eight weeks, indicated by a few bubbles rising to the surface. The speed will depend on the storage temperature: 68 to 72°F (20 to 22°C) is safest to avoid spoilage.

More vegetables may be added in this recipe for the first couple of weeks of the brining process, provided the brine is kept strong enough — at 10 percent. Go ahead and test it with an egg! (An egg in its shell will float to the top of the brine if the brine is salty enough.)

The cucumbers are ready when they are a consistent olive green colour, translucent throughout, and without white spots. Before using them for pickles, they should be desalted by soaking for 12 to 24 hours in large quantities of fresh water that is changed several times or in equal parts water and vinegar.

fertilizer in a band around the plants when they blossom. Cover the fertilizer with soil so the leaves don't flop down on it and get burned. Mulch between the mounds for weed control.

Eggplant/ aubergine

Set out a few transplants before your last frost date and surround them with plastic water bottles. Put others in later, when the soil is warm. Set plants in the soil just slightly deeper than they were in the seed tray or pot.

Aubergines prefer sun and lots of heat and are drought tol-erant. They don't need a lot of fertilizer. Fertilize them lightly with 5-10-10 at planting time and again when blossoms set.

They taste best when they're young. Pick aubergines when the fruits reach one-third of their full growth or any time after their skins appear glossy.

Horseradish

To start a bed, get some roots from a friend. A horseradish grower won't mind, because the plants expand quickly. In fact, unless you till around it several times a year, horseradish will try to invade neighbouring crops.

You'll need only six root pieces. Plant them in early spring. Prepare the area to a depth of 6 to 8 inches. Dig a hole or furrow 4 to 6 inches deep, add a handful of compost or fertilizer, and top with 2 inches of soil. Push in each root piece at a 45-degree angle. The top of the root should be 2 inches below the soil surface. If you buy roots at a store, one end will be cut on a slant. Be sure to place that end downward.

Jerusalem Artichokes

Jerusalem artichokes are closely related to sunflowers. Their underground tubers are delicious and low in calories.

Aubergines prefer hot, dry weather.

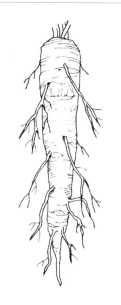

Horseradish is invasive; plant it where it won't crowd out other vegetables.

Jerusalem artichoke is a perennial vegetable that spreads quickly in open soil.

They will grow virtually anywhere and you can plant them as soon as the ground can be worked in spring. They are almost completely free of diseases and pests. They are so prolific that they may take over the whole garden if you don't watch them closely. Any tuber left in the soil will sprout the next year.

Cut six tubers, each with an eye, into quarters for a 25-foot row. Plant them 4 inches deep, spaced 1 foot apart. Leave 3 to 4 feet between rows for tilling. They are mature when they reach 6 feet tall.

They need a long growing season of about 126 days. Harvest them after frost has killed the tops or in the spring before they resprout.

Kale

Kale is a member of the cabbage family. Much like collards and mustard, it is grown for its greens. Sow in May, plant out in July and harvest through the winter. Fertilize it with nitrogen for healthy leaves. Prepare the soil with added compost and animal manure, and boost during the growing season with a side-dressing of comfrey tea, blood meal, or diluted fish emulsion. Kale can be bothered by the cabbage worm. Routine sprayings with *Bacillus thuringiensis* (Bt) after you spot the white cabbage moth should prevent problems.

Leeks

Start leeks indoors early and put them out in the garden as transplants in July. The white part of the leek is caused by blanching and the best way to achieve a white stem is make a hole in the ground using a dibber or old spade handle and drop the seedling in it. Water it liberally and by the end of the summer the leek will have filled the hole. Some varieties mature more quickly than others so it is well worth planting a range of varieties if you like to eat leeks throughout the winter.

Lettuce

Like most greens, lettuce thrives in cool weather and will quickly bolt during a heatwave. The key to a continuous harvest is succession planting. Put lettuce in the rows where peas have finished. Tuck quick-maturing leaf lettuce in the wide spaces between tomatoes, melons, or squash transplants before they spread. Lettuce

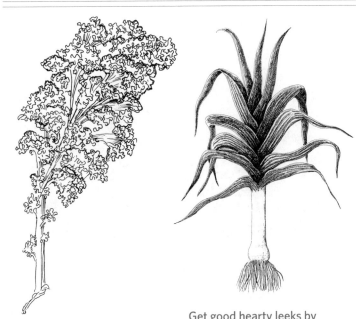

Give kale extra nitrogen for more vigorous leaf growth.

Get good hearty leeks by planting them in holes and filling these with water.

Cut side leaves of leaf lettuce to prolong harvest.

likes nitrogen. The plant's shallow roots must be well supplied with water (1 inch per week) to maintain a mild flavour. If the weather isn't too hot, lettuce will come back when cut down to an inch above the ground. Sprinkle with fertilizer and enjoy a second crop. Cut-and-come-again varieties offer a mix of leaves and are excellent value.

Melons

The culture of melon is similar to that of other members of the squash family. Plants are generally grown in mounds 6 inches apart and are thinned to two or three plants per mound.

Work the soil, and then warm it with black plastic mulch. You can direct-sow or transplant melons. Sow in shallow rows or hills. If planting in rows, place the seeds 1½ to 2 inches deep in groups of three, spacing the groups 18 inches apart. Thin to about 2½ feet by cutting

the stems at the soil line. Avoid planting until the soil warms to 65 to 70°F (18 to 22°C) in the daytime.

Make sure the fruits are supported by a sturdy trellis. Melons thrive in a well-drained, rich, light soil and full sun, and they are sensitive to frost. Their seasons are long, which can be a limiting factor in northern climates. To get them off to a good start, use cloches in the spring to trap heat or plant them in a greenhouse. Water them deeply at least once a week; when they blossom, side-dress with a tablespoon of fertilizer in a band 3 to 4 inches from a plant's stem. Keep leaves from touching the fertilizer by covering it with soil.

The key to a continuous lettuce harvest is succession planting. Put lettuce in the rows where peas have finished.

Mustard

This tasty green is a member of the cabbage family. Mustard greens are peppery with greenish purple leaves.

Direct-sow mustard seeds 1 inch apart in shallow rows. Sow them in early spring and late summer out in the garden,

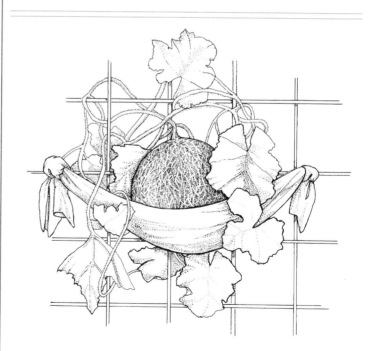

Support developing melons with a "sling" made from tights.

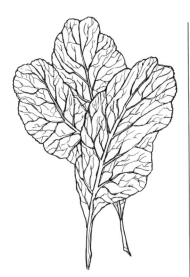

Harvest outer leaves of mustard, and inner leaves will continue to develop.

or during winter in a greenhouse or cold frame. Thin them to about 6 inches apart, separating the rows by 18 to 24 inches. If you want a constant supply, sow them every 10 days. Mustard needs even, steady moisture so water during dry periods.

Harvest the outside leaves when they are 3 to 4 inches long and still tender, leaving the inner leaves to develop. Or you can harvest the entire plant when warm weather sets in. Use leaves 3 to 5 inches long for flavourful salads.

Okra

Okra likes heat so will need to be grown under cover in most of the UK. Soak the seeds 24 hours before sowing to speed germination. Plant them 8 to 10 inches apart in rows 3 to 4 feet apart. Start the seed in pots about five weeks before you plant corn or beans. To keep the plant producing healthily, no pods should be allowed to ripen on the stalk. Young pods are more tender and more nutritious than older pods.

Storing Vegetables in the Garden

It is possible to leave some of your crops in the ground until spring. When the ground begins to freeze in the late autumn, cover such crops as carrots, turnips, and beets with a heavy (18-inch-thick) mulch of hay or straw. Except where the cold is severe (0°F [-18°C] and below), you should be able to pull back the mulch and dig up the crops throughout the winter. Mark where you stop digging each time, so you will know where to start again.

If you are not sure about your lowest winter temperature, try leaving just a few roots in the ground, digging the rest in the autumn to store elsewhere. That way some will be safe for certain, and if you are lucky, you will also have fresh, crisp vegetables right out of the garden in midwinter.

Traditionally, parsnips, horseradish, and salsify are best left in the ground long enough for thorough

freezing, which improves their flavour. Harvested in the late winter or early spring, they provide a great taste treat. *Caution:* Be sure to harvest parsnips before they begin their second growth, because they become poisonous at that time.

Kale withstands extremely cold weather. If the plants are mulched before snow falls, they will keep throughout the winter and be the first crop to grow in the spring. This crop can be important for your family's nutrition, since in late winter and early spring root crops are beginning to lose large amounts of vitamin C.

Celery and Chinese cabbage plants of late-maturing varieties can also be stored in the garden for one to two months. Bank a few inches of soil around the base of the plants at the end of the growing season, then build up the bank to the top of the plants before severe freezing occurs. As the

Keep okra producing by picking all pods before they ripen.

Onions

The key to growing onions successfully is to start early in the season. The cold won't hurt onions, and they need a long time to grow lush, green tops. Warm temperatures and the number of daylight hours signal onions to stop growing, sending their energy down to make bulbs. If you plant late, you may get smaller bulbs.

You can sow seeds indoors, buy started plants, or plant sets. You get the widest choice of varieties if you start your own from seed, but it takes 100 to 120 days to get mature bulbs. Sow seed in early March or plant sets in March/April or overwintering varieties in early November.

Prepare a well-worked soil with a pH of 6.0. The autumn before planting, use compost, manure, or both on the area and till it in. Also incorporate a 5-10-10 fertilizer at a rate of 3 to 4 ounces per square yard.

Onions can go outside as much as a month before the last frost date. Be sure to harden them off first. Plants should be

weather becomes colder, cover the banking with straw or cornstalks held in place with boards.

Plants like celery and Chinese cabbage can also be dug up, keeping a good-sized clump of soil attached to the roots. Place these plants in a trench, a hot bed, or a cold frame or on a dirt or concrete floor in a root cellar. With protection from the weather and insulation with bedding for the outside storage, you may have success keeping these plants until late December. Endive can also be brought inside with roots on, like celery, and kept for a month or two. Tie the leaves together to help blanching. The celery and Chinese cabbage will also blanch in the dark.

Cabbages can be stored in mound-shaped or long pits. Their odour is penetrating, so store alone to avoid spoiling the flavour of other food. When stored this way, they should be dug up with their roots intact and placed head down in the mound and covered with bedding and soil.

Another way to store cabbage plants is upright in a shallow trench, covered by a framework made of boards and stakes driven into the ground or a very thick covering of hay. Cabbages can also be hung up by their roots in a shed where they will not freeze, or keep them wrapped in newspaper in the root cellar.

For healthy, large green tomatoes ready to harvest just before frost, take the suckers off new plants two to three weeks after planting in the spring. Put them in a glass of water for several hours and then plant, watering liberally. These late plants will produce tomatoes timed just right for cold storage.

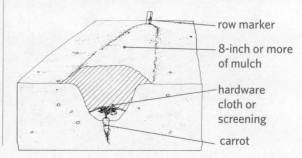

row marker

8-inch or more of mulch

hardware cloth or screening

carrot

set out at about the same level they were growing. Press sets into the soil so they are not more than 1 inch below the surface and 4 to 6 inches apart. You will need about 4 pounds of sets per 100 feet.

For seeds, allow ½ ounce of seed for every 100 feet of row to be sown. Seeds should be placed at a rate of two per inch, in a row to be covered with 1 inch of soil. Use a greater depth for soil that may dry out quickly.

> For maximum-sized onions, pull the soil away from the upper two-thirds of the bulbs.

Scallions, or spring onions, don't form bulbs. Plant them thickly in early spring. Thin them with a small rake when they come up, then let them grow.

Keep onions weed-free. Water them regularly until their tops start to yellow, then withhold water and ease them partially out of the ground. Bend the tops away from the sun, so the bulbs get sunlight. For maximum-sized onions, pull the soil away from the upper two-thirds of the bulbs. Take care when weeding around their shallow roots.

When the tops are dry, lift the bulbs and leave them in the sun to dry, long enough so the dirt on them is dry. Prepare for storage by braiding the long tops or hanging them; or cut off the tops, leaving an inch of stem for each bulb. Curing takes several weeks. Keep onions in a shed or under cover where air circulates freely.

Harvest spring onions when they are pencil-thick, but leave some to grow. They will winter over and come back in spring.

Parsnips

Plant parsnips in early spring, at about the same time as peas and radishes. Like carrots, they require a deeply tilled, well-prepared soil, raked smooth of rocks and clods. They thrive in a soil rich in potassium and phosphorus, so work in a dusting of wood ashes (potash).

Seeds germinate slowly (up to three weeks), even in the best garden conditions. Some

Keeping Onions

Stored onions can be decorative as well as useful if they are plaited. When pulled in the autumn, they should be dried in the garden for a few days. Drying cures them, and without this treatment, they cannot be stored for many months. The thick-stemmed ones must be used quickly; don't store them.

Plaited onions will fall apart as the tops dry if the plait is not given some reinforcement. Cut three pieces of twine about 3 feet long and tie them together at one end. Then plait twine and onion tops together, until within 6 inches of the end of the twine. Wrap one piece of twine fast around the onion stems, then tie to the other two and hang in a dry, cool place. The onions can be clipped off with scissors as needed.

There's a practical advantage to plaiting onions: A spoiled onion in a bag is a smelly nuisance, but it is a dried and hardly noticed part of a of an onion plait.

gardeners soak them overnight or treat the seeds with boiling water before planting. You can start seeds indoors between moist paper towels. Pre-sprouted seeds have a better chance of survival.

Alternatively sow direct in March or April when the soil has warmed up. Sow thinly in rows 12 inches apart and ¾ inch deep.

Keep beds evenly moist but not saturated. Thin to one strong plant every 6 inches when each plant has three or four leaves. Parsnips grow slowly, and mulching with straw is the best way to pamper them. If they receive inadequate moisture during the summer, they'll be tough and likely to split and rot with the autumn rains. During dry spells, water the bed deeply once a week. Parsnips can be left in the ground to harvest during the winter but make sure you have harvested all roots by the end of January.

Peas

For an extended pea season, sow successionally throughout the spring and summer. These are cool-weather plants that dislike hot spells. Sow the first crop in late February/early March under a cloche if the weather is still poor. Make second sowings in March/April for cropping in July and then sow the maincrop in April/May for eating in late summer.

In warm climates, plant peas in wide rows, using a dwarf variety.

Because peas are legumes, they don't need much fertilizer — especially nitrogen. If you do fertilize, mix 5-10-10 fertilizer in the soil a day or two before planting. Sow them in 6-inch-wide drills that are 2 inches deep and space the seeds 2-3 inches apart. Distance between the drills should be equal to the height of the plants.

Peas quickly screen out the sun from hitting weeds, so you never have to weed a good wide row of peas. The shade also

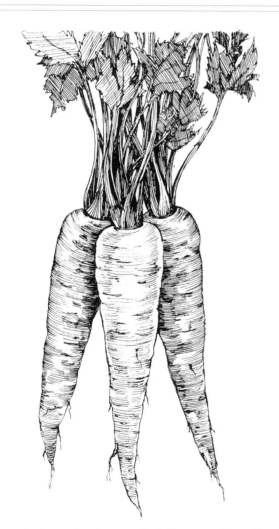

For the sweetest parsnips, leave roots in the ground over the winter and harvest before the following spring.

keeps the soil moist and cool. Peas don't need much staking. You can prop them with piles of hay or plant dwarf varieties that grow to only 15 to 18 inches. You can also stick twigs into the soil so peas can grow on them, or use chicken wire fencing stretched on metal fence posts.

Harvest any time after pods form. You can pick shell peas as soon as the pod is full. Waiting until it begins to bulge is not necessary.

Peppers

Peppers — both hot and sweet — like sunny areas and soil that is warm, dry, fertile, and slightly acidic. Don't plant them where you have used a lot of lime.

Start pepper seeds indoors in a warm place. They need more heat than other crops to get going. Use fertilizer, but in small doses, and put compost or manure under them when you transplant them. Side-dress them with rich, organic fertilizer when they bloom.

When they start to blossom, spray the leaves with a weak mix of warm water and Epsom salts — a form of magnesium. The leaves turn dark green, and you will soon have an abundance of peppers. Most peppers start out green, so for red peppers, wait until the peppers turn colour.

Potatoes

A good potato crop starts with good seed potatoes. Garden stores have certified disease-free seed potatoes. Old potatoes from your root cellar may have disease organisms without showing signs.

When you buy seed potatoes, some will be small. Plant these whole. Cut bigger ones into two or three blocky pieces that have two or three buds, or "eyes." Make these cuts one or two days before planting and leave them in a warm place so the cut pieces have time to heal over and dry out a little. You can douse cut pieces with sulphur immediately after cutting; it helps protect potatoes from rotting. Two

Hot Chilli Pepper Jelly

Could there be a better starter than toasted ciabatta topped with cream cheese and a dollop of hot chilli pepper jelly? It is also a terrific accompaniment to meat or poultry. Use all green peppers or all red ones, so the jelly has a soft colour.

¼ cup chopped jalapeño peppers

¾ cup chopped sweet peppers

6 cups sugar

2½ cups cider vinegar

2 3-ounce pouches liquid pectin

A few drops red or green food colouring (optional)

1. Run the jalapeños and sweet peppers in a blender or food processor until finely ground. Combine with sugar and vinegar in a large saucepan. Bring to a full boil over high heat, stirring constantly, then turn down the heat and simmer for 10 minutes.

2. Strain, returning the liquid to the saucepan. Add about 2 tablespoons of the pepper mixture from the strainer. Return to a boil. Add pectin and the food colouring if you're using it. Bring back to a boil one more time and boil for 1 minute. Ladle into freshly sterilized jam jars with two-part bottling lids, leaving ⅛ inch headroom, and seal. Process in boiling-water bath for 10 minutes.

Yield: Makes about six 8-ounce jars

ounces protects 10 pounds of potatoes. Put both the cut and the whole potatoes in a paper bag, add 1 to 2 tablespoons of sulphur, and shake the bag.

Plant an early crop five or six weeks before last frost. A frost before the plants come up is no problem; the soil will insulate them. But if leaves have popped up and there's a frost warning, cover them with soil. The leaves will grow back in a few days.

Plant your main crop of potatoes after the average last frost day. This planting can go into the root cellar just before the first autumn frost.

Potatoes prefer silt or sandy loam that has good drainage and is high in organic matter. Their preferred pH level is 6.0 to 6.5; a higher level may promote potato scab. Avoid using lime. Get a soil test to find out what you have. If your soil is deficient in phosphorus and potash, add a nutrient supplement such as rock dust. Apply according to package directions.

For bed planting, plant the potatoes under straw, hay, leaves, or other mulch to minimize weeding after sowing. Set up the bed in a rectangle about 6 feet wide and as long as you wish. If heavy rains are a problem in your area, slope the bed to enable drainage.

Place potato chunks, cut-side down, 12 inches from the bed's sides and ends and space them 12 inches apart in each direction. Press them firmly into the soil and top them with a thick layer of straw, hay, or shredded leaves. Weight down the mulch if there is a chance that it might blow away.

For row planting, hoe or dig 12-inch-wide trenches to about 6 inches deep. The rows should be 2 to 3 feet apart. If needed,

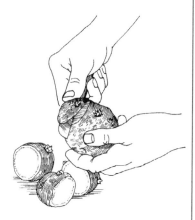

To plant potatoes, cut large ones into chunks with two or three eyes each. Allow cut edges to dry before planting.

Storing the Harvest

When you store your vegetables for winter use, remember that some crops prefer to be kept dry, whereas others like it moist. Garlic does best when you keep it cool but dry. Winter squash such as butternut and dried beans need warm, dry spots. Store the following vegetables in a cool, moist place:

Beetroot, in damp sand

Brussels sprouts, on stems, in damp sand

Cabbage, wrapped in newspaper

Carrots, in damp sand

Celeriac, in damp sand

Celery, planted in a bucket of damp soil

Jerusalem artichokes, in damp sand

Onions, in baskets or braided

Potatoes, in baskets

Swede, in damp sand

Turnips, in damp sand

add 2 inches of compost and work it into the soil. Place potato chunks, cut-side down, 12 inches apart and 3 inches deep. As plants emerge, hoe the soil up to them, gradually filling the trench and building a row-long hill about 8 inches high. Mulch the mounds to keep soil moist and discourage weeds.

Harvest the potatoes in dry periods after the plants are dead and dry. Use a potato hook and work carefully to avoid puncturing the potatoes. Let them dry for 1 to 2 hours before you move them into dark storage. Keep them at 60 to 70°F (15 to 22 °C) if you're using them within a month; 40°F (4°C) if you want to store them for months.

Pumpkins

Pumpkins are easier to grow than to classify. At least three different species are called pumpkins, and all can also correctly be called squash.

Pumpkins dislike being transplanted, so it's best to direct-sow them in hills one to two weeks before the last frost. Plant three seeds per hill, leaving about 4 feet between hills. Keep the area well weeded until the plants begin to make tendrils.

When your thumbnail doesn't easily cut the skin, cut the stem a few inches from the fruit, leaving a good handle. The fruit must be cured, which allows the skin to harden. Field-curing is done by leaving the pumpkins in a bright, sunny dry spot in the garden for 7 to 10 days. Cover them if frost threatens. Store them indoors.

Giant pumpkins require special coddling. Choose a variety such as 'Dill's Atlantic Giant', a proven prizewinner. In the autumn, select a sunny spot 30 feet in diameter and dig manure into the soil. In spring, prepare a hill 8 to 10 feet in diameter and plant four seeds in the centre, watering well. When the seedlings have four to six true leaves, pinch off all but the best plant. Alternatively, you can start seeds indoors or in a cold frame and bring them outside when the soil warms up. Protect the large leaves and vines against wind, and water once or twice a week.

Radishes

Radishes like cool weather, constant moisture, and uninterrupted growth. For a steady supply, make small weekly plantings in April and May, then again in August and September. For succession plantings, keep in mind that the longer the radish, the better it tolerates heat.

Till the radish bed to a depth of 8 inches, mixing in organic matter. Make furrows with a yardstick, spacing them about 3 inches apart, and sow

If mulched with straw, autumn radish varieties can remain in the garden through the winter, to be harvested as you need them.

the seeds at a depth of ½ inch. Space the seeds about 1 inch apart; when 2 inches tall, thin to 3-inch spacing. Most radishes are ready to harvest in less than a month. If mulched with straw, the late sowings can remain in the garden through the winter to be harvested as you need them.

Rhubarb

Three or four root crowns will produce all the rhubarb you can eat.

In the spring, dig planting holes several inches deep and 18 inches apart. Add compost or fertilizer and place a single piece of root in each hole, covering it with about 1 inch of soil. Do not harvest these plants the first year. Add a few side-dressings during the season, so they'll grow lots of tops.

The next season, harvest some stalks when they're 8 to 10 inches tall. Gently pull out and up on the ones you want to tear away from the plant.

Remove tall seedpods from rhubarb to prolong harvest.

Caution: Don't eat the leaves, which are toxic. During the second year, plants may put out tall seedpods. Remove them so the roots will produce tasty stalks all season. The more stalks you harvest, the more the plants will produce. Divide them every four or five years in the autumn or in spring before growth starts. Do this by driving a spade into the middle of a plant and digging up half the root. Fill the hole with compost. This forces the plant to produce younger, better crowns.

Swede

Plant swede in mid-June or about 90 days before your planned harvest, which should occur shortly after the first frost. Sow the seeds about ¼ inch deep with 8-inch spacing. Provide plenty of moisture until the seedlings are growing strong,

Harvest swede after a few frosts.

then mulch well and water deeply once a week.

Harvest swede after a few frosts but before the ground freezes. Cut the tops and store them like carrots in a root cellar or basement. Good roots will keep for up to six months if you store them just above freezing with 90 percent humidity.

Spinach

Spinach is a cool-weather plant and should be direct-sown about one month before the last spring frost; direct-sow autumn crops about one month before the first autumn frost. Set the seeds about 2 inches apart (1 inch in autumn) in shallow rows about 18 inches apart. Thin the seedlings to about 4 inches apart. Repeat sowings every 10 to 14 days to ensure a continual supply. Spinach responds well to fertilizers. Try regular applications of fish emulsion.

Pick the outer leaves as needed or cut the entire plant. Harvest in the cool of the morning and store spinach in the refrigerator until you're ready to use it.

Spinach is one of the earliest cool-weather crops and can also be planted in late summer for autumn harvest.

Squash loves plenty of heat and evenly moist soil.

Squash

The seeds of summer squash (such as courgette and custard squash) germinate best when soil temperatures are above 65°F (18°C). It grows best in raised beds warmed with black plastic mulch for a few weeks before planting. Direct-sow them one to two weeks after the last frost, planting the seeds about 4 inches apart and 1 inch deep in rows 3 to 4 feet apart. For winter-keeping squash, such as butternut, direct-sow pairs of seeds about 1 inch deep, spacing them every 18 inches. Keep them evenly moist, especially after the fruit has begun to set.

Harvest most summer squash when the fruit is 3 to 5 inches long. Summer squash will keep for up to two weeks in the refrigerator.

To harvest winter squash, wait until your thumbnail easily cuts the skin. Cut the stem a few inches from the fruit, then let the fruit cure for 7 to 10 days. Cover it if frost threatens. Stored winter squash can last all winter long.

Sweet Potatoes

Ideally, sweet potatoes should have 130 to 150 frost-free days, with most of them up to 80 to 85°F (27 to 29°C) with moderate to high humidity so will be best grown in the greenhouse in the U.K. Plant them well after the last frost, when the soil is about 70°F (22°C).

Purchase sweet potatoes from a market seven to eight weeks before the last spring frost. Cut them in half lengthwise and lay the pieces cut-side down in aluminium baking trays filled with moist peat moss. Put a covering of the peat moss over the pieces and wrap in a plastic bag.

When the slips (tiny sprouts) appear, remove the plastic and put the plants in a sunny window. After the last frost date, pull each slip and plant it separately. It will grow into a full-sized sweet potato plant.

Sweet potatoes need a long (four- to five-month) growing season.

Plant the slips in raised beds 5 to 6 inches deep and 12 to 15 inches apart. Fertilize them lightly with 5-10-10.

Water young plants generously for the first few days, then infrequently. Just as the vines begin to run along the ground, side-dress once with fertilizer — 1 tablespoon of 5-10-10 per plant.

Dig up the sweet potatoes on a dry day before cold weather. Dry them for 1 hour. To cure, place in a warm, dark, ventilated place for 10 to 14 days.

Tomatoes

Tomatoes don't do well until the soil warms to 65°F (18°C) or more and nighttime temperatures get up into the 50s. They thrive in rich soil with a pH of about 6.5.

To start plants indoors, begin six to seven weeks before the last spring frost. Harden them off before setting them out. Spacing in the garden depends on your method of growing. If you're going to let them sprawl on the ground, each plant needs 4 square feet. For those that will be staked, 3 square feet is adequate. If your soil is wet, set each plant on a mound 4 to 6 inches high. If your soil is dry; create a depression for each plant. Water plants well an hour before transplanting.

Set the plants about 2 inches

Secrets of Tomato Staking

If you stake your tomatoes, place the stake before you transplant, so you don't disturb the roots.

Tie tomato vines loosely to the stake as they grow.

Pinch suckers to encourage strong growth of the main stem.

When the vine reaches the size you want, pinch back the growing tip.

deeper than they were in the pot. Pick off a couple of the lower leaves. If plants are leggy (much stem and few leaves), lay down the plant on its side and bury part of the stem along with the roots. Prune the lower leaves off, leaving just the top leaves exposed. Roots will form later on the stem.

Immediately after transplanting, water the plants well. Mulch four to six weeks later, when the soil is nice and warm. If you let tomato plants sprawl on the ground, a mulch is not necessary.

Pruning is generally not necessary, but staked and trellised plants will be easier to train if they have only one or two main stems. Pruning means pinching off the shoots or suckers that grow out from the stems at their branching points. This encourages larger fruits.

A general yellowing or pale green indicates nitrogen need. Avoid side-dressing with nitrogen until after flowering is well under way. You can then side-dress with a handful of fertilizer or a quart of manure tea around the base of each plant.

Turnips

Direct-sow the seeds late February to August about 1 inch apart in single rows spaced 12 to 15 inches apart.

Thin to 4 inches when the seedlings emerge. Water well during hot weather to prevent splitting. Cover with fleece or cloches to inhibit pests.

Begin to harvest the greens and bottoms when the roots are about 1½ inches across. Pull the entire plant and snip off the top. For best flavour, the roots should be gathered before they exceed 3 inches in diameter.

Freezing Vegetables

If you've ever bought fresh green beans from the supermarket in midwinter and compared them with your own frozen green beans, the merits of freezing should be obvious — there's no comparison in quality. Following are general tips for freezing vegetables:

- Check the seed catalogues and seed packages to be sure you've chosen a variety that freezes well.

- Pick only tender young vegetables ready for table use.

- Wash the vegetables thoroughly by rinsing, repeatedly if necessary. Lift the vegetables out of the water rather than draining the water, which allows the dirt to settle back on them.

- Blanch vegetables (by quickly steaming or immersing in boiling water) before freezing. This procedure sets the colour and stops the action of the enzymes that will otherwise continue to mature the vegetables.

- Cool vegetables promptly after blanching, to keep them crisp.

- Dry vegetables thoroughly after cooling, to prevent the formation of large ice crystals.

- Pack vegetables into freezer bags or containers, leaving at least an inch of headspace if using a rigid container.

Drying Vegetables

1. Blanch washed, cut-up vegetables in steam or boiling water before drying. Fruits can be treated with an antioxidant, if desired.

2. Dry in the sun or in a dehydrator until leathery for fruits or crisp-hard for vegetables.

3. Store in small, airtight containers and keep in the dark.

Springtime Preserving of Stored Crops

After several months, the quality of stored crops may begin to deteriorate, particularly when they are not stored under ideal conditions. As long as they are firm and crisp and have good flavour and colour, their nutritive value is close to that of the fresh crop. When they begin to wither, however, their food value decreases.

Rather than letting these crops continue to deteriorate, you may want to preserve them in midwinter or early spring by bottling, freezing, or drying. The rush of the harvest season is over, plenty of empty bottling jars should now be available if you have been eating vegetables bottled in the autumn, and space in the freezer is opening up.

Now is the time to make and preserve pumpkins, squash, turnips, apple purée, pickled beetroot, or whatever have you. Crops that wintered in the garden or in outside storage should also be preserved now. These winter vegetables and fruits will then be usable throughout the spring and summer — until the next harvest.

Start Bottling!

Home-bottled vegetables are at least as good as store-bought ones, and perhaps better when you have grown them yourself and know exactly how they've been handled and what types of pesticides and fertilizers have (or have not) been used on them. Bottled foods have an advantages over frozen in that they require no expensive equipment to keep them — just a shelf in a cool, dark, dry place.

Good planning is the secret to rewarding and satisfying bottling. Be prepared with all the necessary utensils, ingredients, and information. Set aside more than enough time, so that you don't have to cut corners on processing times. Clear a large surface, since bottling takes space, and organize before starting.

Terms and Processes

It's important to consult a good reference before beginning, but here is a general overview of the terms and processes we've used throughout this book:

Raw or **cold pack.** These phrases are used interchangeably. They refer to prepared but uncooked fruits or vegetables packed in jars to which a hot liquid is added and then processed.

Hot pack. *Hot pack* refers to foods that are precooked to some degree, then put into jars for processing. This makes for more compact packing, particularly with greens. A hot pack sometimes requires less cooking time, since the food is already partially cooked. Sometimes it takes as long or longer because of the denser pack.

Headroom and **headspace.** These terms generally refer to the space between the top of the food and the top of the jar. Generally ½ inch is allowed, with the exception of starchy foods such as corn and peas, which expand more; they require at least 1 inch. Allowing too much headroom means too much air and the possibility of an improper seal. If you have only enough of a fruit or vegetable to fill half a jar, use it fresh or find a smaller jar to fill.

Boiling-water bath. This is the cheapest and easiest method of bottling for preserving high-acid

What You'll Need

- **Spring-Clip or Screw Band bottles such as Kilner jars.** Check for cracks or nicks in the rims; wash thoroughly in hot, soapy water; rinse; and keep hot until ready to fill.

- **Jar lifter**

- **Hot pads**

- **Funnel**

- **Food preparation tools:** knives, chopping boards, saucepan, colander.

- **For boiling-water bath:** deep saucepan with lid and rack; also, a kettle for adding hot water if necessary

- **For pressure bottling:** pressure cooker and rack

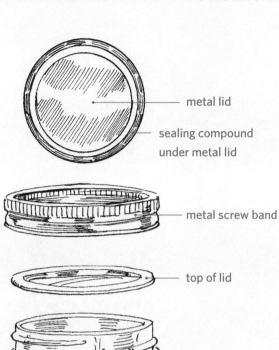

metal lid

sealing compound
under metal lid

metal screw band

top of lid

jar

jar lifter
(for removing jars from the pan)

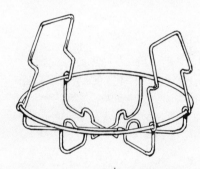

rack
(for boiling-water-bath bottling)

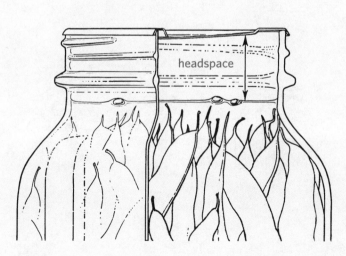

headspace

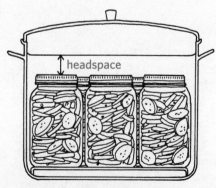

headspace

boiling-water bath;
cutaway shows jars in position

How to Bottle Tomatoes

1. Wash and sort tomatoes. Dip into boiling water for 30 seconds. Remove to cold water to cool for 1 minute.

2. Pull off skins. Cut off stems as well as blemishes and green spots. Cut into sections.

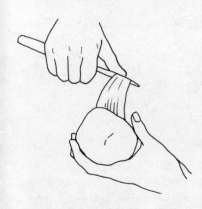

3. Put 2 tablespoons of bottled lemon juice or ½ teaspoon of citric acid per quart of tomatoes in the jars. Pack tomatoes tightly into jars, pushing down so that they are covered by their own juice; leave ½ inch of headspace.

4. Run a rubber spatula or bubble freer around the inside of the jars to release trapped air bubbles.

5. Wipe the jar rims with a clean cloth. Place lids in position and tighten screw bands.

6. Place jars in a boiling-water bath. Cover with 1 to 2 inches of water. Start timing when you have a rolling boil. Process tomatoes for 85 minutes for pints or quarts at elevations below 1,000 feet; see the chart on the next page to adjust for higher altitudes.

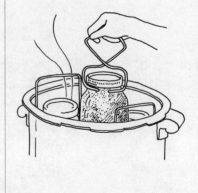

foods. These include all fruits, all pickles, and those vegetables to which sufficient vinegar has been added to raise the acidity level high enough.

Pressure bottling. This is the method to use for all vegetables (except tomatoes, sauerkraut, and pickles). There are several types of pressure cookers, but they all work according to the same principle. The pan has a tight-sealing lid with some type of regulator. When a small amount of water is heated in the cooker (usually 1 to 2 inches of water), it is converted to steam,

Use a pressure cooker to bottle all low-acid vegetables.

which, as it builds up pressure, reaches temperatures substantially higher than boiling.

A Checklist of Precautions

☐ Prime, quality produce is good insurance. Bruises encourage the growth of bacteria.

☐ Wash all produce carefully and completely.

☐ Be sure all equipment and work surfaces are scrupulously clean and in good working order.

☐ Make sure of a good seal.

☐ Don't take shortcuts. Follow directions carefully, so that the result will justify all your time and effort.

☐ Most important, process for the correct time and at the correct temperature. This is the final key and the crucial factor that, along with the seal, cannot be overemphasized.

——— Altitude Adjustment for Boiling-Water-Bath Bottling ———

If you live at an altitude of 1,000 feet or more, you have to increase the processing time in the bottling directions for a boiling-water bath as follows:

Altitude	If processing for 20 minutes or less, increase by	If processing for more than 20 minutes, increase by
1,000 feet	1 minute	2 minutes
2,000 feet	2 minutes	4 minutes
3,000 feet	3 minutes	6 minutes
4,000 feet	4 minutes	8 minutes
5,000 feet	5 minutes	10 minutes

CHAPTER 2

Back Garden Fruits and Nuts

It used to be that nearly everyone had some kind of fruit or nut tree in his or her back garden, and in older gardens, you can still find mature trees that bear fruit reliably every year with little or no care. In Somerset, Worcestershire and Herefordshire, apple and plum trees were commonly planted in domestic gardens and many of these venerable old trees still remain. Scotland continues to have the perfect climate for raspberries and tayberries and pick-your-own farms abound all over the British Isles offering currants, strawberries, gooseberries and other favourites.

At some point in our recent collective history, however, we seem to have decided that the fruit growing in our own gardens and surrounding landscapes (and not purchased from the supermarket or farm shop) is not worth eating. Strolling round those same rural areas and even city neighbourhoods, it is surprising to see plums, crab apples and cherries falling from the trees and rotting on the ground for lack of willing harvesters.

With the renewal of interest in organically grown food, more people are planting fruiting trees, shrubs, and vines in their gardens. Growing fruit can be as easy as potting up a few strawberry plants or putting in a few canes of raspberries and it is much less time-consuming than growing vegetables. You might think that growing fruit requires a designated orchard space, but in fact many traditional fruiting plants can be easily incorporated into ornamental spaces. And there are many traditional ornamental plants that also bear edible fruits (see page 115).

Fortunately, even if you can't grow your own fruit, you can forage for it! Blackberries, sloes, elderberries, even damsons if you're lucky, are common in our hedgerows. Even if all you find is imperfect fruit, you can still make jam with it (see page 90) or maybe even wine (see page 129).

Growing Strawberries

If there is one fruit every grow-your-own gardener should cultivate, it is strawberries. There are varieties for early and late harvesting, prolific cropping and super-sweetness to suit every taste. Although they do best in cool, moist regions, they can be grown in hot, dry regions, especially where windbreaks are provided and supplemental watering is possible during July, August, and September.

Selecting the Right Variety

There are three distinct fruiting habits in strawberries. Summer-bearers produce one large crop of fruit once during the season, usually for about two weeks. Depending on your growing season and region, you can get early-season, midseason, or late-season summer-bearers. Everbearers produce in smaller quantities continually throughout the growing season from early summer to early autumn. Alpine strawberries, the closest descendants of wild strawberries, are perennial and are often grown for edging a border or as ground cover. Unlike the other types of strawberries, they can be grown from seed and will bear fruit throughout the growing season even in shade conditions. Their fruits are small and often intensely flavoured.

How They Grow

Strawberries require two years to produce the best fruit. If you set healthy plants in moist soil in a prepared bed in early spring, they will produce new roots in a few days, followed by several new leaves of normal size.

For most varieties, runners begin to emerge in June, forming new plants that take root near the original plant. New runners grow from the new plants, and in this way a succession of new plants is soon growing around the original.

A Fruiting Glossary

Cane. The woody stem of various berries, grapes, and other plants

Cultivar. A cultivated variety created by cross-pollinating two different plants within a species

Girdle. To remove a strip of material or bark all around a plant, thus cutting off its water and nutrient circulation

Graft. The surgical union of two different plants or trees by attaching a branch (scion) to a rootstock

Pistil. Female parts of a plant

Runner. Horizontal stem with new plants along its length

Scion. The portion of a grafted plant above the rootstock

Self-pollinating. A plant or variety that can be fertilized by pollen from the same variety.

Plants produce blossoms the first year, and these will develop into fruit if not pinched off. Pinching them off will encourage your plants to develop strong root systems and vigorous growth. Your reward will be next season's abundant crop of large, healthy, delicious berries.

In the spring of the fruiting year, buds that developed the previous autumn develop into blossoms. The first one to open on a cluster contains the most pistils and becomes the largest fruit with the most seeds. The next and later ones become successively smaller fruits.

Recommended Strawberries

For Optimum Flavour

'Irresistible' (EM1294) With high levels of sugar and vitamin C, this is simply the sweetest strawberry you will ever grow.

'Sonata' Deliciously sweet and juicy and lasts well once picked without darkening in colour.

For Prolific Fruiting

'Cambridge Favourite' Excellent for jam. Produces a bumper crop of juicy, orange-red fruits of excellent flavour. Ready to pick from June to early July. Suitable for growing in containers.

'Florence' Prolific cropper with exceptional pest and disease resistance. Ideal for a late season harvest as a heavy crop of sweet, dark red fruits are produced from the end of June until the end of July.

'Maxim' Giant strawberries that are exceptionally sweet and high in Vitamin C.

'Pegasus' is a vigorous perennial with white flowers in spring and edible red fruit in summer.

For Small Spaces

'Alice' The perfect choice if you only have room for one variety, as it is troublefree and easy to pick. Flowers in May and fruits from June until early July. Suitable for growing in containers.

'Flamenco' An excellent strawberry for limited space. Produces sweet and juicy fruits over a long picking period. Suitable for growing in containers.

For Early Cropping

'Honeoye' Firm fruits with good flavour

'Mae' (Early) Crops from mid-May

For Late Cropping

'Amelia' (Late) A late cropping strawberry with delicious, natural sweetness. The berries have a regular attractive shape with a bright skin colour and good flavour.

Planting Strawberries

Because your strawberry plants will be growing in the same spot for at least two years, prepare the ground well. The small, shallow-rooted plants will have to receive all their moisture and nourishment from the top few inches of soil.

This soil should be light, rich, slightly acidic (pH of 5.5 to 6.0), and full of rich humus (compost or well-rotted manure) that will hold moisture even during the driest weather. Strawberries grow best in moist soil in full sun.

1. Till soil to a depth of 6 inches, removing weeds and roots. Work 2 inches of organic matter, such as household compost, or well-rotted manure, into the soil.

2. Strawberry plants come in bare-root bundles. Snip the roots to a length of 4 inches before planting, and pull off all but two or three of the youngest leaves on each plant. This action will reduce water loss when the plants are in the ground. As you work, keep the plants in a pan with a little water in the bottom and drape a damp cloth over them.

3. Plant by plunging a trowel straight down into the soil. Pull the handle toward you to open a slit in the ground. Fan out the roots and place them in the opened slit, making sure they don't bend as you set them in. Then set the top of the crown just above the soil line. Any deeper and the crown will rot; any shallower and the roots will dry out. Remove the trowel and firm the soil with the heel of your hand. Give each plant a pint of water to settle the soil.

4. As the plant begins to grow, pinch off all flower buds. Pinch summer-bearers until flowering ceases in early summer. Pinch everbearers for about three months and then stop and allow subsequent flowers to produce berries.

too low

just right

too high

Growth, Care, and Harvest

The matted row system is an easy way to grow a large bed of strawberries. Set rows of strawberry plants 12 inches apart. Let the plants put forth as many runners as they can. As the runners form, arrange them in a roughly circular pattern around the mother plant. Once you've achieved strawberry plants every 3 to 4 inches, snip off additional runners so the plants don't become overcrowded. Although this system produces good crops, the berries are smaller than those grown using the double hill system.

The Double Hill System

The double hill system is a versatile method that is also effective in raised beds. To plant this way, begin by removing any runners from the mother plants. Set your plants 10 to 12 inches apart in paired, hilled rows that are themselves 10 to 12 inches apart. Space the pairs of rows 18 inches apart.

A variation on the hill system requires raised beds, usually of timbers, that are 24 inches wide. Fill the beds with sandy loam amended with compost or rotted manure and adjust the pH to between 6.0 and 6.5. Set plants in twin rows 6 inches from the edge of the timbers and 12 inches apart.

Fertilization

Beginning in the spring of your plants' first year and continuing into autumn, water every other week with a low-analysis fertilizer such as fish emulsion. This will normally supply plants with all the nutrients they need. In some parts of the country, extra phosphorus is needed. In certain soils, applications of trace minerals may be required. From their second season on, fertilize the plants at the beginning of the growing season and when blossoms open.

Watering

While the fruits are ripening, strawberries need about 1 inch of water per week. This watering regimen will produce large,

Strawberry Systems

In the matted row system, arrange runners around the mother plant.

Strawberries trained to a double hill system are less susceptible to fruit rot diseases.

juicy berries. Too much water at this time will yield large fruit that has a watery, diluted flavour. In general, moistening the soil in a way that does not get the leaves wet reduces the spread of foliar diseases.

Cold and Frost Protection

Mulch helps keep moisture in the soil, which protects root systems. It also reduces heaving of soil in late winter and early spring. In areas where the temperatures drop to 0°F (-18°C) without a snow cover, a thick straw mulch can prevent severe damage.

Harvesting

When is it time to pick the berries? As strawberries ripen, the fruit changes colour, from white to pink to red. As the colour changes, sugars are deposited in the fruit. Berries picked before they are fully ready will not have as much sugar as ripe ones. Pick in the cool of the morning, when the berries are firm.

When Will They Ripen?

In mild weather, strawberries mature about 30 days after flowering. In a heat wave, they will mature more rapidly.

Basic Strawberry Jam

Strawberries and sugar, plain and simple. This basic jam is everyone's favourite, especially when it's made from hand-picked, sun-sweetened, home-grown berries.

> 3 lbs washed, stemmed, crushed strawberries
>
> 3 lbs sugar

1. Preheat a boiling-water-bath in which to sterilize eight half-pint jars, and prepare the lids.

2. Combine the berries and sugar in a tall, heavy, non-reactive saucepan or preserving pan.

3. Bring slowly to a boil, stirring occasionally, until sugar dissolves. Boil rapidly until thick, about 40 minutes. As the mixture begins to thicken, stir frequently to prevent scorching.

4. Test for doneness — 220°F (104°C) on a thermometer, or when the jam wrinkles on a cool saucer or spoon.

5. Remove from heat and skim off any foam that has formed during boiling.

6. Pour into the sterilized jars, leaving ¼ inch of headroom. Run a rubber spatula around the insides of the jars to release air bubbles. Wipe the rims of the jars with a clean, damp cloth. Tighten lids.

7. Cool sealed jars. Label and store.

Making Pectin

You can use apples to make your own fruit pectin for use in jam made from strawberries and other low-pectin fruits. Choose hard, tart, ripe apples. Weigh, wash, and cut fine, leaving stems and cores in. Add 1 pint water and 1 tablespoon lemon juice for each pound of apples. Cover and boil rapidly for 30 minutes, stirring occasionally to prevent scorching. Press through a jelly bag or damp cheesecloth, then strain through several layers of cheesecloth without squeezing. Heat liquid back to the boiling point, seal in canning jars, and process in a boiling-water-bath (see page 80) for 10 minutes. To use, mix the pectin and the juice of a low-pectin fruit in equal amounts.

Raspberries and Blackberries

Raspberries and blackberries are prolific, reliable, useful, and long living. They blossom late, so spring frosts never ruin the crop. The diseases and insects that trouble them are easy to control if you buy virus-free and virus-resistant plants. They need little care and are easy to pick (no bending over).

Raspberries

Raspberries are rewarding for the keen gardener because they are expensive to buy in the shops but once established in your garden will reward the effort year after year. They perform best in a sunny or part-shaded site in well-drained soil. They come in both summer-fruiting and autumn-fruiting varieties. The summer-fruiting ones bear fruit that matures in midsummer on canes that have grown the previous season. The canes die within a few weeks after bearing. It is possible to have raspberries throughout the summer by choosing early, mid-season and late-fruiting varieties. The autumn-bearing varieties bear fruit in late summer on canes that are put out in the current year. They put out a large number of canes and are basically self-supporting unlike the summer-fruiting varieties that are best tied to a wire trellis (see page 93).

Yellow raspberries such as 'Allgold' are becoming a popular commodity for their novelty value and exquisite flavour. These berries are so fragile that they are seldom seen in shops. However, they are ideal for growing at home and many fruit lovers regard the ripe yellow raspberry as the finest fruit in the world.

Blackberries

Blackberries are plentiful in our hedgerows all over the British Isles just ripe for the picking, but some claim that the cultivated varieties have a superior flavour so it could be worth finding space for a bramble patch in your garden or allotment. The growth habit is very similar to that of raspberries in that they produce fruit on the previous year's canes.

Choose a good sunny site as the more sun the plants get the more fruit they will produce. Buy the plants from a reputable nursery and plant them in spring or autumn in well-composted soil. Space your plants at 4-foot intervals and cut the plants back to about 6 inches above the ground to get them off to a good start. Water well and apply a thick mulch. To keep your plants producing well over many years, prune them to 18 inches above the ground after they have finished producing fruit for the year. This discourages them from producing the taller spine-bearing runners that do not bear fruit. August and September will be the prime fruit-bearing months. Some of the new varieties such as 'Black Butte' bear

> Blackberries are plentiful in our hedgerows but some claim the cultivated varieties have a superior flavour.

huge fruits ideal for pies. There is also a thornless variety called 'Loch Ness'.

Blackberries freeze well so you can enjoy them throughout the winter. For best results, wash the dark, glossy, ripe berries and dry them well. Fast-freeze them without adding sugar on trays and then pack in freezer bags. They will store well in the freezer for 12 months.

Starting a Raspberry Patch

No fruits are tastier or more perishable than perfectly ripe raspberries, so why not grow them within arm's reach. Get your patch off to a good start by purchasing certified disease-free plants. Those dug from a neighbour's patch may seem economical, but they often carry diseases. Choose a site that has full sun and well-drained soil and is as far as possible from other cultivated or wild raspberries. Don't plant them where you have recently grown aubergines, peppers, potatoes, tomatoes, or strawberries, which are hosts to raspberry diseases. Clear the area of any sod or weeds before you get started.

Recommended Raspberries

Early
Glen Moy Best early fruiting variety. Harvest fruit from mid-June to end July.

Malling Minerva Spine-free and fruits come away from the core easily so it's easy to pick. Sweet flavour and long shelf life.

Early Mid-Season
Malling Jewel Renowned for its old-fashioned juicy fruit with lovely flavour.

Mid-Season
Glen Ample Widely grown for its very high yields of large fruit on spine-free canes. Freezes well. RHS Award of Garden Merit winner.

Julia Good disease resistance. High yields of large fruit freeze well.

Late Season
Glen Doll Harvest from late July to mid-August. High yields of large, sweet fruit on spine-free canes.

Octavia Harvest from mid-July to mid-August. Firm fruit with good flavour and long shelf life.

Tulameen Bred in Canada so good winter hardiness. Long cropping season through July into early August.

Autumn
Autumn All Gold Highly recommended variety that produces large, golden yellow fruits with an exquisite flavour.

Autumn Bliss Justifiably popular variety. Sturdy, short canes rarely need support. Fruits on first year canes from August onwards.

Recommended Blackberries

Most Popular
Loch Ness High yielding variety that produces large, firm, conical berries from late August onwards.

Largest Fruit
Black Butte The berries are almost twice the size of other varieties and they have a firm texture and rich, sweet flavour.

For Edible Landscaping
Loch Maree Double pink flowers add to the value of this thornless variety that bears sweet berries.

Planting a Raspberry Patch

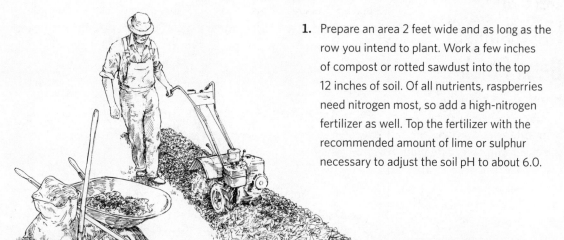

1. Prepare an area 2 feet wide and as long as the row you intend to plant. Work a few inches of compost or rotted sawdust into the top 12 inches of soil. Of all nutrients, raspberries need nitrogen most, so add a high-nitrogen fertilizer as well. Top the fertilizer with the recommended amount of lime or sulphur necessary to adjust the soil pH to about 6.0.

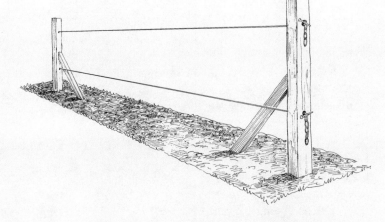

2. Erect a trellis to keep the plants upright. Set a 4 × 4 hardwood post at each end of the row, sunk into the ground at least 2 feet deep and braced. Use 12- to 14-gauge wire, placing one wire 5 feet above the ground and the other 2 feet above the ground.

3. Before planting, soak the roots for a couple of hours in a bucket of water. Dig holes 2 to 3 feet apart in the rows. Set each plant in its hole, spread out the roots, and backfill with the loose soil, making sure the crown is just below ground level. Tamp the soil with your fingers. Cut back all canes nearly to ground level, then pour a gallon of water around each plant.

Care and Harvesting of Berry Patch

Pruning. To keep your patch productive, cut each dead cane to ground level. You'll recognize the dead ones by their pallid colour and brittleness. Insects and diseases overwinter in the old canes, so burn them as soon as possible.

As your berry patch ages, more pruning becomes necessary because the plants produce too many new canes each year. Cut off all the weak new canes when you remove the old ones, and thin out the strong, healthy canes if they are closer together than 6 inches.

Keep rows of red and yellow raspberries and upright blackberries no more than 2 feet in width, and those of trailing blackberries no more than a foot and a half wide. This permits easier harvesting and pruning and also allows better air circulation.

Harvesting. Raspberries ripen a few weeks before blackberries, and the long ripening season of both lets you enjoy fresh picking every day for several weeks. If you want to further extend the season, plant early, mid-season, and autumn-bearing raspberry cultivars. Use only small containers for picking raspberries, because too many piled together will crush those on the bottom. Avoid handling the berries any more than is absolutely necessary, and move freshly picked berries out of the sun as soon as possible because the heat will spoil them.

Steps for Success in the Berry Patch

First Year

Prepare the soil carefully and plant the berries 2 feet apart. If you set out bare-root plants, cut back the tops to 2 inches above the ground after planting, but leave potted plants unpruned. Water potted and bare-root plants with a liquid fertilizer, then mulch.

Second Year

Spring Cut back all plants that didn't make a strong showing the previous year to 2 inches above ground level. Add to the mulch, and apply a light helping of plant food.

Autumn Cut back tops of plants so canes are about 4 feet tall. This makes a stiff plant that doesn't fall over in winter. Install a fence or other support.

Third Year and Thereafter

Spring Add fertilizer and fresh mulch. Trim out any broken canes.

Early summer Mow or pull out tips or sucker plants growing in the wrong places. Cut off and burn wilted tops. Remove any sick-looking plants.

Late summer Cut to ground level and remove all canes that bore fruit. Cut out weak canes and thin remaining canes to 6 inches apart.

Late autumn Cut back canes to 4 to 5 feet in height for winter. Tighten wire supports if necessary.

Few items are as easy or rewarding to preserve as fruit, and almost all fruits are suitable for freezing. The requirements are simple:

- Pick or process small quantities in order to avoid temporary loathing caused by processing huge quantities at a time.

- All fruit should be ripe when preserved, unlike vegetables, which are at their best when slightly immature.

- A mellow flavour in peaches, plums, figs, and some berries is acquired by letting the fruit sit at room temperature to mature overnight. Apples may require several days to develop maximum flavour. Pears are usually picked green and allowed to ripen in the dark for several days.

- Freeze only fruit that you would want to eat fresh. Bruised or slightly overripe fruit makes excellent jam or jelly.

- Prepare fruits for freezing much as you would for the table. Wash the fruit gently in cool water. Don't let fruits soak, or they will become waterlogged.

- Avoid iron utensils, which may darken fruits. Use stainless steel or enamelware instead.

- Consider adding ascorbic acid (vitamin C) or lemon juice to fruits that darken quickly after being peeled (like peaches and apples).

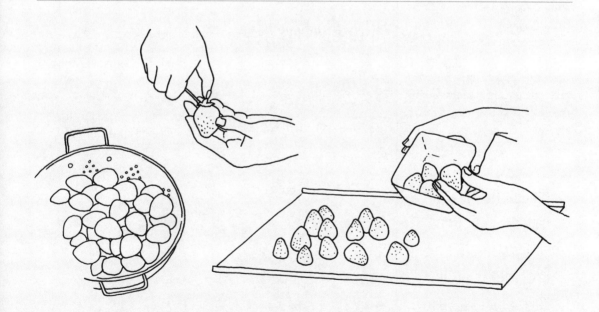

Wash and stem berries, flash-freeze on a metal sheet, then transfer to freezer bags or containers.

Blueberries

Blueberries are increasingly popular in the UK as their culinary value and health benefits become more widely understood. Heath and moorland are home to wild bilberries that are delicious eaten from the bush or taken home to cook with. Cultivated varieties are well worth growing.

The highbush varieties are best suited to the climate of the British Isles, but there are three types of blueberry commonly grown for their fruit in other parts of the world: the hardy lowbush, the popular highbush, and the rabbit-eye, which grows in the southern United States.

All blueberries do best in acidic soil, pH 4.5 to 5.0. If your soil tests from 5.5 to 6.0, mix sphagnum peat moss with the soil around the plants. Composted pine needles or oak leaves, or compost made from pine or oak bark also helps to achieve a more acidic soil. After planting, mulch your plants with pine needles, oak leaves, or shavings from oak or pine as an annual mulch to help maintain the soil's acidity.

> Blueberries can be planted in autumn, but a warm afternoon in spring is preferable. Plant as soon as the ground can be worked.

Planting and Care of Blueberries

Blueberry plants from the nursery come bare-rooted, container-grown, or balled-and-burlapped. Place bare roots in a trench and mound soil or damp peat moss around them until ready to plant. They can be planted in autumn, but a warm afternoon in spring is preferable. Plant as soon as the ground can be worked. Prune off any damaged or long roots, any weak or broken wood, and all flower buds, because fruiting the first year may stunt the growth of the bush.

Rich Blueberry Pie

¾ cup granulated sugar

3 tablespoons cornstarch

⅛ teaspoon salt

2 cups blueberries (fresh or frozen)

¼ cup water

1 tablespoon butter

1 tablespoon lemon juice

2 cups fresh blueberries

Baked 9-inch pie shell

Whipped cream (optional)

1. Combine the sugar, cornstarch, and salt in a medium-sized saucepan. Add the 2 cups of fresh or frozen (thawed) berries and water. Cook over medium heat, stirring constantly, until mixture boils, thickens, and clears. Remove from heat and stir in the butter and lemon juice. Cool.

2. Place the 2 cups of fresh berries into the pie shell and top with the cooked mixture. Chill. Serve with whipped cream.

Yield: One 9-inch pie

Top Varieties

Birgitte A late season variety ripening towards the end of August. Upright bushes will eventually reach 6 ft tall. Large, light blue and sweet flavoured fruits have a crisp texture and are ideal for freezing or for eating straight from the bush.

Bluecrop Very large richly flavoured berries. Harvest from end July. Forms a medium-sized spreading bush that is tolerant of frost.

Chandler This attractive low-growing bush is perfect for growing in a container on a patio. Large fruits measure

up to ¾ inches in diameter. Ripens from early August until mid-September. Carries sweet-smelling, creamy-white flowers in spring. Autumn colour.

Earliblue Large, light blue, sweet berries hang in clusters from early July. A stout bush growing to 6 ft high.

Ozark Blue This is a late season variety producing large fruits that are ripe in late August. They are a beautiful light blue and have excellent flavour. This vigorous plant gives consistently high yields and will mature into a tall, upright bush producing up to 15 lbs of fruit when mature, although not if it is grown in a container.

Spartan This plant has a vigorous, upright, open growth habit and bears large very firm fruit

Tophat This highbush lowbush cross is good for container growth as it is dwarf in habit and will reach a height and diameter of no more than 2 ft. Firm berries are bright blue and small to medium size.

The **highbush** grows 6 to 15 feet high and produces large berries in midsummer and later. It is less hardy than the lowbush, but perfectly hardy for all parts of the British Isles. Yields vary widely among the cultivars, but most gardeners can expect 5 to 15 pounds of fruit per bush.

The hardiest of the three types, the **lowbush** are the blueberries everyone loves to pick from the wild. Lowbush blueberries are hardy enough to be grown commercially in extremely cold regions. Homegrown lowbushes will yield about half a pound of berries for each foot of row.

The **rabbit-eye** blueberry cannot stand low winter temperatures, so the plants are suitable only for warm frost-free zones. They need a chilling period, however, so they cannot be grown in tropical climates. Rabbit-eyes grow on drier soils than the highbush kinds will tolerate, but in hot climates, most need some type of irrigation. They are very productive, often yielding 20 pounds of fruit per bush.

1. Plant your bushes 1 to 2 inches deeper than they were in the nursery and 4 to 6 feet apart in rows spaced 8 to 10 feet apart. In large plantings, do not separate cultivars by more than two rows from others with similar ripening seasons.

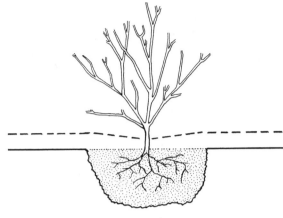

2. After you put a plant in its hole, fill the hole three-quarters full of soil or a 50-50 loam and sand mixture, and then flood it with water. After the water seeps out, fill the remainder of the hole and pack it gently with your feet. Water the plant with a starter solution, then add a layer of an acidic mulch such as pine needles.

3. If irrigation is necessary, water during the early morning but don't wet the bushes when berries are beginning to ripen. You can use ground flooding or a soaker hose. Apply an inch of water each time.

Fertilizing

Fertilize blueberries with blood meal or well-rotted manure about a month after planting and again in midsummer. Thereafter, fertilize twice a year, at the beginning of flowering and again five to six weeks later. Use combinations of the materials to provide balanced fertilization. Don't use bonemeal or wood ashes as they tend to sweeten the soil.

Planting time. Remove all weak, diseased, and broken wood and all flower buds.

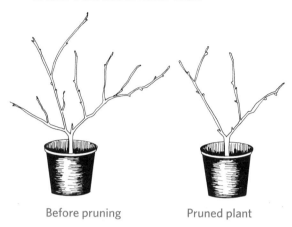

Before pruning   Pruned plant

After one year. Again prune any diseased or broken wood. Vigorous plants may be allowed to bear up to half a pound of fruit (20 to 30 flower buds). Remove any additional buds.

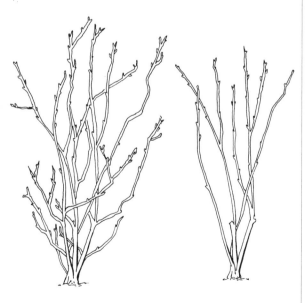

Two- to five-year-old plant, before pruning   Pruned plant

After two to five years. Continue similar pruning. If the plants appear vigorous, do not remove more flower buds than necessary during pruning. The emphasis should be on producing healthy bushes and not on fruit production.

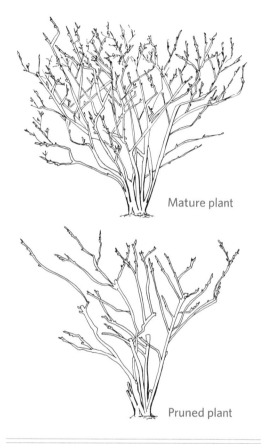

Mature plant

Pruned plant

Older bushes. Blueberry bushes that have been neglected may be rejuvenated through severe pruning. Cut these back to the ground, leaving only short, 2- to 3-inch stubs. The whole bush may be done at once, or half the bush can be done one year and the other half in the following year. By using the first method, the entire crop is lost for one season. The second method allows the plant to bear a portion of the crop each year.

Grapes

In the British Isles, dessert grapes will need to be grown in a greenhouse or conservatory to ripen successfully and produce sweet fruit, but wine grapes can be cultivated outdoors in sheltered, sunny locations. If you plan to grow rows of vines, choose a south-facing slope where the angle of the hillside is sloped to trap the sun. Do not plant outdoor grapes at high altitude.

Grapes need an abundance of heat and sun to grow and produce well. They are one of the last fruit plants to start growth in the spring, and they bloom much later than any of the tree fruits. Gardeners in the British Isles will see the benefits of planting them in heat pockets — spots where buildings, walls, or hills form corners that trap the southern and eastern sun. You can also try mulching them with black plastic or crushed rock.

Very dry, very wet, and very rich soils are bad for grapes. Leaner soils yield comparatively modest crops that mature earlier and have considerable sugar in the berry.

A vineyard should be plowed deeply and well worked so the soil is thoroughly pulverized and weed-free. These conditions do make erosion a significant risk. If your slope is steep, take specialist advice to ensure you plant the most advantageous contour rows for your vines.

Soil Needs

Grapevines grow in many soil types. Well-drained, deep, fertile loams are excellent, yet grapes thrive on soils containing clay, slate, gravel, shale, and sand. Gravelly soils generally drain well, and they absorb and reflect the sun's warmth, providing heat for the vines.

Planting and Supporting Grapevines

As a general rule, grapes should be planted as early in the spring as the soil can be worked. In dry, hot regions it can be advantageous to plant vines in the autumn so they get established before the long hot days of summer begin.

Order your grape stock from a nursery as nearby as possible; if you can, pick out and pick up the plants yourself. The best stock is strong, sturdy, one-year-old plants with large, fibrous root systems; two-year-old plants are more expensive and will not bear any sooner. Dig a good hole in worked-up soil, large enough to spread out the vine's roots comfortably. Pack the soil firmly around the roots, leaving no air spaces that could increase the chances of disease. Plant the vines at the same

The Best Fertilizer for Grapes

The best fertilizer for grapes is well-rotted manure, or garden compost, and it should be applied as a mulch during the growing season. In autumn, apply well-rotted manure at the rate of 15 to 20 pounds per 100 square feet. In most cases, no other fertilization is required. Vineyards given this treatment consistently yield up to 30 percent more fruit than those fertilized with commercial preparations.

depth they grew in the nursery, then prune them back to a single stem two or three buds tall. If it is early spring and the soil is moist, you need not water. Later in the spring you may want to water the stock well after planting. You will need a trellis.

Space most hybrid cultivars 8 to 10 feet apart in the row, with the rows 10 to 11 feet from each other. Less vigorous vines can be closer together — 7 to 8 feet apart in the row. If your grape selection is not self-pollinating, it will need a partner nearby to produce well.

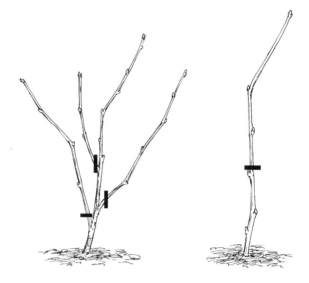

After planting, prune back the vines to a single stem two or three buds tall.

Vineyard Soil and Grape Quality

All grapes have an affection for gravel, flint, slate, or stony soils. One reason why hillsides are so good for grapes is that erosion has scoured the land to its poorest, stoniest constituents. The best acres are so infertile and stony that a corn farmer wouldn't take them as a gift. But soil that produces great grapes (and fine wines) must offer a number of qualities that help grapes flourish. Here are some characteristics of productive vineyard soil:

- Good soil drainage. This is crucial. Grapes do not like wet feet.

- Soil pH appropriate to the variety.

- Soil depth of at least 30 inches, due to the deep-rooting habits of grapes.

- Proper soil preparation. Loosen, break up, and mix soil layers well below ordinary cultivation depth.

A Gallery of Great Grapes

Indoor Grapes

Alicante

Good flavour from these oval, jet black grapes that come with a fine blue bloom. Heavy cropping and very free setting. Excellent flavour.

Black Hamburgh

Ideal for the cold greenhouse or conservatory where it is best planted in the ground rather than a pot. Ripens early in the season and will colour well even in a sunless summer. The grapes are sweet and juicy and the handsome bunches are filled with large, black fruits. The only disadvantage is that this old variety is susceptible to diseases such as botrytis and powdery mildew.

Buckland Sweetwater

An early cropping fruit that grows on a compact vine. Very fine, sweet flavour, from pale green fruits that ripen to almost amber. Heavy cropping. Excellent for pot culture.

Chasselas Rose

Ideal for the cold greenhouse. Well flavoured grapes in long bunches that ripen early. Makes a wine similar to still champagne. Very deep pink-tinged grapes.

Foster's Seedling

Very large bunches of flavourful grapes. Green or yellow to amber. A heavy cropper that sets freely.

Golden Champion

Richly flavoured, golden yellow grapes that ripen in most summers but need full sun and regular feeding. Harvest in October.

Gros Maroc

Deepest blue, large fruits, easily ripened, excellent flavour. Picking October.

Madeleine Angevine

An excellent, early white grape for dessert use primarily although it also makes a superb wine. Heavy crops ripen in late September. Very hardy and ideal for the marginal, colder areas.

Madresfield Court

Very high quality, black fruit. Excellent flavour. An early ripening Muscat type.

Muscat d'Alexandria

This fine flavoured green grape ripens well in an unheated greenhouse or conservatory in September. When established it produces full bunches that have delicious aromatic sweetness when ripe. Suitable for dessert use or for wine making. Self fertile so will produce a crop without a pollinator.

Royal Muscadine

Regarded as the ultimate quality dessert or table grape. Very large sparkling white fruits, fleshy, juicy and thin skinned with a very sweet flavour.

Outdoor Grapes

Bacchus

Well filled bunches of the palest jade-white fruits provide a full-bodied, well-rounded, flavoursome wine. Outdoor, crops well.

Bianca

A white dessert grape with excellent flavour. Suitable for growing in a sunny site, ideally against a south-facing wall. High disease resistance.

Boskoop Glory

A heavy cropping variety with large bunches of high quality grapes. Pale black or almost blue. Ready for picking in September or October. An excellent variety from Boskoop, Netherlands. Very good, sweet flavour.

Brandt

Vigorous grape that produces heavy crops of small fruits that have a very good flavour, sweet and juicy. Ripening in mid October, the fruits are dark red to almost blue. Very hardy and disease resistant. Excellent variety for vigorous wall cover with the added bonus of fiery red autumnal foliage.

Dornfelder

An excellent outdoor variety bred in Germany which is proving to be very reliable in the UK. Large bunches of even sumptuously coloured blue black fruits that self thin during maturity. Sweet flavour when ripe, making it a good dessert variety, but it can also be used to make an excellent red wine. Good autumn foliage.

Early van der Laan

A Dutch variety with pale yellow to green grapes. Excellent for dessert and wine. Early regular crop of quality fruit.

Flame

A highly popular seedless red variety with a sweet flavour and producing well filled bunches. An ideal counterpart to the green 'Lakemont Seedless'.

Fragola

The strawberry grape. The fruits are produced in small bunches of very large fruits. A perfect musk flavour with an enticing hint of strawberry. Truly delicious dessert grapes. Beautiful golden autumn leaves. A superb wall cultivar where the heavy crop is displayed at its best.

Lakemont Seedless

This white seedless grape can be grown outdoors against a sunny wall in all areas except far northern regions of the British Isles. It is also suitable for indoor cultivation. Large bunches of pale yellow green fruits with a good muscat flavour that set evenly. Has shown some resistance to mildew. Reliable cropper good yields when well-established.

Madeleine Sylvaner

A white hybrid grape. Produces regular crops of well flavoured grapes that make excellent wine. Especially good under cold conditions. Highly recommended.

Pruning and Training Grapes

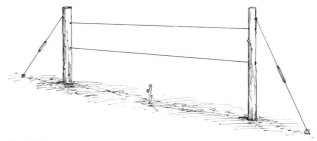

Pruning is a very important part of grape culture and one that must not be neglected. Because of the grape's tendency to grow vigorously, a lot of wood must be cut away each year. Grapevines that are overgrown become so dense that the sun cannot reach into the areas where fruit should form. The easiest way for beginners to manage a garden vineyard is with a two-wire fence using a trellis system. With this type of training, each mature vine should produce 12 to 15 pounds (30 to 60 bunches) of grapes per year. If more bunches are produced, remove the surplus before the grapes develop to avoid overbearing and thus weakening the plant. In this way, your vines should go on producing for 50 years or longer.

First Year

Staple smooth 9- or 10-gauge wire to sturdy posts, and brace the posts with wire to keep horizontal wires from sagging. Centre the plants between posts, about 8 feet apart, in rows 8 feet apart.

Cut back bare-root vines after planting so each is only 5 to 6 inches long and contains just two or three fat buds. This encourages root growth. If you planted potted vines, omit this cutting back. Water the vines frequently and allow them to grow freely the first year.

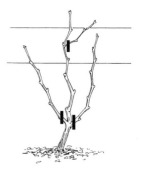

Muller Thurgau

Early to mid-season variety providing excellent quality, golden berries of good, sweet flavour for dessert. Also provides a hock type wine with a good bouquet. Highly recommended.

Phoenix

An excellent quality white grape bred in Germany. These very productive plants have good sized grapes on large packed bunches, that will need thinning. When fully ripe they have a light Muscat aroma and an excellent flavour when eaten fresh as well as making the ideal white wine grape. Suitable for a sunny site, ideally a south-facing wall. Ripens in September, good resistance to mildew. Heavy cropping variety with large bunches of high quality grapes. Pale black or almost blue. Ready for picking in September.

Perlette

If you prefer green grapes to red then Perlette is a first-class choice, being virtually seedless, with a sweet taste and thin skin. An early variety, it ripens well outside in the UK given some shelter. The plants are problem free and easy to grow.

Precoce de Malingre

A prolific, early golden grape for wine and dessert use. Excellent flavoured large, oval fruits.

Sieve Villard

Easy to grow with very heavy crops that have a useful resistance to mildew. Quality white grapes that blend well with Muller Thurgau to make a delicious wine.

Second Year

Very early in the spring, before the buds start to swell, cut back the vine to a single stem with no branches. This will encourage faster growth.

During the year, allow four side branches to grow (two in each direction) and train them along the wires. They will grasp the wires with their tendrils. Pinch off all buds that start to grow in other directions.

By the end of the second year, if growth has been good, the space along both wires should be filled. These vines should then bloom and produce a few grapes the third year.

Third Year

During the year, allow only four more canes to grow from buds along the main stem. Train these to grow along the ground parallel to the four on the wires. These four will eventually replace the first four.

In late winter following the third growing season, cut off the canes that produced that year and tie the new canes to the wires. Trim off all excess growth except the four new canes.

The Secrets of Great Homemade Wine

The byword among travelled wine drinkers is that any wine tastes best in the region (and with the regional food) it comes from. If that's true, then homemade wines must taste best when drunk at home. Not many gourmet experiences are available to us for the pound or so that homemade wine costs.

The secret of the wine is the grapes it's made from. The winemaker's role is to protect and preserve the quality of good grapes right into the bottle. Jim Mitchell, of Sakonnet Vineyards in Rhode Island, USA quotes these maxims:

1. All great wines have four important elements: first, the grape; second, the climate; third, the soil; and fourth, the skill of the winemaker — in that order.

2. The best wines are made as far north as that grape variety will grow.

3. To produce great wines, the vines must suffer, rather like athletes.

The elements for great wine, then, are the same for the home winemaker as for commercial wineries: The right grape variety in the right climate and soil achieves the right balance of sugar, acid, pH, and flavour components. When all these things come together, the results can be spectacular indeed.

Whatever your property, there is a variety of grape that will produce the most excellent wine possible. Your task, long before the first bottles come to life in your cellar, is to identify that vine.

The British climate

Grape vines like summers that are warm and long, so our summers are not ideal for wine making on a large scale. Growing popular French grape varieties isn't an option. You have to grow the non-standard varieties that are especially suited to our conditions (see below). Plant only the sunniest and most favourable sites (usually south-facing slopes).

Wine grapes

Chardonnay Grown widely for sparkling wines but also produces a good still white wine.

Dornfelder One of the few grapes that proves good red wine can be made in the U.K. Wines are usually fresh and fruity more like Syrah or Gamay than Cabernet Sauvignon.

Huxelrebe This is a 'muscat' style with good sugar levels. It has a high natural acidity and strong aromas of elderflower. Produces very fruity white wines that age well.

Ortega This vine suits our climate, although it is prone to disease. When ripe it produces white wines that are rich and zesty with good balance. Good for blending.

Pinot Noir Grows well in the English climate and in good years some excellent quality red wines can be made.

Reichensteiner It is reliable but a little bland and is often used for blending in both still and sparkling white wines, having good sugar levels.

Rondo Produces wines with very good colour and style and overtones of classic red varieties. It blends well with other varieties and can be likened to a cross between Tempranillo and Syrah.

Schönburger This grape is very successful in the the British Isles, producing white wines with low acidity but high sugar levels and good Muscat tones. Its wines are distinctive, full-bodied and delicately flavoured.

Seyval Blanc A good grape for blending that is well suited to oak aging and used for still or sparkling white wines.

Siegerrebe A small berried and intensely aromatic variety. It ripens sometimes to excessive levels and has a very dominating flavour. It is often used to bolster blended white wines.

Calculating the Size of a Vineyard

Assumptions

1. A mature grapevine yields 8 to 12 pounds of grapes.
2. 11 to 12 pounds of grapes yield a gallon of finished wine.
3. Vines are planted 6 feet apart in rows 10 feet apart.

x = gallons of wine desired
z = number of vines in each row
a = number of rows
y = pounds of grapes per vine: 8 for low-yielding varieties; 10 for medium-yielding varieties; 12 for high-yielding vines.

Calculation

To determine the number of vines needed to make x gallons of wine: $\dfrac{11x}{y}$

Example: For 25 gal. of high-yield variety:

$$\frac{11 \times 25}{12} = 22.9 \text{ or } 23 \text{ vines}$$

Only you know whether your property allows for a square, rectangular, or odd-shaped vineyard. Assuming that space is not constricted, you can achieve a good-looking rectangular arrangement by having about as many rows as vines in a row.

Fruit Trees

What could be better than sweet, sun-warmed, fruit picked ripe from the tree just yards from the back door? Plan well and your home orchard will produce quantities of fruit year after year.

The Home Orchard

When you are involved in a home orchard that will quite likely last a lifetime or more, you naturally want to get it right. Mistakes made early have a way of coming back to haunt you.

Even if you can't plant everything you want the first year, make a plan so you will have the best possible trees growing in the best possible locations. Give your trees full sun, plenty of room to grow, and well-drained soil.

A dwarf fruit tree grows less vigorously than a standard tree, is smaller at maturity, and begins to produce blossoms and fruits at an earlier age.

It helps to sketch the orchard on paper to start with. First, measure the area where your orchard will be and match it up to the gridlines of graph paper. Note objects that you will have to work around, such as buildings, large boulders, property lines, footpaths, inhospitable neighbouring plants, and anything else that might influence planting decisions.

After you have chosen the number and varieties of trees you want to plant, draw in each tree based on the crown diameter of the mature tree, leaving enough space for them to grow without crowding.

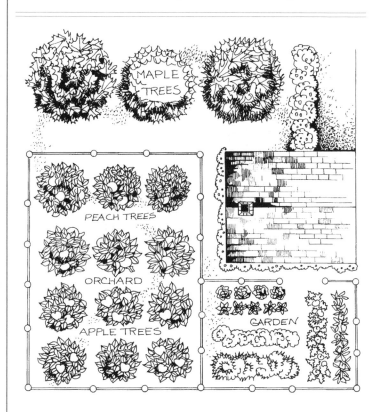

Sketch your entire property, showing house, gardens, and existing trees, and then plan the placement of your orchard. Keep in mind as you sketch which trees need to be near each other for cross-pollination.

Think Small: Planting a Dwarf Fruit Orchard

The fruits produced by dwarf trees are every bit as large and tasty as those on standard-sized trees. The basic differences between standard and dwarf trees are in their growth habits. A dwarf fruit tree grows less vigorously than a standard tree, is smaller at maturity, and begins to produce blossoms and fruits at an earlier age, as soon as the second year after planting. There are other advantages as well. In the space needed by four standard-sized apple trees, planted 40 × 40 feet, you can plant 30 to 40 dwarf trees without crowding them. This lets you plant early, midseason, and late-ripening varieties to extend the harvest period.

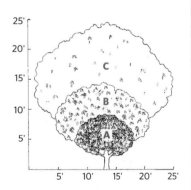

Dwarf (A) and semidwarf (B) fruit trees take up less space and produce fruit earlier than standard (C) trees do.

How Big Are They?

The following are approximate diameters of some full-grown fruit trees. When you plant them, allow enough additional room so that you will be able to walk through them, and so that light can reach the entire exterior of each tree.

Fruit Tree	Crown Diameter	Fruit Tree	Crown Diameter
Apple		**Pear**	
Standard	25–35 feet	Standard	18 feet
Semidwarf	15–20 feet	Dwarf	8 feet
Dwarf	7–10 feet		
		Plum	
Apricot		Standard	18 feet
Standard	18 feet	Dwarf	8 feet
Dwarf	8 feet		
		Quince	12 feet
Peach			
Standard	18 feet		
Dwarf	8 feet		

Recommended Fruit Varieties

Apple

Braeburn Capable of producing heavy crops of round, bi-coloured tasty, crisp fruits.

Bramley's Seedling Classic British cooking apple that ripens in October and stores well.

Cox's Orange Pippin Considered by many to be the finest flavoured eating apple. Pick during the autumn and store for best eating between November and January.

Diva Prolific even in its first year of fruiting. Delicious sweet yet tangy flavour.

Egremont Russet Bronze-skinned heavy cropping variety with distinctive nutty flavour.

Pinova Delicious smooth-skinned fruits are ready to eat from September. Troublefree for the home gardener.

Red Falstaff Sweet, tangy flavour. Dwarf variety deal for growing in a container on a patio.

Encouraging Pollination

Nearly all fruit trees do better with a mate. Although a few are self-fertile, which means that a single tree can bear fruit by itself, most need what is known as cross-pollination and require a partner nearby. In order to cross-pollinate each other, the trees must be in the same family group. Apples cannot pollinate pears, nor can pears pollinate plums. You therefore need at least two different varieties of each species of fruit tree you plant.

Most ornamentals, vegetables, and fruit trees are pollinated by insects — primarily bees. As a rule, bees should not have to fly more than 500 to 600 feet to bring about the mating of two blossoms.

When only one kind of fruit tree is blooming and no suitable partner is blossoming anywhere in the neighbourhood, here's a tip: Drive to an abandoned farm or ask a neighbouring gardener if you can have a few branches from a fruit tree that always blossoms at the same time as yours. Bring the branches home and put them in a bucket of water under the tree. The bees will take over from there.

When bees are scarce, you can sometimes pollinate a few of your fruit trees yourself. Take a small artist's paintbrush and gently dust the pollen from the flowers into a teacup. Then brush it carefully onto the blossoms of an adjoining tree.

If you do this, mark the limbs to show which ones you have treated. Or, if you have the energy, you can pollinate the entire tree. It takes only a short time to pollinate a small orchard of dwarf trees, since you need to dust only one bloom in a cluster.

> When you have only one kind of fruit tree, you can borrow branches to increase the odds of cross-pollination.

Apricot

Bergecot Late-cropping variety. Juicy sweet-flavoured fruit is ready to pick late August in the south of England.

Petit Muscat Fine-flavoured walnut-sized fruit ready to pick in mid-August.

Tomcot Heavy crop of large crimson-tinged fruit ready to harvest around the middle of July.

Cherry

Crown Morello A good sour cherry ideal for a north-facing wall. Productive tree with compact growth and excellent spring blossom.

Merton Glory Large, juicy fruit that is yellow-orange skinned and white-fleshed. Not self-fertile so needs to be grown alongside another cherry.

Peach

Avalon Pride Large, juicy fruit from early August. Resistant to peach leaf curl disease.

Pear

Concorde Excellent self-fertile pear with delicious fruit ready to pick in September.

Invincible Fruit has a rich aromatic flavour and ripens in early October.

Plum

Victoria The classic English plum excellent for crumble and jams.

Quince

Large, butter yellow fruit ripens in October.

Planting a Fruit Tree in Three Simple Steps

Quick root development is important for any newly planted tree, so plant early in the season, as soon as the soil has dried enough to crumble easily in your hand. A tree planted this spring will reward you with harvests of luscious fruit in the years to come, the first crop in some cases appearing as soon as next summer.

If the tree is branched, choose three or four healthy branches starting 2 feet above ground level and shorten them to just a few inches. Each one should end in an outward-pointing bud. Then cut away any other branches and cut off the top of the trunk just above the uppermost branch. If the tree is not branched, simply cut back the trunk to 3 feet high.

1. Soak bare roots in a bucketful of water for a few hours to plump them up. Before planting, trim back long or frayed roots to just a few inches.

2. Add any soil amendments, such as bonemeal (for good root development) and lime (if soil is acidic), over an area as wide as the spread of the mature tree and then dig a hole in the centre. Arrange the roots over a small mound at the centre of the planting hole. Adjust the height of the mound so that tree will stand roughly 2 inches higher than the old soil line on the trunk. If the tree is branched, position it with the lowest branch facing southwest. As this branch grows, it will shade the trunk and lessen the chance of sunscald. If the site is windy, lean the tree slightly into the wind.

3. As you fill the hole, bounce the tree up and down slightly to settle the soil among the roots. After you've filled in the hole, construct a soil dike around the base of the tree to form a catch basin for water — 2 feet out from the trunk in all directions should be sufficient. Spread compost or manure over the catch basin and then a layer of straw or leaf mulch. Drench the soil to settle the tree in place.

Water generously once a week through August. Be sure to weed the catch basin diligently, as weeds will compete with the tree for nutrients and water.

Pruning a Fruit Tree in Four Steps

A tree that has reached its mature size and is yielding fruit requires regular pruning to stay healthy and productive. Although you'll remove some fruit buds and, hence, potential fruits as you prune, the quality of those that remain will be better.

In addition, pruning maintains a balance between fruiting and non-fruiting growth. After you prune, the tree will respond with a flush of leafy shoots that provide new fruit-bearing wood and nourish developing fruits.

The best time to prune a tree is from late autumn until its blossoms open in spring. Where winters are severely cold, wait until after midwinter to avoid cold damage in the cut area.

continued on next page ▶

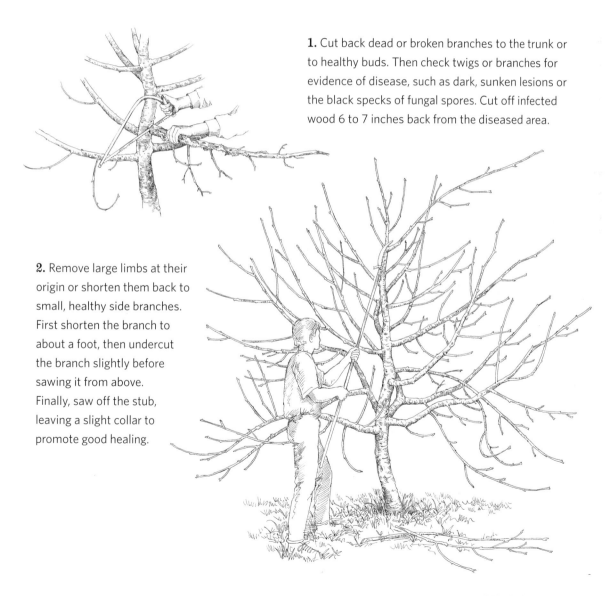

1. Cut back dead or broken branches to the trunk or to healthy buds. Then check twigs or branches for evidence of disease, such as dark, sunken lesions or the black specks of fungal spores. Cut off infected wood 6 to 7 inches back from the diseased area.

2. Remove large limbs at their origin or shorten them back to small, healthy side branches. First shorten the branch to about a foot, then undercut the branch slightly before sawing it from above. Finally, saw off the stub, leaving a slight collar to promote good healing.

▶ *continued from previous page*

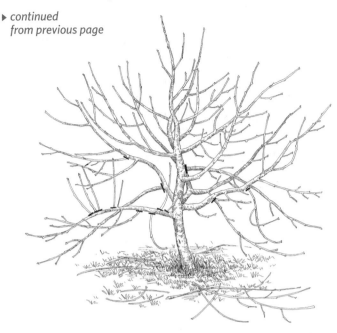

3. Take out most of the water sprouts, or suckers (overly vigorous, vertical branches that produce only a few, poor-quality fruits and shade the interior of the tree), at their base. If there are many water sprouts, leave a few to protect the tree from sunscald. In addition, shorten branches that droop downward, and remove any twiggy branches growing from the undersides of limbs.

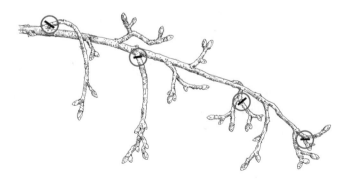

4. Only on apple and pear trees, thin out crowded spurs (fat, stubby growths on which these trees bear most of their fruit). Cut them back to strong buds. If they are crowded, remove a few so that fruit will be evenly distributed, but not packed, along the branches.

Harvest time in the Orchard

How can you tell when a fruit is ripe? Most varieties of tree fruits fall from the tree soon after ripening, so the fruit is ready as soon as it will separate from the branch with an easy twist. Most fruits change colour as they ripen. If you are in doubt about the ripeness of an apple or pear, cut one open. If the seeds are dark brown, the fruit is ready to be picked. Only pears, a few varieties of peaches, and winter apples that finish ripening in storage should be picked before they are tree ripened.

Pick on a dry day, if possible. If the fruit is wet, it may quickly begin to spoil. Put the fruit in a cool place as soon as possible after you pick it.

Ordinary plastic buckets are satisfactory for picking cherries and plums. For apricots, peaches, nectarines, pears, and apples, try the bags used by commercial growers. They hang like knapsacks on the front and are easy to use, even when you are working from a ladder. You can dump the fruit into baskets without bruising it or removing the bag.

Pick each fruit by hand, and never club or shake it from the tree. Bend the fruit upward and twist it gently. If it is ripe, the stem will separate easily from the tree and stay on the fruit. Never pull out the stem, for it will leave a hole where rot will develop.

Old-Fashioned Peach Preserves

This recipe is an all-time favourite, maybe because it is so hard to get real peach flavour in any season but summer. The almond extract accentuates the peach flavour.

½ teaspoon ascorbic acid (crystals, powder, or crushed tablets)

1 quart water

3½ pounds (about 7 large) peaches, peeled, pitted, and chopped

5 cups granulated sugar

¼ cup lemon juice

¾ teaspoon almond extract

1. In a large, non-reactive bowl, prepare an acid bath by adding the ascorbic acid to the water.

2. Dip the peaches in the acid bath; drain well. Combine the fruit, sugar, and lemon juice in a preserving pan or large, heavy saucepan. Cook over medium heat, stirring to dissolve the sugar. Bring to a boil.

Pollination Requirements of Fruit Trees

Apples. Two or more different cultivars are recommended for pollination. If several apples belonging to the same family group are planted together, plant another cultivar nearby.

Peaches. Many peach cultivars are self-fertile, but several of the most popular kinds are not. It is a good idea to plant two different cultivars for insurance.

Pears. Two or more different cultivars are recommended for good crops.

Plums. There are several families of plums, and two different cultivars within the same family are necessary for pollination.

Sour cherries. Sour cherries are one of the few fruits that nearly always self-pollinate well, so one tree is all you need.

Sweet cherries. Two or more different cultivars are necessary. Sour cherries are not good pollinators for sweet cherries because they often bloom at different times.

3. Boil slowly, stirring constantly, until mixture thickens and fruit is translucent and reaches 220°F (104°C) on a cooking thermometer.

4. Stir in the almond extract.

5. Remove from heat and skim off any foam with a metal spoon. Ladle into sterile jars, allowing ¼ inch of headroom. Run a rubber spatula around the insides of the jars to release air bubbles. Wipe the rims of the jars with a clean, damp cloth. Place lids in position and tighten screw bands.

6. Process in a boiling-water-bath (see page 80) for 5 minutes, adjusting for altitude, if necessary.

Yield: 7 pints

It's all in the Thinning

Here's a trick little used by home gardeners that could make you the envy of your neighbours: If you want your tree to produce its best fruit and bear big crops every year, simply thin the little fruits as soon as they reach marble size. The tree's strength and energy will then be diverted to the remaining fruits, which will grow much larger.

Peaches, apples, pears, and the large fruited plums all benefit from thinning, but don't bother to thin cherries, crab apples, small pears, or small fruited plums. How many should you pluck off? Try leaving only one fruit in a cluster and about 6 to 7 inches between each fruit.

Painful as it is to throw away perfectly good apples, pears, and peaches, you won't mind doing it when you see how much bigger and better the fruit is — and when you find that you actually have more pounds of usable fruit than you would have picked otherwise.

Bottling Apple Purée

Even though it takes time to make apple purée, it yields such a wonderful finished product that you may find it well worth your time. work on the basis that 21 pounds of apples will yield 14 pints of apple purée.

Wash, peel, and quarter apples. Put in a heavy-bottomed saucepan with 2 inches of water. Cover and cook until soft, stirring occasionally to prevent scorching. Add sugar to taste. Begin preheating water in boiling-water bath and preparing jars and lids.

If desired, pass softened apples through a hand-operated strainer or food processor. Reheat sauce to boiling.

Pack hot apple purée in hot, clean jars, leaving half an inch of headspace. Process each pint jar for 15 minutes and 2-pint jars for 20 minutes.

Storage of Common Apple Varieties

Variety	Storage Period	
	Normal (months)	Maximum (months)
Braeburn	2-3	4
Blenheim Orange	2-3	4
Bramley's Seedling	3-4	5
Charles Ross	1-2	3
Cox's Orange Pippin	2-3	4
Diva	1-2	3
Egremont Russet	1-2	3
George Cave	1	1
Howgate Wonder	3-4	5
James Grieve	1	1
Jonagold	3-4	5
Pinova	3-4	6
Red Falstaff	3-4	5
Reverend W. Wilks	1	1
Worcester Pearmain	3-4	5

Consider Edible Landscaping

Garden plants have traditionally been pigeonholed into one of two categories: utilitarian, for providing food, or ornamental, for providing beauty.

That choice need not be made; you can have both! You can select, plant, and grow trees, shrubs, and climbers that provide delicious fruits without skimping on aesthetics.

In the last few decades, even the humble vegetable garden has been recognized for its untapped beauty. Ornamental vegetables, such as 'Scarlet Runner' beans and 'Rainbow' chard, have segued out of the vegetable garden and into the flower bed, and the flavours of edible flowers, such as spicy nasturtiums, are now more appreciated.

The time has come for fruit trees, shrubs, and climbers to come into their own as ornamentals. "Edible landscaping" works especially well with fruits. Why? Because fruit-bearing trees, shrubs, and vines become permanent fixtures in the landscape, their branching patterns, their bark, and their trunks enduring throughout the year and looking more dramatic with time. Many fruiting plants are spectacular ornaments and especially so in certain seasons: Just look at peach branches studded in spring with powder puffs of pink blossoms, or quince branches in autumn bowing under the weight of their butter yellow fruit. Crab apples and medlars are among those plants that bear delectable fruits

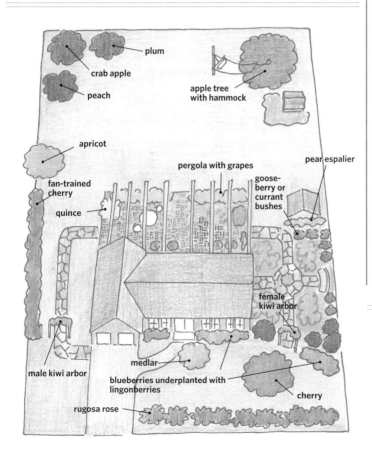

plum

crab apple

peach

apple tree
with hammock

apricot

pergola with grapes

pear espalier

fan-trained
cherry

goose-
berry or
currant
bushes

quince

female
kiwi arbor

male kiwi arbor

medlar

blueberries underplanted with
lingonberries

cherry

rugosa rose

Many ornamental plants also bear delicious fruits (and many edible plants are beautiful in their own right). In this illustration, the homeowners have opted for fruiting plants rather than more traditional ornamental plantings.

yet have actually been planted most often as ornamentals, their gustatory offerings unknowingly overlooked or ignored.

One nice feature of this kind of landscaping is that eating the fruit doesn't ruin the scenery, something that's *not* the case when you landscape with annual vegetables like lettuce. A quince's fruits cling to its branches for weeks and bear in such profusion that the tree's festive look lingers well into autumn despite a gardener's picking and eating plenty of their bounty. Perhaps the biggest bonus is that you get to eat homegrown fruits, nature's original desserts.

For more information on edible landscaping, read *Landscaping with Fruit* by Lee Reich, from which much of this section was excerpted.

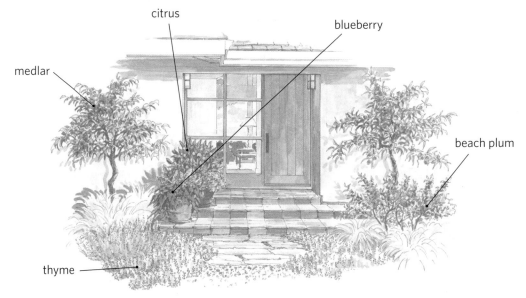

citrus

blueberry

medlar

beach plum

thyme

Edible front garden

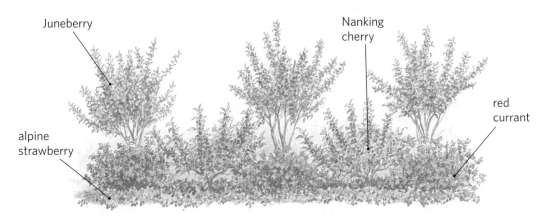

Juneberry

Nanking cherry

alpine strawberry

red currant

Edible hedge

An Overview of Edible Landscape Plants

Common Name	Latin Name	Yield	Hardiness Zones	Pollination Needs	Landscape Use	Most Prominent Ornamental Qualities
Alpine strawberry	*Fragaria vesca*	½ cup per plant	3–10	self-fruitful	ground cover or low border	low mounds or lines of greenery
Apple and crab apple	*Malus* spp.	60–300 pounds per tree	3–9	cross-pollination needed	specimen or shade tree	blossoms, tree form
Apricot	*Prunus armeniaca* var. *armeniaca*	150 pounds per tree	5–9	most varieties are self-fruitful	specimen or shade tree	blossoms, tree form
Autumn olive	*Elaeagnus umbellata*	30 pounds per bush	3–7	partially self-fertile	specimen shrub or hedge	leaves, fruits
Beach plum	*Prunus maritima*	highly variable	3–8	cross-pollination needed	part of shrub border	blossoms
Blackberry	*Rubus* spp.	3 pounds per plant	5–8	self-fruitful	train along a fence or trellis, or tie up to a pole	blossoms, leaves
Blueberry, highbush	*Vaccinium corymbosum*	7 pounds per plant	4–7	self-fruitful, but cross-pollination increases yield and berry size	shrub border, foundation planting, or hedge	blossoms, leaves in summer and autumn, canes in autumn
Blueberry, lowbush	*Vaccinium angustifolium*	5–10 pounds per 100 square feet	3–7	self-fruitful, but cross-pollination increases yield and berry size	ground cover	blossoms, leaves in summer and autumn, canes in autumn

Common Name	Latin Name	Yield	Hardiness Zones	Pollination Needs	Landscape Use	Most Prominent Ornamental Qualities
Blueberry, rabbit-eye	Vaccinium asheii	15 pounds per plant	7-9	self-fruitful, but cross-pollination increases yield and berry size	specimen shrub, foundation planting, or hedge	blossoms, leaves in summer and autumn, canes in autumn
Cherry, cornelian	Cornus mas	30-50 pounds per plant	4-8	self-fruitful, but cross-pollination increases yield	shade tree	blossoms, leaves in summer and autumn, fruits in summer, bark in winter
Cherry, Nanking	Prunus tomentosa	15-25 pounds per bush	3-6	cross-pollination needed	shrub border, hedge	blossoms in spring, fruits in early summer
Cherry, wild	Prunus avium	300 pounds per full-sized tree	5-9	cross-pollination needed for most varieties	specimen or shade tree	blossoms, tree form
Cherry, Kentish red	Prunus cerasus	100 pounds per tree	4-8	self-fruitful	small specimen tree	blossoms
Currant, buffalo	Ribes odoratum	4-8 pounds per shrub	4-8	self-fruitful, but cross-pollination increases yield	shrub border, hedge	blossoms
Currant, red, white, or pink	Ribes petraeum, R. rubrum, R. sativum	3-10 pounds per shrub	3-7	self-fruitful	hedge, foundation planting, or espalier	blossoms, leaves in summer, fruits

Common Name	Latin Name	Yield	Hardiness Zones	Pollination Needs	Landscape Use	Most Prominent Ornamental Qualities
Grape	*Vitis vinifera*	10–30 pounds per vine	7–10	self-fruitful	train over an arbour or fence	canopy of leafy branches, trunk (with age)
Grape, Northern fox	*Vitis labrusca*	10–30 pounds per vine	3–7	self-fruitful	train over an arbour or fence	canopy of leafy branches, trunk (with age)
Grape, muscadine	*Vitis rotundifolia*	10–30 pounds per vine	7–9	cross-pollination needed for most varieties	train over an arbour or fence	canopy of leafy branches, trunk (with age)
Gumi	*Elaeagnus multiflora*	10 pounds per shrub	4–9	self-fruitful	hedge	leaves in summer, fruits
Hackberry	*Celtis australis*	not known	7–9	self-fruitful	specimen or shade tree	bark, tree form
	Celtis laevigata	not known	5–11	self-fruitful	specimen or shade tree	bark, tree form, leaves in autumn
	Celtis occidentalis	not known	2–9	self-fruitful	specimen or shade tree	bark, tree form
	Celtis reticulata	not known	4–10	self-fruitful	specimen or shade tree	bark, tree form

Common Name	Latin Name	Yield	Hardiness Zones	Pollination Needs	Landscape Use	Most Prominent Ornamental Qualities
Black huckleberry	*Gaylussacia baccata*	not known	3–8	probably partially self-fruitful, but cross-pollination increases yield	foundation planting or mixed shrubbery	blossoms
Jujube	*Ziziphus jujuba*	60 pounds per plant	6–9	cross-pollination needed for most varieties	specimen plant or hedge	leaves in summer
Juneberry	*Amelanchier canadensis*	10 pounds per plant	3–8	self-fruitful, except for white-fruited varieties	hedge or loose, naturalistic plantings, specimen trees or shrubs	blossoms, form of tree or shrub, autumn colour, bark in winter
Kiwi fruit	*Actinidia deliciosa*	50–200 pounds per plant	7–9	cross-pollination needed	climbing vine for arbours and trellises	canopy of leafy branches, trunk (with age)
Kiwi fruit, golden	*Actinidia chinensis*	50–200 pounds per plant	8–10	cross-pollination needed	climbing vine for arbours and trellises	canopy of leafy branches, trunk (with age)
Kiwi fruit, hardy or tara vine	*Actinidia arguta*	50–200 pounds per plant	4–9	cross-pollination needed	climbing vine for arbours and trellises	canopy of leafy branches, trunk (with age)

Common Name	Latin Name	Yield	Hardiness Zones	Pollination Needs	Landscape Use	Most Prominent Ornamental Qualities
Kiwi fruit, super-hardy	*Actinidia kolomikta*	50–200 pounds per plant	3–7	cross-pollination needed	climbing vine for arbours and trellises	canopy of leafy branches, variegated leaves, trunk (with age)
Lingonberry	*Vaccinium vitisidaea*	5–10 pounds per 100 square feet	4–7	self-fruitful, but cross-pollination increases yield	ground cover	evergreen leaves, blossoms (two seasons), fruits
Maypop	*Passiflora incarnata*	12 fruits per plant	5–10	cross-pollination needed	climbing vine for arbours and trellises	blossoms
Medlar	*Mespilus germanica*	20 pounds per tree	5–8	self-fruitful	specimen tree planted singly or in a mixed border	blossoms, autumn colour of leaves
Mulberry, black	*Morus nigra*	5–25 pounds per plant	7–10	self-fruitful	specimen or shade tree	tree form
Mulberry, red	*Morus rubra*	5–25 pounds per plant	5–8	self-fruitful	specimen or shade tree	tree form
Mulberry, white	*Morus alba*	5–25 pounds per plant	5–8	self-fruitful	specimen or shade tree	glossy leaves

Common Name	Latin Name	Yield	Hardiness Zones	Pollination Needs	Landscape Use	Most Prominent Ornamental Qualities
Pawpaw	*Asimina triloba*	25 pounds per plant	4–8	cross-pollination needed	specimen or shade tree	leaves all summer and in autumn
Peach	*Prunus persica*	50–150 pounds per tree	5–9	most varieties are self-fruitful	small tree, mixed border	blossoms
Pear, sand	*Pyrus pyrifolia*	60–300 pounds per tree	4–9	cross-pollination needed for most varieties	specimen or shade tree	blossoms, leaves in summer and autumn
Pear, wild	*Pyrus communis*	60–300 pounds per tree	4–9	cross-pollination needed for most varieties	specimen or shade tree	blossoms, leaves in summer and autumn
Persimmon, American	*Diospyros virginiana*	50–100 pounds per tree	4–10	some varieties are self-fruitful	specimen or shade tree	tree form, leaves in summer and autumn, fruit
Persimmon	*Diospyros kaki*	40–400 pounds per tree	7–10	some varieties are self-fruitful	specimen or shade tree	tree form, fruits
Plum	*Prunus domestica*	75 pounds per tree	4–8	self-fruitful, but cross-pollination increases yield	specimen or shade tree	blossoms
Plum, Japanese	*Prunus salicina*	75 pounds per tree	6–10	cross-pollination needed	specimen or shade tree	blossoms

Common Name	Latin Name	Yield	Hardiness Zones	Pollination Needs	Landscape Use	Most Prominent Ornamental Qualities
Quince	*Cydonia oblonga*	75 pounds per plant	5–9	self-fruitful	small specimen tree or shrub, shrub border	blossoms, fruits
Raisin tree, Japanese	*Hovenia dulcis*	5–10 pounds per plant	6–10	self-fruitful	specimen or shade tree	leafy form
Rose hips						
apple rose	*Rosa villosa*	4 pounds per plant	5–10	self-fruitful	shrub border, hedge	blossoms, fruits
dog rose	*Rosa canina*	4 pounds per plant	3–10	self-fruitful	shrub border, trained on fence or post	flowers, fruits
Japanese rose	*Rosa moyesii*	4 pounds per plant	5–10	self-fruitful	shrub border, trained on fence or post	flowers, fruits, leaves in summer
prickly rose	*Rosa acicularis*	4 pounds per plant	2–9	self-fruitful	shrub border	flowers, fruits
Ramanas rose	*Rosa rugosa*	4 pounds per plant	3–10	self-fruitful	shrub border, hedge	flowers, fruits

Common Name	Latin Name	Yield	Hardiness Zones	Pollination Needs	Landscape Use	Most Prominent Ornamental Qualities
sweet briar rose	*Rosa eglanteria*	4 pounds per plant	4–10	self-fruitful	shrub border, trained on fence or post	blossoms, fruits
Oleaster	*Elaeagnus angustifolia*	20 pounds per plant	2–7	self-fruitful	specimen tree, large hedge	leaves in summer, fruits ('King Red')
Sea buckthorn	*Hippophae rhamnoides*	20 pounds per plant	3–7	cross-pollination needed	specimen hedge, shrub border	leaves in summer, fruits
Shipova	× *Sorbopyrus auricularis*	50 pounds per tree	4–9	probably self-fruitful	specimen tree	blossoms, leaves in summer
Sorbus						
Korean mountain ash	*Sorbus alnifolia*	30 pounds per tree	4–7	self-fruitful	specimen or shade tree	leaves in summer and autumn, fruits
service tree	*Sorbus domestica*	30 pounds per tree	6–10	self-fruitful	specimen or shade tree	leaves in summer and autumn
whitebeam	*Sorbus aria*	30 pounds per tree	5–9	self-fruitful	specimen or shade tree	leaves in summer and autumn, fruits
Yu's mountain ash	*Sorbus yuana*	30 pounds per tree	4–7	self-fruitful	specimen or shade tree	leaves in summer and autumn, fruits
Checkerberry	*Gaultheria procumbens*	not known	3–6	self-fruitful	ground cover	evergreen leaves, fruits

Subtropical Fruits

Once you've caught the fruit "bug," you might want to try growing subtropical fruits, a possibility even for cold climates if you plant them in pots. In addition to getting to eat these luscious, exotic fruits, you achieve a special landscape effect, one that can evoke, depending on the plants, the lusher, warmer climate of, say, mountainous Asia or the sunny, warmer climate of the Mediterranean.

Winter care is where these subtropical fruits part ways with temperate-zone fruits. Subtropical fruits cannot be left outdoors where winters are cold. Just how much cold can be tolerated depends on the particular fruit and is spelled out below for each. The favoured winter home for these plants is a sunny window in a cool room, a barely heated basement, a conservatory, or — the Ritz of winter quarters for subtropicals — a cool greenhouse. Subtropical fruits that are evergreen require some light in winter. The cooler the temperature, the less light they can get by with. Of course, don't make the temperature so cool as to harm a plant.

Citrus (*Citrus* spp., various species that include oranges, lemons, and limes): Hardiness variable, generally require winter protection. Mandarins are among the most hardy, tolerating some frost, and Key limes are the least hardy. Many varieties exist of each of these other citrus fruits, and the smorgasbord has been further expanded with hybrids within this genus and even within the related genus of kumquats, resulting in such tongue twisters as citrangequats. All are beautiful plants with glossy, dark green, evergreen leaves that set off the fragrant white flowers and then the usually bright yellow or orange fruits. The only citrus to avoid is the one most commonly grown in pots, the calamondin, which is practically inedible yet no prettier or easier to grow than any other citrus.

Most citrus will bear fruit without cross-pollination and require little pruning beyond some cuts to let in light among the branches and to balance the top with the roots lost when repotting. No need to harvest fruits just as soon as they ripen,

Lemons

which is when they are fully coloured, because the ripe fruits keep well hanging on the plant for a while — and look very decorative doing so.

Feijoa (*Acca sellowiana,* also commonly known as pineapple guava): This green, torpedo-shaped fruit has a flavour that combines the best of pineapple, strawberry, and mint. The plant has downy, evergreen leaves and flowers whose fleshy, purple-tinged white petals enclose a bottlebrush centre of dark pink stamens. The petals, incidentally, are also edible and delicious, minty and very sweet.

Prune lightly, only as much as is needed to balance root loss when repotting and to keep the plant correctly sized to its pot. A few varieties exist and most require cross-pollination for fruit set. You can tell when the fruit is ripe by the slight colour change or, more dramatically, because it falls from the plant.

Orange

Fig (*Ficus carica*): If you've never tasted a fresh fig, you're in for a treat, a juicy, sweet treat that tastes very different from the more familiar dried product. The plant is deciduous and lush when in leaf even though it's native to Mediterranean climates. Figs are very easy to fruit in pots because they tolerate all kinds of pruning, most varieties do not need pollination, and many varieties bloom on new growth. Encourage vigorous growth and protect the old stems through winter and you'll get two crops from some varieties: the first, earlier crop on the previous year's stem growth and the second, late-summer crop on new shoots. Prune one-crop varieties more severely to encourage vigorous new growth on which fruits are borne.

'Brown Turkey', 'Brunswick', 'Violetta' and 'White Marseilles' are among the recommended varieties, but there are many, many more from which to choose. Delay harvest until the fruit is very soft and drooping, at which point it usually has a "tear" in its eye.

Kumquat (*Fortunella japonica, F. crassifolia*): Kumquat is a citrus relative bearing small, orange fruits that are unique in that you eat the whole thing, skin and all. It is the skin that is sweet and the flesh that is tart. 'Nagami' is the usual, oblong-shaped market variety; the less common

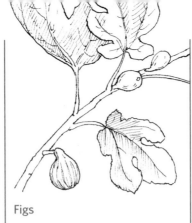

Figs

'Meiwa' is round and not so tart. The shiny, dark green, evergreen leaves form a perfect backdrop for the heavenly scented white flowers and then the orange fruits. The plant requires neither cross-pollination nor more than a little pruning to contain it, shape it, and thin out crowded branches. Harvest when the fruit is fully coloured.

Passionfruit (*Passiflora* spp.): This evergreen vine yields a breathtakingly beautiful flower, fragrant in some species, as well as an egg-shaped, highly aromatic fruit. Most commonly eaten is the purple granadilla, *P. edulis,* a self-fruitful plant bearing a fruit the size and shape of an egg but purple. Within the tough, inedible skin is a cavity filled with numerous edible seeds, each surrounded by an ambrosial sac of jelly. Other passionfruits, such as yellow passionfruit (*P. edulis* var. *flavicarpa*) and red granadilla (*P. coccinea*), do need cross-pollination. Passionfruits bear

flowers in the leaf axils of new growth, so new growth is always needed for continued flowering. Coax new growth and contain the plant by pruning in late winter, cutting back all weak stems and shortening by at least half any vigorous stems. Also provide some sort of support for the vines, which cling by tendrils. Harvest by picking up dropped fruits.

Pomegranate (*Punica granatum*): This familiar and ancient fruit grows on an extremely attractive shrub with glossy, bright green leaves that naturally drop in autumn and flamboyant flowers that look like scarlet crepe paper that's been crumpled into and is bursting out of a scarlet funnel. It is native to western Asia and prefers dry climates and the abundant summer heat you get in Mediterranean regions. Prune lightly, thinning out dense growth, shortening lanky growth, and removing excess suckers from ground level. Many varieties exist — some sweet, some pink, and some almost seedless — in addition to the variety called 'Wonderful', which usually graces supermarket shelves. Pomegranate is partially self-fertile, so planting two or more varieties increases fruit set. Harvest in late summer when fruit is fully coloured and makes a metallic sound when tapped.

Drying Fruits

Fruits should be dried when they are fully ripe and at their most flavourful — just before they become overripe. For best flavour, allow fruits to ripen on the tree or vine.

Some fruits can be dried whole, but fruits sliced as thin as possible or chopped into very small pieces will retain the best colour, flavour, and nutritional value during drying. Cut pieces uniformly so they will dry evenly.

Some fruits tend to darken when cut up. Treating them with an antioxidant will prevent darkening and will also reduce the amount of vitamin C lost during drying. Both this step and sulphuring are considered unnecessary by many who want to dry fruits as naturally as possible.

For a different taste treat, many people like the confection-like taste of fruit that has been dipped in a solution of 1 cup sugar, 1 cup honey, and 3 cups warm water. Drain well before drying. A less sweet dip to try is pineapple juice.

Fruits should be covered with a layer of cheesecloth before

Drying Fruits

Fruit	Cutting	Dipping	Dehydrator (hours)*	Sun (days)	Appearance when dry	1 cup dry = cups cooked	Cooking time (minutes)
Apples	slice	ascorbic	6–8	2–3	leathery	1¼	30
Apricots	slice, chop	fruit juice, ascorbic	8–12	2–3	leathery	1½	30–45
Bananas	slice	fruit juice, ascorbic	6–8	2	crisp	1	eat dry
Berries	split skins	—	12–24	2–4	hard	1½	30–45
Cherries	pit, chop	—	12–24	2–4	hard	1½	30–45
Figs	pierce	—	36–48	5–6	wrinkled	—	—
Grapes	pierce	—	24–48	3–5	wrinkled	—	—
Peaches	slice, chop	ascorbic	10–12	2–3	leathery	1¼	20–30
Pears	slice, chop	ascorbic	12–18	2–3	leathery	1½	20–30
Persimmons	slice	—	18–24	3–5	chewy	1½	20–30
Pineapple	slice	—	24–36	3–4	chewy	1½	30–45
Plums	pierce	—	36–48	4–5	wrinkled	1½	20–30
Rhubarb	slice	—	8–12	1–2	hard	2	30–40
Strawberries	slice	—	8–12	1–2	hard	1¼	30–40

* These are guidelines; follow manufacturer's directions for commercial dehydrators.

drying outdoors to protect them from insects and birds. Prop the cheesecloth up to keep it from touching the fruit and place the trays in full sun where there is good air circulation. Take the trays inside at night.

Fruits to be dried in a dehydrator can be sliced directly onto the dehydrator trays and dried at approximately 120 to 130°F (49 to 54°C) until no moisture is left in the centre of the pieces. Stir the pieces and rotate the trays top to bottom and front to back once or twice during drying, if necessary, for

> **Dried fruit will keep well for a year or more in a dark place, but light will destroy its colour and flavour.**

even drying. At the end of the recommended drying time, cool a few of the pieces and cut or bite through the centre. If they are not dry, continue drying another few hours.

When it is dry, the fruit should be cooled, then stored in plastic containers or small glass jars. Store containers in a cool, dry, dark place. In a few days, check for condensation on the inside of the containers. If condensation is found, the fruit is not thoroughly dry and must be returned to the dehydrator. Dried fruit will keep well for a year or more in a dark place, but light will destroy its colour and flavour.

Dried fruits can be eaten as snacks or soaked overnight in water and then served as a cooked fruit.

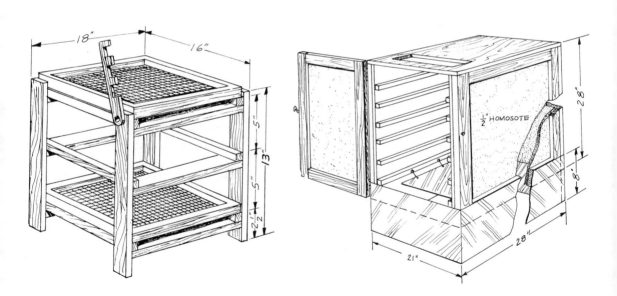

A dryer that can be used in a home oven

A dryer that can be used over a heat source

Country Wines

Country wines are those made with homegrown ingredients; they may not have the balance and complexity of wines from the great châteaux, but they can be surprisingly good and are delightful to use for drinking and cooking. You can make wine from many easy-to-find fruits and plants, such as peaches, grapes, herbs, and even dandelions.

Country wines come from diverse traditions. Most countries have favourite methods and ingredients that have accompanied people all over the world. Most recipes follow the same basic principles: Mix fruit juices, sugar, and yeast; allow the mixture to ferment away from air; wait patiently. In a few months, a new wine will be ready for tasting.

Winemaking Ingredients

Yeast. Bread yeast should not be used for winemaking; commercial wine yeasts yield superior results and are inexpensive. Wine yeasts come in several specific varieties for different kinds of wines. They give you a firmer sediment than does bread yeast, which makes racking easier and more efficient.

Yeast nutrient. A natural "vitamin pill" helps the yeast develop efficiently. Especially useful for honey-based wines.

Pectic enzyme. With honey wines and wines made from certain high-pectin fruits, clarity can be a problem even after diligent racking. Cloudiness probably results from too much pectin — the same substance that turns fruit juice into jam. Adding pectic enzyme to these wines solves the problem; it digests the pectin that keeps the wine from clearing.

Acid blend. This commercial formula provides nutrients essential for fermentation as well as the acid component that gives wines their character. Some older recipes use citrus fruit or juice for this purpose.

Campden tablets. These tablets release sulphur dioxide gas when dissolved. They are used to sanitize the winemaking equipment and to ensure that wild yeasts and bacteria that would interfere with the wine yeast are not present.

Tannin. A component of the skins and stems of some fruits — especially red fruits, such as grapes, plums, apples, and elderberries — tannins give wine a certain zip by creating a hint of dryness in the mouth when you drink it. Equally important, tannins improve a wine's keeping qualities. Traditional winemakers used raisins or a tablespoon of strong tea.

Winemaking Equipment

The following tools are the basics of the winemaker's kit. The plastic fermentation vessel isn't essential, but it is a favourite modern convenience. It comes with its own fermentation lock, which makes the airtight, secondary fermentation easier. Many other gadgets, from hydrometers (to measure the alcohol content of the wine) to corkers, are widely available in specialty stores and catalogues. They are not necessary but are fun to acquire if you are going to make more than a few trial batches.

- 2-gallon plastic bucket. Even if you are making only 1 gallon of wine, you need a container large enough to allow room for active fermentation.
- Plastic cover for bucket.
- Siphon tube. About 4 to 6 feet of narrow, clear-plastic tubing.
- 1-gallon glass jugs or plastic fermentation vessels.
- Fermentation lock.
- Wine bottles. New or used.
- Corks. Must be purchased new each time.
- Mallet. For pounding corks.
- Strainer.

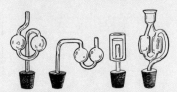

A collapsible plastic fermentation vessel (top) and fermentation locks top the list of useful winemaking equipment.

Cleanliness in every aspect of the winemaking process is extremely important. Equipment must be sanitized. Bacteria that cause spoilage or turn wine to vinegar always lurk in the background. Sanitizing every piece of equipment greatly improves the taste and keeping quality of wine. You can also use a 10 percent bleach solution to sanitize equipment (which then must be rinsed well in hot water three times) or Campden tablets (see page 129).

Basic Steps in Winemaking

Winemaking is an adventure to be enjoyed from the first crushing of the fruit to the last sip of your homemade vintage. Use fresh fruit and flavouring; read all the basic steps of the recipe before you begin.

Primary Fermentation

During this first step, the basic ingredients — fruit, juice, sweetener, yeast — are combined into must. The must sits and ferments vigorously as the yeast takes on oxygen and reproduces.

2-4 pounds fruit
1 cup granulated sugar
1 gallon boiled water
Citric acid or acid blend (if specified in recipe)
1 Campden tablet, crushed
1 teaspoon yeast or yeast starter culture

Yeast Starter Culture (optional)

1½ cups tepid fruit juice (orange juice or juice from the fruit in the wine recipe)
1 package (5–7 grams) wine yeast
1 teaspoon yeast nutrient

1. Sanitize all equipment. Rinse thoroughly with hot tap water. You will need the following materials:

   - 2- to 3-gallon plastic container (for primary fermenter)
   - plastic cover with fermentation lock
   - strainer (if specified in recipe)
   - siphon tube
   - 1-gallon glass container

2. Bruise the fruit; placing fruit in a straining bag makes the later removal of the pulp much easier. Place in the plastic container.

3. Add sugar, water, and acid, according to recipe directions.

4. Add the Campden tablet; let sit for 24 hours to work and dissipate before adding yeast.

5. Make yeast starter culture (optional). This helps the yeast develop more rapidly and efficiently (just as with breadmaking). In a small, sanitized container, combine the fruit juice, wine yeast, and yeast nutrient; cover and shake vigorously. Let stand at room temperature for 1 to 3 hours, until it becomes bubbly.

6. Add yeast or yeast starter culture to the must. Cover; attach the fermentation lock.

7. Allow must to ferment according to time in recipe, usually three to five days; it should work actively and may develop a "cap" or layer of solids floating on top.

8. Punch a hole in the cap if recipe calls for it, taking care not to push the solids back down into the liquid.

9. Strain, if directed in recipe. Most wines do not need to be strained; the racking process usually separates the wine from its cap and lees (sediment).

10. Insert the siphon tube to 1 inch above sediment. Rack (siphon) wine into the clean gallon jar.

11. Discard lees and cap that are left behind in the fermentation vessel.

Secondary Fermentation

By the secondary fermentation, the liquid is now called wine; it is racked into a clean vessel and sealed with a fermentation lock. It will now sit again to ferment until clear, while the yeast converts the sugars to alcohol and carbon dioxide. For some wines, the racking and airlocked fermentation process needs to be performed a third time.

1. Sanitize all equipment. Rinse thoroughly with hot tap water. You will need the following:

   - 1-gallon plastic or glass container (for secondary fermenter)
   - fermentation lock
   - siphon tube

Bigger Batches

If you increase the ingredients in your wine recipe to make a larger amount of wine — say, 5 gallons instead of 1 — you do not have to use additional starter culture. The yeast in the wine is alive and growing, and it will continue to grow in the must until it has converted the sugar to the maximum concentration of alcohol that a given yeast will tolerate. Once the alcohol content reaches that point, fermentation will stop and whatever sugar remains in the solution gives the wine its sweetness. Dry wines have little sugar remaining in them; sweet ones have more.

2. Fill the container almost to the rim. Attach fermentation lock to the spout of the plastic container or rubber stopper; this will allow carbon dioxide to escape without letting any air in.

3. Let the wine sit to work until clear, anywhere from two weeks to several months. This fermentation will not be nearly as vigorous as the first one.

4. Rack again into a clean container, if necessary, for further clarification.

Bottling

You could store your wine in a jug, but regular wine bottles are much nicer and keep the wine better for longer.

1. Gather equipment and sanitizing materials:

   • wine bottles

   • siphon tube

   • corks

   • mallet or corker (alternatively, country wines can be capped as beer is)

Sanitize wine bottles and the siphon tube. Rinse three times in hot tap water.

2. Using the siphon tube, rack wine into bottles.

When selecting wine bottles, look for high-quality, dark green bottles. Thick glass and deep indentation denote quality.

3. Insert corks one-quarter of the way into bottles. Allow to sit for one to two weeks. If the corks pop, the wine may not be completely fermented, and it may need to go back into an airlocked container for another period of fermentation.

4. If the corks have not popped after the first two weeks, cover them with thick cardboard to prevent chipping the bottles, and use a mallet to tap them firmly into the bottles.

5. Cellar in a cool, dark place, usually for at least six months, before sampling. Wine is best stored on its side, with the neck of the bottle slightly lower than the bottom; this keeps the cork moist and swollen, so that it prevents air from entering the bottle. Be sure to label each bottle before you store it.

Peach Wine

The peachy flavour of this wine makes it lovely for sipping or for making coolers. Use very ripe fruit; greener fruits have more pectin, making the wine more difficult to clear.

3–3½ pounds ripe peaches (about 10 peaches)

4 pints water, boiled and cooled

3 pounds granulated sugar

1 teaspoon acid blend

½ teaspoon tannin or 1 tablespoon strong tea

1 Campden tablet (optional)

1 package (5-7 grams) wine yeast

1 teaspoon yeast nutrient

1½ cups tepid orange juice

1-2 teaspoons pectic enzyme

1. Wash the peaches and slice them into a 2-gallon plastic container; toss in the pips too. Add the cooled water, in which you've dissolved 1½ pounds of the sugar, the acid blend, the tannin, and the Campden tablet, if desired. Wait 24 hours before proceeding.

2. Make a yeast starter culture by combining the wine yeast and yeast nutrient with the orange juice. Cover, shake vigorously, and let stand until bubbly, about 1 to 3 hours. Add to the must.

3. Add the pectic enzyme; ferment for 3 days.

4. Rack or strain the wine into another container. Discard the solids.

5. Boil the remaining sugar in water to cover; let cool and add it to the other ingredients with enough water to make 1 gallon. Ferment for 10 days, or until the energetic bubbling slows down. Rack the wine into a 1-gallon, airlocked fermentation vessel; ferment to completion.

6. Bottle, cork, and cellar your wine. Wait at least three months before serving.

Yield: 1 gallon

Grape Melomel

A type of mead and also known as "pyment" this fine country wine was popular in ancient Egypt, where wild grapes and honey abounded.

Optimum Serving Temperatures

Type of Wine	Temperature
Robust red wines	60–65°F (16–18°C)
Light red wines	55–60°F (13–16°C)
Robust white wines	55–60°F (13–16°C)
Light white wines	50–55°F (10–13°C)

3 pounds light honey

3 pounds Concord grapes

1 Campden tablet (optional)

1 packet (5-7 grams) champagne yeast

1 teaspoon yeast nutrient

1½ cups tepid orange juice

1 teaspoon pectic enzyme

1. Remove impurities from the honey by boiling 1 part honey with 2 parts water in a large, nonreactive pot and skimming off the foam. Cool.

2. In a 2-gallon plastic container, crush the grapes.

3. Add the honey-and-water mixture. Pour in water to top off to 1 gallon, if needed. Add a Campden tablet, if desired. Let the mixture stand for 24 hours, well covered, stirring two or three times in an up-and-down motion to introduce oxygen into the mixture.

4. Make a yeast starter culture by combining the champagne yeast and yeast nutrient with the orange juice. Cover, shake vigorously, and let stand until bubbly, 1 to 3 hours. Incorporate into the must. Add the pectic enzyme.

5. Ferment for five days and strain out the solids. Transfer the liquid to an airlocked vessel.

6. Rack after two weeks. When all fermentation has ceased, bottle, cork, and cellar the wine. Wait six months or more before opening.

Yield: About 1 gallon

Herb or Dried-Flower-Petal Wine

Many delicious wines are made from herbs or flower petals. When using fresh herbs or petals, increase the amount to 1 to 4 pints, depending on your taste and how strongly flavoured the herb or flower is.

- 2 ounces dried herbs or flower petals
- 1 quart water
- 1 pound minced sultanas or other light raisins, or juice of 3½–4 pounds grapes
- 1 teaspoon citric acid or 2 teaspoons acid blend
- 1 teaspoon tannin
- 1 Campden tablet (optional)
- 1 package (5–7 grams) wine yeast
- 1½ cups tepid orange juice
- 2¼ pounds granulated sugar for dry wines, 2¾ for sweet

1. Place the herbs in an enamel or glass saucepan with the water. Bring the mixture to a boil; simmer for 20 minutes.

2. Transfer to a 2-gallon plastic container. Add the raisins, citric acid, and tannin. Allow the mixture to cool. Add a Campden tablet, if desired, and let the mixture sit, covered, for 24 hours.

3. Make a yeast starter culture by combining the wine yeast and yeast nutrient with the orange juice. Cover, shake vigorously, and let stand until bubbly (1 to 3 hours); add to the must.

4. Loosely cover the pulp and allow it to ferment for three days. Rack the liquid into a 1-gallon fermentation vessel that can be fitted with an airlock. Add the desired amount of sugar and water to make 1 gallon. Fit the airlock and let the wine ferment to completion, three to four weeks.

Wine Words

Body. The texture and fullness of a wine, the way it feels in your mouth.

Bouquet. The rich, complex aroma that develops in wines as they age.

Cap. The somewhat firm layer of grapes or other solids that rise to the surface during the first fermentation.

Cellar. To store wine while it ages, usually in a cool, dark place.

Lees. The sediment of solids and yeast cells in the fermentation vessel.

Mead. Any wine whose primary fermenting sugar is honey.

Melomel. A wine sweetened with honey but flavoured with fruit.

Must. The first stage of wine, when there are large particles of fruit and yeast in the mixture.

Nose. The aroma or bouquet of wine when it is swirled in a wineglass.

Racking. The use of a siphon to transfer wine from a fermentation vessel to a clean container, leaving behind solids and sediments.

5. Bottle, cork, and cellar the wine.

Yield: 1 gallon

Note: Whenever you use flowers in wine or cooking, make sure they come from edible plants. The oleander bloom is toxic, as are the flowers of lily of the valley. If you aren't sure that it's edible, don't use it.

Traditional Methods

A container made airtight by a plate and a handful of dried beans to hold it down, and our great-grandfathers were in the winemaking business. They probably nicked a little bread yeast from the kitchen to get the fermentation process started, then waited patiently for nature to take its course. If their wine was cloudy after repeated siphoning and straining over several months' time, they added a dried eggshell or two to clear the mixture. They siphoned the liquid into jugs or bottles a few days later, driving the cork home with a block of wood and a hammer.

Flavourings for Herb or Flower Wine

To get you started, here are some ingredients that may be used in the Herb or Dried-Flower-Petal Wine recipe on page 134:

- agrimony
- bramble tips
- burnet
- coltsfoot
- coltsfoot flowers
- cowslip flowers

- dandelion
- elderflowers
- rhubarb stalks
- lemon balm
- rosemary
- rose petals

Coltsfoot

Agrimony

Juicing Apples

The heady fragrance of fresh sweet apple juice running from the press evokes mellow autumn days, fallen leaves, and the brisk country air cleared by early-morning frost. Make your juice outside, preferably on a cool, breezy day. Pour the washed apples into the hopper and grind them, cores, skin, and all. Catch the fresh juice in a clean container and you're on your way to a tasty treat of your own making.

Making Apple Juice

Apple juice is the fresh, untreated juice of pressed, ground apples. To prevent contamination or spoilage, all materials and equipment used must be sanitized.

1. Apple harvest and "sweating". Harvest or buy mature, ripe, sound apples. Store the apples in a clean area for a few days to several weeks, sweating them until they yield slightly to the pressure of a firm squeeze. Keep different varieties of apples separate if you want to make a balanced blend after pressing.

2. Selecting apples for blending. You can make a good blended juice by experimenting with different combinations (see chart below, which will help you choose apple varieties suitable for juicing):

- Neutral or low-acid base: 40 to 60 percent of the total apples. The bland, sweet juice will blend happily with sharper and more aromatic apples.

- Medium- to high-acid base: Tart apples can make up 10 to 20 percent of the total.

- Aromatic: 10 to 20 percent of fragrant apples will give your cider a nice bouquet.

- Astringent (tannin): 5 to 20 percent of the total juice. Go easy with tannin; too much will sour the cider.

Common Apple Varieties for Single Juices and Blends

- Blenheim Orange
- Bramley
- Bramley and Spartan
- Cox and Bramley
- Crispin
- Discovery
- Egremont Russet
- Golden Delicious

- Grenadier
- Howgate Wonder
- Idared
- James Grieve
- Jonagold
- Jupiter
- Katy

- Kids Orange Red
- Red Delicious
- Red Pippin
- Royal Gala
- Spartan
- Sunset
- Worcester Pearmain

3. Milling or grinding. Just before grinding, wash the apples in a large tub of clear, cool water. Squirt a garden hose directly on them; use a high-pressure setting. Place the washed apples into the hopper of a grinder and reduce them to a fine, mushy pomace. If this is your first apple juicing experience, keep the apple varieties, the pomace, and the juice separate and blend to taste later. Press the pomace immediately.

4. Pressing. Using a single-tub screw press or ratchet press, place the nylon press bag in the tub and fill it with apple pomace. Do not use galvanized or metal scoops, which react with the acid in the pomace. Tie or fold the bag closed. Slowly apply increasing pressure to the pulp. As the juice flows out, tighten the screw or pump the ratchet to bring the pressure up again.

Catch the fresh juice in a clean stainless-steel, plastic, or unchipped enamel container. Do not allow the cider to come into contact with other metals. If you are planning to blend the juices from different varieties, keep the pressed-out juices separate.

5. Blending the juices. Take 2-pint samples of each kind of juice. Use a measuring cup to figure exact amounts, and try to achieve a good balance of flavours. Taste-test for tannin (acid) content first. Add small amounts of high-tannin cider to the neutral or low-acid cider base until the level of astringency pleases you. Add aromatic juice, and then cautiously blend in the high-acid juice until the juice is lively, fragrant, and well balanced. Repeat, using the same proportions to blend in greater quantities.

6. Filtering. To correct faintly hazy, natural sweet juice, pass it through a light layer of cheesecloth or nylon mesh. This step will remove impurities and flecks of pomace.

7. Storage. Refrigerate juice in clean glass or plastic jugs or in waxed cardboard containers. It will taste fresh for two to four weeks. After refrigeration, the preferred method of preserving cider is freezing. Allow 2 inches of headroom in containers for expansion during freezing. Defrost the cider for a day in the refrigerator before drinking it.

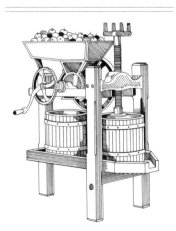

Pack the washed apples into the hopper and grind them, cores, skin, and all.

Getting Started with Apple Juice

- **Grinder.** Usually an oak frame set with stainless-steel or aluminium cutters or rollers, with a hopper on top that can accommodate several pounds of fruit. Grinders are usually hand-powered.

- **Cider press.** A single-tub, hand-operated screw press or ratchet system.

- **Pressing bags and cloths.** Most are made of nylon.

- **Filter cloth.** A layer of cheesecloth or nylon filter cloth.

- **Primary container.** A bucket, bowl, or vat made of stainless steel, polyethylene plastic, glass, or unchipped enamel.

- **Plastic siphon tubing (optional).** A 4-foot section of ¼-inch plastic tubing will help you fill jugs and bottles.

- **Storage containers.** Clean plastic or glass bottles with screw tops.

Vinegars

Making flavoured vinegars, whether spiced, herbal, or fruited, takes little effort and yields impressive results. Infused vinegars add nuances of flavour to your cooking, look great in pretty bottles, and make wonderful culinary gifts.

Making Flavoured Vinegars

Many flavoured vinegars can be made right in the bottles in which you will store them or give them away — as long as you have enough time at your disposal to allow the flavour to gradually build during the steeping process. Simply insert the flavouring ingredients into the bottle, add the vinegar — and wait for about a week.

If, however, you suddenly decide in mid-December that you want to give your friends some marvellous herb or spice vinegar for the holidays, you can speed up the process. To do this, first bruise your seasoning ingredients: Crush them with a garlic press, pepper mill, or mortar and pestle. (In the case of fresh herbs, just crumple them a bit.) Place them in a glass jar with a cover (a mayonnaise jar works well), heat the vinegar to the boiling point, and add it to the jar. Put on the lid and store at room temperature.

Start tasting the vinegar in a day or two. When the flavour is just right, strain out the flavouring ingredients. If the vinegar is cloudy, run it through coffee filters until it's clear. Put some of the seasoning ingredients, this time left whole, into gift bottles, and pour in the vinegar.

Fruit vinegars, such as raspberry, are best made by cooking the main ingredients briefly in the vinegar, then steeping. No matter which method you use, there's very little effort involved and the rewards are tremendous.

All vinegars will keep indefinitely. If you plan to keep them for a long time, though, it's wise to sterilize the vinegar you use as a base.

Base Vinegars

Your choice of vinegar will affect the flavour and colour of the final product. Red wine vinegar adds to the colour of raspberry vinegar; white wine vinegar shows off herbs, lemon peel, and spices; and so forth. Distilled white vinegar is fine for such unsubtle uses as hot pepper and pungent garlic vinegars. Experiment according to your own preferences.

Making Vinegar

To make flavoured vinegars from scratch, you start with the vinegar itself. This requires a large container, a "mother", and liquid to process. The mother is a cloudy or filmy substance that is present in vinegars that have not been sterilized. You can buy a vinegar kit from specialty culinary stores or look for a cloudy deposit or a light film on the top of the vinegar that you have. Add leftover wine or cider to the mother and set aside at room temperature. It takes about two weeks for the mother to make vinegar of whatever you've added.

> All vinegars will keep indefinitely.

Raspberry Vinegar

Many people consider raspberry the best of all flavoured vinegars. Don't omit the sugar or honey; this vinegar needs a touch of sweetening to bring out its full flavour.

2-2½ cups fresh red raspberries, lightly mashed (frozen raspberries can be used, but if they're presweetened, don't add the sugar or honey)

2 cups red wine vinegar

2 tablespoons sugar or honey

1. Combine all ingredients in the top of a nonreactive double boiler. Place over boiling water, reduce the heat, and cook over barely simmering water, uncovered, for 10 minutes.

2. Pour into a large screw-top jar. Store for three weeks, then strain to separate the vinegar from the berries, pressing gently on the berries to extract the juice. If your vinegar is cloudy, pour it through a coffee filter. Pour into bottles, adding a few fresh berries.

Yield: About 2 cups

Note: Manufacturers of some of the commercial raspberry vinegars, also market excellent raspberry syrups that you can find in many delicatessens. A little of these added to a good quality red wine vinegar will give you an instant raspberry vinegar that may not be exactly like homemade but is still very good.

Variations

Blueberry Vinegar: This fabulous fruit vinegar is made in exactly the same way as the raspberry vinegar. Use your choice of red or white wine vinegar. The red will give a darker colour, but it will have a purplish tinge. For an appealing presentation, bottle the finished vinegar with a few large fresh blueberries and a small cinnamon stick.

Peach, Apricot, or Nectarine Vinegar: Follow the procedure for raspberry vinegar, but use white wine vinegar as the base. Peel apricots, peaches, or nectarines before using by dipping them briefly into boiling water, then removing the skin with your fingers. If the fruits are big, cut them into chunks.

Using Fruit Vinegar

Can you imagine peach vinegar sprinkled on a fruit salad, raspberry vinegar mixed with mayonnaise and used in a chicken salad, and perfect leaves of cos lettuce sprinkled with a few edible flowers and dressed in blueberry vinaigrette? Fruit vinegars add a special touch to light marinades and dressings; blend them with mild oils so that their delicate flavours won't be overwhelmed.

Go Nuts

Wild nut trees are less abundant than they once were but our woodlands, copses and hedgerows are still home to sweet chestnuts, cobs and even walnuts. It's still enjoyable to head into the woods on a crisp, autumn day and beat the squirrels to the nuts hidden among the newly fallen leaves.

Once home, the harvest should be laid out in a dry place such as the attic floor in preparation for winter cracking. Although blights, weather, and heavy cutting of the nut trees for their valuable timber have taken their toll nut gathering is still an essential autumn marker.

To make up for the shortage in the wild, gardeners are planting nut trees in increasing numbers at home. Because they grow so large, though, it's important to plan carefully when planting on a small suburban plot. Nut trees are logical companions to fruit trees, but unlike fruits, you can easily store the nut harvest for months or even years without processing it.

Nuts are an excellent source of protein and other nutrients. Recently developed cultivars are hardier, bear younger, and, best of all, produce nuts that are larger, tastier, and crack more easily than their wild ancestors. If you like nuts and have the right climate and enough space, consider planting a nut tree or two.

Improved Cultivars

Nut breeding has progressed less rapidly than fruit and berry development, both because there has not been as much interest in improving them and because they take such a long time to bear. The most progress has been made with almonds, cobs and filberts, pecans, walnuts, and other nuts

---

> Nuts are logical companions to fruits, but unlike fruits, you can easily store them for months or even years without processing.

grown commercially. Recently, however, some excellent cultivars of black walnuts, chestnuts, and hickories have been developed specially for the home gardener. Still, many of the nut trees being sold are simply seedlings from ordinary wild trees.

Your Tree in a Nutshell

If you like the idea of raising wild nuts and are not in a hurry, you might as well grow your own. It's easy — just imitate the squirrels. A large number of nut trees owe their existence to these active little creatures as they stashed away huge numbers of nuts and then forgot where they hid them. Like the squirrels, all you need to do is dig a small hole and bury a nut an inch or so deep. Either plant it where you want the tree to grow permanently or plant a bed of seeds and transplant them after they have grown for two or three years.

Autumn is the time that the squirrels do their planting, and it's the best time for us, too. Most nuts sprout well only if they have been frozen for a few days first, so if you forget to plant them in the autumn, you can do it in the spring after freezing each nut for a week inside a small container of water in the freezer. They may not sprout quite as fast as if the shells had softened in the ground during the winter, however.

Whenever you establish your nut plantation, protect the nuts with a wire screen or a scattering of mothballs, particularly if your garden is home to squirrels. They may forget where they've hidden their own nuts, but they'll have no trouble finding yours and hauling them away.

Don't worry if your new tree doesn't appear the same week the dandelions bloom, or even with the first sprouts of corn. It may be midsummer before it finally bursts through the soil. As soon as it does pop up, it will grow rapidly however, and may be 2 or 3 feet tall within six or eight weeks. The nut itself carries enough nutrients to get the tree off to a good start, so don't feed it anything or it may keep growing too late in the season and be killed by winter cold.

If you transplant nut trees, don't wait until they get large. Most grow tremendous taproots that head speedily toward the centre of the earth, so don't attempt to move them after they get much more than 3 or 4 feet tall. If you should break or bend the taproot in the process of transplanting, the tree is likely to die. The best time to transplant is in early spring.

Planting and Culture

Since some of the new cultivars are as superior to wild nuts as named apples are to wild, sour ones, if the cultivars will grow in your climate, consider planting them rather than seedling trees. Planting a nut tree is much the same as planting a fruit tree. When you are choosing a location, however, keep in mind the eventual size of the tree. Filberts remain nicely within fruit tree dimensions, but most other species become 50 or more feet tall and nearly as wide. Give them enough room, and don't plant them beneath overhead power lines or too close to your house. The falling nuts can become a nuisance, too, so plant away from streets, pavements, roofs, and any lawns that will be mowed in late autumn. Nuts are hard on mowers too.

Nut trees grow best in well-drained, deep soil. After the first year they benefit from annual spring applications of a fertilizer that is rich in nitrogen. To imitate the conditions of the lush forest floor, apply a thick, organic mulch when the trees

Plant in Pairs

Although a single black walnut tree can produce nuts, the general consensus among horticulturists is that they benefit from having a companion. Most other nut trees definitely need a partner, and to be compatible, the partner must be of the same species. The two should be within 100 feet of each other, because nearly all nuts are pollinated by wind instead of bees.

If you are planting all cultivars rather than seedlings, plant two different cultivars or a few seedling trees of the same species to pollinate them. In other words, if you plant a red filbert, plant another filbert hybrid, such as purple-leaved filbert or some wild filberts to pollinate it. Two red flberts would not pollinate each other because they both originated from the same tree. Each seedling tree is different, however, so they will pollinate any other seedling or hybrid of the same species.

are still young. Grafted cultivars take much less time to produce their first crop than do seedling trees, which may require eight years or more to bear their first few nuts.

Because even a hybrid nut tree still closely resembles its wild relatives, it needs no special care. For a strong tree, prune it to have one central trunk with no branches for the first 8 feet. Diseases and insects seldom infest garden nut trees. This is fortunate, because spraying such large trees is not easy.

Harvesting

When the nuts begin to fall off the tree, they are mature and ready to pick. Squir-rels don't always wait for them to fall, though, so it is best to begin collecting as soon as the squir-rels do. If you are careful not to damage the limbs, you can shake most nuts from the trees. In fact, walnuts are often harvested commercially by mechanical shakers. The entire crop of most nut trees can be gathered at one time, although some, like walnuts, may need several pickings. Don't let nuts stay on the ground for any length of time after they fall because they deteriorate rapidly.

Nuts need to be dried thoroughly before their meats ripen enough to eat. Spread them out, one layer deep, on benches in a greenhouse or garage, on warm attic floors, or, best of all, on raised screens where the air can circulate all around them. Turn them occasionally so they will dry on all sides.

After drying the nuts completely, store them in hessian bags, boxes, or barrels in a cool place, making sure the storage area is squirrelproof.

It would be wrong not to mention some of the bad habits of nut trees. Some kinds are not the best trees to plant as close neighbours to other plantings. Black walnut, for example, gives off a toxic substance that eliminates competition by killing certain nearby plants, especially evergreens. They don't have this poisonous effect on grass and many other plants, however.

Other Uses for Nuts

Eating nuts is one of the most enjoyable ways to use them, of course, but they also have other uses. The shells are made into ornaments and jewellery or burned to make a fragrant smoke used for smoking meat or to make activated charcoal, a product used in filters and gas masks. Wood from nut trees is among the most prized in the world. Windmill propellers used to be made from butternut, one of the strongest lightweight woods known. Gun stocks, fine furniture, and many other products are made from black walnut. Hickory, known for its great strength, is used for skis, tool handles, and much more. Chestnut trees, too, are valued for their fine wood.

Nuts for the Back Garden

Included here are nut trees that are practical for domestic gardens in the UK and USA. The cultivation advice includes information on areas where the trees appear to do best and are most widely grown, although they may succeed in other areas under the right conditions.

Black Walnuts (*Juglans nigra*)

The native black walnut is a valuable forest tree in the USA where it is also widely grown for its nut crop. Although it is hardy throughout the British Isles it struggles to bear fruit there particularly in western regions where rainfall is high. Most cultivars have nuts that crack more easily and have larger and better-flavoured meats than the wild kinds, but the trees are less hardy. Not everyone cares for the black walnut's unusual flavour, but its fans use it to flavour cakes, ice cream, and other desserts.

In addition to the different strains of seedlings that vary widely across the country, the following cultivars are among the most popular currently available through nurseries: Bowser, Cornell, Elmer Meyers, Emma Kay, Ohio, Patterson, Ridgeway, Snyder, Sparrow, Stabler, Stambaugh, Thomas Black, Thomas Meyers, Vendersloot, Victoria, and Weschke. Patterson and Weschke are among the most hardy.

Butternut (*Juglans cinerea*)

Like dried corn, beans, and smoked meat, butternuts were one of the staple foods that helped the Iroquois Indians live well through the hard northern winters of the USA but sadly the butternut has failed to thrive in the British Isles so far.

The butternut is one of the hardiest nut trees, and its oily meat is one of the most flavourful nuts. New hybrids and selections of native trees produce nuts that are larger and easier to crack than the wild ones. Even the wild ones crack easily if you

Black walnut

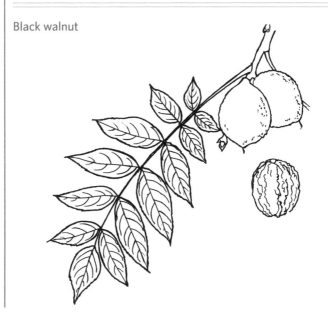

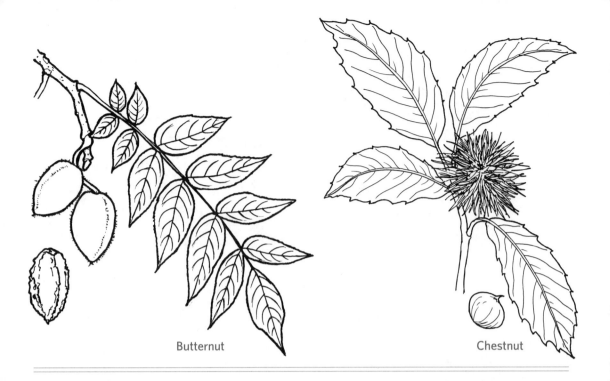

Butternut

Chestnut

pour boiling water over them, let them stand for 15 minutes, and then drain. With one easy hammer blow you can then pop apart the halves intact.

Butternut blooms are easily damaged in late-spring frosts, and even if they are not harmed, the trees are likely to bear abundantly one year and then take a few years off.

Some improved varieties are now being sold: Ayers, Bountiful (Stark), Chamberlin, Chambers, Corner, Craxezy, Creighton, George Elmer, Kenworthy, Mitchell, Van Syckle, and Weschke. Ayers has very large nuts; Mitchell begins to bear at an early age; Chamberlin and George Elmer are among the most hardy.

The buartnut tree (*Juglans × bixbyi*), a cross between the Japanese heartnut and the butternut, combines the hardiness and good flavour of the latter with the easy cracking, high yields, and disease resistance of the former. Several hybrids are now on the market. Among them are Coble's No. 1, Corsan, Dunoka, Fioka, Hopkins, and Wallick.

The Chestnut Family (*Castanea*)

The sweet chestnut (*Castanea sativa*) has flourished in the British Isles and continental Europe for centuries and many ancient specimens can still be found. Its edible nuts are eaten roasted, used by confectioners and even ground to make flour, a particularly in the Cevennes region of France. Native to southeastern Europe and Asia Minor, a mature tree can reach a height of 60 feet or more so it will not be the right tree for every garden but nonetheless makes a magnificent addition to the landscape where space allows. Recommended cultivars of *Castanea sativa* include Maraval and Marron de Lyon. *Castanea dentata* (American chestnut) was an important part of North American colonial life. During cold winter nights, the nuts popped in many a colonial fireplace, and holidays were never complete without chestnut dressing for the turkey or goose.

In New England there is still a belief that a blacksmith shop should stand "under a spreading chestnut tree."

When the blight of the early 1900s wiped out nearly every chestnut tree, a search began for blight-resistant varieties. Trees were introduced from China, Japan, Manchuria, and Spain, and some were successfully crossed with the few remaining American species. Many of the resulting new hybrids are now producing quality nuts.

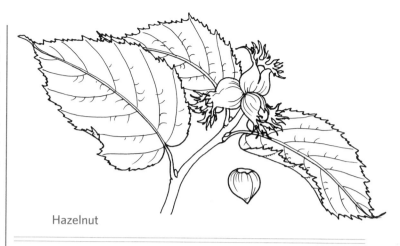

Hazelnut

Filbert and cob (Corylus)

Corylus avellana is parent with Corylus maxima of many different cultivars of filbert and cobnut. These will be familiar to everyone who has ever bought a bag of mixed nuts for the Christmas holidays. Corylus avellana is a native of southern Europe, originating probably in Italy. The nuts of the filbert are slightly longer and narrower than the cob. Recommended cultivars for British gardeners include Ennis, Kentish Cob, Gunslebert, and Red Filbert. Most of North America's commercial filbert production is in the Pacific Northwest, with Barcelona, Daviana, and Duchilly the leading cultivars. They seldom do well in the rest of the continent, however.

An American cousin of the filbert, Corylus americana, grows wild in hedgerows all over the northern United States and southern Canada. The small nuts are favourites of chipmunks and squirrels.

Filbert trees have the advantage of maturing to a size that fits well into most gardens. The trees grow from 10 to 15 feet tall, or about the size of semidwarf apples. Plant them about 20 feet apart. Unlike most other nut trees, they don't have a long taproot, so they are easy to transplant. Soils suitable for fruit trees usually suit the filbert, too, but fertilize it only lightly so it doesn't grow too fast.

Filbert trees root easily from layers and root suckers, so even cultivars are seldom grafted. If you buy a tree, you may want to propagate it in this way to increase your plantings. Some crosses have been made between the European filbert and the hardy wild American hazelnut.

These "filazels" are available in the USA under cultivar names such as Gellatly, Minnesota F2, Peace River Cross, and the Fred Ashworth Crosses, which are reputed to be among the hardiest.

Hickory and Pecan (Carya)

As the botanical name shows, hickories and pecans are closely related, even though they grow in different climatic zones. The relationship, however, has permitted some worthwhile hybrids between them to be developed.

> The round filbert is familiar to everyone who has ever bought a bag of mixed nuts at Christmas.

Of the two, hickory trees are hardy over a wider area. It grows well in the British Isles, especially Cornwall, but sadly offers low yields of nuts. In the USA they are seldom offered commercially, but are much enjoyed by those lucky enough to live in the same habitat. The shagbark hickory (*Carya ovata*), the best of dozens of native American hickories, has the disadvantage of a very tough shell and a small meat that usually breaks in cracking. Many new cultivars, which are selections of these wild trees, are now available in the USA. These bear nuts at a younger age, and the nuts are larger and easier to crack. The hardiness of the new kinds isn't always known for sure, however, and thus far not many are being grafted and offered for sale. Davis, Grainger, Neilson, Porter, Weschecke, and Wilcox are some that are available in the USA.

Shellbark hickory (*Carya laciniosa*) cultivars are slightly less hardy than shagbarks. In the British Isles they only produce a good crop after a hot summer. US cultivars include Abundance, Anderson, Eureka, Henry, Kaskaskia, Missouri Mammoth, and Richmond Furnace.

Pecans (*Carya illinoinensis*) need a long season to develop their nuts, so the trees are limited mostly to the southeastern United States and Mexico. Unlike most other North American trees, the pecan has been cultivated commercially for many years.

Pecans keep for only a few months in ordinary storage but store well for a year or more at temperatures below freezing.

Some pecan cultivars currently being grown are Apache, Barton, Cape Fear, Choctaw, Major, Missouri, Nutcracker, Pawnee, Rocket 800, Schley, Sioux, Starking Hardy Giant, Stuart, and Surecrop (Stark).

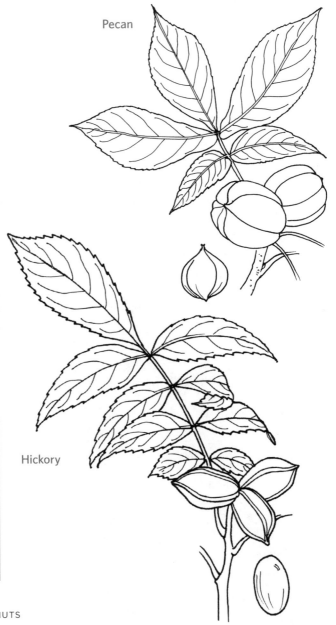

Pecan

Hickory

In an effort to combine the flavour of pecans with the hardiness of hickories, horticulturists have created hybrid "hicans." Among those available in the USA are Burlington, Burton, Gerardi, Henke, Jackson, Pleas, and Underwood. All can be grown farther north than pecans, but the different cultivars vary widely in hardiness.

Walnut (*Juglans regia*)

Walnuts have been grown in Great Britain for centuries. They were considered far too tender for all of North America except the warm regions of the West Coast until a missionary, Reverend Paul Crath, discovered a strain growing wild in the cold mountains of Poland. He brought several thousand seeds to Ontario in the 1930s and found they grew well there. They succeeded so well, in fact, that within only a few years the Carpathian strain he introduced was being grown in some of the coldest regions of North America.

Walnuts are without doubt the most popular of all nuts both to eat straight from the shell and to enjoy as an ingredient in countless appetizing desserts. Unfortunately, a few people get mouth ulcers from eating walnuts and have to sacrifice a real delicacy. Perhaps a variety without this unpleasant side effect will someday be developed, so everyone can enjoy this delicious nut.

Recommended cultivars for the British Isles include Broadview, Buccaneer, Franquette and Rita. Cultivars suitable for Zones 7 and 8 in the USA include Champion, Kentucky Giant, Kwik Krop Stark, Lockport, Serr, Spurgeon, Sunland, and Super. In California, Franquette and Hartley are widely grown commercially.

Most American nurseries offer only seedling trees of the Carpathian walnut, but those that specialize in nut trees have some good cultivars available. Some of these are Ambassador, Ashworth (one of the hardiest), Broadview, Chopaka, Fately, Gurney, Hansen, Lake, McKinster, Russian, and Somers.

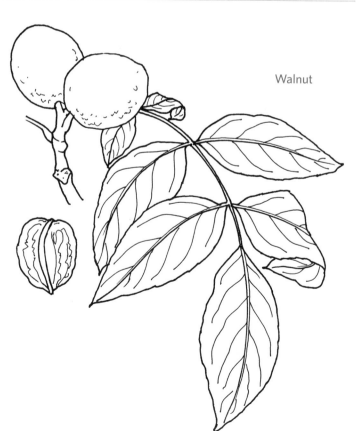

Walnut

SAGE

APPLE MINT

VALERIAN

CHAPTER 3

Easy, Fragrant Herbs

Imagine growing your own herbal tea — peppermint, lemon balm, lavender, chamomile. Or how about running out to the back garden for a handful of chives or a snip of rosemary whenever you need it? Or having a whole cupboard full of dried seasonings, like sage, rosemary, thyme, and parsley, to flavour dinners through the winter and give away as gifts?

Many people don't realize that the herbs and herbal teas they find in high street shops are often at least six months old, and because their essential oils have volatilized, they've lost a lot of their flavour by the time you take them home. You can often find fresh herbs in the produce section, but at an exorbitant price, especially considering how simple and inexpensive it is to grow them yourself.

Herbs are probably the easiest garden plants to grow. For the most part, they require very little attention, average soils, and no additional watering after they're established (in fact, some herbs actually resent being watered, and their flavour is less pungent because of it). In addition to providing tasty teas and seasonings, herbs can be every bit as ornamental as traditional garden perennials are.

Once you've caught the herb-growing bug, you can learn to preserve them by drying or freezing them and to create herbed oils and butters as well as herbal vinegars. Learning about decoctions and infusions (see page 171) can help you get the most of the herbs you grow in your garden, especially if your goal is to brew the best cup of tea you've ever had!

Gardening with Herbs

You can find most of the basic herbs you want already started as plug plants at your garden centre. Growing your own from seed is pretty much like propagating other seeds, with a few changes.

First, herb seeds are usually tiny. After levelling off your soil mix, sprinkle the herb seeds on the surface and just tamp them down. You don't have to bury the tiny ones. Be sure to keep them moist and in a warm spot. The other big difference is that they seem to take for-ever to germinate. Two to three weeks is not uncommon.

Another way to get perennial herbs like chives, oregano, and tarragon is to divide an existing plant. In early spring, or after the growing season in autumn, drive a trowel or spade through the plant and remove a chunk for your garden. Keep the roots moist as you move them, and transplant them immediately.

You can grow a good collection of the basic herbs in one or two hanging baskets, in a corner of your vegetable garden, in pots or window boxes, or mixed in a flowerbed. The best advice is to put your herbs as close to the kitchen as you can. You'll use them more if you don't have to make a special trip to the garden for a few leaves of basil or chives.

Caring for Herbs

Herbs like five to eight hours of sunshine every day and well-drained soil that is rich in organic matter. The exception is mint, which likes damp, partly shady areas.

If you fertilized the soil at planting time, you shouldn't need more during the growing season. Too much fertilizing makes herbs big and rangy, when what you're after is compact, bushy plants with greater concentrations of flavourful oils.

Most herbs are at their best as they begin to flower. Pick the tender leaves and pick off the flowers to encourage continued growth. Herbs grow best if they are not allowed to set seeds. Prune them to control their size and shape as you harvest them for your own use.

A large pot is easy to move if you set it on a mobile stand.

Grow Your Own Ginger

Fresh ginger is a staple of Asian cuisine, and both ginger and its botanical cousin, turmeric, are surprisingly easy to grow at home. The part of the plant that's normally eaten grows underground — a subterranean stem called a rhizome, which bears buds that grow into stems and narrow leaves. Eventually it flowers, and the pure white blooms — as many as 15, borne in a leafy conelike structure at the end of a cane — are delightfully fragrant.

To grow ginger, start with a visit to the supermarket. Purchase a piece of fresh ginger that's at least 2 to 3 inches long and bears several buds or "eyes." Select a shallow, wide pot and fill three-quarters of it with moist potting mix. Bury the rhizome shallowly, covering it with just an inch or two of soil. Keep the soil moist and put the pot in a place that's warm and brightly lit, but out of direct sun.

The ginger plant grows tall quickly and resembles bamboo — in six weeks, it can be as tall as 3 feet! Although the rhizome can be harvested after just a few months, it doesn't develop its full flavour until the plant is mature, which can take up to a year. If you live in a cold climate, bring the container indoors in autumn and water only sparingly through the winter (no more than once a month); the plant should receive just enough water to keep it alive but in a dormant state. The foliage may die back, but it will resprout in spring.

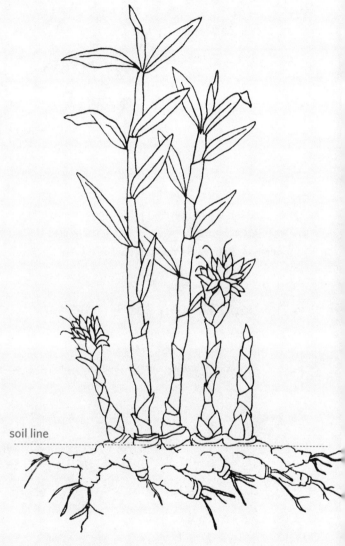

soil line

An Easy and Fragrant Kitchen Border

Plant this herb garden near the kitchen door for easy access. The number in parentheses refers to the number of plants required.

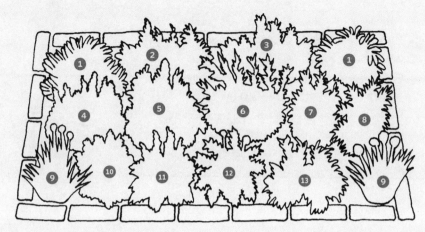

1. Sage (2)
2. Peppermint (1, surrounded by a root barrier; it will spread)
3. Spearmint (1, surrounded by a root barrier; it will spread)
4. Oregano (1)
5. Marjoram (1)
6. Tarragon (1)
7. Lemon balm (1)
8. Rosemary (1)
9. Chives (2)
10. Upright thyme (1)
11. Lemon thyme (1)
12. Burnet (1)
13. French thyme (1)

A Cold and Flu Garden

When cooler winter weather arrives, colds and flu often arrive, too. You can plant a garden that provides the ingredients of a herbal broth (see page 156) to treat your cold or flu. This plan can take up quite a large space. Peppermint becomes invasive, so plant it in a large tub or container with drainage holes in the bottom and sink it into the ground. Butterflies are drawn to echinacea and yarrow.

1. Thyme (4)
2. Garlic cloves (9)
3. Cayenne pepper (3)
4. Yarrow (1)
5. Echinacea (2)
6. Peppermint (1)
7. Rosemary (2)

Preserving Herbs

When you are ready to harvest, choose a dry day and pick after the dew has evaporated. The essential oil concentration is said to be highest in the morning. Remember, essential oils give a plant its fragrance, flavour, and any health benefits attributed to the herb.

Because the oil content is higher in a plant before flowering, many herb gardeners recommend picking herbs before the plant flowers. But I've harvested them at all stages of growth. The best way is to experiment with different times. You might prefer the more delicate flavour of small, new leaves, especially for the more pungent herbs.

The easiest way to clean herbs for harvesting is to rinse them with a garden hose. Set the hose to a light spray or mist. Soak the plants well and let them dry in the sun before you harvest. If you choose instead to rinse them after cutting, use a salad spinner to remove excess water.

Drying Herbs

Herbs have been used to improve health, enhance the taste of food and freshen dwelling places for as long as civilisations have dwelled on earth. Herbs are easy to grow, often can be found in the wild (such as mints), and are easy to dry. Most are picked just before the flowers open or when the leaves are still young and tender. As the plants mature, the oils that produce the odours and flavours become less intense.

Herbs should be dried at cooler temperatures than fruits and vegetables to protect their delicate flavours and aromas. They should never be dried in full sun; rather, place them in the shade, where there is good circulation of warm air, or dry them in a dehydrator. Strong-flavoured herbs should be dried separately from herbs that might pick up their flavours. Wash picked herbs only if they're dirty or have been treated with chemicals.

Store completely dried herbs in labelled, tightly sealed jars.

Hang small bundles of herbs to dry in a dark, airy place.

then stored in small, tightly closed containers.

Jars or packages should be as small as possible to retain maximum flavour and aroma, and well filled to exclude air. Store in a dark, cool closet or cabinet. Dried herbs will keep their flavour for several months but should be discarded after a year.

Most satisfactory, of course, is not to store herbs, but to have them fresh and ready for use. Every kitchen should have a pot or two or three of herbs. Start them outside in summer, and then pot them up before the first frosts. The bigger the pot, the more productive the herbs will be. To start with, try parsley, chives, and basil. Give them as much sunshine as possible, keep them cut back regularly, and water them, and they will reward you with a constant supply of goodness.

Herb seeds should be allowed to develop and partially dry on the plant. Do not let them dry completely, however, or the pod will burst, spilling out the seeds to the ground. To finish drying, remove the seeds from the plants, spread them in a thin layer on trays, and dry them in the shade or in a dehydrator set at 95°F (35°C).

To dry herb leaves, spread them in a thin layer over drying trays and dry them in a shady area or in a dehydrator set at 95°F (35°C) or lower until the leaves are crisp enough to crumble in the hands. Herb leaves also can be dried by tying stalks together with a string and hanging them upside down in a shady, well-ventilated area. This time-honoured method is more picturesque, but there is some loss of flavour and aroma during the longer drying time. The dried leaves should be removed from their stalks and left whole,

Herbs should be dried at cooler temperatures than fruits and vegetables to protect their delicate flavours and aromas. They should never be dried in full sun.

Microwave-Drying Herbs

A microwave oven will enable you to dry herbs in a matter of minutes, rather than the hours, days, or weeks previously required. There will no longer be the worry of dust contamination from hanging herbs to dry them. Best of all, you can do as much or as little as you are inclined to do. For instance, if you have over-picked a fresh herb to use in a dish, you can easily dry the remainder without wasting a bit of it.

Microwave-drying of herbs requires the same preparation as you would use to dry them in an oven or a dehydrator. If there is dirt on the herb you are drying, wash it carefully to avoid bruising the leaves, then dry thoroughly. You can use a salad spinner to dry large amounts of herbs at one time. Drying garlic or chillies in the microwave is not recommended, as both contain too much water to dry properly. All other herb seeds, leaves, and flowers can be dried in the microwave.

Since the amount of herb you are drying will vary from time to time, no definitive guidelines can be given regarding time involved in the process. Once you have separated the leaves, seeds, or flowers from the stems and cleaned them, if needed, you are ready to begin. Dry one herb at a time. Spread a single layer on a double thickness of paper toweling and put it into the oven. Microwave on high power for 1 to 2 minutes at a time, redistributing the herbs for more even drying at each interval. After the second or third time, the herbs will be noticeably drier. Continue this interval timing, but in ½- to 1-minute intervals, until the herbs are completely dry. Be cautious; once dried, herbs can catch on fire. Let them cool, then pack them into airtight containers.

A Guide to Dried Herbs

Herb	Part Dried	Use
Anise	Seed	Sweet rolls, salads, biscuit batter
Basil	Leaves	Tomato dishes, soups, stews, meat pies
Bay	Leaves	Soups, stews, spaghetti sauce
Celery	Leaves	Soups, casseroles, salads
Chervil	Leaves	Eggs, cheese dishes, salads
Chillies	Pods	Soups, stews
Chives	Leaves	Omelettes, salads, casseroles
Cumin	Seed	Cheese spread, bread dough, sausages
Dill	Flowers, seed	Stews, cabbage, pickles
Fennel	Leaves, seed	Soups, casseroles, sweets, rolls, biscuits
Garlic	Bulb	Italian foods, omelettes, chilli
Marjoram	Leaves	Lamb dishes, sausages, stews
Mint	Leaves	Mint jelly, lemonade, roast lamb
Oregano	Flowers	Tomato dishes, spaghetti sauce, pork, wild game
Parsley	Leaves	Soups, sauces, vegetables
Rosemary	Leaves	Salads, lamb dishes, vegetables
Sage	Leaves	Sausages, cheese, poultry, omelettes
Savory	Leaves	Bean dishes, stuffing
Tarragon	Leaves	Tomato dishes, salads, vinegar
Thyme	Leaves	Meat loaf, lamb dishes, onion soup

Freezing, Oils and Butters

It's a good idea to dry some of your herbs — but don't stop there. Try some of the many other methods that can be used to catch their flavours.

Freezing them is one of the easiest and most satisfactory methods of keeping herbs. Wash them well, and then spread them out until they are dry and wilted. (This may take several hours.) Cut or chop them into the form you want for cooking, pack them in jars, and freeze them. With most herbs, flavour and colour will be preserved. Try this first with chives and parsley, then move on to others.

Herb butters, too, can be made when herbs are most plentiful and frozen for later use. They are handy for adding flavour to vegetables as well as for the most conventional use with bread and rolls. Chop herbs very fine, then mix with butter in a ratio of 1 part herbs to 2 to 3 parts butter, depending on your taste. Tarragon, chives, parsley, and rosemary are some to try, and combinations are recommended as you become more familiar with them.

The herbs and butter should be blended with a fork and left in the refrigerator for a few days to enable the flavour to spread through the butter. Then pack it for freezing.

Herbal Broth

Most people have trouble avoiding a cold or flu at some time during the winter. This broth will provide you with herbal comfort when you're ill. It is flavourful, warming, and packed with vitamins.

- 6 garlic cloves, minced
- 1 tablespoon olive oil
- 2 cups water or vegetable stock
- 1 teaspoon finely chopped fresh cayenne pepper or ½ teaspoon cayenne powder
- 1 teaspoon finely chopped fresh rosemary or ½ teaspoon dried
- ½ teaspoon fresh thyme or ¼ teaspoon dried
- Pinch to ¼ teaspoon salt, if the vegetable broth is unsalted

Add the garlic to the olive oil and sauté over high heat briefly, until the garlic starts to change colour. Add the water, turn down the heat to medium-low, and simmer for 20 minutes. Add all of the herbs and salt to taste. Simmer for 5 more minutes. Sip slowly.

Yield: About 2 cups

32 Essential Herbs

There are endless possibilities of herbs to grow, but here are 32 of the most popular ones you'll find at your local nursery, along with tips on how to use them.

Basil

Basil is a tender annual very sensitive to frost. Sow the seed directly into the garden after the soil is warm, with an extra dose of compost. Plant it in full sun and water it weekly in dry weather.

This fast-growing plant grows to 2 feet. To keep the plant bushy, pinch out the blooms or the tips of each stem before it flowers. Harvest the leaves throughout the summer.

To dry basil, harvest just before it blooms. Hang, screen-dry, or freeze.

Pesto

Pesto is an Italian basil sauce that is fabulous on pasta, hot or cold. It also enlivens grilled fish, steamed vegetables, bruschetta, and omelettes. Experiment with substituting parsley or other herbs for some of the basil, and try using walnuts in place of the pine nuts.

2 cups fresh basil leaves
Pinch of salt
1 or 2 cloves garlic
½ cup grated Parmesan or Romano cheese
½ cup extra-virgin olive oil
¼ to ½ cup pine nuts

Using a food processor, preferably with a plastic blade, combine the basil leaves, salt, and peeled garlic cloves until a coarse paste is formed. Add the grated cheese and process to blend. With the processor running, slowly pour in the oil in a thin stream. Add the pine nuts and process until smooth.

Use immediately or store in the refrigerator with a ½-inch coating of olive oil on top. To freeze pesto, prepare without the cheese and cover with ½ inch of olive oil; add the cheese after thawing. To make it easy to use small amounts of pesto, freeze it in ice cube trays. When frozen, transfer the cubes to plastic freezer bags for storage.

Yield: About 2 cups

> ### Freeze small amounts of pesto in ice cube trays, then transfer them to freezer bags.

Basil

Bay

Bay is a slow-growing evergreen shrub with aromatic leaves. A sun-loving plant, it is a tender perennial that must go indoors during winter in cold climates. It is difficult to propagate. Bay can grow to a height of 10 feet.

Bay

Burnet

Burnet's cucumber-flavoured leaves are used in drinks, soups, and salads. It is easily grown from seed. Burnet grows 1 to 2 feet tall in sun or light shade and slightly alkaline soil.

Burnet

Catmint (Catnip)

Beloved by felines, catmint is used in tea by humans as a cough remedy and as an aid to digestion. The plants are 2 to 3 feet high. Easily grown in sun or light shade, catmint tolerates most soils.

Catmint

Chamomile

Tea made from chamomile blossoms is used as a soothing tranquilizer; it is also

Chamomile

Edible Flowers

Many flowers not only are lovely to look at, but they also add delicate texture or taste to foods. Use them as garnishes or to decorate a cake. Some favourites are borage, calendula, chive blossoms, clove pinks, elderflowers, lavender, mints, nasturtium, rose petals, and violets. Larger flowers, such as daylilies and squash blossoms, may be stuffed or fried. For culinary purposes, be sure to use organically grown flowers that are free from pesticides. See page 30 for more edible flower ideas.

used as a tonic. Chamomile grows easily from seed or divisions. It grows up to 10 inches with a spreading growth habit.

Chives

These small, onion-like plants are useful in salads, soups, and egg dishes. Hardy perennials, they reach 12 to 18 inches in height. Cut off the mauve-blue flower heads to keep the plants growing, but leave them on later in the season for foraging bees.

Chives prefer full sun, rich soil, and plentiful water. Mulch around the plants to keep out weeds and grasses.

Harvest chives as soon as the spears are a few inches long. Snipping out entire spears

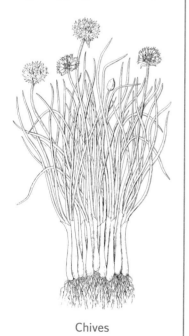

Chives

encourages tender new growth. Chives do not dry well. Freeze them for winter use.

Costmary (Bible Leaf)

Its fragrant leaves with a minty flavour were pressed and used as bookmarks in Bibles during colonial days. Today, costmary is used as a garnish, in tea, and for potpourri. Propagate by root division. The plants grow 2 to 3 feet high. Costmary likes sun and ordinary garden soil.

Costmary

Dill

Dill is a hardy annual that grows 2 to 3 feet tall; plant in groupings to keep it supported in windy weather.

Sow seed directly in the garden. Dill does best in full sun

Dill

in sandy or loamy, well-drained soil that is slightly acidic (pH 5.8 to 6.5). Enrich soil with compost or well-rotted manure for best growth. Dill reseeds itself easily.

Both dillweed and dill seed are used in cooking; the weed is mild, but the seeds are pungent. Harvest dillweed any time, but its volatile oils are highest just before flowering. Cut seed heads when the majority of seeds are formed, even though some flowers are still blooming. Thresh the seeds after drying.

Echinacea (Coneflower)

Echinacea is widely used to stimulate or support the body's immune system. A perennial that loves full sun, echinacea grows to about 3 feet, spreading gradually. Butterflies love this plant. When the blossoms are finished, they dry out and reseed themselves; remove the spent blooms if you don't want this to occur. To harvest, dig the roots after blooming, usually in early autumn. Harvest only two- to four-year-old roots, making sure that you leave enough plants for future use. Wash and dry, then chop coarsely. Store thoroughly dried roots in a tightly covered glass container away from heat and light.

Echinacea

In addition to its healing properties, echinacea has beautiful blooms that attract butterflies.

Make an Echinacea Tincture

Tinctures are a simple and useful way to make the healing properties of herbs available to you. Use the instructions below to make a basic echinacea tincture. At the first sign of a cold or flu's onset, herbal experts recommend 30 drops of tincture every 3 hours for the first two days only. You will need pure grain alcohol but if you cannot get hold of this look for the highest-proof brand of vodka or brandy. If you do not want to ingest alcohol, place drops of tincture in a small amount of warm water and stir to evaporate the alcohol.

1. Combine ¾ cup alcohol with ¾ cup distilled water in a jar with a tight-fitting lid.

2. Add 1½ ounces of dried echinacea.

3. Replace the lid and set the jar in a cool, dark spot.

4. Shake the mixture daily for two weeks.

5. Strain the mixture to remove the herb. Do it quickly, or the alcohol will evaporate. Try pouring the mixture into a strainer lined with an unbleached coffee filter and place it in the refrigerator to slow alcohol evaporation. Then squeeze the filter to remove as much liquid as possible. Store in a cool place, in a dark-coloured glass bottle with an eyedropper fitted into the lid. Label, including the type of tincture and the date.

Cautions. Echinacea can cause adverse reactions in people who are allergic to sunflowers. Do not use it if you have a severe systemic immune disorder or a collagen disease such as lupus or scleroderma. Echinacea should be used with caution by pregnant women. Always, always make a positive identification of any plant before using it.

Fennel

Herb fennel is a hardy biennial that becomes a perennial in favourable climates. It reaches 3 to 5 feet. Fennel prefers a rich, well-drained soil in full sun. Add lime if your soil pH is below 6.0. Harvest leaves just before the plant flowers. Fennel adversely affects the growth of other plants nearby. It is related to dill, and the two should not be interplanted because they may cross-pollinate, resulting in dilly fennel or fennelly dill!

Fennel

Feverfew

Biennial or perennial. As the name implies, this hardy medicinal herb is credited with many beneficial properties. It is easily grown from seed or division, and the plant reaches 2 to 3 feet. It does best in sun or light shade and a well-drained soil.

Feverfew

Garlic

This pungent herb is grown for the flavour of its corms, or cloves. Garlic needs full sun, rich soil, a pH between 6.0 and

Garlic

6.8, and even moisture. Plant it in autumn at about the time of first frost for a summer harvest or in spring to harvest an autumn crop. Harvest before flowering, when the stalks start to turn brown. Dig up the plant carefully, brush off dirt, and spread out the heads to dry.

Horehound

The leaves are dried for tea and used fresh in cough syrup. Grown from seed, cuttings, or division, the plants reach 1 to 2 feet. Horehound needs full sun and dry, sandy soil.

Horehound

Plaiting Garlic

Plaiting garlic heads is the best way to preserve them, because air can circulate around the hung plaits.

The soft-necked variety works best. Start making the plaits as soon as you pull the heads from the ground, so the stems are still pliable. Brush off soil rather than rinsing off the heads. Be sure to use heads that have their leaves attached.

Beginning a plait

On a flat surface, start with three fat heads and plait their leaves together. Then add other heads (like French-plaiting hair). For plaits you plan to give away, or if you care a lot about the appearance of a plait, put the heads so closely together that the leaves don't show. You can use light wire to reinforce the plaits. When you've done as many heads as you want, plait the last of the leaves and tie off with raffia or twine, forming a loop for hanging. Hang in a well-ventilated area.

Finished plait

Lavender

An aromatic herb used fresh or dried in sachets and pillows, lavender grows from seeds, cuttings, or divisions. Plant it in a protected location in northern areas. It prefers lime soil. Lavender produces the loveliest blossoms and fragrant oil. Plants grow to 1 to 2 feet.

Lavender

Hyssop

A hardy, ancient herb used as a purifying tea and for medicine, hyssop is said to cure all manner of ailments from head lice to shortness of breath. Start by seed or division. The plant grows to 3 feet. Hyssop prefers full sun and well-drained, alkaline soil.

Hyssop

Lemon Balm

The lemon-scented leaves are used dried or fresh for tea, jelly, and flavouring. The plant attracts bees. Start from cuttings or division. Plants grow 1 to 3 feet high. Plant lemon balm in sun or light shade and well-drained soil.

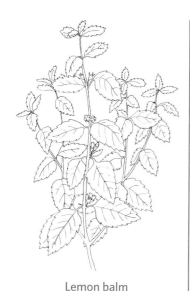

Lemon balm

Lemon Verbena

Lemon verbena is a tender, aromatic perennial that cannot stand frost, so it must be used as a houseplant during winter in cold regions. Its leaves drop

Lemon verbena

in autumn, but they return promptly. It is fragrant and grows to 10 inches.

Lovage

The celery-flavoured leaves and stalks are used in soups, salads, and similar dishes. Lovage grows well from seed in partial shade and moist, fertile soil. Mature plants may be 4 to 6 feet high.

Lovage

Marjoram

Marjoram is a tender perennial. In cold climates, it is grown as an annual. The plant reaches 8 to 12 inches and thrives in a light, rich soil with neutral pH in full sun. It has a shallow root system, so mulching around the plant helps retain soil moisture and keep down the weeds. Marjoram is highly aromatic, and its flavour improves with drying. Harvest just before the flowers open.

Marjoram

Herbes de Provence

This is a blend of summer herbs from the south of France. Use in soups, stews, and chicken dishes; with tomatoes and sauces; or in anything even remotely Mediterranean.

- 2 teaspoons dried thyme
- 1 teaspoon dried basil
- 1 teaspoon dried marjoram
- 1 teaspoon dried rosemary
- 1 teaspoon dried savory
- ½ teaspoon ground fennel
- ½ teaspoon dried lavender flowers

Combine all ingredients; store in an airtight container.

Yield: About ¼ cup

Mint

Mints are hardy perennials that often attain 3 feet. They are notorious spreaders. They prefer a moist, rich soil and thrive in full sun to partial shade. Harvest throughout the summer by cutting stalks just above the first set of leaves, as soon as the flower buds appear. Hang to dry for 10 to 14 days.

Mint

Oregano

Oregano, or wild marjoram, is a hardy perennial reaching 18 to 30 inches. The plant grows in ordinary soil but prefers well-drained, sandy loam. If the pH is below 6.0, add lime and calcium. Oregano likes full sun away from winds. Mulch where winters are severe. Propagate by seed, divisions, or cuttings. The seeds are slow to germinate; it's best to set out young plants. Space them 15 inches apart. Cut the stems an inch from the ground in autumn, just before the flowers open, and hang to dry.

Oregano

Parsley

There are two main types — flat parsley and curly parsley. Both herbs are a hardy biennial, often grown as an annual. The plants reach 12 to 18 inches and thrive in moist, rich soil. They prefer full sun but survive in part shade. Seeds take three to four weeks to germinate, so it is best to set out young plants, spacing them 8 to 10 inches apart. Pick parsley fresh throughout the growing season. Cut the leaves in the autumn and dry or freeze them.

Curly parsley

Flat parsley

Pennyroyal

This old-time medicinal herb was used for flavouring and to cure a variety of illnesses. It has also been found efficacious when used as an insect repellent. Grow pennyroyal from seed, cuttings, or root divisions. The plants grow 1 foot high and prefer shade and a moist soil.

Pennyroyal

Rosemary

Rosemary is used as both an aromatic and a flavouring herb in sauces, soups, and teas. This tender perennial evergreen shrub grows to 2 to 6 feet, depending on climate. Rosemary must be sheltered or grown in containers and taken indoors in winter in cold areas. It thrives best in warm climates and prefers moist, well-drained, alkaline soil. Apply lime or wood ashes to acid soil below pH 6.5. Grow rosemary from cuttings, root divisions, or layering, since seed germination is poor. Harvest all season or hang to dry for a winter supply.

Rosemary

Rue

Rue is a bitter medicinal herb used for centuries as an antidote to many poisons. It is easily grown from seed, but the

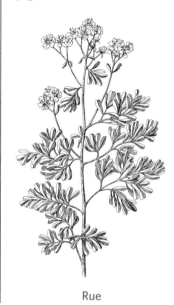

Rue

Facts about Herbs

- Dried herbs are more potent than fresh — 1 teaspoon dried equals 1 tablespoon fresh.

- To store fresh herbs, wrap them in barely damp paper towels, place inside resealable plastic bags, and keep refrigerated.

- Add herbs about 30 minutes before the end of cooking time; simmer slowly to release flavour and retain volatile oils.

- The chopped leaves of fresh herbs may be frozen with water into ice cubes and then stored in labelled, airtight freezer bags. Use to impart an herbal flavour to soups or stews.

- Use herbs in moderation. Some may be overpowering if too much is used.

ancient Greeks believed that a plant stolen from a neighbour's garden had more power than one acquired honestly. Plants grow 2 to 3 feet high and thrive in an alkaline soil, in sun or partial shade.

Sage

Sage is a hardy but short-lived perennial growing to about 2 feet. The mature stems become woody and should be pruned. Because the plant takes a long time to mature, transplants are usually set out. Space them 2 feet apart in a well-drained, rich soil and full sun. Add lime if pH is below 5.8. Water sage well while it is young. Harvest sparingly the first season; increase yearly. Pick leaves anytime, but

Sage

Harvest sage frequently to keep the plant from becoming woody.

harvest two crops a year — one in June and another in autumn — to keep the plants less woody. Hang in small bunches to dry.

Scented Geraniums

The leaves of rose geraniums are used in jelly and to make tea. Most varieties are grown primarily as scented houseplants. These geraniums are not frost hardy. Started from cuttings, they prefer full sun and well-drained soil.

Scented geranium

Sorrel

Sorrel leaves have a sour, acidic, citrus flavour and are used in soups and salads. Sorrel grows easily from seeds or division, prefers acidic soil, and often becomes a weed. Plants grow to 2 feet in sun to partial shade.

Sorrel

Sweet Woodruff

Used in Germany for many centuries to flavour May wine, it has also been used as an ointment, in perfume, and as an internal medicine. Placed in drawers, it repels insects and gives sheets and towels a pleasant scent. Sweet woodruff likes acid soil. It is difficult to grow from seed, so buy plants instead. The top may be cut and dried anytime; the fragrance

Sweet woodruff

Bouquet Garni

This traditional French herbal mixture will enhance any soup or stew. Tie sprigs of fresh herbs together in little "bouquets," or use dried herbs and make up pouches to pop into the pot.

1 tablespoon fresh parsley

1 teaspoon fresh marjoram

1 teaspoon fresh summer savory

1 teaspoon fresh thyme

1 bay leaf

Cut a 4-inch square of cheesecloth and lay it flat. Pile herbs into the middle. Gather up the corners of the cheesecloth and tie with a length of string. Store in a closed container until ready to use.

Yield: 1 bouquet

Variation: You can vary the recipe by adding rosemary, basil, celery seed, or tarragon.

appears only after drying. Plants grow to 8 inches high.

Tarragon

Tarragon is a perennial. The French variety has the best flavour and is preferred to Russian tarragon, which is weedy and lacks essential oils. Tarragon grows 2 to 3 feet tall and tends to sprawl. Because it rarely sets seed, propagate by cuttings or divisions. Tarragon prospers in fertile soil, sun, and moisture. Mulch the roots in late autumn and divide every three to four years. Harvest throughout the summer. To dry, cut the stalks a few inches from the ground in early autumn. Hang or screen-dry.

Tarragon

Thyme

The many varieties of this perennial include lemon thyme, creeping thyme, and garden or common thyme. Most have orna-

Thyme

mental, culinary, and aromatic qualities. Thyme is a short plant, growing only 8 to 12 inches tall, and is used as a ground cover or in rock gardens. It flourishes in sandy, dry soils in full sun. Propagate by seeds, divisions, or cuttings, but the seeds are slow to germinate. Space thyme 15 inches apart. Rejuvenate an older plant by digging it up in early spring and dividing it. Fertilize with compost or seaweed. Harvest the leaves throughout summer. To dry, cut stems just as flowers start to open. Hang in small bunches. Harvest sparingly the first year.

Watercress

Watercress is used for garnish and flavouring. If you have a shallow, slow-moving pond or stream where there is no threat of flood, you can try growing this flavourful, low-growing herb. Propagated by division, it can be easily transplanted from one stream to another.

Watercress

Making More Herbs

Once you've got a couple of herb plants, there's nothing to stop you from having many more! Here are three easy ways to make more plants for your herb garden:

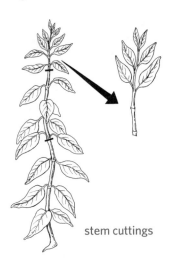

stem cuttings

Two or three 3- to 6-inch cuttings can be obtained from **one healthy stem** (above). Strip off the leaves from the bottom third or half of each cutting, dip the cutting in rooting powder (optional), and insert it into a pot of moistened perlite.

To make **root cuttings,** dig up the donor plant and slice sections from the root system. (If you want to keep the donor plant, as well as the cuttings, don't slice very large sections.) Bury the sections in moistened perlite.

root cuttings

Simple layering can produce new herb plants. After partly slitting a stem, lay it in a hole (one preferably amended with compost) adjacent to the donor plant and tack it down to prevent it from working itself loose from the soil. In time, new roots will form on the buried section. When a good root system has developed, the new plant can be cut from the donor and transplanted.

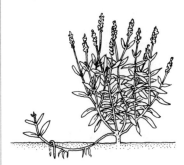

simple layering

Making Herbal Vinegars

Herbal vinegars are incredibly easy and inexpensive to make. Use a delicate rice wine vinegar with a subtle herb like chervil for a gentle hint of summer's glory. Combine a robust red wine vinegar with garlic, rosemary, marjoram, and black peppercorns, and enjoy extra gusto in a hearty bean soup.

The most common mistake people make when creating herbal vinegars is not using enough herbs. To achieve the best effect, use about 1 cup of loosely packed fresh herb leaves to 2 cups of vinegar. For dried herbs, use ½ cup of leaves to 2 cups of vinegar.

After cleaning the herbs, place them in a clean, sterilized jar and bruise them slightly with a spoon. Pour vinegar over the herbs and cover the jar tightly. Do not heat. Let the mixture steep in a dark place at room temperature. Shake the jar every couple of days and after a week, taste it. If the flavour is not strong enough, let it stand for another one to three weeks, checking the flavour weekly. If a stronger flavour is desired, repeat the steeping process with fresh herbs. When the flavour is right, strain, fill clean sterilized bottles, cap tightly, and label.

Basil and Other Single-Herb Vinegars

Follow this basic pattern for any fresh herb vinegar. Dill and chervil make nice alternatives, and tarragon makes one of the best vinegars. Chive makes a subtle vinegar; be sure to use a lot of it in the bottles. For small-leaved herbs, such as thyme, use an extra sprig or two.

    4 large sprigs fresh basil
    2 cups white wine vinegar

1. Place the basil sprigs into a pint bottle (or divide between two smaller bottles) and pour in the vinegar. Seal.

2. Store for two to three weeks before using.

Yield: 2 cups

Bouquet Garni Vinegar

This vinegar takes on the flavours of a classic French herbal combination. It is ideal in marinades for beef and for dressing roasted vegetables.

    1 cup sprigs of parsley
    ½ cup bay leaves
    ½ cup sprigs of rosemary
    ½ cup sprigs of thyme
    1 quart white wine vinegar

Using a wooden spoon, pack the parsley, bay leaf, rosemary, and thyme into a glass jar. Cover with the vinegar, seal with plastic wrap, and screw on the lid. Allow to steep for four to six weeks.

Yield: 4½ cups

Mixed Herb Vinegar

Here is an all-natural, instant salad dressing. Just whisk it with olive oil, and you're ready to dress the salad.

- ¾ cup chopped fresh basil
- ¾ cup chopped fresh marjoram
- ½ cup chopped fresh rosemary
- ½ cup chopped fresh savory
- ½ cup chopped fresh thyme
- 1 quart white wine vinegar

Using a wooden spoon, pack the basil, marjoram, rosemary, savory, and thyme into a glass jar. Cover with vinegar, seal with plastic wrap, and screw on the lid. Allow to steep for four to six weeks.

Yield: 4¼ cups

What Goes with What?

As a rule, stronger flavours go with strong vinegars and subtler flavours with more delicate vinegars. When you anticipate lovely colour from your herbs or petals, a white wine vinegar would usually be the best choice. Here are some great combinations.

Red Wine Vinegar
- Rosemary, savory, sage, basil, bay, and garlic
- Sage, parsley, and shallots
- Raspberries and thyme
- Red pepper, hot red chilli peppers, garlic, rosemary, and tarragon

White Wine Vinegar
- Dill, basil, tarragon, and lemon balm
- Savory, tarragon, chervil, basil, and chives
- Blackberries and lavender flowers
- Green onions, green peppercorns, thyme, marjoram, and a bay leaf

Apple Cider Vinegar
- Horseradish, shallots, and hot red peppers
- Dill, mustard seeds, lemon balm, and garlic

Sherry Vinegar
- Parsley, thyme, rosemary, and a bay leaf
- Apricots and allspice berries

Champagne Vinegar
- Pears and hyssop
- Rose flowers and lemon balm

Herbal Tea

There's a knack to brewing the perfect cup of herbal tea that tastes, smells, and looks inviting and has the strength to heal or refresh without calling to mind a dose of medicine. Packaged China teas with clearly spelled-out directions don't pose much of a problem. But because herbal teas are brewed from petals, roots, seeds, flowers, or leaves — alone or in combination — they require more know-how. Once you master a few simple methods, it's easy to brew a perfect cup of herbal tea.

Depending on the type of herbal tea you're brewing, you'll use one of two methods — infusion or decoction. For either method, brew the tea in a covered container; an open container allows volatile oils to escape.

Brewing by Infusion

Most teas made from leaves, petals, and flowers are prepared by infusion — steeping in boiling water. Infusion allows the oils in these parts of the herb to be released gently; if the herbs were boiled, the oils would evaporate.

Brewing by Decoction

The decoction method — simmering herbs for several minutes — is used mainly for teas made from seeds, roots, and bark whose active ingredients are more difficult to release. Herbal teas prepared by decoction generally tend to stay fresher than do teas prepared by infusion.

Basic Infusion of Leaves, Petals or Flowers

Bruise freshly picked herb leaves gently by crushing them in a clean cloth. The bruising will help release aromatic oils. Some herbal tea experts say infused herbs should be removed and discarded after brewing. Others believe the tea can steep for as long as a day or two. If you allow the herbs to sit, use boiling water to warm up cold tea and/or dilute it if it has become too strong.

- 1 teaspoon dried herbs (or 3 teaspoons freshly picked herbs)
- 1 cup boiling water

Rinse teapot with boiling water (to heat it). Place herbs in the pot, pour in boiling water, and allow mixture to steep for 5 to 10 minutes, or until the delicate flavours are released. Strain and serve.

Yield: 1 cup

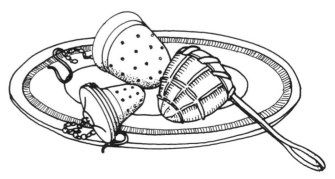

Basic Decoction of Seeds

Seeds should be well crushed to bring out their oils. A mortar and pestle work best, or wrap the seeds in a clean cloth and crush them with a wooden mallet or rolling pin.

2 cups water

1 tablespoon seeds

Bring water to a boil over high heat. Add seeds, reduce temperature, and allow mixture to simmer gently for 5 to 10 minutes. Strain the tea, then serve.

Yield: 2 cups

Lavender Mint Tea

Lavender adds a pleasant but not too flowery contrast to the sweetness of mint.

1 teaspoon fresh lavender flowers or ½ teaspoon dried

1½–2 tablespoons fresh mint leaves or 2 teaspoons dried

1 cup boiling water

In a teapot, combine the lavender flowers and mint. Pour boiling water over mixture; steep 5 minutes.

Yield: 1 cup

Variation: For more interesting blends, add rosemary, lemon balm or lemon verbena, and rose geranium.

Peppermint Punch

Tea punches are economical, low in sugar, and high in fruity flavour.

6 bags peppermint tea (4 tablespoons dried peppermint leaves)

4 pints water

1 tablespoon honey

1 quart cranberry juice cocktail

Juice of 1 lime

Sprigs of fresh mint

1. Place the tea bags in a jug. Bring the water to a boil; immediately pour water and honey into the jug. Let steep for 30 minutes.

2. Remove the tea bags. Add the cranberry and lime juices; chill. Serve in tall glasses over ice, garnished with a sprig of mint.

Yield: 6 pints; 10 to 12 servings

15 Herbs That Make Delicious Tea

1. Anise hyssop
2. Basil
3. Calendula
4. Catnip or catmint
5. Chamomile
6. Lavender
7. Lemon balm
8. 'Lemon Gem' and 'Orange Gem' marigolds
9. Lemon verbena
10. Mints
11. Monarda (bee balm)
12. Pineapple sage
13. Rosemary
14. Sage
15. Scented geraniums

	Hardy Perennial	Tender Perennial	Annual or Biennial	Under 1 foot	1–3 feet	3–5 feet	Over 5 feet	Dry	Wet to Moist	Direct Sunlight	Shade or Partial Shade	Seeds	Stem Cuttings	Root Divisions	Leaves	Roots	Flowers	Berries, Seeds
Agrimony	•				•	•		•		•	•	•		•	•		•	
Alfalfa	•				•				•	•		•			•			•
Angelica			•			•	•		•	•	•	•		•	•	•		•
Anise			•		•			•		•		•			•			•
Basil			•		•				•	•	•	•			•			
Bay		•				•	•	•	•	•			•		•			
Bearberry	•			•				•		•	•		•	•	•			
Bee balm	•				•				•	•	•	•	•	•	•		•	
Betony	•				•			•	•	•		•		•	•			
Bilberry	•				•			•	•	•			•	•				•
Birch	•						•	•	•	•		•	•		•			
Black cohosh	•						•	•		•				•		•		
Blackberry		•				•	•	•		•	•	•	•	•	•			
Blue cohosh	•				•				•		•	•		•		•		
Borage			•		•			•		•	•	•			•		•	
Burdock			•				•	•		•		•				•		•
Burnet	•				•			•		•		•		•	•			
Calendula			•	•	•			•		•		•					•	
Caraway			•		•			•		•		•						•
Catnip	•				•				•	•	•	•	•	•	•			
Cayenne	•	•				•			•	•		•						•
Chamomile	•			•				•		•		•		•			•	
Chicory	•					•		•		•		•				•		
Chrysanthemum	•			•	•	•		•	•	•		•	•	•			•	

	Hardy Perennial	Tender Perennial	Annual or Biennial	Under 1 foot	1–3 feet	3–5 feet	Over 5 feet	Dry	Wet to Moist	Direct Sunlight	Shade or Partial Shade	Seeds	Stem Cuttings	Root Divisions	Leaves	Roots	Flowers	Berries, Seeds
Cicely	•				•				•		•	•		•	•			
Clover	•				•				•	•		•					•	
Coltsfoot	•			•					•	•		•		•	•		•	
Comfrey	•				•				•	•	•	•		•	•	•		
Coriander			•		•			•		•	•	•						•
Dandelion	•			•				•	•	•		•			•	•		
Dill			•			•		•		•		•			•			•
Echinacea	•				•		•	•		•		•					•	
Elder	•						•		•	•		•	•	•	•		•	
Elecampane	•						•		•	•			•	•			•	
Ephedra	•				•			•		•		•			•			
Fennel	•					•		•	•	•		•		•	•			•
Fenugreek			•		•			•		•		•			•			•
Feverfew	•				•			•		•	•	•	•	•	•		•	
Flax			•		•				•	•		•						•
Fraxinella	•				•			•		•	•	•			•	•		•
Garlic	•				•				•	•	•	•			cloves			
Geranium		•			•	•			•	•				•	•			
Ginger		•			•				•		•			•			•	
Ginkgo biloba	•						•		•	•	•	•	•		•	(tincture)		
Ginseng	•			•				•	•		•	•					•	
Goldenrod	•				•	•		•		•	•	•	•	•	•		•	
Gotu kola		•		•					•		•			•	•	•	•	
Hawthorn	•				•	•			•	•	•	•	•				•	•
Hibiscus		•	•		•	•	•		•	•		•					•	
Hollyhock			•				•		•	•	•	•					•	

	Hardy Perennial	Tender Perennial	Annual or Biennial	Under 1 foot	1–3 feet	3–5 feet	Over 5 feet	Dry	Wet to Moist	Direct Sunlight	Shade or Partial Shade	Seeds	Stem Cuttings	Root Divisions	Leaves	Roots	Flowers	Berries, Seeds
Hops		•					•		•	•	•	•	•		•		•	•
Horehound	•				•			•		•		•	•	•	•			
Hyssop	•				•			•		•		•		•	•		•	
Jasmine		•				•	•	•	•	•	•	•	•				•	
Juniper	•						•	•		•		•	•					•
Labrador tea		•			•				•	•		•			•		•	
Lavender	•				•			•		•		•	•				•	
Lemon balm	•				•	•		•		•	•	•	•	•	•			
Lemon verbena		•				•	•	•		•		•	•		•			
Licorice		•			•			•		•			•	•		•		
Linden	•						•		•	•		•	•				•	
Lovage	•					•	•		•	•		•		•		•		
Marjoram		•			•				•	•		•	•	•	•			
Marsh mallow	•					•			•	•		•	•	•		•		
Meadowsweet	•						•		•	•	•	•		•	•	•	•	
Milk thistle			•		•			•		•		•			•			•
Mint	•				•	•			•		•	•		•	•			
Mugwort	•				•	•		•	•	•	•	•			•		•	
Mullein			•			•	•	•		•		•			•		•	
Nettle	•				•	•			•	•		•		•	•			
New Jersey tea	•				•			•		•		•	•	•	•			
Oregano	•				•			•		•	•	•	•		•			
Oregon grape	•					•		•			•	•	•				•	
Parsley			•	•					•		•	•			•			
Pennyroyal	•				•				•	•	•	•	•		•			
Raspberry			•				•		•	•			•	•	•			
Rose	•	•		•	•	•	•		•	•		•	•				•	•
Rosemary		•			•	•	•	•		•	•	•	•		•		•	

	Hardy Perennial	Tender Perennial	Annual or Biennial	Under 1 foot	1–3 feet	3–5 feet	Over 5 feet	Dry	Wet to Moist	Direct Sunlight	Shade or Partial Shade	Seeds	Stem Cuttings	Root Divisions	Leaves	Roots	Flowers	Berries, Seeds
Sage	•				•				•	•	•	•	•	•	•			
Sarsaparilla		•		•					•		•	•		•		•		
Sassafras	•						•	•	•	•		•	•		•	•		
Savory	•		•	•	•			•		•		•	•		•			
Saw palmetto		•					•		•	•		•						•
Skullcap	•			•	•				•	•	•			•	•		• (tincture)	•
Speedwell	•			•				•	•	•	•	•		•	•			•
Strawberry		•		•					•	•		•	•		•			
Sweet woodruff	•			•					•		•	•			•			
Tansy	•					•			•	•		•			•			
Thyme	•			•				•		•		•	•	•	•			
Valerian	•				•			•	•	•		•		•		•		
Violet	•			•					•	•	•	•		•	•		•	
White willow	•						•		•	•			•		•			
Wintergreen	•			•				•	•		•	•	•		•			
Yarrow	•				•			•		•		•		•	•			
Yerba maté		•					•	•			•	•	•		•			

Herb	Annual/ Perennial	Part to Harvest	Sweet	Savory	Tea	Classic Uses/Recipes
			Uses			
Anise	A	stems, leaves, seeds	•			pastry, cookies
Basil	A	stems, leaves		•		pesto, tomatoes
Bay leaf	P	leaves		•		stocks, stews, marinades
Caraway	A	seeds	•	•		breads, cheese, cabbage
Chamomile	A/P	flowers			•	calming tea
Chervil	A	stems, leaves		•		eggs, salads
Chives	P	stems		•		salads, soups, cheese
Coriander	A	stems, leaves		•		curries, salsas, salads
Dill	A	leaves, flowers, seeds		•		pickles, salads, soups
Fennel	A/P	seeds, leaves, stems		•	•	fish, stews, tea
Garlic	P	bulbs		•		sauces, soups, shrimps
Horehound	P	leaves, stems	•		•	horehound sweets, tea
Lavender	P	flowers	•	•	•	Provençal, teas
Lemon balm	P	stems, leaves	•	•	•	salad dressings, fish
Lemon verbena	P	leaves	•	•	•	sauces, tea, desserts
Lovage	P	leaves, stems	•	•	•	soups, fish
Marjoram	A/P	leaves, stems		•		meat, stocks, salads
Mint	P	leaves, stems	•	•	•	jelly, drinks, peas, sweets
Oregano	P	leaves, stems		•		pasta, sauces, stews
Parsley	P	leaves, stems		•		salads, soups, sauces, garnish
Rosemary	P	leaves, stems		•	•	lamb, eggs, game, stuffing
Saffron	P	stigma/styles		•		sauces, breads, fish, rice
Sage	P	leaves		•		poultry, stuffing, cheese
Savory	A/P	stems, leaves		•		beans, meat
Shallots	P	bulbs		•		sauces, soups
Sorrel	P	leaves		•		soups, sauces
Tarragon	P	leaves, stems		•		eggs, sauces, chicken
Thyme	P	leaves, stems		•		fish, meat, soups

CHAPTER 4

Homegrown Grains

There's nothing more redolent of home than a loaf of freshly baked bread. And how much homelier would it be if that bread were made from wheat or corn you'd grown and milled yourself? Like anything else you grow in your garden, grains taste better when they're fresh. Their flavour is sweeter, nuttier, and more complex than that of grains that have sat on a shelf for months, never mind grains that have been ground into flour and then stored for an indeterminate amount of time. When you grow your own grain, you're able to grind it right when you need it, capturing as much of the flavour as possible.

Depending on how much bread and pasta you eat, you may not have enough land to grow all the wheat needed to feed your family week in week out. But that doesn't mean you couldn't start with a "pancake patch" — a small patch of wheat to use for making pancakes at the weekends.Or maybe enough corn to eat during the summer and make popcorn for family film night through the winter. Of course, you could also plant enough corn to freeze the extra and eat through the winter (see page 185).

Grain isn't just for eating, though. It's also a necessary ingredient in beer making, and fresh grains impart a unique flavour to the brew. Once you've got your pancake patch established, why not try your hand at growing and malting barley for making your own homebrew (see pages 206 and 209)?

Growing Grains

When it comes to growing grains, following two simple rules will keep the experience positive: first, think through the entire process before you begin; and second, start small.

Preparing the ground and getting the seed in is only the first step in a long process. Each step requires time and energy and planning. You don't want to spend the summer admiring your sea of gold only to realize at harvest time that you don't know how you're going to cut the grain fast enough to keep ahead of the birds and the thunderstorms. Before you drop the first seed to the ground, you need to answer these questions:

- How much grain do I want to harvest?

- How will I control the weeds in my grain?

- In case of drought, will I water or give up the crop?

- How will I harvest the grain? Will I need help?

- How will I thresh, winnow, and hull the grain?

- Where can I store my grain to protect it from bugs, rats, and heat?

Which Grain to Grow?

If you're a beginner and want success, your first grain crop should be **corn** (**maize**). Consider the advantage: If you're already a gardener, you're probably growing corn, and you only have to let a few ears go past their prime to have a grain crop. There's no worry about dealing with hulls when you grow corn — just husks, and they're easily stripped away. It's easy, too, to twist dried corn off the ear. And you'll be delighted with the corn and cornmeal recipes in this book and wonder why you waited so long to try growing corn.

If you're a bit more ambitious, try **wheat** (or triticale). It's very easy to grow, and you can harvest, thresh, store, and grind wheat in small amounts with little difficulty.

Like those who have experimented with wheat, you will probably grow fond of having a wheat crop and want one each year. Ah, the thrill of biting into a piece of wholemeal bread and knowing that it is "your" bread, from planting to oven. And don't forget the many other dishes for which wheat is the base.

Rye is the crop for the fainthearted. It is almost immune to failure. It's hardy, so there's little danger from frosts, and will grow in poor soil. It's a good cover crop, makes a fine green manure to turn under to replenish the soil, and is easy to harvest, thresh, and grind.

Other grains involve one more step, and it can be a difficult one. The grains have hulls that must be removed, or at least minimized.

Millet hulls easily. Simply rub a handful of grain between your hands and the thin hulls will rub off.

Barley has a hull that fits firmly into the crease of each grain and is hard to remove. The commercial method of wearing this down is called "pearling." You can pearl small amounts of your own barley crop by popping it into the blender.

Buckwheat, not a true grain, has a kernel shaped like a beechnut and covered with a hard, inedible hull. By grinding the buckwheat, then sifting out pieces of the hull, a flour can be produced.

Oats are one of the easiest grains to grow and the hardest to hull. If you're growing oats for chickens or rabbits or horses, they'll handle the problem by ignoring the hull. If you're growing oats to eat, find a method of hulling before you start or choose a hull-less variety.

Rice can be raised at home, but it is a challenge. It's a delicious grain that can be used in many ways, all of which most of us would forgo if we had to raise our own rice.

Remember that all of these can be purchased, ready for cooking or grinding, at natural-food stores, and some of them are available in your supermarket. They are generally inexpensive, far less costly than foods that have been processed.

If you buy grains at places other than food stores, make certain they have not been chemically treated in some way to prepare them for planting.

Planting the Grains

	Per 1,000 Sq. Ft.		Per Acre		Hull	When to Plant	Soil	Yield
	Plant, lbs.	Harvest, Pounds	Plant, Pounds	Harvest, Bushels				Pounds per Bushel
Barley	2–3	25–65	75–100	40	H	early spring, late autumn	sweet	48
Buckwheat	1	33	36–48	15–20	H	after last frost	sandy, fast-draining	48
Corn/maize	1–2 oz. per 100 ft. row	6–8 doz. ears	12	750–1500 doz. ears	N	after last frost	light, sandy loam	56 shelled
Millet	1	55	30–35	15–60	H	after last frost	will grow in poor soil	48
Oats	2	50	80–100	60	H	early spring, late autumn	will grow in poor soil	32 (varies)
Rice	3–4	60–80	140	65	H	soil and air must be warm	area must be flooded	45
Rye	3	40–45	90–120	30	N	winter: early autumn. spring: early spring	will grow in poor soil	60
Triticale	3–6	35	100–180	20–35	N	early spring	well-drained, sandy loam	60
Wheat	3–6	40	100–180	20–50	N	winter: early autumn. spring: early spring	well-drained sandy loam	60

Back Garden Corn (maize)

In Europe, it's maize; South Africans call it *mielie* or *mealie*; early Virginia colonists in the USA wrote home about learning to grow *pagatour*. Call it what you will, you can't get away from corn.

Even if, by some quirk of nature or orthodonture, you were indifferent to chewing it from fresh steamed ears in summer, never touched polenta, and go to the cinema without a packet of popcorn, you'd still get your share of corn. It would take a lot of doing to avoid corn flour, corn tortillas, and corn oil. And the person who doesn't go for corn flakes with milk may be the same person who sips a little whiskey after dinner.

Commercial growers choose from the tremendous number of corn varieties according to their highly specific purposes — cattle feed, starch, oil, and so on. On the smaller, garden scale, you can plant one or two varieties that will successfully serve all your intentions.

For the home gardener, the most important distinction is between field corn and sweet corn. Unless you're growing corn for animals as well as people, growing sweet corn exclusively is probably your better choice. You can use it not only for eating fresh, but also for drying and grinding into meal. If you want to get more serious, you can try growing corn especially for cornmeal — sometimes called "flint" corn. These varieties were developed for shelling after 100 or more days and are usually left on the stalk until after several frosts.

Growing Corn

Begin preparing the corn bed in autumn. Apply at least an inch of compost or rotted manure and work it into the soil with a garden fork. To encourage worm activity, mulch the bed before a hard freeze.

Sowing. In spring, remove the mulch to let the soil begin heating and apply some finished compost. Cover the corn beds with black plastic at least a week before sowing. Sow the seeds 1 inch deep and 8 inches apart down the centre of a 30-inch bed. To ensure good pollination, plant each variety in blocks of four short rows rather than a single long row. Sow new blocks every two weeks for successive harvests throughout the season.

After sowing, keep the soil moist and install a fabric floating row cover supported by hoops to maintain soil temperature and protect seedlings against frost. Remove the cover when night temperatures are consistently above 60°F (16°C).

Growing. Corn is a heavy feeder, particularly of nitrogen. Yet for a

Field Corn

Field corn is a term that lumps dent, flint, and flour corn into one category. The names are unimaginative but accurate:

Dent corn has a dent in each kernel when dry.

Flint corn has rock-hard kernels.

Flour corn makes the best-quality corn flour.

If you're a beginner and want to ensure success, your first crop should be corn.

plant of its large size, corn does not have a very deep or extensive root system: A good blast of wind can flatten a corn plant. This means that corn needs deeply tilled, fertile soil with readily available nutrients. This combination allows the plant to produce roots that compensate in density for what they lack in range.

Like other plants with relatively shallow roots, corn is sensitive to fluctuations in soil moisture, which stress a plant. Regular and shallow (about 1½ inches) cultivation controls weeds while making nutrients available. Water regularly and fertilize every two weeks with a complete organic fertilizer, such as fish emulsion.

Harvesting. It's easy to know when to pick a tomato, but knowing when to harvest corn is a little trickier. The secret is to examine the silk at the top of the ear. A ripe ear of corn has a small amount of pliant, greenish silk near the top of the husk, with dry, brownish silk at the ends.

The time of day to pick is another concern, and it's one about which you'll hear different advice. Very soon after picking, the sugar in corn begins turning to starch. Some people like to pick their corn a few minutes before it gets dropped into the cooking pot. The theory is that the faster an ear of corn moves from the garden to the plate, the sweeter it will taste. It makes sense. Yet corn actually has its highest sugar content in the

Corn for Popping

Popcorn, as well as field corn and ornamental corn, has a higher starch content than sweet corn, but the growing requirements for all these are the same as for sweet corn. The difference is in the harvesting. For a kernel to pop, it must have just the right amount of moisture inside it, and this balance is influenced by curing.

Harvest the ears before a hard frost, when the husks have dried and the kernels are plump, well coloured, and shiny. Remove the husks and spread out the ears in a cool, well-ventilated space. After they've cured for about a month, test-pop some kernels. If they pop nicely, remove the kernels from the cobs and store them in dark glass containers. If they pop weakly, they still contain too much moisture. Continue curing, but test-pop every few days, because you don't want them to get *too* dry.

Popcorn comes in many varieties, from red and blue to white and yellow. Popcorn takes longer to mature than sweet corn, so you need to choose a variety that has enough time to develop in a typical growing season.

'Red Strawberry' has tiny, red jewel-like kernels carried on compact strawberry-shaped ears. It is suitable for the British climate and you pop it by placing the entire cob in the microwave. Watch it explode with fluffy, white, popped corn. Apply sugar or salt as desired and it's ready to eat.

early morning, not just before the evening meal. A good idea, then, is to pick corn early in the morning, before it's warmed by the sun, and refrigerate it in the husk until supper.

To harvest field corn, allow the husks to dry completely. Commercial growers try to dry to a water content of 12 to 13 percent; you'll know when your corn is dry enough because the kernels will shell easily, and as they come off the cob, small flakes from the cob will drop into your hand. Unlike most other corns, you can harvest field corn after a few frosts. Husk the ears and bring them to a cool, dry, well-ventilated space to finish drying. Store kernels on the cob or rub them off and store in covered glass containers.

How to Dry Corn

Pick fully mature sweet corn. After husking, immerse the ears in boiling water for three minutes. Drain and plunge them into ice water for three minutes. This process sets the milk in the kernels. It also keeps the corn from fermenting or smelling as it dries.

Cut the corn from the cobs and spread it onto baking trays. Place these in an oven at the lowest setting, in a food dehydrator, or in a protected spot in the sun. Turn occasionally as the corn dries. In the oven it will be a matter of hours; in your dehydrator, follow the times given in the instructions. If you dry the corn outside, put it in a covered, well-ventilated area. Remember to bring all the trays inside every afternoon before the sun goes down so the evening dew won't remoisten the kernels and leave them thoroughly confused about whether they're supposed to be dry or wet. You'll know the corn is dried when it has become very hard and has turned an orange-brown colour. Be careful, if you use the oven, not to let the kernels become overly brown from heat. After the corn is dried and cool, store it in an airtight container in a cool, dry place. It will keep almost indefinitely.

Storing Corn for Grinding

Corn, like any other grain, keeps better in its whole state, so don't grind it into meal too much in advance of using it. The degermed cornmeal on supermarket shelves lasts almost forever because the process used in refining it takes away the germ, that portion of the grain that supports life and contains

The kernels of fully dry corn come off the cob easily.

oil, flavour, and nutrients. It lasts forever, but who wants it?

Your cornmeal, ground from the whole grain, is highly perishable because the fat in the germ can go rancid. How fast that happens depends on the temperature at which you store the meal. In your freezer, cornmeal will keep for several months in an airtight package; stored in the cupboard in midsummer, it may not last for two weeks. If you have a home flour mill, the best way to get good flavour and nutrition is to grind small batches at a time, storing only a few cups in the refrigerator for immediate use.

Freezing Corn

1. Husk corn and remove silk from fresh ears.

2. For whole-kernel corn, blanch for 4 minutes in boiling water. For corn on the cob, blanch small ears 7 minutes, medium ears 9 minutes, and large ears 11 minutes.

3. Cool immediately in cold water. Drain well.

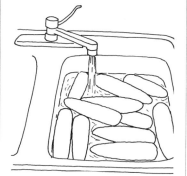

4. For whole-kernel corn, cut kernels from the cob at about two-thirds their depth.

5. Pack into containers or freezer bags, leaving 1 to 2 inches of headspace. Seal, label, and freeze.

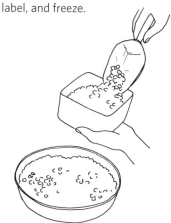

6. For corn on the cob, pack corn into freezer bags after blanching and cooling, expelling as much air as possible. Seal, label, and freeze.

Plant Your Own Wheat Field

If you're heavily into gardening and enjoy making your own bread, then sooner or later you'll want to try growing your own wheat, if only to get yourself away from the commercial process that grows a perfectly good grain, scrapes off the bran, peels out the germ, bleaches the flour, and then sells all those things back to you separately.

When you try, you will discover that although wheat grows fairly easily you need a lot of land to keep yourself in bread for the year, particularly if you are gardening in the British Isles (and the further west you live, the more difficult you will find it).

In the United States, growing wheat is a much more viable option. In fact, one gardener in Vermont attests to having planted 30 pounds of winter wheat on ⅛ acre and harvesting 250 pounds of grain in July.

Before you enthusiastically plan to put in enough wheat on your first try to make all the bread you expect to need for the next year, consider a small trial area for the first year. This test run will allow you to learn how the grain behaves, what its cultivation problems are, how long it takes you to handle it, how it's affected by varying climate conditions, and so on.

Selecting Seed

Once you've decided how much to plant and your ground is prepared, you'll have to decide what type to plant. In the UK, wheat is planted in the autumn and harvested the following August Winter wheat is planted in the or September. In the USA, winter wheat is planted in autumn and harvested from June to late July. It's fine for bread and biscuits. Spring wheat is planted in the spring, harvested in the autumn.

Commercial Wheats and their Uses

Class	Hard Red Spring	Malacca or Hereward	Hard Red Winter	Durum	Soft Red Winter	Riband, Consort, Claire
Where Grown	North-central states of USA	England	Southern half of Great Plains, USA	North-central states, esp. N. Dakota, USA	Eastern states, USA	England
Use	Bread	Bread	Bread	Pasta	Pastry, biscuits, crackers	Cakes, biscuits

It yields less than winter wheat but has a higher gluten content, so it's better for breads.

Both spring and winter wheat are further divided into soft wheat (lacking a high gluten content and used primarily for pastries and cheese biscuits), hard wheat (with a high gluten content, used for breads), and durum wheat (a spring crop, used for pasta). The variety you select will depend on where you live.

Planting Wheat

Plant winter wheat to allow for six to eight weeks of growth before the soil freezes. This gives time for good root growth. If the wheat is planted too early, it may smother itself the following spring and could be vulnerable to some late-summer insects that would be stopped by cool weather a little later. If winter wheat is planted too late, the roots may

---

Spring wheat should be planted as early as the ground can be worked. Do the initial plowing in the autumn and then till and sow in the spring.

---

not develop enough to stand the cold, and the wheat will not winter well. This decision may depend somewhat on the quality of your soil; some researchers believe excessively wet land that puddles and freezes chokes the plant when it freezes over, depriving it of oxygen. At least theoretically, then, dryer land would support wheat at lower temperatures.

Spring wheat should be planted as early as the ground can be worked. Do the initial ploughing in the autumn and then till and sow in the spring.

To ensure a fairly evenly distributed crop, calculate the amount of seed you'll need, divide it into two piles, and broadcast one part in one direction, such as east and west, and the remainder in another, such as north and south. A cyclone crank seeder will do an even job, but for a small plot, broadcasting by hand is fine, and for planting in rows, it is probably the best approach.

Cover the seed by rotovating or raking it in to a depth of 1 to 1½ inches for spring wheat, 2 to 2½ inches for winter wheat. Then roll it with a lawn roller, or in a small area, put down a plank and walk on it to firm the bed and increase the contact between the seed and the soil.

With an autumn planting and cooperative weather, the wheat should be 5 to 6 inches tall by

---

Pick a few grains and pop them into your mouth. If they're soft and doughy, the grain is not yet ready. When the grains are firm and crunchy, it's time to harvest.

---

winter. The following spring, as early as you can get on the land without wallowing in mud, roll the wheat again. This is an old practice that increases the number of stems emerging from one crown by squashing the crown and stimulating the plant to grow more stalks. The process is called *tillering*. After tillering, just keep the weeds down, if you can, and enjoy watching your wheat grow until it's time to harvest.

As you admire your rows of wheat, you'll notice in midsummer (later for spring wheat) a change in them. The colour of the stalks turns from green to anything from yellow to brown. The heads, heavy with grain, tip toward the earth. It's time to test the grain. Pick a head, pick out a few grains, and pop them into your mouth. If they are soft and doughy, the grain is not yet ready. Keep testing daily. One day the grains will be firm and crunchy. It's time to harvest.

Harvesting

At harvest, how should you cut the wheat? If you have a very small plot, you won't. Instead, you'll just pick the heads of wheat off the stems. It goes quickly if your wheat field is no larger than about 6 feet wide by 25 feet long.

Using a scythe. If you like the traditional way of doing things and are going to harvest a larger amount of grain, you might try to find a scythe and cradle. The scythe itself is not unusual. What is different is the cradle, a series of long wooden fingers mounted above the scythe blade. The scythe cuts the wheat, and then the cradle carries it to the end of each swing and deposits it in a neat pile, stacked so that all of the heads are grouped together in each pile. You can cut with the scythe alone — it's easy to find one — but you'll waste a lot of time picking up the cut wheat and arranging it so it can be handled easily.

Harvesting with a sickle. Another possible tool for cutting small amounts of grain is the sickle. It's a matter of grab and cut, grab and cut. If you're right-handed, you'll hold a handful in your left hand and swing the sickle with the right to cut the plants at nearly ground level. It's possible to kneel or

Using a scythe and cradle is an old-fashioned but efficient way to harvest wheat.

After wheat is harvested, it should be tied into sheaves, which are then piled into shocks for curing.

crouch in various positions to avoid getting too tired. As you cut handfuls, lay them in small piles with all heads pointed in the same direction.

Binding sheaves. The next step is to bind the grain into sheaves, each about 12 to 14 inches in circumference — a bunch you can hold comfortably in your two hands. Bind the same day you cut the wheat. It's nice to have two people taking turns cutting and sheaving. You can bind with cord or baler's twine or even with some of the wheat stems, twisting them in a way that holds the bundle firm.

Making shocks from sheaves. When 8 to 12 sheaves are piled together they form a *shock* (also called a shook or a stook). To make a shock, push the bases of two sheaves firmly in the ground at about a 60-degree angle, leaning toward each other, then mesh the tops of the two sheaves for stability. Mesh two more and place them at right angles to the first pair, forming a square. Pile as many as 8 or 10 more around them. A cheesecloth "hat" on top of the shock discourages hungry birds. The shocks are left in the field for a week to 10 days, curing, even during wet spells. Rain will not harm the grain.

Threshing wheat in a large, clean dustbin helps keep the released grains contained.

Threshing

Then it's time to thresh the grain, to separate the straw and chaff from it. You can go about it in a number of ways.

One method is flailing. A flail consists of one piece of wood about 3 feet long, which is the handle, attached with a leather thong to a shorter piece about 2 feet long. The shorter piece is flung at the grain repeatedly, shattering a few heads each time. When using this method, you can expect to produce about 3 pounds of wheat in 20 to 25 minutes. That's slow work. Also, there's a trick to learning to swing the flail without rapping yourself on the head.

Another way is to beat the individual sheaves inside a large, clean dustbin. In two hours a thresher can produce a bin full of wheat, but with a lot of chaff and even solid heads in it. This is faster than flailing but produces far more debris that has to be separated from the wheat.

Winnowing

The usual method for winnowing is pouring the grain from one container to another, letting either the wind or the breeze from an electric fan push the lighter chaff out of the grain, but it's nearly impossible to get the grain perfectly clean with this method, and you end up picking out a lot of debris by hand.

Storing

The way you store grain depends on how much you're dealing with. Storing it properly means protecting it from heat, light, and moisture, as well as rats, mice, and insects. You can keep a small amount of grain in plastic bags in the freezer practically forever; but it takes more effort to store larger amounts.

The general recommendation is to store hard winter or spring wheat with less than a 10 percent moisture content, a moisture level that is actually difficult to attain without additional drying. Five-gallon metal or plastic bins with tightly fitting lids are ideal for storing all grains. One hundred pounds of grain can be stored in three of these containers. Dustbins are not good for storage because making them airtight is difficult.

While these bins will prevent new insects from getting into the grain, you must take another step to eliminate any eggs or larvae already in the grain. A simple method is to heat the grain in the oven for 30 minutes at 140°F (60°C), which also will help reduce the moisture content. If you're not sure about the accuracy of your oven's thermostat, check it against an oven thermometer; temperatures higher than 140°F (60°C) may damage the grain.

Grinding

Some books suggest using a blender, but that gives poor results. You can't make nice fine flour, only a coarse meal with particles of uneven size. At first, buying an inexpensive, hand-

Winnowing can be done with an electric fan.

cranked mill sounds promising and romantic — back to nature all the way. But how much flour are you going to be grinding? You'd have to grind all afternoon to get enough flour for six loaves of bread, and that's apt to discourage you from baking at all after the first few tries.

When grinding grain, avoid the temptation to grind large amounts for future use. Grind what you need for perhaps a week, with the unused portion to be refrigerated in an airtight container. Whole grains can be stored for months without loss of taste or nutrition. This is not true of whole-grain flour.

Selecting a Flour Mill

Will it handle in a reasonable amount of time the amount of flour you expect to grind?

Does it grind without overheating the grain?

Is it easy to clean?

Can it be adjusted to grind different grains into varying degrees of coarseness?

Is it easy to use?

Will replacement parts be available if you need them?

Is it manufactured by a reputable company that will honour the warranty?

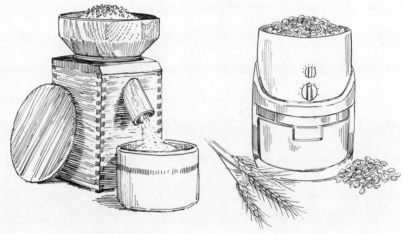

Electric stone grinder

Electric impact mill

Stand mixer attachment

Hand-cranked burr grinder

Cooking with Grains

First, remember that whole grain, like any fresh produce from the garden, must be completely clean before you cook it. Nothing will turn off those who eat what you prepare faster than biting into a mouthful of grit or chaff or even a little stone.

The easiest way to clean any grain (rice always seems to need it most) is by putting it in a large pan and running water over it, tilting the pan to run off the dust and chaff that weren't winnowed away, swirling your fingers through the grain to catch any bits of stone, and finally draining it in a sieve or colander.

The second thing to remember is that while whole grains take longer to cook than highly refined ones, you don't want to cook them into mush. Most whole grains cook to perfect tenderness in 45 minutes to an hour, at most.

Salt Sparingly

A word about salt. Every time you turn around, someone is warning you not to use so much salt and saying you get all you need for a week from one dill pickle. Here's the good news. When you cook with whole grains, you can easily use much less salt than you ever have before. Recipes calling for as much as a teaspoonful of salt work perfectly well with only ¼ teaspoonful.

The problem comes when you are using the salt to make the food have any taste at all. If you think about it, you realize that white flour, polished rice, highly refined grains, and the products made from them don't have much taste except for the seasonings added to them. When the recipe on a package of white rice calls for a teaspoon of salt to cook a single cup of rice, it's because otherwise the rice hasn't any flavour. But whole grains have their own flavour. You may add a bit of salt so that they taste salted, but you don't have to add it so they'll have taste. In fact, too much salt obscures the good flavours.

Secrets of Serving

Here's a final suggestion on how to incorporate grains into the diets of people who still think oats grow in little Os and corn and wheat grow in squares inside red-checked boxes. Do it the same way you'd approach any difficult task — very carefully. Most of us hate to admit it, but we resist change. This statement may even include you. A person who is accustomed to food that's bland to the taste and effortless to chew is not going to gobble up his or her first slice of sprouted wheat bread shouting, "Yum, more please." More likely, he's going to feed it to the dog and head for the neighbour's in search of chocolate. And if, after reading this chapter, you get all excited and run out and buy eight different grains and serve them all for supper tonight, your neighbour is probably going to be visited by your whole family.

The way to do it is to create as little anxiety as possible. Nobody should feel that he or she must like anything. All the familiar old favourites shouldn't be replaced suddenly with strange casseroles and dark breads. And no one, especially children, should fear that if they don't like the wheat soup, they'll get no supper at all. Instead, include a whole-grain dish along with the food you usually serve, with as little fanfare as possible. If somebody doesn't like it, refrain from commenting. And never scream, "How come nobody in this house ever wants to eat anything but chips and vanilla ice cream?"

Don't get preachy about nutrition. But don't give up, either. Continue to include whole grains in each meal, beginning with the more familiar ones like corn and rice. Cornbread made from whole-kernel cornmeal couldn't possibly offend anyone, and brown rice is a gentle introduction to a grain without all its nutrients refined away. Save the less familiar grains such as millet and whole cooked rye for later. When you come up with something you like especially well yourself or something that seems to appeal to others, make it again. In time the people you cook for will come to enjoy and often prefer whole grains.

Sprouting Grains and Beans

The seeds that you store, such as the grains and dried legumes, can be sprouted to provide fresh vegetables for salads, casseroles, and soups. Sprouts can be roasted, ground up, and used to enrich breads, biscuits, and other baked goods. Sprouting greatly increases the food value of the seed and its digestibility, because some of the fats

Nutritional Values

Food (100 g, or 3.5 oz.)	Calories	Protein (g)	Fat (g)	Carbohydrates (g)	Calcium (mg)	Iron (mg)	Vit. A (I.U.)	Thiamine (mg)	Riboflavin (mg)	Niacin (mg)
Barley, pearled	349	8.2	1.0	78.8	16	2.0	0	0.12	0.05	3.1
Buckwheat	335	11.7	2.4	72.9	114	3.1	0	0.60	—	4.4
Bulgur, hard winter wheat	354	11.2	1.5	75.7	29	3.7	0	0.28	0.14	4.5
Corn, field	348	8.9	3.9	72.2	22	2.1	490	0.37	0.12	2.2
Cornmeal, 1 cup	435	11	5	90	24	2.9	620	0.46	0.13	2.4
Oats (oatmeal or rolled oats)	390	14.2	7.4	68.2	53	4.5	0	0.60	0.14	1
Rice, brown	360	7.5	1.9	77.4	32	1.6	0	0.34	0.06	4.7
Rice, white milled	363	6.7	0.4	80.4	24	2.9*	0	0.44*	—	3.5
Rye	334	12.1	1.7	73.4	38	3.7	0	0.43	0.22	1.6
Wheat, hard red spring	330	14.0	2.2	69.1	36	3.1	0	0.57	0.12	4.3
Wheat, hard red winter	330	12.3	1.8	71.7	46	3.4	0	0.52	0.12	4.3
Wheat, soft red winter	326	10.2	2	72.1	42	3.5	0	0.43	0.11	—

* Enriched white rice

This table is based on information in the *USDA Composition of Foods, Agriculture Handbook 8.*

and starches are converted to vitamins and sugar. A dry seed becomes a homegrown vegetable in your kitchen any time of the year.

Sprouting is simple. The easiest method is to put a few seeds into a clean, large Kilner jar. Use about ¼ cup of large seeds, such as beans, and less of the small seeds like alfalfa. Cover the top of the jar with a piece of cheesecloth or fine-screen wire, held in place by a screw band. Fill with water and soak overnight.

The next day, pour off the water and rinse the seeds with cool, fresh water. The cheesecloth acts as a sieve on top of the jar. Pour off all excess water and put the jar in a dark place, such as a kitchen cabinet. The temperature should be warm but not hot; seeds may turn rancid at over 80°F (27°C).

Rinse the seeds several times a day with fresh water, always pouring it off, leaving the seeds damp but not soaking. In three or four days, you will have nutritious sprouts ready to serve raw in salads or in cooked dishes. Store unused sprouts in the refrigerator to keep them fresh for several days.

Large bean sprouts such as those of kidney beans and soybeans will need to be steamed for 10 to 15 minutes to tenderize them before using. Sprouted grains to be used in recipes such as breads can be roasted and

Sprouting grains in a Kilner jar

ground before you use them.

Seeds will not sprout well if they have been heated at over 130°F (54°C) as part of a drying process or in order to destroy insects. If you intend to use some of your wheat or other grains for sprouting or for planting, do not use this heat treatment on them.

When buying seeds for sprouting, be sure that they are pure, untreated seeds suitable for eating. Many seeds sold for planting have been treated with fungicides — they will still sprout, but they are poisonous.

Note that sprouted seeds have

been implicated in foodborne outbreaks including *Salmonella* and *E. coli*. Young children, the elderly, and other individuals who may have compromised immune systems are advised against eating raw sprouts. Raw sprouts present food safety problems because conditions under which they are produced — growing time, temperature, water activity, pH (a measure of acidity), and nutrients — are ideal for the rapid growth of bacteria. Even sprouts grown in the home present a risk if eaten raw; many outbreaks have been attributed to contaminated seed.

Cooking with Cornmeal

The number of dishes one can create with cornmeal boggles the mind. If you've been indifferent to it until now, it's probably because you've had only the degermed kind, which has a texture like beach sand and not much more taste. When you grind your own cornmeal or buy it fresh and still containing the germ, you will find it has a fluffy consistency and a rich taste utterly unlike anything you've tasted before. Your home flour mill will also grind corn. Although you sometimes hear that a blender can also do the job, the resulting meal is coarse and irregular.

To double the variety of cornmeal recipes, try toasting the meal lightly by stirring it over low heat in a heavy skillet or heating it on the lowest setting on a baking tray in the oven, stirring often, just until it begins to turn colour. All recipes taste quite different made with toasted cornmeal. Often, since toasting removes moisture from the meal, you'll find you have to increase the moisture content of a recipe. Just relax and add a little milk or water until you have your usual consistency.

> If you've been indifferent to cornmeal, it's probably because you've had only the degermed kind, which has a texture like beach sand and not much more taste.

Corn Bread

This recipe is based on one used at the Moosewood Restaurant in New York, whose cooking and recipes have probably done more to spread enthusiasm for whole foods than any other single effort. The difference is that this recipe uses wholemeal flour and cornmeal; Moosewood's uses unbleached white flour. The wholemeal flour produces a darker corn bread. If you'd prefer yours to be pale, substitute an equal amount of unbleached white flour for the wholemeal in the recipe.

    1 cup cornmeal
    1 cup wholemeal flour
    2 teaspoons baking powder
    ½ teaspoon baking soda
    ½ teaspoon salt
    ¼ cup honey
    1 cup buttermilk
    1 egg
    3 tablespoons melted butter

Sift together the dry ingredients and beat together the liquids, then stir everything together. Be thorough but do not overmix or the corn bread will be tough. Spread the batter in a greased 8-inch-square pan and bake about 20 minutes in a 425°F (218°C) oven.

Yield: 8 generous servings

Cornmeal Pancakes

These are American-style pancakes with a little cornmeal added — a good way to introduce the sceptical to cornmeal.

    ¾ cup unbleached white flour
    ¾ cup fine cornmeal
    ¼ teaspoon salt
    1½ teaspoons baking powder
    2 eggs, beaten
    1¼ cups milk
    2 tablespoons melted butter

Sift together the dry ingredients; combine the liquids. Stir the liquids into the dry ingredients quickly, mixing only until blended. Don't worry about lumps. Cook on a lightly greased hot frying pan and serve at once. You can make these as thick or as thin as you like. Allow the batter to stand for a few minutes to make a thicker pancake; thin it out with more milk for a thinner version.

Yield: 4 servings

Polenta

This is a close Italian cousin to cornmeal that has become a popular and versatile dish. Try making it simply and dress it up with different cheeses, meat sauce, or a spicy fresh tomato sauce. This version, however, is good enough to eat by itself with a fresh green salad.

- 4 cups water
- 1 cup yellow cornmeal
- 1 teaspoon salt
- 2 tablespoons butter or olive oil
- 1 teaspoon dried oregano
- ½ cup grated Parmesan cheese
- Freshly ground black pepper

1. In a small bowl, combine 1 cup of the water and the cornmeal.

   In a saucepan, bring the remaining 3 cups of water to a boil, then pour in the moistened cornmeal and salt, stirring constantly with a whisk so that lumps do not form. Cook over low heat until thickened and smooth. Remove from heat and let sit, covered, for 5 minutes.

2. Add butter, oregano, and Parmesan, mixing well. Add pepper to taste and serve with your favourite sauce, or stir in another cheese, such as fontina or sharp cheddar.

Yield: 4 servings

Topping Polenta

There's just no end to what you can put on top of polenta. Try a fresh, lightly cooked tomato-onion sauce made with fresh plum tomatoes from your garden and a light sprinkling of freshly grated cheese.

A completely different approach is to sauté a variety of fresh vegetables in a little oil and serve them over the polenta. A mixture of courgette, green onion, green pepper, and chunks of fresh tomato complements the corn taste beautifully.

Or melt some cheese on top of the polenta and use no other sauces.

An Italian friend suggests the following sauce as one that is wonderful with polenta, and can be cooked even while you are stirring the latter. (And you might want to make a double recipe of the polenta to go with this much sauce.)

- Olive oil
- 2 cups chopped onions
- 3 cups tomato purée
- ⅛ teaspoon sage
- ⅛ teaspoon thyme
- ½ cup chopped and grilled mushrooms
- ½ teaspoon salt
- ¼ teaspoon freshly ground black pepper
- 2 cloves garlic, crushed
- 3 tablespoons minced parsley
- 1 cup grated Parmesan cheese

Pour ⅛-inch layer of olive oil in frying pan and heat. Sauté onions until golden. Add tomato purée, sage, thyme, mushrooms, salt, and pepper and simmer for 30 minutes, stirring occasionally. Add garlic and simmer for 5 more minutes. Add parsley and stir.

The serving can be varied by placing polenta on a platter and covering with sauce, then sprinkling with cheese, or by making two layers of polenta, each topped with sauce and cheese.

Basics of Making Bread

Making bread is not difficult. Like other activities that we soon enough take for granted (such as driving a car and planting a garden), several steps must be linked in sequence. That sequence, however, is somewhat flexible.

There are few rules in baking, few measurements that must be precise. Making bread intimidates people because the behaviour of yeast mystifies them (they don't quite trust it) and the steps seem long and complex. But after you have done it a few times, you will assimilate this process until you can make bread with a light heart and confidence.

Let's take one good, simple bread from start to finish, elaborating upon each step so as to dispel the mystique. These instructions are given in detail, but the procedure is quite simple and is applicable to almost every yeast bread.

About Yeast

Baker's yeast is usually available in one of two forms.

Active yeast: granulated yeast that must be activated in water.
1 packet = 1 tablespoon

Compressed yeast: moist, live yeast sold in small cakes. Must be used within 2 weeks.
1 cake = 1 packet of dry yeast

Easy, Basic, and Good White Bread

Assemble all the ingredients before starting.

   2 cups warm water
   2 tablespoons honey
   1 tablespoon active dry yeast
   2 tablespoons vegetable oil
   2 teaspoons salt
5-6 cups unbleached bread flour
   2 tablespoons raw wheat germ
   ½ cup powdered milk

Proofing Yeast

1. The most critical judgment you make comes at the very beginning, when you test the temperature of the water in which you dissolve the yeast. It should be warm, not tepid and not hot — around 100°F (38°C). If you have a thermometer, use it. If not, run the water over your wrist; if it feels definitely but not uncomfortably warm, it's okay.

2. Put 2 cups warm water in a large mixing bowl. Add the honey and the dry yeast. Stir. Set aside for a few minutes; it will take about 3 to 15 minutes, depending on the temperature of the water. As the grains of yeast activate, they begin to foam.

Combining Ingredients

1. When the yeast is bubbly, add the oil, the salt, and 2 cups of the flour. Beat this mixture extremely well; this stimulates early development of gluten, the magic ingredient in the flour that gives bread

Breadmaking Supplies & Equipment

Necessities

- Yeast or some other leavening agent (usually)
- Water
- Flour
- Bowl or other container
- Wooden or similar strong spoon
- Two knives and a fork (for some kinds of mixing)
- Surface for kneading
- Something to bake on or in (pan, baking tray, roasting dish)
- Something to cover dough (towel, shirt, pillowcase, plastic wrap)
- Oven (woodburner, fireplace, outdoor fire)
- Measuring cup
- Measuring spoons

Helpful to Have

- A second bowl
- Electric mixer or hand beater
- Loaf tins
- Sharp knife
- Rubber spatula
- Single-edged knife for slashing loaves
- Pancake turner
- Pastry scraper
- Pastry brush
- Wire rack
- Reliable oven and/or good oven thermometer
- Instant-read thermometer
- Pastry blender

Options & Frills

- Two pastry brushes: one for melted butter, one for glazes
- Bread pans in many sizes, a variety of casseroles, soufflé dishes, tube pan, fluted moulds, special French bread pan
- A large, convenient surface to use solely for kneading bread
- Heavy-duty electric mixer with dough hook
- Plant mister for spraying

lightness and a fine texture. If you have an electric mixer, use it to beat the mixture on medium speed for 2 minutes or longer. Otherwise, beat it with a wooden spoon, at least 200 strokes. When you have finished beating, the surface of the dough may have a glossy look — this is a good sign.

2. Add the wheat germ and powdered milk and mix them in. Then add 2 to 3 cups more of the flour, a little at a time, mixing with a wooden spoon until the dough is too stiff to stir and pulls away from the sides of the bowl.

Kneading

1. Kneading is like dancing — almost any way you do it will be okay. A delicate touch is fine, but it will take longer to produce a state of elasticity. Energy and decisiveness will get you there more quickly. If you have a heavy-duty mixer with a dough hook, you can use it to knead. If you are kneading by hand, choose a kneading surface (bread board, tabletop, or other clean surface) that is about the level of your wrists when your arms are hanging at your sides. Any-

thing higher will tire your shoulders.

2. Sprinkle the kneading surface with flour. Dip your hands in flour. Turn the dough out of the bowl onto the surface. Move the dough around to coat the outside with flour, patting it into a cohesive mass. Begin to knead.

3. Take the far side of the dough and fold it toward you, stretching the dough and then folding it as though you were folding a sheet of paper. With the heels of your (floury) hands, push the folded portion down and away from you. Give the whole piece of dough a quarter turn, fold, and push. Repeat. Each time you will be folding and pushing a different segment of the dough. Do it again and again. Ten minutes is a good target.

   The dough will be rough and sticky at first. You may have to keep dipping your hands and sprinkling flour onto the dough and onto the board; add only as much flour as you need to keep the dough from being too sticky to work with. Too much flour makes a dry loaf; you want to end up with a dough

that is smooth but still soft and pliable. When you push it, it springs back. Eventually, it will become smooth and satiny.

First Rise

1. Rub a large bowl with soft butter or brush it with melted butter. (Oil tends to be absorbed by the dough, which then sticks to the bowl.) Place the dough in the bowl and turn it until all sides are coated with a thin layer of butter, or brush the top of the dough with melted butter. Cover the bowl with a kitchen towel.

2. Place the bowl in a warm, draught-free spot. Many people recommend the inside of the oven. If your oven has no pilot light, preheat it for half a minute, turn it off, and put the bowl inside. Or put the bowl in the oven with a pan of hot water on the shelf below.

3. Let the dough rise until it has doubled in size. You can test it by poking a finger into the top of the dough, about an inch down. If the hole you have made remains, it has risen enough. This can take anywhere from 45 minutes to several hours. If the dough

gets away from you and rises too much more than double, it's best to punch it down and let it rise again in the bowl before you proceed.

Punching Down

Give the dough a good punch with your fist. This is called punching down the dough. Take the dough over to the lightly floured work surface and tip or pull it out of the bowl. Knead it a few times to press out gas bubbles, then take a sharp knife and cut the dough into two equal pieces. Cover them with a towel and do something else for 5 to 15 minutes while the dough rests.

Preparing Pans

Grease two 8- or 9-inch loaf tins. Use soft or melted butter, preferably unsalted. If you don't have loaf tins or prefer free-form loaves, grease a baking sheet and sprinkle it lightly with cornmeal.

Shaping

Take one piece of dough, pat it with your hands into a rough ball, and flatten it to a size about twice as wide as your loaf tin and slightly longer. Fold the two long sides under so that they meet in the middle

of the bottom. Tuck the two short ends under. Gently press the loaf against the board to help the folded dough stick to itself. Place the shaped dough in a loaf tin or on the baking sheet. It should fill the tin no more than half full. Repeat this process with the remaining piece of dough. Brush the tops of the loaves with soft or melted butter.

Second Rise and Baking

1. Cover the tins or baking sheet with a towel and put the loaves in a draft-free place to rise again until they double in size, usu-ally 45 minutes to an hour. Meanwhile, preheat the oven to 375°F (191°C).

2. Place tins in the oven and bake about 25 to 30 minutes. Resist the impulse to open the oven door and peek during the first 15 to 20 minutes.

Testing for Doneness

When the bread has baked almost the minimum baking time, take a look. If the loaves are well browned and the sides have shrunk slightly from the sides of the tins, remove them from the oven. Tap the bottom of a tin to release a loaf.

Bread Ingredients

- Salt
- Milk
- Powdered milk or evaporated milk
- Eggs
- Butter and oil

- A variety of flours and meals
- Several kinds of sweeteners
- Fruits, nuts, seeds
- Alcohols and liqueurs (occasionally)

Turn out the loaf into your other, oven-gloved hand. Give the bottom of the loaf a tap; if it makes a hollow sound, it is done. If it makes a dull thud, bake a few minutes longer.

Finishing the Bread

1. When done, turn out the loaves on a wire rack to cool. If you like a softer crust, brush the loaves with melted butter or cover the loaves with a towel as they cool on the rack.

2. Bread doesn't slice well when it's hot, but the suspense may be too strong to let you wait. Don't be disappointed if it's a bit doughy inside. The texture will improve as the bread cools. In any event, be sure to wait until the bread is thoroughly cool before wrapping it. Happy eating!

Yield: 2 loaves

Note: Wholemeal and rye flours make dough that is stickier and less elastic than white-flour dough. It has been kneaded enough when it feels resilient. When rising wholemeal and rye dough, covering with a dampened towel helps prevent a crust from forming on the top.

Your Favourite Bread Tin

If you don't have the tin called for in a recipe or want to make individual portions of quick bread, use a different container; porcelain, earthenware, and metal will work. The times are meant as a guide. Watch the bread carefully.

Pan Size/Type	Approximate Baking Time
1-cup porcelain ramekin	15–20 minutes
3-cup pie dish	15–20 minutes
9- by 5-inch loaf tin	about 1 hour
5½- by 3-inch loaf tin	30–40 minutes
1-quart casserole	40–50 minutes

Types of Bread

Yeast bread may be the first thing that comes to mind when you think of homemade bread, but many other types are worth trying and tasting as you explore and expand your breadmaking skills.

Batter: Batter bread is beaten, not kneaded. With a heavy-duty mixer, you can make superb breads with little effort. They have a coarse crumb, a chewy texture, and a cratered surface like a lava flow. They have a yeasty flavour (they need more yeast because the gluten that supports rising is not completely developed by kneading).

Quick: Quick breads are almost effortless. Most are sweeter than many yeast breads, contain fruit and/or nuts, and are leavened with baking powder and/or baking soda. They have a crumbly, often crunchy texture.

Sourdough: Yeast-leavened breads are relatively recent. For thousands of years, people leavened bread by tearing off a piece of dough and using it to start the next day's batch. These breads, which require use of a sourdough starter, are coarser and chewier and have a heavier crust than yeast breads.

Quick Breads

Guests coming and time is running short? Quick breads are the perfect way to say "welcome" with fresh goods from the oven. Quick breads, risen with baking powder or soda instead of yeast, are fun to make and, because they are so easy, lend themselves to experimentation. Bake them fruit-studded and herb-scented as tea loaves, or whip up some savoury dinner breads with shredded vegetables, sausage, and peppers. Leftovers, spread with unsalted butter or cream cheese, make wonderful breakfast or lunchbox treats.

Basic Quick Bread

This basic recipe can be enhanced with different flours, spices, nuts, seeds, and fruits. It is not very interesting as it stands, so use it as a guide to create your own special breads.

1½ cups bread flour

½ tablespoon baking powder

½ teaspoon salt

¼ cup butter or margarine, softened

½ cup sugar

1 egg

¾ cup milk

In a large bowl, combine the flour, baking powder, and salt. In another bowl, cream the butter and sugar. Stir in the egg and mix well. Stir in the milk and add the liquid mixture quickly to the dry ingredients. Stir just enough to moisten completely. Spoon the mixture into a greased 9- by 5-inch loaf pan and bake at 350°F (177°C) until a tester comes out clean. Cool in the pan for 10 minutes and then remove to a wire rack to cool completely.

Yield: 1 loaf

Additions: Be creative! Stir in fresh or dried fruit and nuts. If you use fruit purée, use a little less fat. If you add or substitute an acidic ingredient, such as apple purée or buttermilk, compensate for it by adding ½ teaspoon baking soda.

Homemade Pasta

Fresh pasta has a taste and texture so much richer than those of dried pasta that it's worth the extra preparation time.

Simple Fresh Pasta

2¼ cups plain flour

3 large eggs

½ teaspoon salt (optional)

1. Mound the flour on a smooth work surface or in a very large bowl and make a well in the centre.

2. Beat the eggs and pour them into the centre of the flour (adding salt, if desired). Using a fork or your hands, combine the mixture until it is blended and a ball forms.

3. Continue kneading until the dough is smooth and supple — about 5 minutes longer. (If the dough feels too sticky, sprinkle it with 1 tablespoon flour and knead the flour into the ball. If the dough feels too hard, add *1 drop at a time* of beaten egg or vegetable oil.)

4. Lightly grease a piece of plastic wrap with vegetable oil. Place the dough in

Pasta dough can be made quickly and easily in a food processor.

the wrap and let it rest for at least 30 minutes before rolling it out.

Mixing in a Food Processor

1. Place the flour in the food processor bowl, and with the motor running, add the eggs one at a time.

2. Process until the mixture forms a ball.

3. If the dough seems too sticky, add 1 tablespoon flour and process for 10 seconds until incorporated.

Then process for 40 to 60 seconds longer.

4. Remove the dough and wrap it in greased plastic wrap. Allow the dough to rest for at least 15 minutes before rolling it out.

Rolling by Hand

1. To make the dough more manageable, divide it into four pieces and place them on a lightly floured surface.

2. Roll each piece into a rectangle. The dough should be ⅛ inch thick for noo-

dles or ¹⁄₁₆ inch thick for ravioli, cannelloni, tortellini, lasagna, manicotti, and any other "stuffed" recipe. (If you lay the rectangle on a clean tea towel and you can see the design of the towel through the dough, the dough is approximately ¹⁄₁₆ inch thick.)

3. *To make noodles,* roll the rectangle lengthwise like a swiss roll and slice off ⅛-, ¼-, or ½-inch widths for noodles or 2- to 4-inch widths for lasagna.

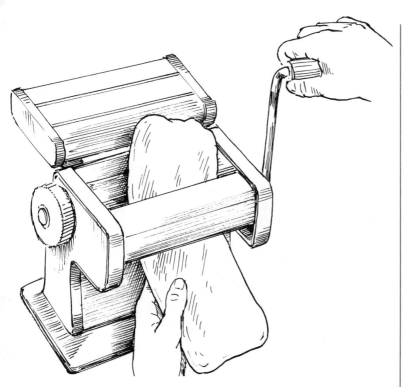

Although pasta dough can be rolled out by hand, it's much easier to get thin pasta when you use a machine.

Rolling by Machine

1. Cut the rested dough into four pieces; flatten and lightly flour each piece as required. Keep all but one piece wrapped in the plastic to prevent them from drying out.

2. Set the pasta machine at the widest setting and run a piece of the flattened dough through the machine. Repeat at this width four times, folding the dough in half each time.

3. The dough will now be thoroughly kneaded, and the rollers can be set closer together for each successive rolling to obtain the desired thickness.

4. Once the pasta has reached the desired thickness, allow the sheet to stiffen somewhat (without drying out) before running it through the cutter. Repeat for the remaining pieces of dough.

Yield: 1 pound

Variations

- Substitute semolina durum wheat flour for the whole amount of plain flour and use four eggs.

- Use only two eggs and add ½ cup puréed vegetables, such as spinach, broccoli,

To make cannelloni or manicotti, cut the rectangle into 4-inch squares and drop them into a large pot of boiling water. When the squares come to the top, remove them immediately and place them on a clean towel. When the excess moisture has been removed, lay the squares on a tablecloth and fold the cloth so that it comes between all the squares. They must not be touching. If the pasta is not going to be used during the next hour, place the folded tablecloth in a plastic bag and refrigerate the pasta for up to two days.

To make ravioli, cut the rectangle into 1½- to 2-inch squares, fill the squares with a prepared stuffing, top each with another square and crimp the edges, and then place them in a single layer on a lightly oiled or floured tray. Refrigerate until ready to use, or freeze. When they are frozen, pack them into plastic bags and seal. Cook in the frozen state.

beetroots, carrots, or red or yellow peppers. Combine the vegetables with the eggs before adding them to the flour.

- Substitute wholemeal, buckwheat, triticale, rye, or semolina flour for 1 cup of the plain flour and add ½ cup puréed vegetables.
- Add ¼ to ½ cup chopped fresh herb, such as parsley, basil, lemon thyme, or tarragon (a strong flavour — try 2 to 4 tablespoons the first time). If using dried herbs, add only 2 to 3 tablespoons.

Cooking Perfect Pasta

Allow ¼ pound of pasta per person. Use 8 to 12 pints of water to every pound of pasta; cook in a large pot with room to spare. (The extra space prevents the pasta from sticking together and helps it cook faster.) The addition of 1 teaspoon of oil will keep the strands from sticking.

Bring the water to a rolling boil over high heat (add 1 tablespoon of salt, if desired) and put in the pasta all at once. Using a wooden fork, stir gently to separate the strands or shapes. Return the water to a rolling boil; keep the pot uncovered and lower the heat to medium to prevent it from boiling over.

The pasta is done when it is tender but firm. The Italians call this *al dente* — firm to the bite. Cooking time varies according to the pasta: thick or thin, small or large, dried or fresh. If it's homemade (fresh or dried), it may take as little as 2 minutes, so check frequently. When commercial dried pasta is used, follow the directions on the package, but choose the shorter time listed and start testing (by tasting) several minutes before the end. This way, you'll be assured of getting perfectly cooked al dente pasta.

Drain pasta in a colander and serve immediately. When cooking manicotti, lasagna, or shells, drain and deposit on a clean tea towel to blot dry before use in a stuffed recipe. Do not rinse pasta unless it is to be chilled for a cold salad.

Grow Your Own Beer

Homebrew enthusiasts today can buy most of what they need from specialist suppliers, and this is a great convenience for all concerned. But if you have a little land, or even a sunny patio, you can grow enough of your own hops, herbs, and adjuncts to make a real contribution to the flavour, aroma, and uniqueness of your homebrew. Everything you need to make beer can be grown in garden-sized plots, including grains for malting.

Barley in Your Back Garden

Growing some of your own grains for homebrewing will seem excessive to some people, but it's really not that complicated. If you're lucky enough to have a garden or allotment of 800 square feet you can easily produce enough barley in one year for five full all-grain, 5-gallon batches. It can produce enough for at least 30 home-brew batches if you use a partial-mash recipe.

The greatest advantage of home-malting (whether or not you grow the grain yourself) — beyond the simple satisfaction of the act — is that you can bring the cost of brewing a batch of beer down to almost nothing. Unmalted grain costs pennies a pound. With a little work, you can transform the humble material into the finest, freshest beer-making malt available.

Barley is the king of all beer-making grains. Most barley is now used for animal feed. The barley grown for malting is mostly bearded six-row varieties in the Upper Midwest region of the USA and two-row varieties grown in the Pacific Northwest

Small Plot, Big Yield

A plot of ground measuring just 20 × 40 feet will produce a bushel of barley in one planting. Since a bushel weighs approximately 47 pounds, one crop of barley on an average garden plot can produce the grain ingredients for up to five batches of all-grain beer or 30 or more batches of extract or partial mash. On a smaller scale, if growing intensively in good garden soil in raised beds with frequent watering and good sun, a grower can expect roughly 5 to 15 pounds of grain per 10- × 10-foot bed.

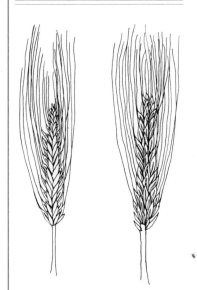

two-row barley   six-row barley

The greatest advantage of home-malting (whether or not you grow the grain yourself) is that you can bring the cost of brewing a batch of beer down to almost nothing.

and Great Plains regions of the USA, and in Europe. The terms *six-row* and *two-row* refer to the number of rows of seeds on the spike of the seedhead.

Harvest. When the grain is ready to harvest, the stalks should be golden; the individual grains should be hardening and difficult to dent with a fingernail but not brittle. They will have lost about 30 percent of their water content at this point. The ears will be bent over. The grains will be pale yellow and will easily pull off the head. Wait until the grains are perfectly mature before cutting the stalks and curing them in the field. The stalks will need to be threshed (bashing bundles of grain to separate the grains from the dried seedheads) and winnowed (using a fan to blow away the chaff) before they can be used for malting. Store the grain in hessian sacks in a cool cellar until it's needed.

Homegrown Hops

Although hops aren't grains like barley, they are a major ingredient in beermaking. They are also attractive plants that make great arbours, wreaths, and arrangements. Every homebrewer who owns a piece of land should try his or her hand at growing a few hop vines.

When you grow your own hops, you can pick them at their absolute peak of readiness. As soon as hops are picked, they start to lose the essential oils needed for good flavour and aroma. The best way to know that hops haven't been sitting on a shelf for a year is to grow your own. Commercial whole hops, the least processed form available, have been cut down, run through a packing machine, dried, baled, shipped, repackaged, and shipped again before reaching the homebrew store. Inevitably, some of the hops' bitter resins and essential oils are lost during processing. Your own hops will never have to run the gauntlet, making them

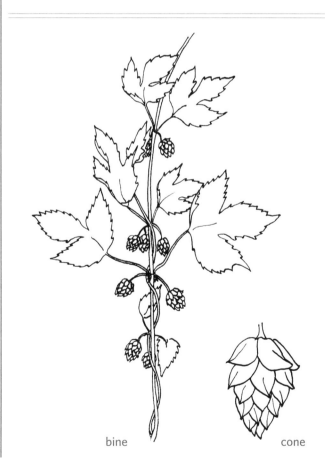

bine   cone

fresher, more aromatic, and better for brewing than any you could buy. The aroma alone will be enough to convert you, to say nothing of the flavour.

Harvest. Hop cones should be picked at their peak of readiness, which means that you have to pay attention to how they are developing. The most obvious sign of readiness is the development of lupulin glands — small yellow grains clinging to the base of the bracts. A mature hop cone will be heavy with this yellow powder. When you begin to suspect that the hops are nearing maturity, pick a cone and pull or cut it open. The lupulin should be a dark yellow-gold, and there should be a strong hop aroma.

If you want to dry your crop, do it as quickly as possible after the harvest, to preserve the essential hop oils. Warmth, no sunlight, and good air circulation are all that's required. Once the hops are picked, they should never again be placed in direct sunlight, or even strong artificial light. Light-struck hops will impart an unpleasant off-flavour to beer.

Once the hops are completely dry, seal in freezer bags with as much air as possible squeezed out. If you plan to use the hops right away, you can place them in the refrigerator. Otherwise, freeze all bags.

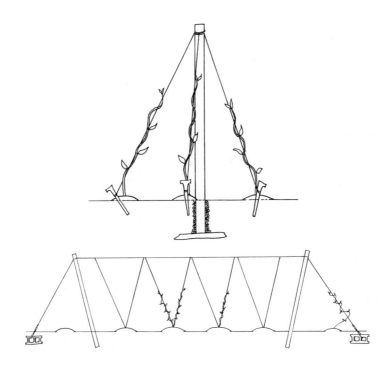

Hops are easily grown on trellises in small spaces.

Basic Barley Malting

Barley malting is best done in late autumn or winter, when temperatures are cold. The temperature of the malting area should be around 50°F (10°C), if not cooler. There are two reasons for this, both having to do with the final quality of the malt. Warm temperatures cause germinating barley to bolt, or grow very rapidly into a green shoot. Warm temperatures also encourage moulds, mildews, and fungi that can grow on wet grain.

To malt barley, you'll need some basic equipment. Some of the items on the list are handy but optional; others are vital. This basic malting procedure is for 5 pounds of barley grain.

- Two 5-gallon plastic buckets
- One 5-gallon plastic bucket with ⅛-inch holes drilled in the bottom
- Close-fitting (but not air-tight) lid for the plastic bucket with holes
- Large metal or plastic spoon
- Thermometer
- Notebook (for recording procedures)
- 20-pound scale (optional)
- Aquarium pump with air stone (buy a new one rather than reusing an old one; algae and fish waste don't mix with beer).

1. **Clean the grain.** Weigh out 5 pounds of barley and pour it into a 5-gallon bucket. Fill the bucket with water, stir the grain, and allow the chaff and debris to float to the top. Pour off the debris and repeat with fresh water as needed.

2. **Steep the grain for a total of 72 hours.** Cover the grain with at least half a gallon of water at 50°F (10°C). Change the steeping water after 2 hours (by pouring the grain and water through the perfo-

Malting Equipment

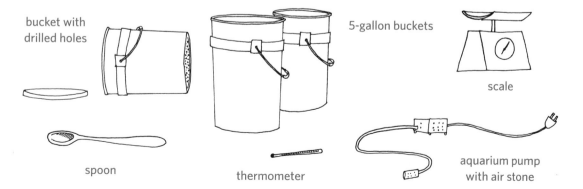

bucket with drilled holes

5-gallon buckets

scale

spoon

thermometer

aquarium pump with air stone

rated bucket into the second 5-gallon bucket), and every 12 hours thereafter. If an aquarium pump and air stone are used, the water needs to be changed just once every 24 hours.

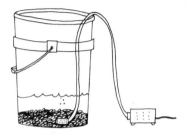

Steeping the grain

3. **Germination.** Drain the grain thoroughly in the sieve bucket (the one with holes drilled in the bottom). Pour about a gallon of water into the 5-gallon bucket, then put the air stone into the water and turn on the pump. Set the sieve bucket full of grain into the plastic bucket. The temperature of the grain should never exceed 68°F (20°C). After about three days of germination, rootlets will begin to grow, and the acrospire, or shoot, should be visible as a bulge under the husk. Once the acrospire has grown to two-thirds the length of the grain, it should be couched.

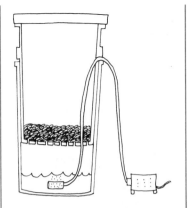

Germinating grain

4. **Couching.** This process prevents the acrospire from growing by denying it oxygen and allows enzymes to convert the grain starches into fermentable sugars. Turn off the aquarium pump and seal the sieve bucket with a lid. Turn the germinating mass once a day to prevent heat and carbon dioxide build-up. Couch the grain for one to three days.

5. **Kilning.** To make a dark malt, use a home oven at the lowest setting possible. Spread out the grain on a baking sheet, place the sheet in the oven, and leave the door slightly ajar. It should take about 48 hours to dry 5 pounds of wet malt.

To make a pale malt, a professional dehydrator with more exact temperature control is recommended.

6. **Roasting.** Once the malt has been dried, it can be spread in a ¾-inch layer on a baking sheet and roasted in the oven. All home-roasted grains should be allowed to cool after roasting and stored in a cool, dry place to mellow for five to seven days before brewing.

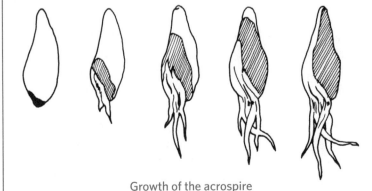

Growth of the acrospire

Roasting times vary according to the kind of malt you're producing. Here are a few examples:

Toasted malt. Roast the dry, kilned malt at 350°F (177°C) for 10 to 15 minutes.

Munich malt. Roast the dry, kilned malt at 350°F (177°C) for 20 minutes, until it's lightly toasted.

Black patent malt. Start with dry, finished malt. Spread the malt very thinly and roast at 350°F (177°C) for 1 hour and 20 minutes. Stir often to prevent burning. (A certain amount of smoke in the kitchen is inevitable, however.)

Basic Homebrew

Learning a basic recipe is a must and this one is intended to produce a Continental-style lager that will please most palates.

   5 gallons brewing water; 4 gallons chilled, 1 gallon at room temperature

   2 tins (3⅓ to 4 pounds each) unhopped amber malt concentrate

   ½ cup plus 1 tablespoon corn sugar

   1 packet lager yeast

   ½–1 pound crystal malt

   1½–3 ounces hops pellets

Preparation

Thorough preparation is essential to the success of any home-

Basic Brewing Ingredients

- **Water.** 5 gallons. Bottled springwater or tap water that is pre-boiled may be used. Boil 6 gallons of tap water, uncovered, for 15 to 20 minutes. Cover and let cool. Siphon the water into sanitized containers. For most types of beer, a pH of 5.0 to 5.5 is best; adding gypsum or Burton Water Salts will lower the pH of brewing water. Burton Water Salts also treats water with minerals for optimal beermaking.

- **Malt concentrate.** 6 to 8 pounds of malt concentrate, a molasses-like syrup made from malted barley sugar. Available in amber, dark, and light.

- **Hops.** 1½ to 3 ounces of hops pellets, depending on desired bitterness. Hops is an herb that flavours the beer.

- **Yeast.** Brewer's yeast, available in dry and liquid form, usually comes in amounts that are right for one batch.

- **Crystal malt.** Toasted, malted barley for imparting a mellow flavour.

- **Corn sugar.** A small amount of corn sugar to add at bottling time to produce carbonation.

brewing effort — it cannot be overstressed. Preparation includes cleaning and sanitizing all equipment and procuring all necessary supplies before beginning. *It is best to use baking soda and warm water for cleaning brewmaking equipment, as soap leaves a residue that can harm the beer.* Be sure to allocate sufficient time for each step.

Besides the above ingredients, you'll need the following equipment:

- Chlorine sanitizing solution
- Large saucepan
- Long-handled spoon
- Grain bag
- Kilner jar
- Primary fermenter with fermentation lock
- Aluminium foil
- Carboy
- Bottling bucket
- Bottles

1. Prepare chlorine sanitizing solution according to package instructions, or use homemade solution. *Plastic items should be dipped into the solution but should not be allowed to soak; they may pick up and transmit an unpleasant chlorine taste. All items should be rinsed three times in very hot tap water after being sanitized.*

2. Wash the saucepan and the spoon. These need not be sanitized, because they will be in contact with only the boiling wort.

3. Wash and sanitize the Kilner jar and a piece of aluminium foil large enough to cover the mouth of the jar. Rinse, and then let the jar drain by placing it upside down on clean paper towels.

4. Wash and sanitize the primary fermenter, its lid, and the fermentation lock.

Steeping and Primary Fermentation

It is a good idea to read and understand all these steps before you begin to work. They will take you from preparation of the yeast through the start of the fermentation process.

1. Have the 4 gallons of chilled brewing water ready. Pour the remaining gallon into the saucepan.

2. To prepare the yeast: In a small saucepan, measure 2¼ cups of the brewing water. Heat it to steaming. Add 1 tablespoon of the malt concentrate and 1 level tablespoon of the corn sugar; stir until dissolved. Increase heat and simmer for 10 minutes. Let cool until lukewarm.

3. Pour the mixture into the sanitized Kilner jar. Add the yeast; gently swirl the jar to mix. Cover the jar with aluminium foil; set aside.

4. Heat the water in the saucepan until it is steaming but not quite boiling. Meanwhile, pour the crystal malt into the grain bag; tie it off to prevent spillage, then lower it into the pan. The crystal malt will begin to flavour the water and prepare the grain for cooking. Remove the saucepan from the heat; remove the grain bag and set it in a clean container.

Step 4

5. Add the remaining malt concentrate to the hot water. Stir until it is dissolved.

6. Return the saucepan to high heat; heat the mixture until it is almost boiling. Return the grain bag to the hot mixture. Stir frequently but gently.

7. Vigorously pour the 4 gallons of chilled brewing water into the primary fermenter. (Vigorous pouring will aerate the water.) Cover the fermenter.

8. When the mixture in the saucepan is heated almost to boiling, remove from heat and transfer the grain bag to the primary fermenter.

9. Stir the grain bag and the water briefly; replace the cover. Add the hops pellets to the hot mixture in the saucepan; stir. Return the pot to high heat; stir frequently.

Read this paragraph carefully.

Now that all the ingredients have been added to the saucepan and the grain bag has been removed, you will bring the mixture to a boil. As the mixture approaches boiling, a froth will form on the surface. When it reaches the boiling point, it will vigorously foam to as much as twice its normal volume. This foaming is the reason for using such a large pot for what seems to be such a relatively small amount of liquid. An overflow of hot foam can scald you badly on contact; at best, it will make a sweet foamy mess all over your stove.

After foam-up occurs, the froth will die down of its own accord and the liquid will maintain a rolling boil. Stir occasionally during this time. Let it boil about 20 minutes from foam-up.

10. After 20 minutes of boiling, remove the pan from the heat. Let the mixture cool in the pot until the outside of the pan feels cool. You can hasten this step by placing the pan in a sink full of cold water, being careful not to let any of the sink water get into the pot. As the mixture is cooling, remove the grain bag from the fermenter and discard the grain. Clean the grain bag immediately in warm water; it can be reused almost indefinitely.

11. When the outside of the pot feels cool, dry the outside and pour the mixture into the water in the fermenter. The mixture should not be stone-cold, but if it is too warm, the heat will kill the yeast preparation. Stir the contents (now called the wort) of the fermenter to mix well.

12. By this time, the yeast preparation in the Kilner jar should be actively working. Swirl the jar gently and carefully pour the preparation into the wort. Cover the fermenter. Put

Air Is the Enemy

Remember that in brewing, air is the enemy. Once the wort is in the fermenter, a delicate process is taking place. Living yeast is consuming sugar and producing alcohol and carbon dioxide. The environment in the fermenter is the perfect place for this to happen. It is vital to keep aeration of the fermenting wort to a minimum. Whenever you move, siphon, skim, stir, or otherwise disturb the process (as you sometimes must), take care to cause the least possible agitation. Fermenting beer is a living thing — nurture it.

the fermentation lock in place, following directions for its proper use.

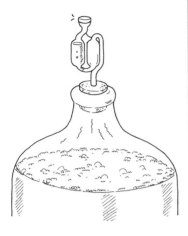

Step 12

13. Place the fermenter in a location that maintains a fairly constant temperature of about 65 to 70°F (18 to 21°C). When yeast becomes active, move the fermenter to a cooler (45 to 50°F [7 to 10°C]) location. *Note:* When making ale, do not move the fermenter to a cooler location.

14. The time that the wort will spend in the fermenter in its primary fermentation will depend largely on ambient temperature and on such conditions as initial water temperature and the type of yeast used. After as little as two days or as many as seven, the foam head on top of the

wort will collapse and the top of the wort will be visible. (Resist the temptation to lift the lid and examine the wort too often. Any opening of the lid invites the invasion of unwanted micro-organisms that can spoil the beer. The bubbling of outgoing carbon dioxide through the fermentation lock will let you know that things are progressing well.) When the bubbling slows to one bubble every 90 seconds, it is time to siphon the wort into the glass carboy.

Secondary Fermentation

The second fermentation will take longer than the first and will complete the principal production of alcohol in the wort. It will also contribute much of the flavour and char-

acter to the beer. The steps to accomplish the second fermentation are very simple, but you must follow them carefully so as not to spoil the wort.

1. Wash the carboy thoroughly, sanitize it with a chlorine solution, and rinse it thoroughly with hot water three times. Wash, sanitize, and rinse the carboy's fermentation lock, rubber stopper, and siphoning tube.

2. Use the siphoning tube to transfer the wort between fermenters. To do this, set the primary fermenter on a surface above the carboy.

3. Start the siphon: Fill the tube completely with water, using your thumbs to seal the ends of the tube. While holding your thumb over one end of the tube, place the other end

Step 4

into the fermenter. Let the water flow into a catch container. When beer starts to flow out of the tube, stop the end again, using your thumb.

4. Insert the tube into the carboy, with the end of the tube at the bottom of the carboy. Release your thumb and let the flow resume.

5. It will take several minutes for the wort to flow from the fermenter into the carboy. During this time, hold the tube in the fermenter as steadily as possible to prevent bubbles or agitation. Channeling the wort against the side of the carboy helps.

6. When you begin to hear sucking noises from the inflow of the tube, stop the siphon and remove the siphon hose.

7. If necessary, add brewing water to the carboy until the top of the wort is about 1 inch below the lip of the carboy. Insert the rubber stopper (which should not touch the wort) and fermentation lock into the top of the carboy right away.

8. Place the carboy in a location with a steady temperature of 40 to 50°F (4 to 10°C) and minimal light exposure. (You can cover it with a lightproof cover, such as a coat or black plastic bag.)

9. Leave the carboy undisturbed and listen for the bubbles through the fermentation lock. These will occur less frequently than during the primary fermentation, but they will come.

10. Thoroughly wash the siphon hose and the fermenter. These need not be sanitized at this time, but they must be kept clean. They will be used again before the job is done.

11. The secondary fermentation will take anywhere from two to six weeks. It is complete when bubbles have just about stopped rising to the top of the wort and a ⅛-inch-wide ring of bubbles has formed at the surface.

12. You should wait at least one week after secondary fermentation is done to let the sediment settle, and you may wait an additional week to suit your convenience.

13. During this waiting period, make sure that all of your bottling supplies and equipment are ready. It's best to thoroughly wash the bottles well in advance, so that they are ready to be sanitized and rinsed right before they are needed for bottling.

Where Do I Get That?

Equipment and ingredients for beermaking are often available in home wine and beer supply stores; check your local Yellow Pages under "Brewing Supplies" or "Winemaking Supplies." You may also obtain information about brewing and supplies from the Craft Brewing Association (see Resources, page 336).

Many homebrewers learn more about making beer by joining a homebrew club. Ask about clubs when you visit a local supplier, or contact the Craft Brewing Association.

Bottling and Storage

It's no secret — bottling beer is tedious. Enlist a friend to help and to keep you company. *Be sure to read this section through entirely before starting any of the following procedures.* Practise the bottling procedure with water in the fermenter before you actually attempt to bottle beer. It can be a bit tricky, and it is better to learn on water than to waste beer.

1. If you haven't already, thoroughly wash the bottles and make sure that the other supplies and ingredients are ready. Have corn sugar at hand, the bottling bucket clean, the bottle caps ready, and the siphon tube and filler wand clean. Make sure that the bottle capper has been adjusted to the proper setting, so that the caps crimp properly onto the bottles; practise on some empties.

2. Sanitize and rinse three times with hot tap water everything that will come into contact with the beer: the bottling bucket, the siphon hose, the stainless-steel spoon, the bottle caps, and the bottles.

3. In a small saucepan, heat 1 cup of water. When it is steaming, dissolve ½ cup of corn sugar in it; bring the mixture to a boil, stirring frequently. Remove from heat, cover the pan, and let cool.

4. Siphon the beer out of the carboy into the bottling bucket, leaving the sediment behind. Try to aerate the beer as little as possible.

5. Gently pour the cool sugar solution into the beer in the bottling bucket. Slowly and without agitation, stir to mix thoroughly.

6. Place the bucket on a surface above the one on which the bottles will rest as they fill. Some spillage is inevitable, so choose your

location carefully. Clean the area thoroughly.

7. *Think through steps 8 through 11 and plan how to most efficiently and quickly accomplish them in your work area.*

8. Sanitize the bottling bucket spigot. Attach the tube to the spigot; attach the filler wand to the other end of the tube.

9. Open the spigot to start the beer flowing.

10. Position a bottle and place the filler wand down to the bottom of the bottle. Press the wand gently against the bottom of the bottle and let beer flow in until it reaches the mouth of the bottle. Lift up the wand to stop the flow of beer. As you remove the wand from the bottle, the level of the beer in the bottle will drop down to the appropriate height.

11. Place a bottle cap over the mouth of the bottle and position it in the capper. Press down on the handle of the capper until the cap is firmly sealed on the bottle. Set aside the full bottle.

12. Repeat steps 10 and 11 with the remaining bottles.

13. Thoroughly wash all of the equipment you have used and store it in a clean, dry place. You will get years of use out of most of the gear if it is properly maintained.

14. Once the beer is bottled, it should be stored for six weeks before tasting. You may want to label and date the beer. Wipe dry the full bottles; place them upright in crates. Put the crates in a cool, dark place.

15. During storage, the little remaining yeast is processing the corn sugar that you added at bottling and producing a little more alcohol and carbon dioxide. This carbonates the beer so that it will foam when you open it. After six weeks, the beer is ready to taste. It will improve even more over time, but it is ready for a first taste now.

Yield: About 48 bottles

Fresh Hop Ale

This recipe uses fresh hops, right off the vine. Fresh hops should be used only for aroma or dry hopping, since their full flavour and bitterness are developed in the drying process. The rule of thumb is to use six times the amount of fresh hops as dry.

2¼ pounds dry amber spray malt

¾ pound 40°L crystal malt

½ pound toasted malt

¼ pound Special B malt

Serving Beer

Do not chill the beer too much. If you intend your beer to resemble bottled German or French beer, naturally you will refrigerate it. Just don't make it icy cold, or you won't be able to taste it properly.

If you have an bitter ale flavour in mind, you may not want to refrigerate it at all. If you can store your ale at cellar temperature, about 55 to 60°F (13 to 16°C), you will find that the lack of chill enhances the ale taste.

Use a large, uncoloured beer glass or mug. Tilt the glass slightly and pour the beer gently down the side. Pour in one smooth, continuous motion without stopping. Continue to pour until you see sediment approach the mouth of the bottle. At that point, stop pouring.

If you are tasting a six-week-old beer for the first time, the richer, fuller complexities of the hops will not yet have matured. After the first bottle, put away the rest for a couple of months. You'll be pleased at how much it improves.

1½ gallons cold water

3⅓ pounds amber malt extract syrup

½ ounce Centennial hops (for bittering)

¾ ounce Cascades hops (for flavour)

3 ounces Willamette fresh hops (for aroma)

Wyeast 1028 London ale or Whitbread ale yeast

⅔ cup corn sugar (for priming)

1. Crush malts and add the water. Bring to a slow boil over 30 minutes. Strain and sparge (rinse residual sugars) with ½ gallon of 170°F (77°C) water. Add extract and return to a boil. Add Chinook hops and boil for 45 minutes.

2. Add Cascades flavouring hops and boil for 5 minutes.

3. Add the fresh Willamette aroma hops and boil for a final 10 minutes.

4. Strain hot wort into a fermenter containing 1½ gallons of chilled water. Rinse hops with ½ gallon boiled water. Top up to 5 gallons.

5. Pitch yeast when cool.

6. Ferment at ale temperatures (65 to 70°F [18 to 21°C]).

7. Bottle with priming sugar when fermentation ceases (7 to 10 days). It should be ready to drink in two weeks.

Yield: 5 gallons

Dandelion Bitter

If you have a lawn, dandelions have probably given you a lot of pain over the years. Why not take revenge by using this traditional bittering herb for brewing? This ale is bright brown-orange and cloudy, with a sour piquancy unlike that of hops.

1 pound dandelion leaves, blossoms, and roots

1½ gallons cold water

½ pound toasted malt

½ pound 60°L crystal malt

3¾ pounds Cooper's Bitter kit

2 pounds Munton's light dry malt extract

1 ounce East Kent Goldings hop plugs (for flavouring)

½ ounce homegrown Willamette fresh hops (for aroma)

½ ounce Willamette dry hops (for flavouring)

Wyeast 1028 London ale or Whitbread ale yeast

⅔ cup corn sugar (for priming)

1. Clean the dandelions very thoroughly in several changes of water, removing any twigs or other debris.

2. Add the malts to the water and bring to a slow boil over 30 minutes. Strain and rinse with ½ gallon of 170°F (77°C) water. Add the extracts and return the mixture to a boil. Add dandelions and boil for 45 minutes.

3. Add East Kent Goldings hops for flavouring. Boil for 15 minutes. Add fresh Willamette hops for aroma during the last 2 minutes of the boil.

4. Strain hot wort into a fermenter containing 1½ gallons of chilled water. Rinse hops with ½ gallon boiled water. Top up to 5 gallons.

5. Pitch yeast when wort cools to 70°F (21°C).

6. Ferment at ale temperatures (65 to 70°F [18 to 21°C]). When primary fermentation slows, add Willamette dry hops to fermenter.

7. Bottle with priming sugar when fermentation ceases (7 to 10 days). It should be ready to drink in two weeks.

Yield: 5 gallons

Pale Horse Pale Ale

Pale ale is an amber- to copper-coloured bitter, malty beer of medium body and alcoholic strength.

- 5 gallons brewing water (1½ gallons chilled)
- 3⅓ pounds Black Rock East India Pale Ale kit
- 3⅓ pounds amber malt extract syrup
- ½ ounce East Kent Goldings hop plug
- ½ ounce Fuggles hop plug (for aroma)
- 1 packet Whitbread ale yeast
- ⅔ cup corn sugar

1. In a large saucepan, bring 1½ gallons of the water to a boil. Remove from heat, add the Black Rock and amber extracts, and return to a boil. Boil for 60 minutes.

2. Add the East Kent Goldings hop plug and boil for 15 minutes. Remove from heat; add the Fuggles hop plug. Steep for 5 minutes.

3. Strain hot wort into a fermenter containing the chilled water. Rinse hops with ½ gallon boiled water. Top off up to 5 gallons.

4. Add yeast to wort when cool.

5. Ferment at ale temperatures (60 to 70°F [16 to 21°C]). Bottle when fermentation ceases (7 to 10 days), using corn sugar for priming. Ale should be ready to drink in two weeks.

Yield: 5 gallons

Brown Ale

This mellow, dark ale uses a barley-rich malt, which gives it a distinctive nutty flavour that is very drinkable.

- 5½ gallons brewing water
- 20 ounces Russian malt beverage concentrate (contains rye and barley malt, rye flour, and clear water)
- 3 pounds Laaglander light dry malt extract
- 1½ ounces Northern Brewer hops pellets
- 1 packet Red Star dry ale yeast
- 5¼ ounces cane sugar

1. In a large saucepan, bring the water, malt concentrate, and dry malt extract to a boil. Boil for 4 minutes.

2. Add the hops. Boil for 70 minutes longer. Remove from heat and allow to cool.

Modifying Recipes for Homegrown Ingredients

Remember that the ingredients you grow and make at home can have some different characteristics from store-bought ingredients because they are so much fresher.

Hops. Homegrown hops tend to be much stronger than commercial ones because they're not dried, so use fewer of them.

Herbs. Unlike hops, herbs become more concentrated when they're dried. Use twice as much of a fresh herb as you would a dried herb, to allow for the concentration of flavour.

Malts. No adjustment for quantity needs to be made when using homemade malts rather than commercial ones.

3. Transfer the mixture to the primary fermenter and top off up to 5½ gallons. Pitch yeast.

4. When primary fermentation subsides, rack to a secondary fermenter. Add ¾ ounce of the cane sugar.

5. When fermentation is complete, prime with the remaining cane sugar. Bottle.

Yield: 5½ gallons

CHAPTER 5

Poultry for Eggs and Meat

It's amazing how many people have never had a truly fresh egg. Hens that live a healthy life with fresh air, good food, and clean water (not to mention access to open space and green fields) lay eggs that are firmer, more deeply coloured, harder-shelled, and, most important, more nutritious than those of their factory-farmed counterparts.

Chickens are among the easiest animals to keep in a small amount of space. In a quarter-acre garden, a family can keep as many as a dozen chickens (see page 14). Since a flock that size would produce as many as a dozen eggs per day, though, you might want to start with fewer (perhaps three or four hens), unless you have a ready supply of customers to buy the surplus eggs.

Another benefit of keeping chickens and letting them roam the backyard is that they can help with pest control, picking vine weevils off the shrubs and snapping up snails and slugs in the vegetable garden (with some supervision to make sure they don't start attacking the strawberries). Besides — chickens are just such fun to watch.

If you're serious about being self-sufficient and want to try your hand at raising poultry — chickens, ducks, or geese — for meat, spend some time thinking about the realities of raising an animal you plan to eat. First, there are the logistics. Who will slaughter the animal? If you're raising animals for the first time, definitely seek out a professional in your area who can either do the job for you or at least lead you through the process. And don't under-estimate how attached you can become to a chicken. You just might find yourself with a long-term pet instead of dinner.

Keep Chickens!

If you've never reared livestock before, keeping chickens is a great start. They're easy to look after, they don't need a lot of space, and they don't cost a lot of money to buy or to feed. Everything you learn about feeding, housing, and caring for your chickens will help you later if you decide to raise some other kind of animal.

People have raised chickens for at least 5,000 years. All chickens belong to the genus *Gallus,* the Latin word for rooster. The naturalist Charles Darwin traced all chickens back tens of thousands of years to a single extant breed, the wild red jungle fowl of Southeast Asia (*Gallus gallus*). These fowl look like today's brown Leghorns, only smaller.

Wild jungle fowl are homebodies, preferring to live and forage in one place as long as possible. This trait made taming wild fowl an easy task. All people had to do was provide a suitable place for the chickens to live and make sure that the flock got plenty to eat. As a reward, they had ready access to fresh eggs and meat.

Early chickens didn't lay many eggs, though, and they made pitifully scrawny meat birds. Over time, chicken keepers selected breeders from those that laid best, grew fastest, and developed the most muscle — and thus came about today's domestic chickens. The Romans called household chickens *Gallus domesticus*, a term scientists still use.

Different people who have kept chickens over the years valued different traits, which led to the development of many different breeds. In 1868, Darwin took inventory of the world's chicken population and found only 13 breeds. Now we have many times that number. Most of today's breeds were developed during the twentieth century, when chickens became the most popular domestic food animal. In recent years, there has been renewed interest in heritage breeds, as well.

Getting Started

How much it costs to get started depends on such factors as the kind of chickens you want and how common they are in your area, how simple or elaborate their housing will be, and whether you already have facilities you can use or modify.

Chickens must be housed to protect them from predators and harsh weather, but the housing need not be fancy. An unused toolshed or the corner of a barn or other outbuilding can provide comfortable quarters. If your garden isn't fenced, you'll need to put up one. A good fence keeps dogs and other predators away from your chickens and keeps the flock from bothering your vegetable patch or your neighbours' flower beds.

In deciding where to put your chickens, consider whether crowing may bother the neighbours. Male chickens — called roosters or cockerels — are well known for their inclination to crow at dawn. Ancient peoples believed they crow to scare away evil spirits lurking in the dark. Cockerels occasionally crow during the day, and if two cockerels are within hearing distance, they will periodically engage in an impromptu crowing contest. A rooster rarely crows during the dark of night, unless he is disturbed by a sound or a light.

If the sound of crowing might cause a problem in your area, consider keeping hens without a rooster. Although the occasional neighbour may complain about hen sounds, the loudest noise a hen makes is a brief cackle after she's laid an egg. Contented hens "sing" to themselves by making a soft, pleasant sound to which few people could object.

Without a rooster, hens will still lay eggs. The rooster's function is not to make hens lay eggs but to fertilize the eggs so they can develop into chicks. Without a rooster, you won't be able to hatch the eggs your hens lay.

Comparing Drawbacks and Benefits

Rearing chickens has some downsides. One is the dust they stir up, which can get pretty unpleasant if they are housed in an outbuilding where equipment is stored. Another is their propensity to scratch, which becomes a problem if they get into a bed of newly planted seedlings. Chickens also produce plenty of droppings that, if not properly managed, will start to smell and attract flies.

Before you acquire chickens, make sure that you and your family are not allergic to them. You can find this out ahead of time by visiting a poultry show at your county fair or spending a few hours helping a friend or neighbour care for his or her chickens. If you have an allergic reaction, you will have avoided the expense and heartache of setting up a flock you immediately have to get rid of.

Until you raise your own chickens, it may be hard to believe that people become attached to their chickens and have difficulty letting them go when it's time to butcher meat birds or replace old layers with younger, more efficient hens. The only alternative, though, is to run a retirement home for chickens, which gets pretty expensive, and the birds will still get old and die eventually. You'll have to come to grips with the loss.

For many people, the upside of raising chickens far outweighs the downside.

- Chickens provide wholesome eggs and meat for your family, and you can take pride in knowing that the flock that puts food on your table lives under pleasant conditions.

- Raising chickens is educational. By watching chickens interact with each other, you will learn something about how all birds live and behave.

- Chickens are attractive. They come in all sizes, shapes, and colours. You can find a breed that appeals to your aesthetic sensibilities.

Caring for a home flock takes a few minutes each day to provide feed and water and to collect eggs. In hot or cold weather, these jobs must be done twice daily, seven days a week. If you raise chickens for meat, the project will be finished in two to three months. If you raise hens for eggs, you must care for them year-round. As long as you keep in mind that your flock relies on you for its survival, raising chickens is a breeze.

Choosing the Right Breed

No one knows for sure how many breeds of chicken may be found throughout the world. Some breeds that once existed have become extinct, new ones have been developed, and forgotten ones have been rediscovered. Only a fraction of the breeds known throughout the world are found in the British Isles.

Egg Breeds

All hens lay eggs, but some breeds lay more eggs than others. The best laying hen will yield about 24 dozen eggs per year. The best layers are smallish breeds that produce white-shelled eggs. These breeds originated near the Mediterranean Sea, hence their classification as Mediterranean. Examples are Minorca, Ancona, and Leghorn, respectively named after the Spanish island of Minorca and the Italian seaport towns of Ancona and Leghorn (Livorno).

Leghorn is the breed used commercially to produce white eggs for the supermarket. Leghorns are inherently nervous, flighty birds that are unlikely to calm down unless you spend a lot of time taming them. The most efficient layers are crosses between breeds or strains within a breed. The strains used to create commercial layers are often kept secret, but you can be sure a Leghorn is involved.

Most layers produce white eggs, but some lay brown eggs. Brown-egg layers are calmer than Leghorns and therefore more fun to raise.

After a year or two, the laying ability of hens decreases. Unless you choose to keep your spent hens as pets, the best place for them is the stew pot.

Meat Breeds

Good layers are scrawny, because they put all their energy into making eggs instead of meat. If you want to have homegrown meat, rear a meat breed.

The various terms for chicken meat depend on the stage at which the bird is butchered. Broilers and fryers weigh about 3½ pounds and are suitable for frying or barbecuing. Roasters weigh 4 to 6 pounds and are usually roasted in the oven.

For meat purposes, most people prefer to raise white-feathered breeds, because they look cleaner than dark-feathered birds after plucking. The best breeds for meat grow plump fast. The longer a chicken takes to get big enough to butcher, the more it eats. The more it eats, the more it costs to feed.

A slow-growing broiler therefore costs more per pound than a fast grower.

Most meat breeds are in the English class, which includes Australorp, Orpington, and Cornish. Of these, the most popular is Cornish, which originated in Cornwall, England. The ideal Cornish hen weighs exactly 1 pound dressed. The fastest-growing broilers result from a cross between Cornish and New Hampshire or White Plymouth Rock. The Rock-Cornish cross is the most popular meat hybrid. Those 1-pound Cornish hens you see in the supermar-

Meat Classes

Rock-Cornish game hen: Not a game bird and not necessarily a hen, but a Cornish, Rock-Cornish, or any Cornish-cross bird, usually five to six weeks old, weighing between 1 and 1½ pounds.

Broiler or fryer: A young, tender chicken, usually weighing 4 to 4½ pounds live weight, less than 13 weeks of age, with soft, pliable, smooth-textured skin and flexible breastbone; suitable for almost any kind of cooking.

Roaster: A young, tender chicken, usually weighing 6 to 8 pounds live weight, three to five months of age, with soft, pliable, smooth-textured skin and a breastbone that's less flexible than that of a broiler or fryer. This class of chicken is suitable for roasting whole.

ket are actually four-week-old Rock-Cornish crosses, and they may not be hens but cockerels (young cocks).

A Rock-Cornish eats just 2 pounds of feed for each pound of weight it gains. By comparison, a hybrid layer eats three times as much to gain the same weight. You can see, then, why it doesn't make much sense to raise a laying breed for meat or a meat breed for eggs. If you want both eggs and meat, you could keep a flock of layers and raise occasional fryers, or you could raise a dual-purpose breed.

Egg Breeds

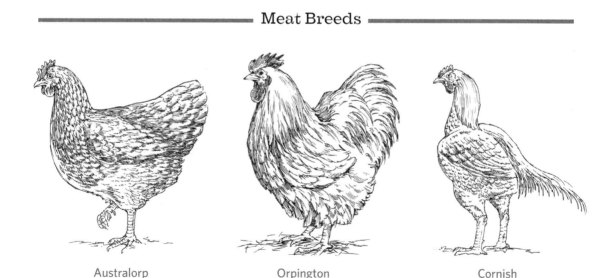

Minorca   Ancona   Leghorn

Meat Breeds

Australorp   Orpington   Cornish

Dual-Purpose Breeds

New Hampshire

Plymouth Rock

Rhode Island Red

Endangered Breeds

Chantecler

Dominique

Dual-Purpose Breeds

Dual-purpose breeds kept for both meat and eggs don't lay quite as well as a laying breed and aren't quite as fast growing as a meat breed, but they lay better than a meat breed and grow plumper faster than a laying breed. Most dual-purpose chickens are classified as American, because they originated in the United States. They have familiar names like Rhode Island Red, Plymouth Rock, Delaware, and New Hampshire. All American breeds lay brown-shelled eggs.

Some hybrids make good dual-purpose chickens. One is the Black Sex Link, a cross between a Rhode Island Red rooster and a Barred Plymouth Rock hen. Another is the Red Sex Link, a cross between a Rhode Island cockerel and a White Leghorn hen. (A sex link is a hybrid whose chicks may be sexed by their colour or feather growth.) Red Sex Links lay better than Black Sex Links, but their eggs are smaller and dressed birds weigh nearly 1 pound less.

Each hatchery has its favourite hybrid. Although hybrids are generally more efficient at producing meat and eggs than a pure breed, they will not reproduce themselves. If you want more of the same, you have to buy new chicks.

Endangered Breeds

Many dual-purpose breeds once commonly found in back gardens are now endangered. Because these chickens have not been bred for factory-like production, they've retained their ability to survive harsh conditions, desire to forage, and resistance to disease.

Organizations like The Poultry Club and The Traditional British Fowl Company keep track of breeds and varieties it believes are in particular danger of becoming extinct and encourages breeders to join its poultry conservation project. Rare American breeds include Dominique, sometimes incorrectly called "Dominecker," the old-est American breed. A few years ago, it almost disappeared, but it is now coming back thanks to the efforts of conservation breeders. Canada's oldest breed, the Chantecler, experienced a similar fortunate turn of fate.

In the UK, The Rare Poultry Society specializes in tracking and conserving rare breeds that do not have their own breed club or society in this country. It was established in 1969 in order to support breeds lost between the two world wars.

Exhibition Breeds

Exhibition chickens are bred for beauty rather than their ability to efficiently produce meat or eggs. Some of the same breeds kept for meat and eggs are also popular for exhibition, although the strains are different. Commercial strains used for egg or meat production are often hybrids, but even the pure production breeds are not necessarily true to type. Exhibition strains, on the other hand, are more true to type but less efficient at producing eggs or meat.

Even among the exhibition breeds, some lay better than others. Exhibition breeds in the Mediterranean class lay better than most other show breeds, even though they don't lay as well as production flocks of the same breed. Similarly, among exhibition birds, the Cornish and Cochin are more suitable

> Because dual-purpose breeds have not been bred for factory-like production, they've retained their ability to survive harsh conditions, desire to forage, and resistance to disease.

than many others for meat production.

Bantams are miniature exhibition chickens weighing 1 to 2 pounds. They are popular because they eat less and require less space than larger chickens. The shrill crowing of a bantam cockerel, however, is much more likely to irritate neighbours than the lower-pitched crowing of a large rooster.

Egg Production

A pullet starts laying when she is 20 to 24 weeks old. Her first eggs are quite small, and she will lay only one egg every three or four days. By the time she is 30 weeks old, her eggs will be normal in size and she will lay about two eggs every three days.

When a pullet is born, she carries in her body as many as 4,000 ova, or undeveloped yolks. When the pullet reaches laying age, one by one the ova grow into full-size yolks and drop into a 2-foot-long tube called the oviduct.

As a yolk travels through the oviduct, it becomes surrounded by egg white and encased in a shell. About 24 hours after it starts its journey, it is a complete egg ready to be laid.

A hen cannot lay more eggs than the total number of ova inside her body. From the day she enters this world, each female chick carries with her the beginnings of all the eggs she can possibly lay during her lifetime. Few hens, however, live long enough to lay more than 1,000 of the possible 4,000 they started with.

The Life of a Layer

A good laying hen produces about 20 dozen eggs in her first year. At 18 months of age, she stops laying and goes into a moult, during which her old feathers gradually fall out and are replaced with new ones. Chickens moult once a year, usually in the autumn, and the process generally takes two to three months. Because a hen needs all her energy to grow replacement feathers during the moult, she lays few eggs or none at all. Once her new feathers are

in, she looks sleek and shiny, and she begins laying again.

After her first moult, a hen lays larger but fewer eggs. During her second year, she will lay 16 to 18 dozen eggs. Some hens may lay more, others fewer. Exactly how many eggs a hen lays depends on many factors, including breed and strain, how well the flock is managed, and the weather. Hens lay best when the temperature is between 45 and 80°F (7 and 27°C). When the weather is much colder or much warmer, hens lay fewer eggs than usual. In warm weather, hens lay smaller eggs with thinner shells.

All hens stop laying in winter, not because the weather is cold but because there are fewer daylight hours in winter than in summer. When the number of daylight hours falls below 14, hens stop laying. If your henhouse is wired for electricity, you can keep your hens laying year-round by installing a 60-watt lightbulb. Use the light in combination with daylight hours to provide at least 14 hours of light each day.

Layers versus Lazy Hens

You can improve your flock's overall laying average by culling and slaughtering the lazy layers. The hens you cull can be used for stewing or making chicken soup. When your flock reaches peak production, at about 30 weeks of age, you

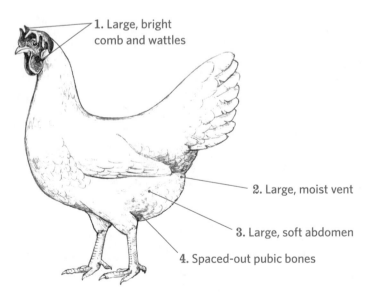

1. Large, bright comb and wattles

2. Large, moist vent

3. Large, soft abdomen

4. Spaced-out pubic bones

The four-point examination of a good laying hen.

can easily tell by looking at your hens and by handling them which ones are candidates for culling.

- Look at their combs and wattles. Lazy layers have smaller combs and wattles than good layers.

- Pick up each hen and look at her vent. A good layer has a large, moist vent. A lazy layer has a tight, dry vent.

- Place your hand on the hen's abdomen. It should feel round, soft, and pliable, not small and hard.

- With your fingers, find the hen's two pubic bones, which are located between her keel (breastbone) and her vent. In a good layer, you can easily press two or three fingers between the pubic bones and three fingers between the keel and the pubic bones. If the pubic bones are close and tight, the hen is not a good layer.

The Bleaching Sequence

If you raise a yellow-skinned breed, you can sort out the less productive hens by the colour of their skin after they have been laying awhile. The

Bleaching Sequence

Body Part	Number of Eggs Required to Bleach	Approximate Weeks to Lay That Many Eggs
Vent	0-10	1-2
Eye ring	8-10	2-2½
Earlobe	8-12	2½-3
Beak	35	5-8
Bottom of feet	50-60	8
Front of shank	90-100	10

same pigment that makes egg yolks yellow colours the skin of yellow-skinned breeds. When a hen starts laying, the skin of her various body parts bleaches out in a certain order. When she stops laying, the colour returns in reverse order. You can therefore tell how long a yellow-skinned hen has been laying, or how long ago she stopped laying, by the colour of the exposed skin on her beak and legs.

Replacement Pullets

A hen lays best during her first year. As she gets older, she lays fewer and fewer eggs. If you raise chickens primarily for eggs, you have the same concern as commercial producers — a time will come when the cost

of feeding the hens is greater than the value of the eggs they lay. For this reason, commercial producers rarely keep hens more than two years.

To keep those eggs rolling in, buy or hatch a batch of chicks every year or two. As soon as the replacement pullets start laying, get rid of the hens. If you replace your hens every year, you might sell your old flock, which will still lay fairly well for at least another year. If you replace your hens every two years or more, you can sell or use them yourself as stewing hens.

Add a batch of chicks every year or two to keep the flock producing eggs.

Collecting and Storing Eggs

An egg is at its best the moment it is laid, after which its quality gradually declines. Properly collecting and storing eggs slows that decline.

Collect eggs often so they won't get dirty or cracked. Pullets sometimes lay their first few eggs on the floor. A floor egg is usually soiled and sometimes gets trampled and cracked. Well-managed pullets soon figure out what the nests are for. If they continue laying on the floor, perhaps not enough nests are available for the number of pullets in the flock.

Eggs also get dirty when a hen with soiled or muddy feet enters the nest. Eggs crack when two hens try to lay in the same nest or when a hen accidentally kicks an egg as she leaves the nest. The more often you collect eggs, the less chance they will get dirty or cracked.

Further collection keeps eggs from starting to spoil in warm weather and from freezing in cold weather. Try to collect eggs at least twice a day. Since most eggs are laid in the morning, around noon is a good time for your first collection.

Discard eggs with dirty or cracked shells, which may contain harmful bacteria. If you are going to sell or hatch your eggs, sort out any that are larger or smaller than the rest or have weird shapes or wrinkled shells. You can keep the oddballs for your own culinary use. (And by the way, it's normal to occasionally find an extremely small egg with no yolk or an extra-large egg with more than one yolk.)

Store eggs in clean cartons, large end up so the yolk remains centred within the white. Where you store your eggs depends on whether they will be used for eating or hatching. If you plan to hatch them, store them in a cool, dry place, but not in the refrigerator. If you plan to eat them or sell them for eating, store them in the refrigerator as soon as possible after they are laid.

The egg rack on a refrigerator door is not a good place to store eggs. Every time you open the refrigerator, eggs on the door get blasted with warm air. When you shut the door, the eggs get jarred. The best place to keep eggs is on the lowest shelf of the refrigerator, where the temperature is coldest. Raw eggs in a carton on the lowest shelf keep well for four weeks.

Nutritional Value

Eggs have been called the perfect food. One egg contains almost all the nutrients necessary for life. The only essential nutrient it lacks is vitamin C. Most of an egg's fat, and all the cholesterol, is in the yolk. To reduce the cholesterol in an egg recipe, such as scrambled eggs or omelets, use two egg whites instead of one whole egg for half the eggs in the recipe. If the recipe calls for four eggs, for example, use two whole eggs plus four egg whites.

To eliminate cholesterol in a recipe for cakes, cookies, or muffins, substitute two egg whites and 1 teaspoon of vegetable oil for each whole egg in the recipe. In a recipe calling for two eggs, for example, use two egg whites plus 2 teaspoons of vegetable oil. If the recipe already has oil in it, you may omit the extra 2 teaspoons.

Determining Freshness

Sometimes you'll find eggs in a place you haven't looked before, so you can't tell how long they've been there. One way to determine whether an egg is fresh is to put it in cold water. A fresh egg sinks, because it contains little air. As time goes by, moisture evaporates through the shell, creating an air space at the large end of the egg. The older the egg, the larger the air space will be. If the air space is big enough to make the egg float, the egg is too old to eat.

Another way to tell if an egg is fresh is to use a light to examine the air space, the yolk, and the white. This examination is called candling, because it was once done by using candles. These days an electric light is used, but the process is still called candling. A good pen torch is ideal for candling.

Candle eggs in a dark room. Grasp each egg by its small end and hold it at a slant, large end against the light, so you can see its contents through the shell. In a fresh egg, the air space is no more than ⅛ inch deep. The yolk is a barely visible shadow that hardly moves when you give the egg a quick twist. In an old or stale egg, the air space is large and sometimes irregular in shape, and the yolk is a plainly visible shadow that moves freely when you give the egg a twist.

Occasionally, you may see a small, dark spot near the yolk or floating in the white. This spot is a bit of blood or flesh that got into the egg while it was being formed. Even though blood spots and meat spots are harmless,

Gauging Egg Quality

Fresh Egg (AA quality) ⅛ inch or less	Ageing Egg (A quality) up to ³⁄₁₆ inch	Old Egg (B quality) over ³⁄₁₆ inch

⅛"   ³⁄₁₆"

Photocopy this gauge, paste it onto a piece of cardboard, and use it as a guide when candling an egg to determine freshness. Remember: In a fresh egg, the air space is no more than ⅛ inch deep.

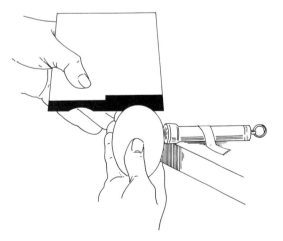

old egg floats

fresh egg sinks

old yolk flattens

fresh yolk stands up

when you sort eggs for hatching or for sale, eliminate those with spots. Customers don't find them appetizing, and eggs with spots may hatch into pullets that lay eggs with spots.

If you aren't sure what you are seeing when you candle an egg, break the egg into a dish and examine it. Soon you will be able to correlate what you see through the shell with what you see in the dish.

When you break a fresh egg into a dish, the white is compact and firmly holds up the yolk. In an ageing egg, the white is runny and the yolk flattens out. Try comparing one of your home-grown eggs with a store-bought egg — it's easy to tell which is fresher.

Eggs with spots may hatch into pullets that lay eggs with spots.

Shell Colour

A hen's eggs have a specific shell colour. All her eggs might be white, light brown, dark brown, speckled, blue, or green. The colour of the shell has nothing to do with the nutritional value of the contents.

Hens of the Mediterranean breeds lay white-shelled eggs. Since Mediterraneans are the most efficient layers, they are preferred by commercial egg producers. Many consumers prefer eggs with white shells because that's what they're used to seeing.

American breeds lay brown-shelled eggs. Since the Americans are dual purpose, they're popular in backyard flocks. Some consumers prefer brown eggs because they look home-grown. Brown eggs come in every shade from a dark reddish colour to a light tan that appears almost pink.

Blue-shelled eggs are laid by a South American breed called Araucana and its relative, the Ameraucana. Because the eggs are so pretty, these breeds are sometimes called "Easter-egg chickens."

Green-shelled eggs are laid by hens bred from a cross between Araucana and a brown-egg breed. Unscrupulous sellers charge outrageous prices for blue or green eggs by falsely claiming that they're lower in cholesterol than white or brown eggs.

Cooking with Fresh Eggs

Hard-boiled eggs have many uses, ranging from picnic garnish to afternoon snack, from main dish at lunch to appetizer before dinner. Actually, the term *hard-boiled* is not accurate. True, the egg is cooked hard, but if it has been boiled, it will be rub-

Seven Ways to Preserve and Store Fresh Eggs

Method	Storage Conditions	Maximum Storage Time
Refrigeration	lowest shelf	5 weeks
Store eggs in closed carton.		
Freezing	0°F (-18°C)	1 year
Freeze only raw eggs with shells removed. Break whole eggs into a bowl. Stir just enough to blend yolks with whites. Press the eggs through a sieve. Unless whites and yolks are thoroughly mixed, add ½ teaspoon salt (for a main dish) or ½ tablespoon honey, corn syrup, or sugar (for a dessert) to each cup of eggs. Freeze in containers.		
Pickling	refrigerate	6 months
Use small and medium eggs and a widemouth jar. Mix pickling solution from vinegar and spices (cloves, cinnamon, dry mustard, salt, and pepper) or use juice from prepared cucumber pickles or pickled beets. Pour boiling solution over peeled hard-cooked eggs in jar. Season small eggs for at least two weeks, medium eggs for at least four weeks.		
Oiling	31°F (-1°C)	7 months
Wait to oil for 24 hours after eggs are laid. Heat white mineral oil to 180°F (82°C) for 20 minutes. Pour into small bowl and let cool to 70°F (21°C). Immerse eggs in oil one by one with tongs or slotted spoon. To remove excess oil, place each egg on a rack and let oil drain for at least 30 minutes.		
Thermostabilization	room temperature or chilled	2 weeks at 68°F (20°C), 8 months at 34°F (1°C)
Thermostabilize eggs the day they are laid. Heat tap water to exactly 130°F (54°C), using a thermometer to determine temperature. Place eggs in a wire basket. Submerge in the water for 15 minutes if eggs are at room temperature, 18 minutes if they were refrigerated. Lift basket, drain, and dry the eggs.		
Thermostabilization and Oiling	34°F (1°C)	8 months
To combine methods, on the same day eggs are laid, heat the oil to 140°F (60°C) and hold at that temperature. Use a pair of tongs to rotate each egg in hot oil for 10 minutes. Set eggs on a rack to drain.		
Water Glass	34°F (1°C)	6 months
"Water glass" is a syrupy sodium silicate solution, available from drugstores. Combine 1 part water glass to 10 parts boiled water. Mix solution thoroughly and let cool. Place eggs in a clean glass jar with a tight-fitting lid. Pour cooled liquid slowly over eggs until they are covered by at least 2 inches. Screw lid onto jar and store in refrigerator, basement, or other cool place.		

How Many Eggs?

Most recipes call for large eggs. If you're using eggs of some other size, use the following chart to figure out how many you need:

	Large	Jumbo	Extra-Large	Medium	Small	Bantam
Number of eggs	1	1	1	1	1	2
	2	2	2	2	3	3
	3	2	3	3	4	5
	4	3	4	5	5	6
	5	4	4	6	7	8
	6	5	5	7	8	10

bery and tough. A more accurate term might be *hard-cooked.*

If you've never tried to peel a hard-boiled fresh egg, you're in for a shock. The contents of a fresh egg fill up nearly the entire shell. When the egg is cooked through, it sticks to the shell. If you try to peel the egg, you'll peel off several layers of white, too. The contents of an egg that's least a week old have shrunk away from the shell, making it easier to peel. Store-bought eggs peel easily because they're usually at least a week old by the time you get them home.

Old eggs have an off-centre yolk, which doesn't look as nice as a centred yolk when the cooked egg is sliced or deviled. The fresher the egg, the more centred the yolk, but the more difficult the egg is to peel. A good compromise is to hard-boil eggs that are 7 to 10 days old. If you want to hard-boil fresher eggs, leave them overnight at room temperature first.

Beating Egg Whites

A gourmet cook beats egg whites only in a copper bowl. Copper from the bowl reacts with con-albumin in the white to stabilize the foam, so the air that's beaten in will not leak right back out. You can get the same results in a glass or stainless-steel bowl by adding an acid ingredient.

Cream of tartar is an acid ingredient. Add ⅛ teaspoon per egg white unless you're making meringue, in which case add ⅛ teaspoon per two egg whites. Lemon juice or vinegar serves the same purpose as cream of tartar.

Egg whites beat up to their greatest volume if the eggs are first warmed to room temperature for about 30 minutes. Because fat inhibits beating, take great care not to get any yolk into the white when you separate the eggs. Properly beaten whites should increase to four times their volume.

Butchering

As butchering time draws near, seek out a fellow small-scale chicken keeper willing to show you how to clean your broilers, or learn the procedure from a good book. If you prefer not to butcher your own birds, perhaps you can find a butcher or slaughterhouse in your area that handles chickens.

Poultry Weights at Various Ages

Type	Age	Weight
Broiler	8–14 weeks	1–2½ pounds
Fryer	14–20 weeks	2½–3½ pounds
Roaster	5–9 months	over 3½ pounds
Capon (desexed male)	6–10 months	over 4 pounds
Fowl	over 9 months	over 3 pounds
Rooster	over 10 months	3–6 pounds

To cut up a chicken, use a sharp, heavy knife and follow these steps:

1. Cut skin between thighs and body.

2. Grasp one leg in each hand, lift the bird, and bend back the legs until the hip joints pop free.

3. Cut away the leg by slicing from the hip, as close as possible to the backbone.

4. If you wish, separate the thigh from the drumstick by cutting through the joint between them.

You can find the joint by flexing the leg and thigh to locate the bending point.

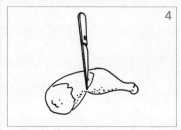

5. On the same side, remove the wing by cutting along the joint inside the "wing pit," over the joint and down around it. Turn the bird over and remove the other leg and wing. To create mini drumsticks, separate the upper, meatier portion of each wing from the lower two bony sections.

6. To divide the body, stand the bird on its neck and cut from the tail toward the neck, along the end of the ribs on one side. Cut along the other side to free the back. Bend the back until it snaps in half; cut along the line of least resistance to separate the ribs from the lower back.

7. Place breast on the cutting board, skin-side down, and cut through the white cartilage at the V of the neck.

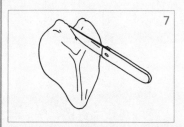

8. Grasp the breast firmly in both hands and bend back each side, pushing with your fingers to snap the breastbone. Cut the breast in half lengthwise along the bone. For boned breasts, place the breast skin-side up on a cutting board. Insert the knife along one side of the bone, and cut the meat away from the bone. Repeat for the other side.

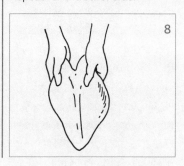

— A Simple Chicken Coop (The "Poulet Chalet") —

Holds:
3 hens
1 nest box
1 roost

The Poulet Chalet is ideal for the British climate and its clean lines and transparent roof make it a favourite, and one that everyone wants to build for their back garden. "My objective was to make a coop that was portable, secure from predators, and easy to maintain and clean," chicken owner Bruce Goodson explains. "So far, I have been very happy that the design has met these objectives." Lightweight and easily picked up by two people gripping the boards on the side, Poulet Chalet is completely portable. The coop is entirely enclosed with wood and screening to make it secure from predators. One side of the roof is hinged at the top, and on the opposite side, half of one of the bottom screens is a hinged door to allow for plenty of access to clean and maintain the coop.

Poulet Chalet houses three chickens comfortably and has plenty of room inside for a light, a feeder, and a waterer. The second level has a sturdy tree-limb roost and a nest box that can be accessed from the outside via a small door located on the outside of the coop. The roost and nest box are located in the upper level of the coop, and chickens use a ramp to reach the lower ground level, where the feeder and waterer are suspended. The ramp is pulled up by a cord to secure the chickens from predators overnight. The chicks can access the yard through a chicken door on the side. The chickens stay warm and comfortable in mild winters. In areas with severe winter weather, the coop could be moved into the garage or barn for added protection against the elements.

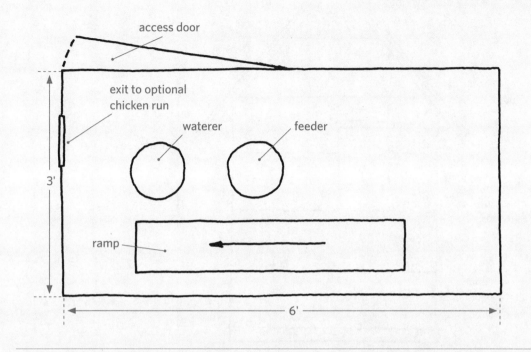

access door

exit to optional
chicken run

waterer

feeder

ramp

3'

6'

FLOOR PLAN: UPPER LEVEL

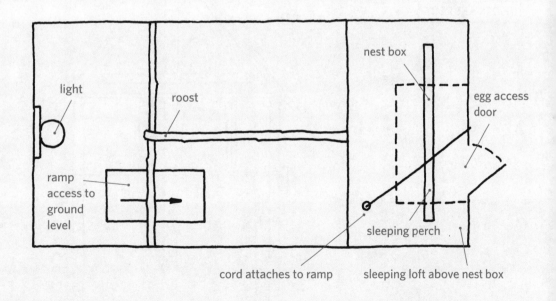

light

roost

nest box

egg access
door

ramp
access to
ground
level

sleeping perch

cord attaches to ramp

sleeping loft above nest box

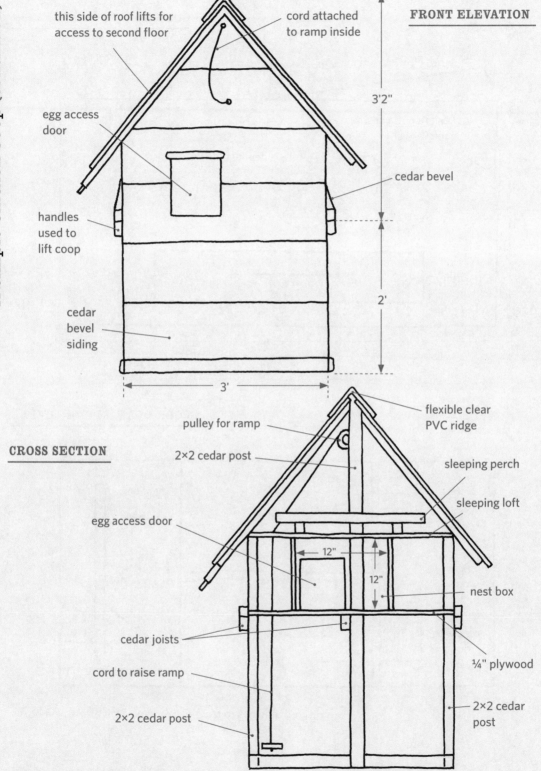

FRONT ELEVATION

this side of roof lifts for access to second floor

cord attached to ramp inside

3'2"

cedar bevel

egg access door

handles used to lift coop

cedar bevel siding

3'

2'

CROSS SECTION

pulley for ramp

2×2 cedar post

egg access door

flexible clear PVC ridge

sleeping perch

sleeping loft

12"

12"

nest box

cedar joists

cord to raise ramp

2×2 cedar post

¼" plywood

2×2 cedar post

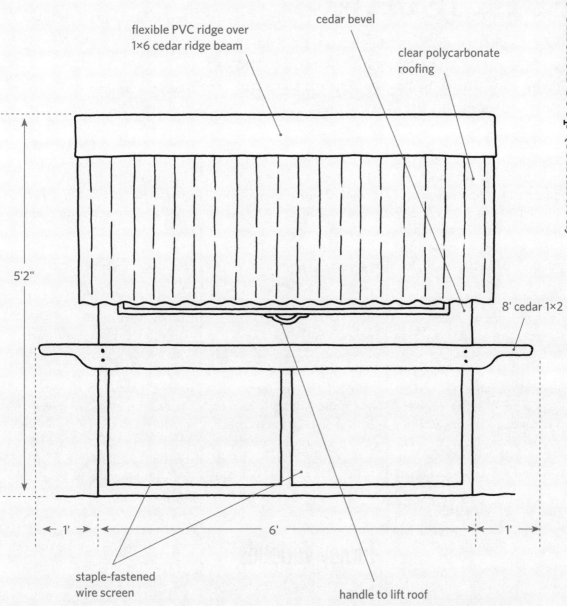

flexible PVC ridge over
1×6 cedar ridge beam

cedar bevel

clear polycarbonate
roofing

8' cedar 1×2

5'2"

1'

6'

1'

staple-fastened
wire screen

handle to lift roof

Turkeys for Christmas

With a gobble-gobble here and a gobble-gobble there, the turkey has pecked its way from the United States to Britain to take pride of place on the Christmas table.

Traditionally, small farmers raised turkeys both for meat production and for pest control (these birds are avid eaters of insects making them the ultimate solution in organic pest control). By 1970, the production of turkeys had dramatically changed from small-scale farm production to large-scale confinement production on an industrial-type farm.

Today, industrial farms produce almost all of the turkeys required to meet the demand for Christmas birds and turkey products ranging from turkey bacon to soup. In the USA, over 99 percent of the breeding stock, which is essentially held by just three multinational companies, is tied to merely a few strains of Broad Breasted White turkeys that can no longer breed naturally.

This movement toward industrial turkey production has left many of the old heritage turkeys, such as the Standard Bronze, the Bourbon Red, and the Narragansett, in trouble. In 1997, the American Livestock Breeds Conservancy (ALBC) considered turkeys to be among the most critically endangered domestic animals and the most vulnerable to extinction.

Since that time, many of the heritage varieties have begun to make a comeback, thanks largely to interest from organizations like Slow Food USA and The Turkey Club UK (see Resources, page 336), which has encouraged small-scale growers to increase the numbers of these endangered birds. The irony is that by creating a market for rare breeds, these growers have been able to keep heritage turkeys from becoming extinct.

Turkey Varieties

By choosing to raise your own turkey, you can ensure that your family is eating a quality bird that was raised well and slaughtered humanely. By choosing to raise a heritage variety, you can play a part in continuing the demand for endangered birds to be kept in production.

Following are four of the breeds that can be purchased from hatcheries in the UK and USA and raised at home.

Standard Bronze. The Standard (or heritage) Bronze was brought to the USA by English colonists and developed there in the 1700s. As colonists began establishing settlements along the eastern seaboard, the turkeys they brought with them crossbred with the eastern wild turkey, yielding a cross that was larger and healthier than the original birds.

The colour of the cross was close to that of its wild forebears (an iridescent reddish brown with flecks of green that glint coppery in the sun), but the moniker Bronze wasn't applied until the 1830s, when a strain developed in the Point Judith area of Rhode Island was dubbed the Point Judith Bronze.

During the late eighteenth and early nineteenth centuries, breeders began selecting for a larger breast and legs, ultimately ending up with the Broad Breasted Bronze. The Broad Breasted quickly dominated the marketplace, and by the 1940s the Standard Bronze was losing its position of prominence in the turkey world.

The Broad Breasted Bronze

was the first variety to be bred up to a point where its large breast and small legs precluded it from mating naturally, thus requiring human intervention. All Broad Breasted Bronze turkeys are the result of artificial insemination.

The Broad Breasted Bronze had a short stint (20 years or so) as the main commercial turkey in North America, only to be replaced by the Broad Breasted White. However, the Bronze maintained some popularity with barnyard and backyard producers. Unfortunately, over the ensuing years the Standard Bronze, which was capable of mating naturally, almost disappeared. Today it is making a comeback in the USA and UK.

Bourbon Red. The Bourbon Red is an older American variety developed in Pennsylvania and Kentucky from crosses of Buff, Bronze, and White Holland turkeys in the late 1800s. It is a large bird with primarily rich chestnut-red plumage laced in black and highlighted by some white on the wings and tails.

The Bourbon Red has remained popular with small producers, thanks to excellent utility traits, such as good foraging capability, a relatively heavy breast, light-coloured pin feathers for a clean carcass, and richly flavoured meat. In fact, the Bourbon has the most breed-

Turkey Varieties

Standard Bronze

Bourbon Red

Narragansett

Broad Breasted White

ing birds of any non-industrial heritage breed, with over 1,500 documented in the 2003 American Livestock Breeds Conservancy census — about double the number from the 1997 census. Part of the Bourbon's rebounding success can be attributed to Slow Food USA, which has placed the Bourbon (as well as the Buff, Standard Bronze, and Narragansett) varieties in its Ark of Taste program (see Slow Food USA's website for more information).

Narragansett. Like the Bronze, the Narragansett, named for Narragansett Bay in Rhode Island, developed in the 1700s from crosses of domestic turkeys brought from Europe with eastern wild turkeys. (In fact, some speculate that it may have been an intermediate between wild turkeys and the Bronze.) Its colouring is similar in pattern to that of the Bronze, but where the Bronze has a coppery tinge on the exposed portion of its feathers, the Narragansett has a steely grey colour.

The Narragansett breed was especially popular in New England during the nineteenth and early twentieth centuries, and it also commanded respect in the Mid-Atlantic states and the Midwest. But by the early 1950s its numbers had plummeted, in spite of the fact that it was known for good meat quality, broodiness, and a calm disposition.

In fact, when the ALBC completed its 1997 census, the organization had found only six breeding birds. By 2003 the Narragansett, with the help of its position in Slow Food USA's Ark of Taste program, had rebounded to 368 breeding birds — the most impressive increase in breeding numbers for any birds checked in the six-year census.

Broad Breasted White. Also called the Large White, this variety has been developed over the past half century specifically for intensive, industrial production. Unfortunately, it is sometimes shown under the name White Holland, though the White Holland is a heritage bird that can still breed naturally.

Broad Breasted Whites were developed from White Holland and some white sports of the Broad Breasted Bronze. They have been selected for decades for efficiently producing the most meat at the least cost, and they are quite remarkable in that ability. The result, however, is a loss of the birds' capacity to mate naturally, so artificial insemination is required to produce fertile eggs.

Broad Breasted Whites generally are not kept beyond one year of age because they have leg problems and are prone to suffering from heart problems such as plaque buildup. Most birds are butchered as soon as they reach marketable weight, between 14 and 18 weeks of age. The one exception is small groups of breeding toms that are milked for sperm used in artificial insemination.

Raising Turkeys

Turkeys are not difficult to raise, but they do require special care to get them off to a good start. Sometimes they are a little slow in learning to eat and drink. Turkeys should be isolated from chickens and other poultry to prevent many diseases. It is important that turkey poults (young turkeys) be kept warm and dry during the first few weeks after hatching; this time is called the brooding period. If you start with good stock and provide good feed, housing, and husbandry, you can raise turkeys successfully.

However, before launching into production, even on a small scale, be aware of the costs. Day-old turkey poults are quite expensive (as hatchlings go), and they consume a considerable amount of feed; thus, the cost of producing full-grown market turkeys is comparatively high.

Before starting a flock, check local bye-laws and regulations. In some urban and suburban areas it may not be possible to keep poultry of any kind. If you live close to neighbours, keep in mind that noise, odour, and possibly fly problems are associated with raising turkeys.

Place your order for poults well in advance of the delivery date, so you can be sure to get the stock you want. The best time to start the small turkey flock is in late May or early June. Starting poults at that time enables you to grow them to the desired market weights just prior to the traditional holiday season, when the demand for turkey is strongest. It also avoids starting poults during the coldest season of the year, which can make brooding (growing young poults) much more difficult.

With good management, you should be able to raise to maturity 85 to 90 percent of the turkeys you start. With the high costs of poults and feed, mortality can become expensive, especially when the birds are lost during the latter part of the growing periods. The following management techniques can help:

- Keep young poults isolated from older turkeys, chickens, and other poultry. Ideally, no other birds should be on the same farm where turkeys are raised.

- Take care to avoid tracking disease organisms from other birds to the turkeys.

- Follow a good control program for mice and rats. These rodents carry disease and are capable of consuming large quantities of feed. Rats can kill young poults, too.

- Watch consumption on a daily basis. One of the first symptoms of a disease problem is a reduction in feed and water consumption.

Wild Turkey

We think of the bird gracing the Christmas dinner table as an American import, yet in an odd twist, the birds that the Pilgrims feasted on at Thanksgiving were actually brought from Europe. Spanish explorers returning from the New World in the late 1400s and early 1500s brought turkeys back with them. In fact, by 1511 Spain's King Ferdinand ordered that every ship returning to Spain should bring back ten turkeys (five toms and five hens). These turkeys were domesticated and spread throughout the continent surprisingly quickly. Later, as colonists crossed the Atlantic in the other direction, the domestic turkey returned with them and recrossed with eastern wild turkeys.

Turkeys did not fare well in the years after Europeans came to the Americas, because they could be lured to piles of corn and other feed placed in fields, making them easy pickings for hunters. Their numbers declined until the 1930s and '40s, when, scientists estimate, there were only about 30,000 left in the wild in the United States and none in Canada. Hunters and wildlife agencies banded together to restore turkey habitat and limit baited hunting sites, and now there are again millions of turkeys throughout most of their traditional range.

Butchering

Turkeys should be finished and ready for processing at 12 to 24 weeks of age for old heritage varieties (which take longer to grow to a marketable size) and 12 to 18 weeks for newer, heavier varieties. Hens are usually processed at younger ages than toms. Turkey broilers or fryer-roasters are usually animals of the same strain used to produce heavier carcasses but are processed at younger ages, such as 8 to 10 weeks old. The precise age for finishing and processing depends on the turkey variety, strain and feeding programme, among other factors.

To assess whether a bird is in prime condition and ready to be processed, see if it is free of pinfeathers. The bird is ready when the feathers are easy to remove. Pinfeathers are immature feathers that do not protrude or may have just pierced the skin.

You must also check the degree of fat covering.

Evaluating Degree of Fat Covering

1. Pull a few feathers from the thinly feathered area of the breast, at a point about halfway between the front end of the breastbone and the base of the wing.

2. Take a fold of skin between the thumb and forefinger of each hand.

3. Examine for thickness and coloration. On a prime turkey, the skin fold is white or yellowish white and quite thick. Well-fattened birds have thick, cream-coloured skin, while underfattened birds have thin skin that is semi-transparent and tends to be reddish.

When you've determined that a turkey is ready for slaughter, seek the advice of an experienced mentor who can demonstrate the butchering process for you. It's important to end an animal's life as quickly and humanely as possible, and slaughtering is a process that shouldn't be tried without some previous instruction.

skin can be skewered to the back and the wing tips folded back under, in toward the body.

Place the turkey, breast up, on a rack in a shallow oven dish. Brush the carcass with butter or olive oil. Roast in an oven set at 325°F (163°C), basting every half hour or so. When a meat thermometer inserted into the thigh registers 180°F (82°C), the bird is done. If the turkey has been stuffed, the stuffing needs to reach a temperature of 160°F (71°C). With large birds, it may be difficult to reach this temperature, so if the bird weighs 24 pounds or more, you should probably cook the stuffing separately.

How to Roast a Turkey

Start by rinsing the turkey and patting it dry. If you're stuffing the turkey, stuff it loosely. Alternatively, salt the cavity and put in a few pieces of celery, carrot, onion, and parsley for flavour. Tie down the legs, or tuck them in the skin flap. The neck

Approximate Roasting Time for Stuffed* Turkey in Preheated 325°F Oven

Ready-to-Cook Weight	Approximate Cooking Time
8–12 pounds	3–3½ hours
12–14 pounds	3½–4 hours
14–18 pounds	4–4¼ hours
18–20 pounds	4¼–4¾ hours
20–24 pounds	4¾–5¼ hours

*Roast an unstuffed turkey ½ hour less than times given.

How to Carve a Turkey

Allow 15 to 30 minutes between roasting and carving. This gives the juices time to be absorbed.

1. **Remove the drumstick and thigh.** To remove drumstick and thigh, press the leg away from the body. The joint connecting the leg to the hip often snaps free or may be severed easily with the point of a knife. Cut dark meat completely from the body by following the body contour carefully with the knife.

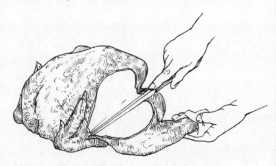

2. **Slice the dark meat.** Place the drumstick and thigh on a cutting surface and cut through the connecting joint. Both pieces may be individually sliced. Tilt the drumstick to a convenient angle, slicing toward the table.

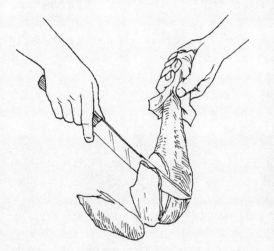

3. **Slice the thigh.** To slice the thigh meat, hold it firmly on a cutting surface with a fork. Cut even slices parallel to the bone.

4. **Remove the breast meat.** Slice off half of the breast at a time by cutting along the keel bone and rib cage with a sharp knife.

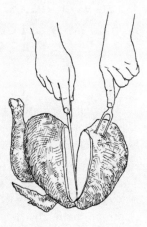

5. **Slice the breast.** Place the halved breast on a cutting surface and slice evenly against the grain of the meat. Repeat with the second half of the breast when additional slices are needed.

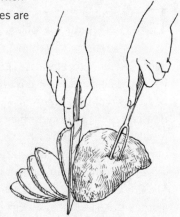

Keeping Ducks and Geese

Keeping ducks and geese is a relatively simple proposition. They prefer to forage for much of their own food in meadows and woodlands, and they require little in the way of housing.

Often, a fence to protect them from wildlife and marauding neighbourhood pets — and to keep them from waddling far afield — will suffice. Ducks and geese do not need a pond to lead a happy life in your back garden, although keeping them on one simplifies their maintenance even further.

All About Ducks

Ducks spend a lot of time in water, nibbling at plants, bugs, and other shoreline inhabitants. If you let them wander in your vegetable garden or flower bed, they will help control garden pests, although you have to take care they don't run out of other things to eat and start attacking your peas or pansies. Muscovies in particular relish slugs, snails, and other creepy-crawlies. In fact, an enterprising Californian organization once had a rent-a-duck service that loaned out Muscovies to local gardeners. Ducks also enjoy chasing flies, in the process offering not only fly control, but also a great deal of entertainment. Ducks also keep mosquitoes from getting beyond the larval stage. Unfortunately, tadpoles will suffer the same fate.

Some breeds of duck are kept primarily for ornamental reasons, whether for their colourful plumage, their comical upright stance, or their diminutive profile. Other breeds are prized for their eggs. Khaki Campbells are particularly known for their laying ability, and their eggs make wonderful baked goods. Any breed may be raised for meat, and putting your excess ducks into the freezer both keeps meat on the family table and keeps down the population at the pond.

Some breeds like to fly around, and occasionally one will fly off into the sunset, but such wanderlust can readily be controlled by clipping a wing. The primary downside to ducks is their eternal quacking. In a neighbourhood where the noise could become a nuisance, the answer is to keep Muscovies, also known as "quackless ducks." Among the other breeds, the male makes little sound, but the female quacks loudly, and each bevy seems to appoint one particularly loud spokesduck to make all the announcements.

Getting Along with Geese

Geese also make a racket with their honking. Usually they holler only with good reason, but a less observant human might not detect that reason: for instance, the cat or weasel the geese have spotted slinking along the fence line. Besides announcing intruders, geese have a tendency to run them off. A lot of people are more afraid of geese than of dogs, probably because they are less familiar with geese and feel intimidated by their flat-footed body charge, indignant feather ruffling, and snakelike hissing.

Even as they fend off intruders, geese can become attached to their owners and are less likely to charge the family dog or cat than roaming pets and wildlife.

Geese are active grazers, preferring to glean much of their own sustenance from growing vegetation. They are often used as economical weeders for certain commercial crops; farmers take advantage of their propensity to favour tender shoots over established plants.

Geese lay enough eggs to reproduce, but no breed of goose lays as many eggs as the laying breeds of duck. Their meat, however, is plentiful and delicious. Goose is a traditional holiday meal, and when roasted correctly, the meat defies its reputation for being greasy. Goose fat rendered in the roasting makes terrific shortening for baking (leaving your guests wondering what your secret ingredient might be), and in the old days, it was used as a flavourful replacement spread for butter. The feathers and down from plucked geese may be saved up and made into comforters, pillows, and warm vests.

Ducks and geese get along well together and may be kept in the same area. Given sufficient living space with water in which to wash themselves, they will remain spanking clean.

Waterfowl Names

Talking about waterfowl can get a bit confusing. A male duck is a **drake,** but a female duck is a **duck.** A male goose is a **gander,** but a female goose is a **goose.** So a drake is a duck, but a duck isn't always a drake; and a gander is a goose, but a goose isn't always a gander. Got it? Dealing with these fowl in groups is much simpler: A bunch of ducks is a **bevy** and a gang of geese is a **gaggle.**

A **hatchling** is a duck or goose fresh out of the egg. If the hatchling is a duck, it is a **duckling;** if it is a goose, it is a **gosling.** A hatchling that survives the first few critical days of life and begins growing feathers is called **started.** When it goes into its first moult (shedding of feathers), it's called **junior** or **green.** A hatchling is considered mature when it has reached one year of age.

Choosing the Right Bird

Numerous breeds of ducks and geese may be found worldwide, and more are created all the time. Others, however, are becoming endangered or extinct. Only a few of the developed breeds are commonly found in the British Isles. Other breeds with much lower populations are kept by fanciers or conservation breeders. Your purpose in keeping waterfowl will to some extent determine which breed is right for you, but in the long run, your best bet is to select the breed you find most visually appealing.

Each breed has been developed for specific characteristics valued by humans. Among

Geese are active grazers, preferring to glean much of their own sustenance from growing vegetation.

ducks, some are efficient at laying eggs, whereas others grow rapidly to provide an economical source of meat. Still others are prized primarily for their unusual plumage, although most breeds are attractive in one way or another. Geese are largely bred for meat, with down as a by-product. But any goose seems elegant on a pond and could be regarded as a discount swan.

Ducks for Eggs

Some breeds of duck have been genetically selected for their outstanding laying habits, but unless this ability is maintained through continued selective breeding, the laying potential of a particular flock may decrease over time. For this reason, not all populations of a breed known for laying are equally up to the task. Some sources offer hybrid layers that are bred for efficient and consistent egg production, but their offspring will not retain the same characteristics and cannot be used to raise ducklings of your own. Since laying stops when nesting begins, the trade-off among laying breeds is that they do not have strong nesting instincts.

Although some ducks lay pale green eggs, most of the laying breeds produce white eggs.

Campbell. Originally bred in England at the turn of the twentieth century, Campbells are fairly active foragers that can withstand cool climates. They weigh around 4 pounds, making them a fair size for eating. The original and most common colour is khaki; the ducklings are dark brown and feather out to a seal-brown colour, and the males' heads and wings turn darker brown. Good layers will produce 240 to 300 eggs a year.

Campbell

Runner. Developed in Scotland from stock originating in the East Indies, where these ducks are put to work gleaning snails and waste grain from rice paddies, Runners have an upright stance that allows them to move around with greater agility than other breeds. They tend to be active and somewhat on the nervous side. Known also as Indian Runners, these ducks weigh

Runner

around 4 pounds and can be expected to lay 140 to 180 eggs per year. They come in many colours, including white, fawn and white, chocolate, black, and blue.

Ducks for Meat

Any breed of duck may be used for meat, although some breeds have been developed to grow faster and larger than others while consuming less feed. You will find that the meat from the ducks you raise yourself is superior in quality to, and less expensive than, store-bought duck meat.

Pekin. A Pekin is a big duck with snow-white feathers and an orange bill and feet. Pekins are not particularly outstand-

Pekin

Ducks and Egg Profile

Breed	Eggs per Year*	Weight per Dozen	Colour
Campbell	250–325	30 ounces	white
Runner	150–300	32 ounces	white
Pekin	125–225	42 ounces	white
Muscovy	50–125	44 ounces	waxy white
Rouen	35–125	40 ounces	green

*The precise number of eggs laid per year varies from strain to strain within each breed.

ing layers and are only fair at nesting and caring for their young. At maturity, they weigh 8 to 10 pounds. Because they have snow-white feathers, they appear cleaner when plucked; their white pinfeathers don't show as much as the pinfeathers of coloured waterfowl. If you order duck in a restaurant, you will most likely be served a Pekin.

Rouen. The Rouen looks like an overstuffed Mallard. At maturity, it averages 9 to 11 pounds. Rouens are docile, tend to be relatively inactive, and are not particularly good layers. Because of their deep breast, they breed best on water, and their egg fertility tends to be low if they breed on land. Thanks to their dark feathers, Rouens are considered to be largely ornamental, although some people claim this breed has the most flavourful meat of any, and its size certainly makes it ideal for roasting.

Muscovy. The Muscovy doesn't look like any other domestic duck and, indeed, is only distantly related to the others. Muscovies are sometimes called quackless ducks, because in contrast to the loud quacking of other female ducks, the Muscovy female speaks in a musical whimper, although she can make a louder sound if startled or frightened. The male's sound is a soft hiss. Ageing males take on a distinctive musky odour, giving this breed its other nickname of "musk duck." Both the males and the females have a mask over the bridge of their beak that features lumpy red warts, called carbuncles.

Muscovies are arboreal, preferring to roost in trees and nest in wide forks or hollow trunks. In confinement, they like to perch at the top of a fence, but they don't always come back down on the right side. To get a good grip while perching on high, these ducks have sharply clawed toes. If you have to carry one of these ducks, try to keep it from paddling its legs so those sharp claws don't slice your skin. Ageing males can be aggressive, usually toward other male

Rouen

Muscovy

Duck Breeds:
Average Mature Weight (in Pounds)

Breed	Male	Female
Campbell	4.5	4.0
Muscovy	12.0	7.0
Pekin	10.0	8.0
Rouen	11.0	9.0
Runner	4.5	4.0

ducks but occasionally toward their keeper. With their powerful wings and sharp claws, they can engage in fierce battles over male dominance.

The male Muscovy matures to be the largest domestic duck, weighing up to 12 pounds. The drakes are thus twice the size of the average female, which tops out at around 7 pounds. Although white Muscovies are more suitable for meat because they have a cleaner appearance when plucked, the original colour is an iridescent greenish black with white patches on the wings. Over the years, Muscovy

The male Muscovy matures to be the largest domestic duck, weighing up to 12 pounds.

fanciers have developed about a dozen additional colours.

Muscovies are an entirely different species from other domestic ducks, and although they will interbreed with others, the resulting offspring will be mules — sterile hybrids that cannot reproduce. Commercial producers may deliberately cross Pekins with Muscovies to produce meat birds called Moulards, which have the large breast of the Muscovy with less fat than the Pekin. Muscovy meat differs in flavour and texture from that of other ducks, in part because it contains less fat.

Being native to Mexico and South America, Muscovies do best in warm climates, although they also do well in moderate zones. They adapt better than other breeds to an environment that lacks a steady source of water for bathing. They are intelligent and curious, and the females can be as friendly as

puppies, making great pets. Both sexes have an enormous appetite for slugs, snails, and baby mice. With their massive bodies and large flat feet, though, they tend to be somewhat destructive to seedlings.

Goose Breeds

Most breeds of domestic goose have been developed for meat, although some have been developed for their odd appearance. The Sebastopol, for instance, has curly feathers that look like a misguided perm. Nearly every breed has a tufted version, meaning that the geese have a puff of extra feathers on top of the head. No breed of goose lays as prolifically as a duck, and although a single goose egg makes a formidable omelette, the eggs are more often used for hatching or for creating craft items, such as decorative jewellery boxes.

Some poultry fanciers prefer geese that are not truly domesticated, such as the diminutive and dauntless Egyptian and the celebrated Canada. Being native to North America, Canada geese require a permit from the United States Fish and Wildlife Service to be kept in confinement.

African. The African is a graceful goose with a knob on top of its head and a dewlap under its chin. The brown variety, with its

African

Chinese

black knob and bill and a brown stripe down the back of its neck, is more common than the white variety with orange knob and bill. Being fairly calm, Africans are easy to confine and tend not to wander. They mature to weigh 18 to 20 pounds. If you are raising geese primarily for meat and are concerned about the fat content, select African or Chinese geese, both of which naturally have less fat than other breeds.

Chinese. The Chinese (or China) goose is similar in appearance to the African but lacks the dewlap. It comes in both white and brown. In contrast to the typical goose honk, this breed emits a higher-pitched *doink* that can be piercing if the bird is upset or irritated. This breed

is most commonly used commercially as weeders. Because Chinese geese are both active and small, they do a good job of seeking out emerging weeds while inflicting little damage on established crops. Thanks to their lightweight and strong wings, they can readily fly over an inadequate fence. Chinese

geese are the best layers among geese and produce a high rate of fertile eggs even when breeding on land rather than on water. They grow relatively fast but are the smallest of domestic geese, reaching a mature weight of only 10 to 12 pounds.

Embden. The Embden most often matures to 20 to 25 pounds but can weigh up to 30 pounds. Because of its size and white feathers, the Embden is the most popular goose to raise for meat. In some countries, this breed was traditionally plucked throughout its life as a perpetual source of down for duvets and pillows, but the plucking of live geese is now considered inhumane. The yellow goslings have patches of grey down when they hatch, and some people claim they can distinguish female from male goslings by their higher ratio of grey to yellow.

Goose Breeds: Average Mature Weight (in Pounds) and Egg Production

Breed	Male	Female	Eggs per Year
African	20	18	20-40
Chinese	12	10	50-100
Embden	25	20	35-50
Pilgrim	14	12	20-40
Toulouse	20	18	35-50
Toulouse, dewlap	26	20	20-40

Embden | Pilgrim | Toulouse

Pilgrim. The Pilgrim goose is only slightly larger than the Chinese. It is the only domestic breed of goose in which the male and female mature to be different colours; the male is white like an Embden and the female is grey like a Toulouse. Because of this plumage pattern, Pilgrim hatchlings may be distinguished by sex on the basis of their down colour: The males are yellow and the females are grey. In recent years, however, this distinction seems to be breaking down, as some flocks reputed to be Pilgrims produced white birds of both sexes. Pilgrims weigh 12 to 14 pounds at maturity and will fly over a fence when attracted to something on the other side.

Toulouse. The Toulouse, named for a town in France, is the common barnyard goose. It has grey plumage set off with white feathers underneath. The Toulouse goose has been developed in two distinct populations. The common barnyard, or production, Toulouse matures to a weight of 18 to 20 pounds. The more massive giant, or dewlap, Toulouse matures to weigh 20 to 26 pounds.

Feed Conversion

A typical feed conversion rate for meat ducks is 1:2½ to 3 pounds, meaning that each duck gains 1 pound of weight for every 2½ to 3 pounds of feed it eats. The feed conversion rate for geese is 1:2 to 3 pounds. The older the birds get, the higher the feed conversion rate, creating a trade-off between economical meat and more of it. To improve the conversion rate, commercially raised waterfowl are encouraged to eat continuously by being kept under lighting 24 hours a day and having their feed troughs topped off several times a day. At the same time, they are discouraged from burning off calories by being confined to a limited area.

Ducks and Geese for Meat

Although some waterfowl breeds have been developed for efficient meat production, any breed is good to eat. If you purchase a duck or goose at the grocery store or butcher shop, the duck would most likely be a Pekin and the goose an Embden. These white-feathered breeds appear cleaner when plucked, because their white pinfeathers don't show as much as the pinfeathers of coloured waterfowl.

Commercially raised waterfowl that are pushed for rapid growth are ready for butchering at an earlier age than most domestic waterfowl. Ducks of the Mallard-derived breeds may be ready as early as 7 weeks, geese at 8 weeks, and Muscovies at 14 weeks. Pasture-raised ducks and geese grow considerably more slowly, taking as much as three times longer to reach size, but are less expensive to raise and have less fat. As with any type of poultry, younger ducks and geese will produce more tender meat than mature birds will.

Feathering Means Butchering Time

Weight gain is only one important factor in determining when a duck or goose is ready for butchering. The other is the stage of the moult. All those feathers that enable ducks and geese to swim comfortably

Using Feathers from Ducks and Geese

One of the advantages of cleaning your own waterfowl is getting the feathers and down as a by-product. The larger feathers may be used for various crafts, while the smaller, softer feathers may be used to make pillows and duvets. However, you'll need the feathers from a lot of birds to make a sizable pillow, let alone a duvet. One goose will give you about ⅓ pound of feathers, and a duck will yield about ⅙ pound. And remember, some of those feathers are too stiff for making pillows.

When saving feathers, discard any that are dirty or have the soft, gooey quill of an immature feather. After each round of butchering, wash your collection of feathers. Place the feathers in a tight-mesh laundry bag and submerge it in lukewarm water with a little washing soda and some detergent or borax. Gently slosh the feathers in the water, and then rinse them in clean lukewarm water. Repeat until the rinse water runs clear. Gently squeeze the bagful of feathers and hang it outside to dry.

Waterfowl have an inner layer of feathers called down, which is extremely soft and light. Just as it keeps ducks and geese warm in cold water, it may be used to create vests and other articles of clothing to keep you warm in cold weather. Down gets its insulating ability from loft, which is its tendency to fluff up. The greater the loft, the greater the down's insulating ability. Goose down has more loft than duck down, which is why it's preferred by Arctic explorers. Because of loft, you may think you have a big bag full of down, but you'll soon find that it's mostly air. If you sneeze, or open a door or window, while you're gathering down, it will float out of the bag and waft through the air. Because down is so difficult to contain, it is often saved in smaller pouches rather than in larger bags. If you are careful while plucking, the down will remain clean and won't require washing. You can find suitable fabric for stuffing with down at many outlets that manufacture or renovate pillows, duvets, and sleeping bags.

> **You'll know the optimum time to pluck a duckling or gosling has passed when the feathers around its neck start falling out.**

in cold water take a long time to remove, and plucking is considerably more difficult if some of those feathers are only partially grown. Plucking is less time-consuming, and the result is more appealing, if a duck or goose is in full feather.

Soon after a duck or goose acquires its first full set of feathers, it begins moulting into adult plumage and won't be back in full feather for another two months or so. You'll know the optimum time to pluck a duckling or gosling has passed when the feathers around its neck start falling out. From then on, the bird won't grow as rapidly as it has been and the feed conversion rate goes up. After this point, feeding waterfowl for meat pur-

poses becomes more costly, the meat becomes tougher, and the meat of Muscovy males takes on an unpleasant, musky flavour.

A duck or goose is in full feather when:

- its flight feathers have grown to their full length and reach the tail

- its plumage is bright and hard looking, and it feels smooth when stroked

- you see no pinfeathers when you ruffle its feathers against the grain

- it has no downy patches along the breastbone or around the vent

When all of these signs are right, a duck or goose is ready to be butchered. If you are doing your own butchering for the first time, try to enlist the help of an experienced person who can guide you, or refer to a good book. If you don't want to do your own butchering, you might find a custom slaughterer willing to handle ducks and geese. Alternatively, a fellow

domestic waterfowl keeper or a local farmer might be willing to kill and pluck your ducks or geese for a small fee. If not having to kill your own waterfowl is important to you, determine before you start whether or not someone in your area can do it instead.

Storing the Meat

Freshly butchered duck or goose must be aged in the refrigerator for 12 to 24 hours before being cooked. If you're not going to use it within the next three days, freeze it after the ageing period until you're ready to cook it. To avoid freezer burn, use freezer storage bags. Most ducks will fit in the 1-gallon size. A Muscovy female should fit in the 2-gallon size. Geese and Muscovy males should fit in the 5-gallon size. Remove as much air from the bag as you can by pressing it out with your hands or by using a smallholder's vacuum device designed for that purpose. Properly sealed and stored at a temperature of 0°F (-18°C) or below, duck and goose meat may be kept frozen for six months with no loss of quality. To thaw a frozen goose or duck before roasting, keep it in the refrigerator for two hours per pound.

A whole duck or goose takes up a lot of freezer space. Unless you intend to stuff and roast

---

Dressed Weight

A duck or goose loses 25 to 30 percent of its live weight after the feathers, feet, head, and entrails have been removed. Heavier breeds lose a smaller percentage than lighter breeds. The breast makes up about 20 percent of the total meat weight; skin and fat make up about 30 percent.

the bird, you can save space by halving or quartering it, or filleting the breasts and cutting up the rest. Muscovy breast makes an exceptionally fine cut and is the most like red meat of any waterfowl. After removing the fillets, you might package the hindquarters for roasting or barbecuing and boil the rest for soup. A great use for excess Muscovy and goose meat is sausage. Small amounts may easily be made into sausage patties, whereas larger amounts might be stuffed into links.

Roasted to Perfection

Properly prepared, a homegrown duck or goose should not be greasy. Although ducks and geese have a lot of fat, the meat itself is pretty lean. All the fat is either just under the skin or near one of the two openings, where it may be easily pulled away by hand.

Proper roasting begins by putting the meat on a rack to keep it out of the pan drippings while the bird roasts. Remove any fat from the cavity and neck openings, and stuff the bird or rub salt inside. Rub the skin with a fresh lemon and then sprinkle with salt. Pierce the skin all over with a meat fork, knife tip, or skewer, taking care not to pierce into the meat. Your

Cooking Methods

The most suitable method of cooking a duck or goose depends on its tenderness, which in turn depends on its age. Fast dry-heat methods, such as roasting, broiling, frying, and barbecuing, are suitable for young, tender birds; slow moist-heat cooking methods, such as pressure cooking and making a fricassee, soup, or stew, are required for older, tougher birds.

goal in piercing is to give the fat a way out through the skin as it melts during roasting. This melted fat will baste the bird as it drips off; no other basting is required. Do not cover the duck or goose with foil during roasting as you would a turkey.

Slow roasting keeps the meat moist. Roast a whole duck at 250°F (121°C) for 3 hours with the breast side down, then for another 45 minutes with the breast up. Roast a goose at 325°F (163°C) for 1½ hours with the breast side down, plus 1½ hours breast up, then increase the temperature to 400°F (204°C) for another 15 minutes to crisp the skin.

Because not all birds are the same size and not all ovens work the same way, the first time around, keep an eye on things to avoid overcooking your meat, which will make it tough and stringy. Once you settle on the correct time range for birds of the size you raise, you can roast by the clock in the future.

When the meat is done, it should be just cooked through and still juicy. You can tell it's done when the leg joints move freely, a knife stabbed into a joint releases juices that flow pink but not bloody, and the meat itself is just barely pinkish. To keep the meat nice and moist, before you carve the bird let it stand at room temperature for 10 to 15 minutes to lock in the juices. During this time, residual heat will cook away any remaining pink. Duck or goose does not have light and dark meat like a chicken or turkey; rather, it is all succulent dark meat.

Properly prepared, a homegrown duck or goose should not be greasy. Although ducks and geese have a lot of fat, the meat itself is pretty lean.

CHAPTER 6

Meat and Dairy

Perhaps the final step in back garden self-sufficiency is the addition of animals for milk and meat. Surprisingly, it takes very little space to begin raising your own meat. Although they're most often thought of as pets, rabbits are the easiest and most efficient way to produce meat in a small space. An ordinary back garden can easily accommodate two pigs (provided the neighbours don't mind and your local bye-laws allow it), and with a quarter acre of open yard or pasture, your family could keep a couple of goats for milk or meat. You'll need a bit more space (at least half an acre) if you're interested in keeping a cow.

If you have the land and desire to keep animals, one way to start is with a short-term commitment. Try buying a young steer or a couple of pigs to raise for the spring and summer, then take to slaughter in late autumn. This way, you can see how caring for an animal suits your lifestyle before you dive in to a years-long commitment with dairy goats or cows. And if, after you've had your steer for the summer, you decide that raising animals isn't for you, you won't be stuck trying to find a home for it.

Even if you don't intend to keep livestock at all, this chapter contains plenty of information you can use when you're buying local meat and milk. You can still play an active role in producing the food you put on your table. You can learn to make yogurt, butter, and several kinds of cheese. You can make your own chorizo, smoked pork chops, sausage, and so much more.

Consider this chapter to be your introduction to back garden animals, but not the definitive guide. It wouldn't be feasible for such a short book to cover in adequate detail *everything* you'd need to know in order to raise a dairy cow successfully, for instance, or to slaughter a chicken humanely. While a vegetable garden or a patch of grain can endure failure without any real harm, "failing" at animal husbandry can result in real harm to the animals. It pays to do your homework before setting out on the path to animal care. If you find yourself getting especially interested in keeping animals, contact people who have some experience through a specialist organization (see Resources, page 336 or at least read an authoritative book.

Goats for Meat and Milk

Goats serve many purposes worldwide. They produce delicious milk, healthful low-fat meat, and fibre for spinning. They are excellent at scrubland control, and they may be used to carry camping supplies on treks or hitched up to help with light chores around the yard. They are inexpensive to maintain, require simple housing, do not take up a lot of space, and are easy to handle and transport.

Scientifically, goats belong to the suborder Ruminantia — that is, they are ruminants, like cows, deer, elk, caribou, moose, giraffes, and antelopes. Ruminants are hoofed animals with four-part stomachs. Within the suborder Ruminantia, goats belong to the family Bovidae, which includes cattle, buffalo, and sheep. Of the six species of goat, only one, *Capra hircus*, is domesticated.

One nice thing about goats is that they do not require elaborate housing. All they need is a shelter that is well ventilated but not drafty and provides protection from sun, wind, rain, and snow. You can easily convert an unused shed into a goat house. Each goat requires at least 15 square feet of space under shelter and 200 square feet outdoors. A miniature goat needs at least 10 square feet under shelter and 130 square feet outdoors. You'll also need a sturdy fence — don't underestimate the ability of a goat to escape over, under, or through an inadequate fence.

Goats are social animals and like the company of other goats, so you'll need at least two. If you will be breeding your goats, the herd will probably grow larger than you initially expect. Plan ahead by providing plenty of space.

Goats are opportunistic eaters, meaning they both graze pasture and browse woodland. Those that harvest at least some of their own food by grazing or browsing will cost less to maintain in hay and commercial goat ration. Each year the average dairy goat eats about 1,500 pounds of hay and 400 pounds of goat ration. Non-dairy goats do well on hay and browse, with little or no ration.

Despite what you may have heard, being opportunistic eaters does not mean goats eat things like tin cans. A goat learns about new things by tasting them with its lips. Young goats like to carry things around in their mouths, as puppies do. If you see a goat with an empty tin, it could be playing with it or eating the label, which, after all, is only paper made from wood. Although the goat may look cute carrying a tin, it's a bad idea to let her do so; the goat may cut her lips or tongue on the sharp rim.

Another myth is that goats are smelly. A goat is no smellier than a dog, unless you keep a breeding buck, which will smell pretty strong during the breeding season. But unless you plan to breed the does, you don't need a buck. And even if you do plan to breed, you may find it more convenient and economical to use someone else's buck if you have only a few does.

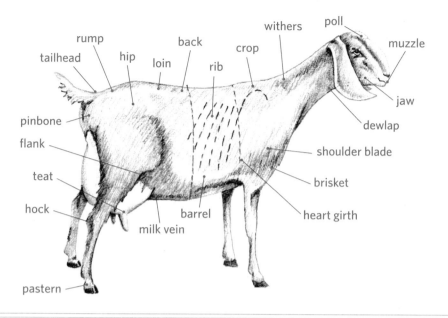

rump · tailhead · hip · back · loin · crop · rib · withers · poll · muzzle · jaw · dewlap · pinbone · flank · teat · hock · shoulder blade · brisket · heart girth · barrel · milk vein · pastern

Why Keep Goats?

So what's your reward for keeping goats? If you raise dairy goats, each doe will give you about 23 gallons of delicious fresh milk every month for 10 months of the year. You and your family might drink the milk or use it to make yogurt, cheese, or ice cream. Surplus milk may be fed to chickens, pigs, calves, or orphaned livestock and wildlife.

From each meat wether (castrated buck), you will get 25 to 40 pounds of tasty, lean meat, which may be baked, fried, grilled, stewed, or barbecued. If you raise fibre goats, from each adult Angora you will get 5 to 7 pounds of mohair twice a year.

From each cashmere goat, you will get just less than 1 pound of down per year.

Each doe you breed will produce one kid or more annually; some does kid twins year after year. Every day, each goat will drop a little more than 1 pound of manure, which makes good fertilizer for the garden.

Buying Goats

More than 200 breeds of goat may be found worldwide. Each breed has characteristics that are useful to humans in different ways. Some are efficient at turning feed into milk or meat, others at turning feed into hair for spinning. Some breeds are small and produce less milk or meat than larger breeds but are easier to keep in small spaces. Your purpose in keeping goats will determine which breed is right for you.

Dairy Goats

A dairy goat is one that produces more milk than it needs to nurse its kids. Here are some of the most common dairy breeds: Alpine, LaMancha, Nubian, Oberhasli, Saanen, and Toggenburg.

Alpine. An Alpine has a long neck and a two-tone coat, with the front end a different colour from the back. A mature doe weighs at least 130 pounds and a mature buck weighs at least 170 pounds.

Alpine

LaMancha

Nubian

Oberhasli

Saanen

Toggenburg

LaMancha. LaManchas come in many colours and are considered to be the calmest of the dairy breeds. A LaMancha is easy to recognize because it has only small ears or no visible ears at all. A mature doe weighs 130 pounds or more; a mature buck weighs 160 pounds or more.

Nubian. Nubians come in many colours and are the most energetic and active of the dairy breeds. You can tell a Nubian from any other goat by its rounded face (called a Roman nose) and long, floppy ears. A mature doe weighs 135 pounds or more; a mature buck weighs 170 pounds or more.

Oberhasli. The Oberhasli looks something like a refined deer. Its coat is bay (reddish brown) with black markings. A mature doe weighs at least 120 pounds and a mature buck weighs at least 150 pounds.

Saanen. A Saanen is all white or cream coloured. A goat of this breed in any other colour is called a Sable. A mature doe weighs 130 pounds or more; a mature buck weighs 170 pounds or more.

Toggenburg. A Toggenburg has white ears, white face stripes, and white legs, setting off a coat that may range in colour from soft brown to deep chocolate. A mature doe weighs 120 pounds or more; a mature buck weighs 150 pounds or more.

Alpines, Oberhaslis, Saanens, and Toggenburgs are closely related and are similar in shape. They all originated in the Swiss Alps and are therefore referred to as the Swiss breeds. These goats have upright ears and straight or slightly dished faces. They may or may not have wattles consisting of two long flaps of hair-covered skin dangling beneath their chin. These breeds thrive in cool climates.

LaManchas and Nubians, on the other hand, originated in warmer climates and are therefore grouped together as tropical or desert breeds. The Nubian originated in Africa, and the LaMancha comes from the west coast of the United States. As a general rule, both breeds are better suited to warm climates than the Swiss breeds.

A dairy goat may be born with horn buds that will eventually grow into horns. Kids with buds are usually disbudded, because mature dairy goats without horns are easier to man-

Traits of a Good Milker

If you buy a young female, or doeling, you can't tell for sure how much milk she will give when she matures, but you can get a good idea by looking at her dam's milk records. An average doe yields about 1,800 pounds, or 225 gallons, of milk per year. A doe's dairy character gives you a fair idea of whether she will be a good milker. Characteristics of does that prove to be good milkers include the following:

- A soft, wide, round udder

- Teats that are the same size, hang evenly, and are high enough not to drag on the ground or get tangled in the doe's legs when she walks

- A well-rounded rib cage, indicating that the doe has plenty of room for feed to fuel milk production

- A strong jaw that closes properly, so the doe has no trouble eating

- Strong, sturdy legs

- Soft skin with a smooth coat

Boer

Spanish

age and are less likely to injure their herdmates or their human handlers. If they are to be registered or shown, they are now allowed to have horns. Goats born without horns are called *polled.*

If your dairy herd includes polled does, make certain your buck is disbudded rather than polled. The polled trait is linked to a gene for infertility; if you breed a polled buck to your polled does, half of their offspring will be incapable of reproducing.

Meat Goats

In many countries, more goats are kept for meat than for any other purpose, and many people prefer goat meat to any other. Since slightly more than half of all goat kids are male and only a few mature bucks are needed for breeding, most young bucks are raised for meat. Surplus goats of any breed may be used for meat, but a breed developed specifically for meat puts on more muscle, and does so more rapidly, than other breeds. In the USA and UK, two types of goat are popular for meat.

Boer. A rewarding meat breed to keep is the Boer goat. Boers originated in South Africa, where they were developed for their rapid growth, large size, high-quality meat, and uniformity of size, meat quality, and colour. The Boer has a white coat, a brown or dark red head with a white blaze, and horns that curve backward and downward. A mature doe weighs 150 to 225 pounds; a mature buck weighs 175 to 325 pounds.

Spanish. More common in the USA, Spanish goats were around long before Boer goats became popular in the United States during the latter part of the twentieth century. At this time, most meat goats were essentially those that were left to roam over brushy range- or forestland in the South and Southwest of the USA to keep the land cleared of brush and undergrowth. These goats are often called Spanish goats because the first feral herds were brought to the USA by Spanish explorers and left behind to furnish meat for future expeditions. Because these goats vary greatly in shape and colour, the term *Spanish* doesn't really refer to a specific breed. Mature does weigh 80 to 100 pounds; bucks weigh 150 to 175 pounds.

African Pygmy

Nigerian Dwarf

Miniature Goats

Miniature goats are smaller than full-sized goats and therefore produce less milk or meat. Minis eat less, require less space, and have scaled-down housing needs that make them ideal for cold climates, where they spend a lot of time indoors. The two miniature breeds are African Pygmy and Nigerian Dwarf.

African Pygmy. Pygmies are blocky, deep, and wide, and their faces are dished. The most common colour is agouti, meaning they have two-tone hairs that give the coat a salt-and-pepper look. The Pygmy has the muscular build of a meat breed. Mature does weigh 35 to 60 pounds, and mature bucks weigh 45 to 70 pounds.

Nigerian Dwarf. The Nigerian Dwarf is a miniature dairy

The milk from minis tastes sweeter than other goat milk because it is higher in fat.

breed. It is smaller and finer-boned than a Pygmy and has longer legs, a longer neck, and shorter, finer hair. Nigerian Dwarfs are lean and angular, with faces that are flat to slightly dished. Dwarfs come in all colours. Mature does weigh 30 to 50 pounds and mature bucks weigh 35 to 60 pounds.

A Dwarf yields about 75 gallons, or 600 pounds, of milk per year, which is one-third the amount you would get from a regular-sized goat.

Despite its stockier build, a Pygmy doe produces about the same amount of milk as a Dwarf. The milk from miniature goats tastes sweeter than other goat milk because it is higher in fat.

Name That Meat

In the UK, juvenile goat meat is sometimes marketed as *kid* while in the United States, most goat meat is marketed as *chevon*, a term coined by combining the French words *chêvre* (goat) and *mouton* (sheep) and used to describe the meat of older kids and adult goats. The pale, tender flesh of milk-fed kids is called *cabrito* (Spanish for "little goat") or occasionally *capretto* (Italian for "little goat" and a term more commonly used in Europe, Great Britain, and Australia).

Goat's Milk

Milk from a doe that is properly cared for tastes exactly like milk from a cow. Although most people in Europe and the USA drink cow's milk, around the world more people drink goat's milk than cow's milk.

Goat's milk, like all milk, contains solids suspended or dissolved in water. Goat's milk is made up of around 87 percent water and 13 percent solids:

- Lactose (milk sugar), which gives us energy

- Milk fat, which warms our body and gives milk its creamy, smooth texture

- Proteins, which help with growth and muscle development

- Minerals, for our general good health

Milking Equipment

Goats are milked in a milk room or milk parlour, which may be built into a corner of your dairy barn or in a separate building. Some people milk their goats in their garage or laundry room. Wherever your milk room is, it should be easy to clean and big enough to hold a milk stand and a few necessary supplies.

A milk stand, homemade or purchased from a dairy goat supplier, gives you a comfortable place to sit while you milk. At the head of the milk stand is a stanchion that locks the doe's head in place so she can't wander away while you are still milking her. Most people feed a doe her ration of concentrate to keep her from fidgeting during milking, but it's better to train your does to be milked without eating. A doe that's used to eating while she's being milked tends to get restless if she finishes eating before you finish milking.

Keep your equipment scrupulously clean to ensure that the milk is healthful and good tasting. Every time you use any of your dairy equipment, rinse it in lukewarm (not hot) water to melt milk fat clinging to the sides. Then scrub everything with hot water mixed with liquid dish detergent and a splash of household chlorine bleach. Use a stiff plastic brush — not a dishcloth (which won't get the equipment clean) or a scouring pad (which causes scratches where bacteria can hide). Rinse the equipment in clean water, then in dairy acid cleaner (which you can obtain from a farm or dairy supply store), then once more in clear water.

You will need the following equipment and supplies for milking.

Equipment. These items are a one-time purchase:

- Spray bottle (for teat dip)
- Strip cup
- Stainless-steel milk bucket
- Dairy strainer or funnel
- Milk storage jars
- Pasteurizer
- Mastitis Test kit
- Milk scale
- Sturdy milking stand with feed cup

Supplies. These items must be replaced as you use them:

- Baby wipes
- Teat dip
- Bag Balm or Corn Huskers lotion
- Milk filters
- Chlorine bleach
- Dairy acid cleaner
- A handful of grain to entice the doe onto the stand

A milk stand may be used for hoof trimming as well as for milking.

Milking a Goat

When a doe gives birth, her body begins producing milk for her kids, a process called freshening. If the doe is a milking breed, she may give more milk than her kids need and continue to produce milk long after the kids are weaned. The amount of milk a doe gives increases for the first 4 weeks after she freshens, then levels off for about 15 weeks, after which production gradually decreases and eventually stops until the doe freshens again to start a new lactation cycle.

A doe's milk is produced and stored in her udder. At the bottom of the udder are two teats, each with a hole at the end through which the milk squirts out. The two most important things to remember when you milk a goat are to keep her calm and not pull down on her teats, both of which can be tricky when you're first learning. Keep the doe calm by singing or talking to her and by remaining calm yourself. Not pulling her teats takes practice. The doe will kick the milk bucket if you pull a teat, pinch her with a fingernail, or pull a hair on her teat. To avoid pulling a doe's hair during milking, and to keep hair and dirt out of the bucket, use clippers to trim the long hairs from her udder, flanks, thighs, tail, and the back part of her belly.

To get milk to squirt from the hole, you must squeeze the teat rather than pull it. The first time you try, chances are milk will not squirt out but will instead go back up into the udder. To force the milk downward, apply pressure at the top of the teat with your thumb and index finger. With the rest of your fingers, gently squeeze the teat to move the milk downward. If you are milking a miniature goat, her tiny teats may have room for only your thumb and two fingers.

After you get out one squirt, release the pressure on the teat to let more milk flow in. Since you will be sitting on the milk stand and facing the doe's tail, work the right teat with your left hand and the left teat with your right hand. Get a steady rhythm

How to Milk

Apply pressure with your thumb and index finger to keep the milk from going back up into the udder.

Use your remaining fingers to move the milk downward into the milk pail.

going by alternating right, left, right, left. Aim the stream into your bucket beneath the doe's udder. At first the milk may squirt up the wall, down your sleeve, or into your face, while the doe dances a little jig on the milk stand. Keep at it and before long you will both handle the job like pros.

When the flow of milk stops, gently bump and massage the udder. If more milk comes down, keep milking. When the udder is empty, the teats will become soft and flat instead of firm and swollen.

If you milk more than one doe, always milk them in the same order every day, starting with the dominant doe and working your way down to the meekest. Your goats will get used to the routine and will know whose turn is next.

As you take each doe to the milk stand, brush her to remove loose hair and wipe her udder with a fresh baby wipe to remove clinging dirt. While you clean the doe's udder, watch for signs of trouble — wounds, lumps, or unusual warmth or coolness. Squirt the first few drops of milk from each side into a cup or small bowl, called a "strip cup" because it is used to examine the first squirt or stripping. Check the stripping to see whether it is lumpy or thick, two signs of mastitis.

When you finish milking each doe, spray the teats with teat dip so bacteria can't enter the openings. Use a brand recommended for goats — some dips used for cows are too harsh for a doe's tender udder. In dry or cold weather, prevent chapping by rubbing the teats and udder with a recommended salve (available from farm supply shops).

Milk Output

Exactly how much milk a doe produces in each cycle depends on her age, breed, ancestry, feeding, health and general well-being, and how often you milk. The more often you milk, the more milk the doe will produce. Most goat keepers milk twice a day, as close to 12 hours apart as possible. If milking twice a day gives you more milk than you can use, milk only once a day. Do it every day at about the same time. If you don't milk regularly, your doe's udder will bag up, or

Milking a large goat

Milking a miniature goat

> **The more often you milk, the more milk the doe will produce. Most goat keepers milk twice a day, as close to 12 hours apart as possible.**

swell with milk. Bagging up signals to the doe that her milk is no longer needed, and the doe dries off.

Milk sold at the grocery shop or supermarket is measured by volume: 1 pint, 1 quart, or ½ gallon. Milk producers measure milk by weight: pounds and tenths of a pound. One pint of water weighs approximately 1 pound, giving rise to the old saying, "A pint's a pound the world around." Milk also weighs approximately 1 pound per pint, although its exact weight depends on the amount of milk fat it contains, which varies by goat and by season.

During the peak of production, a good doe in her prime should give at least 8 pounds of milk (about 1 gallon) per day. She will then gradually taper off to about 2 pounds (1 quart) per day by the end of her lactation cycle. During the entire lactation, the average doe will give you about 1,800 pounds (225

gallons). A miniature doe averages one-third as much milk as a large doe.

Weighing each doe's output helps you manage your goats properly. A sudden decrease in production may mean a doe is unhealthy, is not getting enough to eat, or is in heat.

Weigh milk by hanging the full bucket from a dairy scale. A dairy scale has two indicator arms. Set the arm on the right to zero. With the empty pail hanging from the scale, set the left arm to zero. When you hang a pail of milk on the scale, the left arm automatically deducts the weight of the pail. Use the right arm to weigh other things, such as newborn kids.

If you don't have a scale, you can keep track of each doe's output by volume, although this method is not as accurate as weighing because fresh milk has foam on top and it's hard to tell where the foam stops and the milk starts.

Keep a record of each doe's milk output, noting not only the amount of milk obtained from each milking but also anything that might affect output, such as changes you've made in the doe's ration, rainy weather that has kept your herd from going out to graze, or the time of day you milked (whether earlier or later than usual). At the end of each month, add up each doe's milk output. At the end of her

lactation cycle, add up each doe's total output.

A standard cycle lasts 10 months, or 305 days. To accurately compare the annual output from each doe, or to compare the output of one doe against another, adjust production to a 305-day cycle: Divide the total output by the actual number of days in the cycle, then multiply by 305.

Milk Handling

Milk, especially raw milk, is highly perishable and extremely delicate. Following are some simple steps that will prevent spoilage.

- Cool milk immediately after milking.

- Don't add fresh warm milk to cold milk.

- Never expose milk to sunlight or fluorescent light.

Cooling milk immediately after milking means that it should not be left standing while you finish chores. Ideally, milk should be cooled down to 38°F (3°C) within an hour after leaving the goat. That's quite a rapid drop when you consider that it was over 100°F (38°C) when it left the udder. Home refrigerators aren't cold enough to cool large quantities of milk. Small containers may be cooled in the refrigerator, but anything more than a quart will not cool rapidly enough for good results unless it's immersed in ice water. (Remember, the bottom of the refrigerator is colder than the top part.)

Don't add fresh warm milk to cold milk. If you're accumulating milk for cheesemaking, develop a system for rotating it, perhaps from left to right or one shelf to another, so you know which is freshest.

If you store milk in glass jars, be sure never to leave them in the sun or fluorescent light, as this will change the flavour. In fact, don't leave a container of milk sitting out after a meal in any event. Keep it cold.

Raw Milk versus Pasteurized

If you want to start an interesting (and sometimes heated) discussion in goat rearing circles, just casually bring up the topic of raw milk and stand back.

For obvious reasons, most people never worry about such trifles. They just buy their jug or bag of milk and don't ever have to think about where it came from or how it was treated. For those of us interested in simple living, however, or even just in producing our own dairy products, it's not nearly so simple.

Here's the problem. Milk is the "ideal" food, for animals,

for humans — *and* for bacteria. Milk is extremely delicate. It can attract, incubate, and pass on all sorts of nasty things such as salmonella, toxoplasmosis, Q fever, listeriosis, campylobacteriosis, and others that most of us non-medical people never even hear about. In short, nature's most healthful food can make you very sick.

The Industrial Age answer has been pasteurization — heat-treating the milk to kill or retard most of those threatening organisms. Government regulations now demand that such treatment be performed "for the public good."

This is no doubt a wise policy, for the masses. When you pick up a jug of milk at the store, how would you know if the dairy animals were healthy, if the milker had clean hands or a runny nose, and if proper sanitation measures were taken, without such governmental intervention?

But many goat's-milk drinkers raise their glasses with a different perspective. They know everything about their animals, from age and health status to medical history and what they ate since the last milking. The home milker knows exactly how the milk was handled — how clean the milking area and utensils were, how quickly the milk was cooled and to what temperature, and how long it has been stored. (Usually, it hasn't been stored

> The home milker knows exactly how the milk was handled – how clean the milking area and utensils were, how quickly the milk was cooled and to what temperature, and how long it has been stored.

long. Most milk from the home dairy is probably consumed before commercial milk even leaves the farm, if it's picked up only every two or three days.)

Under these conditions, many people who milk goats feel it isn't necessary to go to the bother of pasteurizing their milk. Also, many people rear goats because they want raw milk. (It's possible to buy raw milk, goat's or cow's, in wholefood shops and goat's milk is often sold as "pet food" for orphaned or sickly young animals.) Some think it tastes better. And some say it's more nutritious.

Pasteurization does have an effect on nutritive value. But raw-milk opponents claim it's very minor and insignificant when compared to the potential dangers of untreated milk. To them those dangers are horrific: They would just as soon drink poison.

One of the potential problems raw-milk opponents often point to is campylobacteriosis, a gastrointestinal disease caused by campylobacter — a bacterium universally present in birds, including domestic poultry. Among the symptoms, which range from mild to severe, are abdominal cramps, diarrhoea, and fever. Apparently, farm families who regularly drink raw milk build up an immunity. Most of the reported cases have involved farm visitors, those unused to raw milk. Raw-milk advocates point out that the incidence is very small — might as well worry about being struck by a meteorite, they say.

In the UK, consumers should be aware that a wide range of pathogens have been reported in raw milk including *Campylobacter*, *Salmonella*, and *E. coli*. While cattle are susceptible to tuberculosis, goats are highly resistant and they have not yet been implicated in tuberculosis outbreaks. And whereas undulant fever is a goat problem in some countries, including Mexico, it hasn't been in the USA.

So, who's right, those who oppose raw milk or those who advocate it? Probably both, in certain situations and under certain circumstances. For example, people with impaired immune systems, such as infants and the elderly, are more at risk for some of the minor diseases that can be passed from goats to humans. In general, most people who feel strongly about this issue, one way or the other, base their decisions more on emotions than on facts. Your personal decision will very likely depend on your psychological makeup: how you regard science and medicine in general, for example, or your attitude toward natural or organic foods, or whether or not you fasten your seat belt.

Milk Sensitivities

Milk gets its sweet taste from the complex sugar lactose. For your body to digest lactose, it needs the enzyme lactase to break down the lactose into two simple sugars: glucose and galactose. About 75 percent of all adults are lactase deficient. They cannot digest lactose, and when they ingest it, the result is bloating, cramps, gas, nausea, and diarrhoea. The problem may be resolved by taking a lactase concentrate, available at most drugstores. Fermentation reduces lactose content by as much as 50 percent, so if you have a problem drinking milk because of lactose intolerance, you may not have a problem eating yogurt.

Not all problems associated with milk are caused by lactase deficiency. About 5 percent

Goat's Milk versus Cow's Milk

Goat's milk does not taste any different from cow's milk. It doesn't look appreciably different. It's somewhat whiter, because it doesn't contain the carotene that gives a yellow tinge to the fat in cow's milk. (Goats convert all carotenes into vitamin A.) It is not richer. It certainly does not smell; if it does, something's wrong.

Most small-scale goat rearers enjoy serving products of their home dairy to sceptical friends and neighbours. The reaction is invariably, "It tastes just like cow's milk!"

People who are accustomed to regular semi-skimmed or skimmed milk are prone to comment on the "richness" of goat's milk. They'd say the same thing about real cow's milk if they had the opportunity to taste it before the cream was separated from it. As with cow's milk, the percentage of butterfat — the source of the richness — varies with breed, stage of lactation, feed, and age. But generally, there is virtually no difference in taste or richness between whole, fresh cow's milk and goat's milk.

of the population is allergic to milk protein. In children, symptoms of milk protein allergy are eczema and digestive problems, including diarrhoea, vomiting, and colic. In adults, milk protein allergy causes a feeling of being bloated and gassy. Since the protein in goat milk is not the same as the protein in cow milk, someone who is sensitive to cow milk protein may have no trouble drinking goat milk. Besides having a different protein makeup, goat milk has proportionally more small fat globules, making it easier to digest than cow milk and therefore leaving less undigested residue in the stomach to cause gas and cramps.

Whole and Skimmed Milk

After goat's milk has been refrigerated for a day or two, its milk fat rises to the surface. Milk fat thinned with a little milk is cream. The milk fat content of goat milk ranges from 2 to 6 percent, depending on genetics, diet, and other factors. An average of 4 percent will give you about 5 tablespoons of milk fat per quart. The milk from Nubians and African Pygmies contains more fat than other milk, and the milk from all does varies in fat content during the lactation cycle. Milk fat content is important in making ice cream, butter, and certain kinds of cheese.

If you are trying to limit the amount of fat in your diet, you may remove the milk fat to create skimmed milk. Store fresh milk in a wide-mouthed container. In about two days, most of the milk fat will rise to the surface, and you can then skim it off.

> Someone who is sensitive to cow's milk protein may have no trouble at all drinking goat's milk.

Sheep for Meat and Milk

For thousands of years, people have raised sheep for three critical reasons: milk, meat, and wool. Of course, other barnyard animals are also able to provide humankind with these items, but sheep have many advantages.

They are much easier to handle than other farm animals, such as cows, horses, and pigs. Moreover, they require little room, they're fairly easy to care for, and they can be trained to follow, come when called, and stand quietly.

Sheep are also earth-friendly. Land that cannot be used to grow vegetables, fruits, or grains is fine for sheep. They eat weeds, grasses, brush, and other plants that grow on poor land, and their digestive system is designed to handle parts of food plants such as corn, rice, and wheat that people cannot eat. Many of the world's most popular cheeses are made from sheep milk. Sheep wool, which can be used to make rugs, blankets, clothing, and other materials, is a renewable resource. Sheep manure fertilizes soil. The fat of a sheep raised for meat can be used to make candles and soap, and the pelt of that sheep can be used to make clothing.

Sheep rely on their owners for food, protection from predators, and regular shearing, but they require less special equipment and housing than any other livestock. One or two lambs or ewes can be raised in a backyard with simple fencing and a small shelter. No sheep should be raised alone. They have a built-in social nature and a flocking instinct and are happiest when they have companions. Bummer (orphaned) lambs, however, are often just as happy around humans as they are with other sheep. Orphaned lambs quickly become attached to the person who feeds them.

Sheep don't need fancy food. In summer, they can live on grass; in winter, they can eat hay supplemented with small amounts of grain. Fresh water, salt, and a mineral and vitamin supplement complete their diet.

Choosing a Breed

If you want to raise sheep, you'll need to know which breeds have the characteristics that are most important for your purposes. The climate in your region will also help you determine which is the best breed for you. If you live in an area with severe winters, choose a breed that can survive in cold weather. If you live in a wet area, look for a breed that tolerates rainy weather. If you live in a desert-like area, you will want a breed that is adapted to hot, dry climates. Look around and see what breeds of sheep are being raised locally — these breeds may also be the best ones for you.

Sheep come in so many breeds that it would take a whole book to describe them all. This section describes some of the most popular breeds, as well as a few minor ones. If you keep in mind your reasons for owning sheep, these brief descriptions will help you decide which breeds are right for you.

Columbia. This American breed was developed by crossing Lincoln rams with Rambouillet ewes. Columbias are large ani-

Sheep Terminology

White face and black face. These terms describe the colour of the wool on the sheep's head and face. Normally, the wool on the lower legs is the same colour as that on the face.

Open face and closed face. These terms are used to describe how much long wool is on the sheep's face. An open-faced sheep has only short, hairlike wool on its face. A closed-faced sheep has long wool on its face. On a closed-faced sheep, the wool may grow all the way down to the animal's nose. Too much wool around the eyes causes the sheep to become "wool blind." The excess wool must be clipped away so that the animal can see.

Prick ear or lop ear. Just as a German shepherd's ears stand up and those of a cocker spaniel hang down, a sheep's ears can stand straight up (prick ear) or hang floppily down (lop ear). Some sheep's ears even stand out to the side.

Polled or horned. Polled sheep have no horns and horned sheep have horns.

Open and black face

Closed and white face

mals that produce heavy, dense fleece and fast-growing lambs. Columbias have a calm temperament and are easy to handle. They have an open, white face and are polled.

Corriedale. Corriedales, noted for their long, productive lives, are distributed worldwide. These large, gentle-tempered sheep have been developed as dual-purpose animals, offering both quality wool and quality meat. A strong herding instinct makes them excellent range animals, as well. They have an open, white face and are polled.

Dorset. The Dorset is considered one of the best choices for a first sheep and is popular in south-west England and parts of the United States. Dorsets are medium-sized and have a very gentle disposition. A Dorset has very little wool on its face, legs, and belly, which makes lambing easier. Its face is usually open, and it is white on both the face and the legs. Both polled and horned types are available.

Dorsets are a fine choice for both wool and meat. Their lightweight fleece is excellent for handspinning, and they have large, muscular bodies and gain weight fast. Dorset ewes are good mothers, and, unusually, Dorsets can lamb in late summer or autumn.

Hampshire. The Hampshire is distributed all over the world.

Common Sheep Breeds

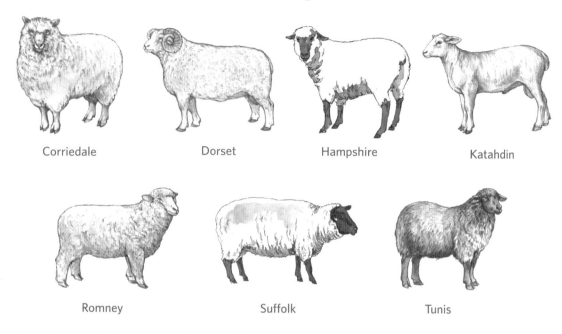

Corriedale   Dorset   Hampshire   Katahdin

Romney   Suffolk   Tunis

It is among the largest of the meat types, and the lambs grow fast. Its face is partially closed; the wool extends about halfway down. It has a black face and legs and is polled. Hampshires have a gentle temperament.

Katahdin. This US breed is an easy-to-raise meat sheep that has hair instead of wool. It does not require shearing, because it sheds its hair coat once a year. Katahdins can tolerate extremes of weather. Except for the fact that Katahdins do not produce wool, they possess all of the ideal traits for a pet or small flock: They are gentle, with a mild temperament; require no shearing; have few prob-lems with lambing; are excellent mothers; and have a natural resistance to parasites. They have an open, white face and are polled.

Polypay. Large and gentle tempered, this synthetic breed is popular in America. Polypays are superior lamb producers with a high rate of twinning, a long breeding season, and good mothering ability. They are also known for having strong flocking instincts, quality meat and wool, and milking ability. They have an open, white face and are polled.

Romney. Like other gentle-tempered sheep breeds, Rom-neys make excellent pets. They are polled and have an open, white face; black points (noses and hooves); and a long, soft fleece that is ideal for hand-spinning. They also produce good market lambs. Romney ewes are quiet, calm mothers. Romneys are best suited to the world's cool, wet regions.

Suffolk. Suffolks are similar to Hampshires and they too are distributed throughout the world. They are large and have fast-growing lambs. They have an open, black face and are polled. Suffolks are usually gentle, but some can be headstrong and difficult for younger children to manage.

Proper Sheep Conformation

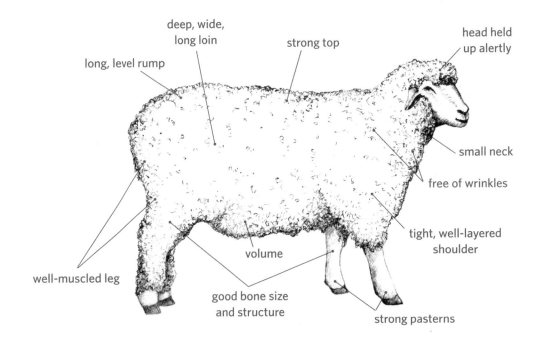

deep, wide,
long loin

strong top

head held
up alertly

long, level rump

small neck

free of wrinkles

tight, well-layered
shoulder

well-muscled leg

volume

good bone size
and structure

strong pasterns

Heritage, Rare, and Minor Breeds

The breeds that have fallen out of favour with industrialized agriculture are referred to as rare, heritage, or minor breeds. Many of these breeds were major breeds just a generation or two ago, but as agriculture has focused on maximum production regardless of an animal's constitution, these old-fashioned breeds have begun to die out. The loss of heritage breeds can have an especially grave impact on small-scale producers, who are usually interested in low-input (less work on the part of the farmer) agriculture. These breeds, although not the most productive in an industrialized system, have traits that make them well suited to low-input farming. Some are dual-purpose, able to produce both meat and fibre. Others are acclimatized to regional environments, such as hot and humid or dry and cool conditions. Many perform well on pasture with little or no supplemental feeding. Others resist disease and parasites. Some have such strong mothering skills that the farmer doesn't have to do much work during lambing season.

Interest today in preserving heritage breeds of livestock, including sheep, is increasing. A driving force in this movement in the UK is the Rare Breeds Survival Trust (RBST). For more information about British sheep breeds, contact the National Sheep Association (see page 336).

> Lamb meat is delicate and tender; the meat from older animals, called mutton, can be used like minced beef.

Tunis. Around for more than 3,000 years, the Tunis is one of the world's oldest sheep breeds. It is a minor breed in the United States but not found in the UK. They are medium sized, hardy, docile, and very good mothers. The reddish tan hair that covers their legs and closed faces is an unusual colour for sheep. They have long, broad, free-swinging lop ears and are polled. Their medium-heavy fleece is popular for handspinning. The Tunis thrives in a warm climate, and the rams can breed in very hot weather. The ewes often produce a good supply of milk.

Culling and Butchering

If you breed sheep, eventually you'll have to cull the flock to improve your stock. Keep the best ewe lambs to replace less productive older ewes. Butcher all ram lambs, unless you intend to raise a breeding ram for your own use or to sell. Unneeded lambs should be butchered at five to six months of age.

When evaluating older ewes for culling, consider age, productivity, and general health. Cull the following types of older ewe:

- Ewes with defective udders
- Ewes with a broken mouth (teeth missing)
- Limping sheep that do not respond to regular trimming and footbaths
- Ewes with insufficient milk and slow-growing lambs

Lamb meat is delicate and tender; the meat from older animals, called mutton, can be minced and used like minced beef. However, mutton is easier to digest than beef is, which makes it a good meat for people who have gastrointestinal difficulties.

You can either take your sheep to a custom packing plant to be slaughtered and butchered or do it yourself. If you want to do it yourself, consult a good manual.

If you're going to work with packers, you'll have to give them some instructions. Consider these guidelines:

- Cut off the lower part of hind legs for soup bones.
- For mutton, have both hind legs smoked for hams.
- For lambs, the hind legs can be left whole, as in the traditional leg of lamb, or cut into sirloin roasts and leg chops.
- The loin, from either mutton or lamb, can be cut as tenderloin into boneless cutlets or as a loin roast.
- Package riblets, spare ribs, and breast meat into 2-pound packages. Riblets, which are sometimes referred to as short ribs, are almost inedible when prepared by most cooking methods, but when prepared in a pressure cooker for about 45 minutes, with 1 inch of water, barbecue sauce, curry sauce, or your favourite marinade in the bottom to start, they are a real delicacy. For lambs, the spareribs and breast can be barbecued or braised. For mutton, these cuts are pretty much waste products.
- For mutton, have the rest boned, trimmed of fat, and ground. Double-wrap in 1-pound packages.
- For lamb, the rack, or rib area, can be cut into lamb chops or left as rack roast. The shoulder can be cut into roasts or chops, and the neck and shank can be used as soup bones.
- If you want kebab meat, make sure that it is cut from the sirloin or loin.

Cattle for Milk and Meat

Rearing cattle, a milk cow, or even just a calf or two can be a profitable and satisfying experience. Cattle are an efficient way to produce food because they can graze on land that won't grow crops and can eat roughage that humans can't.

They can mow the hillside behind your house that is too steep for a garden or survive in a paddock that is too thin or stony to grow any crop other than grass. Cattle provide us with meat or milk while keeping the grass down and the weeds trimmed, which is easy on the eye and yields a neater landscape.

Moreover, getting set up to rear cattle often does not involve much expense, except for the initial fencing to keep them where you want them. And if you don't want to bother with purchasing hay and grain, you can use weaned calves to harvest your grass during the growing season, then send them for butchering when the grass is gone — thus making seasonal use of pasture and creating a "harvest" of meat.

Rearing cattle can also be good for the soul. They are fascinating and entertaining animals; working with cattle is never boring. It can be physically challenging at times, as when delivering a calf in a difficult birth and trying to catch an elusive animal. But for those who enjoy rearing cattle, the chores of caring for them are not really work. Their interaction with these animals is part of their enjoyment of life.

What Do I Need to Rear Cattle?

You can rear a steer in your paddock or smallholding, or you can raise a herd of cattle on a large pasture, on crop stubble after harvest, or on steep rocky hillsides. Cattle can be fed hay and grain or can forage for themselves. Economics and individual circumstances will dictate your methods. If you have pasture, all you'll need is proper fencing to keep the animals in, so they won't trample your flower beds or visit the neighbours.

You will need a reliable source of water and a pen to corral the animals when they need to be handled for vaccinations and other management procedures. If you have a milk cow, you may want a little run-in shed or at least a roof, so you can milk her out of the weather if it's raining or snowing. Most of the time, cattle don't need shelter; their heavy hair coat insulates them against wind, rain, and cold. In hot climates, however, shade in summer is important. A simple roof with one or two walls can provide shade in summer and protection from wind and storm in winter.

The novice cattle rearer may also need advice from time to time from a veterinarian, cattle breeder, farmer or dairyman. Don't be afraid to contact an experienced person to ask questions or to request help.

Cattle provide us with meat or milk while keeping weeds trimmed.

Choosing the Right Kind of Animal

Your choice of calf will depend on how much space you have and what your goals are. Do you want to raise a steer to butcher or sell for beef or a heifer that will grow up to be a cow? A calf can be raised in a small area, even in your back garden, if your local bye-laws permit livestock. But if your goal is to have a cow that someday will have a calf of her own, she'll need more room.

If you are raising a calf to sell, you should probably raise a steer. Steers weigh more than heifers of the same age and bring more money per pound when sold. However, heifers are more flexible — you can raise them as beef or keep them as dairy animals. Dairy heifers are worth more money than beef cattle when they mature. If you want to eventually raise a small herd of cattle, choose a heifer to start with. Her calves will become your herd.

Bull. When a male calf is born, he is considered a bull because he still has male reproductive organs. Most bulls are castrated and become steers. Only the best males are kept as bulls for breeding. A commercial herd may contain no bull calves. A farmer may buy all his bulls from a purebred breeder and not raise any of his own.

Steer. A bull becomes a steer when he is castrated. The steer may still have a small scrotum or his scrotum may be entirely gone, depending on the method used to castrate him. Beef calves are sold as steers.

Heifer. A heifer is a young female animal. Between her

Cattle Names

Steer (castrated male)

Bull (intact male)

Heifer
(unbred female under two years old)

Cow
(female over two years old that has given birth)

hind legs, she has an udder with teats on it that will grow as she matures. A bull or steer calf also has small teats, just as a boy has nipples, but they don't become large. A heifer's vulva is located under her tail, below the rectal opening. The female animal is called a heifer until she is older than two years and has had a calf. After this point, she is called a cow.

Choosing a Dairy Breed

Why keep dairy cattle? Perhaps you want to rear a heifer as a family milk cow or start your own dairy herd. Or maybe you want to raise a dairy heifer to sell. A good young milk cow is worth more than a beef cow; a dairy cow can make more money producing milk than a beef cow can make by producing beef calves.

You can be successful with any of the dairy breeds, but you may want to choose one that is popular in your area, especially if you want to sell your heifers.

Ayrshire. These cattle are red and white. The red can be any shade and is sometimes dark brown. The spots are usually jagged at the edges. Cows are medium sized, weighing 1,200 pounds; bulls weigh 1,800 pounds. Cows are noted for

their good udders, long lives, and hardiness. They manage well without pampering, and they give rich, white milk.

Brown Swiss. Brown Swiss are light or dark brown or grey. Cows weigh 1,400 pounds and bulls weigh 1,900. Brown Swiss are noted for their sturdy ruggedness and long lives. They give milk with high butterfat and protein content.

Guernsey. Guernseys are fawn and white, with yellow skin. The cows weigh 1,100 to 1,200 pounds; bulls weigh 1,700 pounds. Guernsey cows have a good disposition and few problems with calving. Their milk is yellow in colour and rich in butterfat. Heifers mature early and breed quickly.

Holstein. Holstein cattle are black and white or red and white. They are large: Cows weigh 1,500 pounds and bulls weigh 2,000 pounds. A Holstein calf weighs about 90 pounds at birth. The cows produce large volumes of milk that is low in butterfat. Holsteins are the most numerous dairy breed in the United States.

Jersey. Jerseys are fawn coloured or cream, mouse grey, brown, or black, with or without white markings. The tail, muzzle, and tongue are usually black. They are small cattle: Cows weigh 900 to 1,000 pounds and bulls weigh 1,500. Jerseys calve easily and mature quickly and are noted for their fertility. Jerseys produce more milk per pound of body weight than any other breed, and their milk is the richest in butterfat.

Milking Shorthorn. These cattle are red, red and white, white, or roan (a mix of red and white hair). Cows are large, weighing 1,400 to 1,600 pounds; bulls weigh 2,000 pounds or more. They are hardy, noted for long lives and easy calving. Their milk is richer than that of Holsteins but is not as high in butterfat as that of Jerseys or Guernseys.

Dairy Breeds

Ayrshire

Brown Swiss

Guernsey

Holstein

Jersey

Milking Shorthorn

Choosing a Beef Breed

Modern beef breeds are descendants of cattle native to the British Isles, continental Europe, and India. Many of the modern breeds are mixes of these breeds.

British Breeds

British Breeds are those that originated in England, Scotland, and Ireland.

Angus. Angus cattle are black or red and genetically polled (always born hornless). Smaller and finer boned than Herefords, Angus are known for ease in calving because they give birth to small calves. This characteristic makes them popular for crossbreeding with larger, heavily muscled cattle. Angus are noted for early maturity, marbling of meat, and for being good mothers. Angus cows are aggressive in protecting their calves and give more milk than Herefords.

Dexter. Dexters are probably the smallest cattle in the world and are used for milk and beef. The average cow weighs less than 750 pounds and is only 36 to 42 inches tall at the shoulder. Bulls weigh less than 1,000 pounds and are 38 to 44 inches tall. Dexter cattle are quiet and easy to handle, and the cows give rich milk.

Galloway. Galloways are hardy and have a heavy winter coat. Galloway cows live a long time and often produce calves until 15 to 20 years of age. The calves are born easily because they are small, but they grow fast. Most Galloways are black, but some are red, brown, white (with

Parts of a Beef Animal

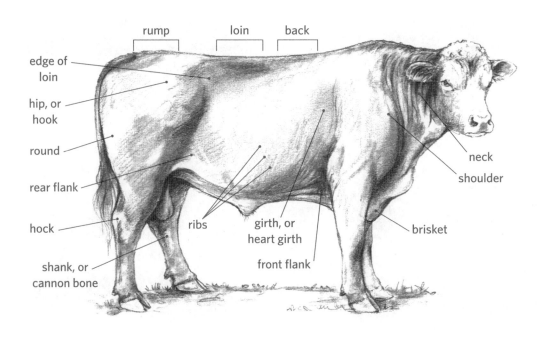

rump · loin · back

edge of loin

hip, or hook

round

rear flank

hock

shank, or cannon bone

ribs

girth, or heart girth

front flank

neck

shoulder

brisket

black ears, muzzle, feet, and teats), or belted (black with a white midsection). All Galloways are polled.

Hereford. The Hereford is well known for its red body and white face which make it instantly recognisble. The feet, belly, flanks, crest (top of neck), and tail switch are white. Other characteristics of the Hereford are a large frame and good bones (heavier bones than those of many breeds). The Hereford has a mellow disposition compared to that of the Angus or some Continental breeds.

The Polled Hereford is identical to the Hereford except that it has no horns.

Highland. These cattle are small, with long, shaggy hair and impressive horns. These hardy cattle do well in cold weather. Their shaggy coats provide protection from insects, and their long forelocks protect their eyes from flies.

Shorthorn. Shorthorn cows have good udders and give a lot of milk. They have few problems with calving. Even though the calves are born small, they grow big quickly. Shorthorn cattle can be red, roan, white, or red-and-white spotted.

Continental (European) Breeds

Many European beef breeds are now raised all over the world. They have become especially popular over the past few decades, adding size and muscle (and sometimes more milk) to crossbred herds.

Charolais. Charolais are white, thick-muscled cattle originally found from France. Cattle farmers like Charolais for crossbreed-

British Beef Breeds

Angus

Hereford

Shorthorn

ing because they are larger than the British breeds.

Chianina. Chianina are the largest cattle in the world. They are white in colour. Due to their size and colour, they make impressive oxen.

Gelbvieh. Gelbvieh cattle are light tan to golden in colour. The calves grow fast, and the heifers mature more quickly than heifers of most other Continental breeds.

Limousin. The Limousin is a red, well-muscled breed. Cattlemen like the Limousin's moderate size and abundance of lean muscle. The small calves are born easily and grow fast.

Continental Beef Breeds

Charolais

Gelbvieh

Limousin

Salers

Simmental

Salers. Salers cattle are horned and dark red. Originally from France, they are popular for crossbreeding because of their good milking ability, fertility, ease of calving, and hardiness.

Simmental. Simmentals are yellow-brown cattle with white markings. They are known for rapid growth and good milk production.

Tarentaise. The Tarentaise is a breed of red cattle with dark ears, nose, and feet. They are moderate-sized animals that are used for milk and meat. They reach maturity early and have good fertility.

Other Continental Breeds. Many other Continental breeds have proved popular among cattle farmers today, such as Maine Anjou, Pinzgauer, Piedmontese, Braunvieh, Normandy, and Romagnola. In general, Continental cattle are larger, leaner, and slower to mature than the British breeds.

Breeds from Near and Far

Some beef cattle breeds originated in other parts of the world.

Brahman. Brahman cattle, which originated in India, are easily recognized by the large hump over the neck and shoulders, loose floppy skin on the dewlap and under the belly, large droopy ears, and horns that curve up and back. They come in a wide variety of colours. Brahmans do well in the southern part of North America because they can withstand heat and are resistant to ticks and other hot-climate insects. They are large cattle, but the calves are small at birth and grow rapidly because the cows give lots of rich milk.

Murray Grey. The Murray Grey is a silver-grey breed from Australia. Murray Greys are gaining popularity in some parts of the world because of their moderate size, gentle disposition, and fast-growing calves. The calves are small at birth but often grow to 700 pounds by weaning.

Texas Longhorn. The Texas Longhorn is descended from wild cattle left by early Spanish settlers in the Southwest USA. Longhorns are moderately sized and are well known for ease of calving, hardiness, long life, and good fertility.

Continental cattle are larger, leaner, and slower to mature than the British breeds

---

Beef Breeds from Near and Far

Brahman

Texas Longhorn

Crossbred Cattle

Crossbreeding is a useful tool for the beef producer. There are numerous breeds and farmers often cross them to create unique cow herds with the traits they want. For example, cattle are raised in a wide variety of environments, from lush green pastures to poor moorland and steep mountains. Each farmer tries to create a type of cow that will do well and raise good calves in his or her situation. No single breed offers all the traits that are important to beef production.

Hybrid Vigour

The most effective genetic advantage in cattle breeding is hybrid vigour, which results when two animals that are different mate. Hybrid vigour

---

Well-marbled meat comes from cattle that have reached puberty.

— displayed by the offspring of such parents — increases the fertility, milk production, and life span of cows and the robustness and health of young calves. With careful crossbreeding, the farmer can develop crossbred cows that will do better than the parent breeds. Good crossbred females make the best beef cows.

Composites

Composite cattle are created from different breeds that have been blended into a uniform type of crossbreed. Several composites have been created in the past few decades, and new ones are being formed all the time. Nearly every breed registered today began as a composite. Brangus, Santa Gertrudis, and Beefmaster are examples of successful composites. More recent blends are the Stabiliser (a British composite breed made up of half native British breeds and half maternal Continental breeds) and the RX3 (a blend of Hereford, Red Angus, and Holstein).

Butchering a Beef

If you're raising a calf to butcher, you will probably want to let it grow to good size. Some people like baby beef (from a calf at weaning age), but if you have enough pasture to raise your calf through its second summer, you will get a lot more meat for your money by letting it grow bigger. The ideal age at which to butcher a steer or a heifer is 1½ to 2 years. At that age, the animal is young enough to be tender and is nearly as large as it will get. Butchering at the end of summer or in the autumn, before you have to feed hay again during winter, makes the grass-fed beef animal economical to raise.

The breed of the animal can be a factor in determining when it is ready to butcher. Beef animals generally do not marble until they reach puberty (or in the case of a steer, the age at which he would have reached puberty if he had been a bull). Different breeds mature at different ages. Angus and Angus-cross cattle often reach puberty at a younger age (and a smaller weight) than do larger-framed cattle, such as Simmental, Charolais, and Limousin.

An Angus-type beef calf may finish faster and be ready to butcher when it is a yearling or a little older. If you feed it longer, it may not get much bigger,

Beef Cuts

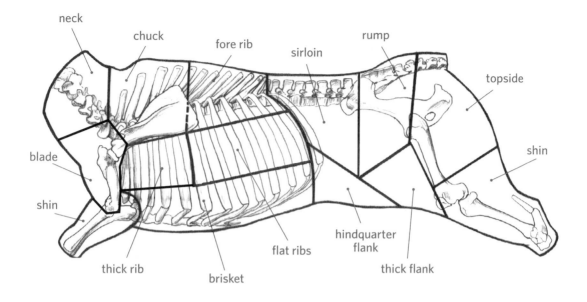

neck
chuck
fore rib
sirloin
rump
topside
blade
shin
shin
thick rib
brisket
flat ribs
hindquarter flank
thick flank

just fatter. A Simmental calf, in contrast, may still be growing and not fill out (carry enough flesh to be in good butchering condition) until it is at least two years old.

Thus, the ideal age at which to butcher your beef animal depends on its breed and on whether it is grass fed or grain fed. Cattle will grow faster and finish more quickly on grain, but at greater cost. Whether you feed grain depends on personal preference (some people prefer grain-fed beef to grass-finished beef, and vice versa) and your situation. If you have lots of pasture, raising grass-fed beef is usually most economical.

You can take cattle to a custom packing plant to be slaughtered and butchered or you can do the butchering yourself.

Raising Pigs

Most people start thinking about keeping a pig as a way to provide quality meat for the family table at moderate cost. When you raise your own pigs, you select them, feed them to an exact slaughter weight, and control the meat processing.

Fattening up a pig for slaughter is a rewarding process. It gives you an assurance of quality and wholesomeness that you can have in no other way. And along with quality control, there is much that you as a home finisher can do to contain costs. Granted, a pig is not all chops, but when it is raised and processed to order, you can expect to maximize the cuts and quality you and your family prefer in meat and meat products.

So where do you begin? Chances are you'll start with one or two feeder pigs — young pigs between 40 and 70 pounds — which you'll feed out to market weight. A 40- to 50-pound feeder pig should reach a harvest weight of 240 to 260 pounds in 120 days or so. If you're getting started in cold or wet weather, look for a pig that's closer to 70 pounds; a larger pig will be better able to cope with harsh conditions. Like many other herd animals, pigs are much more content when they're raised in groups, so you might consider raising two pigs instead of one.

Although they're often portrayed as living waste disposal units, pigs are healthier and produce better meat when they're fed a balanced diet and are given food scraps only as a supplement. Amazingly, a healthy young pig will eat roughly 3 percent of its body weight in food every day, amounting to 10 to 12 bushels of corn and 125 to 150 pounds of protein supplement.

Thinking about Space

One of the first things to consider is where you'll raise the pigs. Some small-scale pig keepers finish their pigs in small "finishing units." These buildings are made up of two parts: a small house and a slatted, floored pen fronting it (the "pig patio" or "pig deck"). The house provides shelter in inclement weather and keeps pigs off the ground, which eliminates or reduces mud and, in the process, keeps parasites in check. The slatted pen allows wastes to work through the floor and away from the hogs.

Other owners prefer to keep their pigs on the ground. If this is your choice, you'll need to provide at least 150 square feet of pen space per pig to keep mud problems from developing. In very wet, low areas, that space amount may have to be tripled. Pig fields become muddy not from the rooting activity of the pigs, which can be controlled with the use of humane nose rings, but from excessive foot traffic and those sharp, pointed hooves. You'll still need a house for shelter (since it will be the animals' only dry retreat in wet or raw weather), not to mention fencing made of pig panels or electric wire.

Pigs in the Garden

Letting pigs into the garden may sound like a recipe for disaster, but not if they're put there with a plan. Where space permits, many pig owners will maintain two separate (often adjacent) garden plots; one will be used for a season and the other will be left fallow. In the fallow plot will go a small hut and one or two growing shoats (young pigs). Their rooting activities will improve soil tilth and help turn under any crop residues,

Tips for Buying Feeder Pigs

- The greatest variety and highest quality of pigs is available in the 40- to 60-pound weight range.

- Crossbred pigs are generally more vigorous and faster growing than purebreds.

- Male pigs should be castrated and healed.

- Buy pigs that have been treated for internal and external parasites.

- Buy pigs that are well past the stress and strain of weaning.

- Bear in mind that while females (gilts) may grow more slowly than barrows (males), they will generally produce leaner carcasses and can be pushed harder with more nutrient-dense rations.

Modern Swine Breeds

In the 1960s breeds such as the Duroc, Hampshire, and Landrace were imported to Britain. They and their crosses are the backbone of the pork industry. Their development and preservation was the loving work of generations of small and mid-size family farmers.

A distinction of sorts is now made between coloured and white breeds of swine. The coloured breeds are noted for their vigour, faster yet leaner growth, and meatier carcasses. The white breeds, on the other hand, are strong in the traits needed for successful pig raising. They milk better than do coloured breeds and, as a group,

and their wastes will enrich the soil. Spent bedding from the hut can be thrown out for them to work into the garden soil, also. A pig patio can be set up adjacent to the garden, so that spoiled vegetables, spent plants, and other garden wastes can be thrown into the pen as a boost to the pigs' rations.

Pig raising is simplest and most efficient in climates without great extremes in temperature or precipitation. The grow-out period will normally be between 90 and 120 days, depending on the starting weight of the pig or pigs, and can usually be fit into the spring or autumn to avoid the weather extremes of a long hot summer or freezing cold winter. Small producers with simple facilities following a seasonal plan of pro-duction can realize two litters per sow per year without taxing their time or resources. And it is reasonable to expect those litters to have a weaning average of eight or nine good pigs.

Traits of Popular Breeds

Breed	Traits
Berkshire	Premium table-quality pork
Black Poland	Especially durable; good for crossbreeding in an outdoor swine operation
Chester White	Hardy white breed; breeds back quickly
Crossbreed	Hybrid vigour boosts hardiness and growth rate
Duroc	Top eating quality; hardy enough to raise outside
Hampshire	Offspring grow rapidly, with exceptional leanness
Landrace	Large litters; docile
Spotted	Excellent mothering ability; large litters
Yorkshire	The mothering breed; large litters

tend to farrow larger litters. They also have the docile nature you need when you are raising and weaning large litters.

Heritage Breeds

Other swine breeds now popular among small farmers are the heritage breeds, and sadly some of these have to be considered truly endangered. They are a valuable group because they include some of the hardiest of all swine genetics and are often among the leanest of the purebreds. Some of these are the Tamworth, a light red breed with erect ears; the Wessex, a hardy black-and-white breed with drooping ears; and the Gloucestershire Old Spot, a large meaty animal with a broad and deep body and large hams. Its white coat has largely defined black spots.

Breeds of Pig

Berkshire

Chester White

Crossbreed

Duroc

Tamworth

Butchering

Today's pig breeds can be fattened up to as much as 260 pounds and still have quite lean and high-yielding carcasses. A pig will normally yield about 70 percent of its liveweight in pork and pork products. A family of four people may find that fattening up two pigs a year will fit their needs: one for slaughter in late winter and another for the autumn.

With your pig fattened up to the desired weight, the next step is the harvest, or slaughtering process. As with any large animal, this is a process that requires a certain level of skill to be accomplished quickly, cleanly, and humanely. For small-scale pig raisers, perhaps the best solution is to find a nearby abbatoir (consider how the pig will be transported) or an experienced local butcher.

Primal Cuts

Primal cuts are large cuts that are often transported to butcher shops for further butchering and sale. There are five primal cuts in the halved hog carcass:

1. The **leg,** which is comparable to the round in beef and produces boneless leg, ham, and ham steaks

2. The **loin,** which can produce blade chops, loin chops, butterfly chops, country-style ribs, back ribs, bacon ranging from lean to streaky, loin roasts, and tenderloin

3. The **spareribs,** which yield both ribs and salt pork

4. The **shoulder,** from which can come casserole cubes, roasts, steaks, ground pork, sausage, and shoulder rolls

5. The **jowl,** which can be cured for seasoning meat or sliced like bacon

No single carcass can produce *all* of the above meats, but the beauty of home processing is that you can give over as much of the carcass as possible to your family's favourite cuts.

Pork Cuts

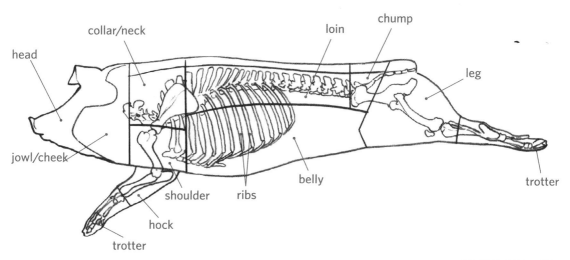

Raising Rabbits

Today, rabbits are mostly raised domestically as pets or for show. However, the culinary traditions of many countries include rabbit as a mainstay, and raising rabbits is a serious option for anyone looking to be completely self-sufficient. If you're considering how to maintain your protein supply on a small property, rabbits may be well worth considering.

First of all, they take up less space than any other kind of meat-producing animal and are relatively inexpensive to feed. Rabbit meat is tender and mild, not to mention higher in protein and lower in fat than chicken, turkey, beef, lamb, or pork. Because they reproduce . . . well, like rabbits . . . it's possible to raise as many as 16 kits (baby rabbits) to harvest weight each year after starting from just one crossbred pair.

Rabbits have other uses on the back garden smallholding in addition to producing meat. Soft rabbit fur is another product that can be used or sold for profit after the rabbit is butchered. Rabbit droppings are an excellent fertilizer for the vegetable garden; try situating the rabbit hutches nearby to making transporting waste a bit easier.

Choosing a Breed

Worldwide, there are 25 species of rabbits. Domestic rabbits that are raised as pets and for fur and meat are descendants of the wild European rabbits. Rabbits were introduced to Britain by the Romans who kept them in fenced-off warrens and harvested their fur and meat.

Selecting a breed is probably the most important decision you will make. Your choice of breed affects many things, such as the size of the cage you will need and when you should first breed young rabbits. Research each of the breeds you're considering so you can choose the one that best suits you.

Crossbred rabbits, which are rabbits that have more than one breed in their family background, are appealing and readily available. However, it's best to begin with purebred rabbits. Purebred rabbits may cost more than crossbred rabbits, but they have many advantages that soon make up for the difference in price:

- A crossbred rabbit costs just as much to house and feed as a purebred.

- If you plan to breed and sell rabbits, purebred young bring a better sale price. You can therefore soon make up the difference in the initial cost of your parent stock (the mother and father).

- If you want to show your rabbits — and showing is fun! — purebred rabbits will qualify to exhibit at more shows.

Meat Breeds

If you are interested in raising rabbits for meat production, consider the large breeds, which weigh from 9 to 11 pounds when mature. Large breeds generally convert feed to meat at a profitable rate, and they yield an ideal fryer — 4 or more pounds — at eight weeks of age, the preferred age for culling. Although not all large breeds are ideal for meat production, the following popular breeds are worth looking into.

Meat Breeds

Californian

Champagne D'Argent

Florida White

New Zealand

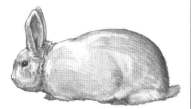

Palomino

Californian. The Californian is an outstanding meat breed, popular in the UK and USA. It is white with black colouring on the feet, tail, ears, and nose.

Champagne D'Argent. One of the oldest rabbit breeds, this silver-coloured rabbit is born completely black and gradually turns silver as it matures. The breed is well regarded for both its meat and its fur.

Florida White. Although the Florida White weighs only 4 to 6 pounds, it is a good meat rabbit. The Florida White was created in the United States.

New Zealand. This breed has long been a top-quality meat producer. It was imported into the UK after the Second World War. Although the breed comes in three colour varieties — red, white, and black — the white variety has proved most popular. New Zealands are known for their full, well-muscled bodies and their ability to become market-ready fryers (4 to 5 pounds liveweight) by eight weeks of age.

Palomino. The Palomino combines an attractive colour with a body type that is well suited for meat production. It was developed in the United States. The breed is available in two colours: golden and lynx.

High-Protein, Low-Calorie Rabbit

Meat	Protein (grams)	Fat (grams)	Moisture (percent)	Calories per Pound
Rabbit	20.8	10.25	27.9	795
Chicken	20	11	67.6	810
Veal	18.8	14	66	910
Turkey	20.1	22.2	58.3	1,190
Beef	16.3	28	55	1,440
Lamb	15.7	27.7	55.8	1,420
Pork	11.9	45	42	2,050

Processing and Preserving Meat

This section covers general procedures for freezing and gives basic methods for curing, smoking, and sausage making. The directions are only examples of techniques. Collect as many recipes for preserving and sausage making as you can, and vary the basic ones given here to suit your taste.

Freezing

Freezing is a method of preserving or storing food in a frozen state during which the growth activity of bacteria, moulds, yeasts, and enzymes is slowed down or stopped. During freezing, water in meat is transformed into ice crystals.

Contrary to popular belief, freezing does not kill all bacteria; bacteria will begin growing again after meat is thawed. Also contrary to general opinion, freezing does not improve the quality of meat; it may temporarily (for up to four to eight weeks of freezing) improve its tenderness, however.

Certain requirements must be met if meat is to be frozen properly; any attempts to ignore them only court failure. Meat must be wrapped in airtight containers — ones that are moisture-, odour-, and vapour-proof. Here's why:

- Moisture (ice crystals) in meat that is allowed to dry out will result in freezer burn.

- Vapours from outside sources must not be allowed to enter the meat and add to moisture already in it.

- Natural meat odours must not be allowed to enter other products in the freezer, and odours from other products should not be allowed to enter the meat.

Getting Started with Freezing Meat

Freezing quantities of meat for storage requires basic equipment and supplies. Here's a list of what you'll find useful:

- Home freezer or access to a large cold storage room

- Containers suitable for freezing including: glazed pottery, plastic boxes, aluminium containers, and tin and tin-enamelled containers (for packing meat)

- Freezer tape (to seal containers)

- Aluminium freezer foil or freezer paper coated with cellophane or polyethylene; polyethylene plastic also works

- Wax paper, not as wrapping, but to separate chops and cuts

- Moisture- and vapour-resistant bags (for wrapping fowl and small pieces of meat)

- Marking pencils (to label packages), rubber bands and freezer ties

How to Wrap Meat for Freezing

Freezers tend to dry meat out. This tendency is a main reason for sealing it in proper wrappings or containers. Wrap meat tightly, also, to squeeze out all possible air, for normal air contains bacteria and other enemies of food. If you pack meat in rigid containers, pack it tightly for the same reason.

So that moisture does not escape through the wrappings and vapour and odours do not penetrate the meat, the proper wrap must be moisture-vapour-resistant paper. If you pack meat in rigid containers, they, too, should be moisture-vapour-resistant. If you're wrapping meat in paper, either the airtight fold or the butcher's wrap will work (see illustrations, page 294). Packages should be sealed with regular freezer tape to cover the seams completely. Unless rigid containers have screw tops or other means of sealing them airtight, their tops, too, should be sealed with freezer tape. When using ziplock freezer bags, be careful to eliminate excess air and close them securely.

Maximum Recommended Freezing Times for Meat

Meat	Cut or Type	Storage Time
Beef	Roasts	12 months
	Steaks or chops	12 months
	Minced	3 months
Veal	Roasts	8 months
	Steaks or chops	9 months
Lamb	Roasts	12 months
	Chops	9 months
Pork	Roasts	8 months
	Chops	4 months
Fish	Fatty fish	3 months
	Lean fish	6 months
	Shellfish	3 months
Minced meat		3 months
Sausage		1–2 months
Whole chicken or turkey		12 months
Whole duck or goose		6 months
Poultry, cut up		9 months
Giblets		3 months
Cured meat		1–2 months

Power Failure!

Your freezer may occasionally lose power because of a breakdown or a power cut. Short power failures will not affect meats. But if the power is off for a day or more, be prepared to take some action.

Place about 25 pounds of dry ice on a sheet of cardboard over the top of the frozen packages in your freezer. Close the freezer tightly. If the freezer is half full, this should keep foods frozen for two or three days. However, check every 24 hours to see if more dry ice is required. If the freezer is practically full, food should remain frozen for three or four days.

Making an Airtight Fold

1. Place food on the shiny side of the freezer paper in the centre of the sheet.

2. Bring two sides over food, keeping edges even. Fold together 1 inch of freezer paper and crease.

3. Continue making narrow folds until the freezer paper is snug against the food.

4. Fold ends toward food in narrow folds, squeezing out air until the package is tight, and tape to secure. The seam is sealed with the fold.

5. Seal with tape. Write the date and contents on the dull side of the freezer paper.

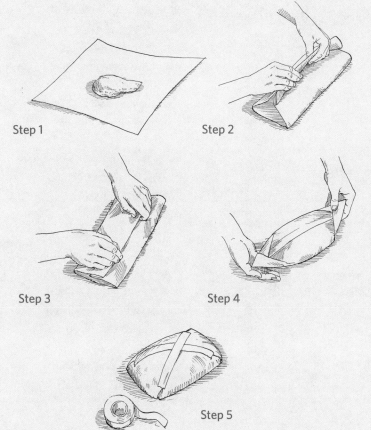

Step 1

Step 2

Step 3

Step 4

Step 5

Making the Butcher's Wrap

1. With the meat at one corner of the paper, roll the paper tightly toward the opposite corner.

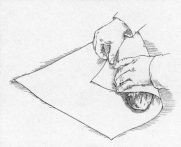

2. Tuck in the sides of the paper and roll to opposite corner.

3. Seal the open edges with freezer tape.

Thawing Meat

Three methods will safely defrost food. The best way is to plan ahead for slow, safe thawing of meat in the refrigerator in its original wrappings; this prevents evaporation of its natural juices. Meat may also be thawed in cold water or in a microwave. Meat may be thawed as it cooks, too. However, unthawed meat requires more time to cook than does meat that has thawed, and partially frozen meat is apt to cook unevenly. Other than that, it should be treated like fresh meat when being cooked. But cook it quickly following removal from the refrigerator, or dormant bacteria will go into action and start spoilage.

In general, small items may defrost overnight, while most foods require a day or two. Large items such as turkeys may take longer: one day for every 5 pounds. For faster defrosting, place food in a leakproof plastic bag and immerse it in cold water. Be careful not to allow leaks, as tissues can absorb water like a sponge, which results in watery food. Check the water often to be sure it stays cold, and change it every 30 minutes. When the food is thawed, refrigerate it until it is ready to be cooked.

Of course, the defrost feature on microwave ovens has greatly simplified and quickened this process. After defrosting in a microwave, you must complete the cooking process immediately, because some areas of the meat become warm and begin to cook during microwaving. In partially cooked food, bacteria might not be destroyed.

Refreezing Meat

It is safe to refreeze meat that has started to thaw, provided ice crystals remain in it. But under no circumstances should meat be refrozen if an off colour or off odour is noticed; destroy it at once without tasting by man or beast! In general, refreezing reduces the quality of meat somewhat, so the refreezing should be noted on the label and the refrozen meat used first. Meat that has been completely thawed should not be refrozen.

Temperatures for Preserving Meats

Temperature range that destroys most bacteria (kill time decreases as temperature increases): 166 to 240°F (74 to 116°C)

Bacteria growth stopped, but some survive: 140 to 166°F (60 to 74°C)

Bacteria may grow; many survive: 120 to 140°F (49 to 60°C)

Danger zone; allows rapid growth of bacteria and toxins: 60 to 120°F (16 to 49°C)

Food-poisoning bacteria may grow; store meat, fish, and poultry no more than a week: 40 to 60°F (4 to 16°C)

Chill meat, fish, game, and poultry under 40°F (4°C) and as close to freezing (without freezing) as possible.

Some food-spoilage bacteria will grow slowly: 32 to 40°F (0 to 4°C)

Freeze point for most liquids and foods: 32°F (0°C)

Bacteria stop growing but may survive: 0 to 32°F (-18 to 0°C)

Store frozen meat, fish, game, and poultry: 0°F (-18°C)

Minimum for fast freezing: 10°F (-12°C)

Making Sausages

The smell of sausages sizzling on the grill is enough to whet even the mildest appetites, but somehow, when the sausages are fresh and homemade, it's even more enticing. And making sausages is easy.

Basic Sausages

These country-style sausages are a good place to start in sausage making. Once you have mastered this basic technique, you will be able to try the variations that follow and create your own recipes.

> 4 feet small (1½-inch diameter) pig or sheep casings
>
> White vinegar
>
> 2½ pounds lean pork butt, chilled
>
> ½ pound pork fat, cut into 1-inch cubes
>
> 1½ teaspoons dried sage
>
> 1½ teaspoons coarse salt
>
> ¾ teaspoon finely ground white or black pepper
>
> ¾ teaspoon sugar
>
> ½ teaspoon crushed red pepper
>
> ½ teaspoon dried thyme
>
> ¼ teaspoon dried summer savory

Preparing the casing. Rinse the casing under cool running water to remove any salt clinging to it. Place in a bowl of cool water; soak for 30 minutes. While you're waiting for the casing to soak, begin preparing the meat (next step).

After soaking, rinse the casing under cool running water. Slip one end of the casing over the faucet nozzle. Hold the casing firmly on the nozzle and then turn on the cold water, gently at first and then more forcefully. This procedure will flush out any salt in the casing and pinpoint any breaks. Should you find a break, simply snip out that small section of the casing.

Place the casing in a bowl of water and add a splash of vinegar — 1 tablespoon of vinegar per cup of water is sufficient. The vinegar will soften the casing and make it more transparent, which in turn will make your sausages more pleasing to the eye. Leave the casing in the vinegar solution until you are ready to use it. Rinse well and drain before stuffing.

Preparing the meat. Cut pork collar into 1-inch cubes. Refrigerate the meat cubes and fat for 30 minutes to firm them up before grinding.

- If you are using a food processor, process the meat and fat to a very fine dice and mix in the seasonings after all of the meat and the fat have been processed.

- If you are using a hand mincer, run the meat and fat through the fine disk (¼ inch or smaller) twice. Mix in the sage, salt, white or black pepper, sugar, red pepper, thyme, and

About Sausage Safety

When making sausages, you must be responsible for providing food that is safe to eat. Here are some rules to follow:

1. Use hot water and dish detergent to scrub all surfaces that will be in contact with the meat. In particular, clean your cutting board very well. Rinse everything thoroughly. When you are finished, wash and sanitize the cutting board (use a mixture of 1 teaspoon chlorine bleach and 1 quart of water as a sanitizing solution).

2. Assemble your utensils and equipment: mincer, sausage funnel, knives, mixing spoons, and a large pan for mixing. Pour boiling water over the mincer and the utensils that will come into contact with the meat. Allow everything to cool completely before proceeding, so as not to raise the temperature of the meat and thus encourage the growth of bacteria.

3. Take off any rings you are wearing and wash your hands carefully. Wash them again if you are called away from your work, such as for a phone call.

savory with your hands between the first and second grindings.

- If you are using an electric mincer with a sausage-stuffing attachment, sprinkle the seasonings over the meat and fat and mix with your hands before grinding, because with this method the grinding and stuffing will be one continuous operation.

Stuffing the sausages. Slide a bit of the prepared casing over the sausage funnel or over the attachment of the electric mincer. Push it along until the entire piece of casing is on the funnel and the end of the casing is even with the funnel opening.

- If you are using an electric stuffer, turn it on and feed the seasoned cubes of meat into the hopper. When the minced meat mixture is flush with the opening of the tube, turn off the mincer. Pull about 2 inches of casing off the tube and tie it into a knot; this will prevent air bubbles from getting into the sausage.

- If you are using a sausage funnel, push the minced meat mixture through with your fingers until it reaches the lip of the opening. Tie off the casing.

Continue stuffing the casing until all the meat has been used. Feed small amounts of meat through the funnel at a time, packing the casing firmly but not to the bursting point. If the casings are packed too firmly, you will be unable to twist off the links without rupturing the casings. Try to maintain an even thickness throughout the length of the casing for a professional finish, and avoid trapping air in it. When all the meat has been used, remove any leftover casing from the funnel.

Sausage-Making Equipment

With one or two exceptions, you probably already have the equipment in your kitchen that you will need to make sausages. Here's a list of the basic tools.

- **Mincer.** An old-fashioned, cast-iron hand mincer like the one in your grandmother's kitchen is still available and is still a bargain, even at today's inflated prices.

- **Power mincer.** If you don't want to mince meat by hand, purchase an electric food mincer with at least two cutting disks.

- **Sausage funnel.** If your mincer doesn't have a sausage-stuffing attachment or if you use a food processor to mince the meat, you will need a sausage funnel to stuff the meat into casings.

- **Knives.** The knife is the most important tool you'll use to make sausages, because so much of the job involves cutting, boning, and trimming the meat. A boning knife aids the cook in removing as much meat as possible from the bone. For slicing, use an 8- to 10-inch chef's knife.

- **Butcher's steel.** This steel or ceramic rod with a handle is used to finely hone a knife blade.

Arrange the links in a single layer on a platter and refrigerate them for at least a couple of hours.

Cooking. Fresh sausages should be cooked slowly and thoroughly because they contain raw pork. (See Cooking Fresh Sausages, opposite.)

Storing. If you are not going to eat the sausages within two days, wrap the links or patties individually in plastic wrap, pack them into a plastic freezer bag, and freeze. Frozen sausages will retain their flavour for about three months. Thaw them completely in the refrigerator before cooking.

Yield: About 3 pounds

Forming the links. Beginning at the tied end of the stuffed casing, grasp about 3 inches of sausage and give it two or three twists in the same direction to form a link. Continue twisting off links until the entire length of casing is done. With a very sharp knife, cut apart the links and cut off any empty casing at the end. The casing will fit the mixture like a glove, and the mixture won't squeeze out. Cooking will firm up the links, so the meat will not pour out even though the ends of the links are open.

Ageing. Sausages taste better if they age, a process that enables the herbs and spices to penetrate the meat more completely.

Sicilian-Style Hot or Sweet Sausages

This recipe provides enough that you can please everybody by making hot and sweet sausages at the same time. Just add crushed red pepper to only half of the sausage mixture.

Version 1

- 5 feet medium (2-inch diameter) pig casing
- 4½ pounds lean pork collar, cubed and chilled
- ½ pound pork fat, cubed and chilled
- 1 tablespoon fennel seed
- 1 tablespoon freshly coarse-ground black pepper
- 2½ teaspoons salt, or to taste
  Crushed red pepper: (½ teaspoon for sweet sausage, to taste for hot sausage)

Missing Links

You don't have to stuff sausage into links; you can use it as bulk sausage and crumble it or shape it into patties for cooking. Stack patties between squares of wax paper and seal in heavy plastic bags for freezing.

Cooking Fresh Sausages

The best way to cook fresh sausages is in a covered, cold skillet with about ½ inch of water. Bring to a boil, then reduce to a simmer; cook until juices run clear. Then drain and fry or grill over medium-high heat, turning frequently, until they are well browned. This technique keeps the casing from bursting. Sausage patties should be cooked over medium-low heat until the juices run clear. Turn the patties once during the cooking time.

Version 2

  Ingredients for Version 1, plus:

- 2 cloves garlic, finely minced
- 1 teaspoon anise seed

1. Prepare the casings (see page 296).
2. Using the coarse disk of a food mincer, mince the meat and fat together.
3. Mix the fennel seed, black pepper, salt, and red pepper together with the meat and fat.
4. Stuff the mixture into the casing. Twist off into 3- to 4-inch links.
5. Refrigerate and use within three days, or freeze.

Yield: 5 pounds

Chorizo

In Spain, spicy chorizo is used alone or to add flavour to many dishes. Smoked or fresh pork can be used. The wine and brandy in the mixture give extra kick to the meat and help extract the flavours of the herbs and spices.

- 5 feet medium (2-inch diameter) pig casings
- 3½ pounds lean collar, cubed
- ½ pound pork fat, cubed
- ¼ cup dry red wine
- 2 tablespoons brandy
- 4 cloves garlic, finely chopped
- 1 tablespoon red wine vinegar
- 2 teaspoons freshly coarse-ground black pepper
- 2 teaspoons salt, or to taste
- 1 teaspoon fennel seed
- 1 teaspoon crushed red pepper

1. Prepare the casings (see page 296).

2. Using the coarse disk of a food mincer, mince the meat and fat together.

3. Mix the wine, brandy, garlic, vinegar, black pepper, salt, fennel seed, and red pepper with the meat.

4. Place the mixture in a large, covered pan. Let sit in the refrigerator for 3 to 4 hours, so the wine and brandy have time to extract the flavours from the herbs and spices and the meat can absorb some of the liquid.

5. Stuff the mixture into the casings. Twist off into 3- to 4-inch links.

6. Refrigerate and use within three days, or freeze.

Yield: 4 pounds

Country Chicken Sausages

Chicken makes light sausages that are very low in fat. Be sure that the chicken is well chilled to begin with, and work quickly, so that it will not get warm during processing. This recipe calls for a traditional "country sausages" combination of ginger, sage, savory, and thyme.

2 feet small (1½-inch diameter) pig or sheep casings

2 pounds chicken meat, chilled

1 teaspoon freshly ground black pepper

1 teaspoon salt, or to taste

½ teaspoon ground ginger

½ teaspoon ground sage

½ teaspoon summer savory

½ teaspoon ground thyme

½ teaspoon cayenne pepper (optional)

1. Prepare the casings (see page 296).

2. Using the fine disk of a food mincer, mince the chicken.

3. Mix the pepper, salt, ginger, sage, savory, thyme, and cayenne, if desired, with the chicken.

4. Using the fine disk of a food mincer, mince the mixture.

5. Stuff the mixture into the casings. Twist off into 2- to 3-inch links.

Yield: 2 pounds

Smoking: Bringing Out Flavour

Smoking is another activity through which one may experiment and bring forth tantalizing flavours that can become hallmarks of a good smoker, and experimentation may help you develop a perfect recipe that is truly "your own".

The main advantages of smoking meat are to impart that distinctive smoky flavour, to drive out any remaining moisture, and to give a favourable colour to the meat's exterior. The amount of smoking, the kinds of chips used for fuel, and the type of cure preceding smoking (such as sugar, honey, or maple) will bring forth that particular flavour you want.

Cold smoking refers to a slow, smouldering smoke that seldom gets above 90°F (32°C). This is the kind of smoke one uses when hams and bacon are smoked. Meat is never cooked during cold smoking, because the smoke never becomes hot enough.

Hot smoking is nothing more than cooking with a very hot smoke. Of course, if anything is cooked, it has to be consumed, bottled, or frozen immediately afterward: Meat that has been hot-smoked cannot be wrapped and stored as it can if it has been smoked with a slow, smouldering smoke.

Types of Smokers

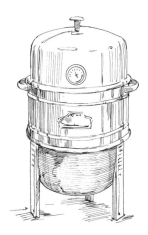  

Vertical water smokers similar to the one on the left use charcoal briquettes; look for a good heat-regulation system. An electric smoker, centre, is temperature-controlled and may require less attention during smoking. Wood-burning smokers such as the one on the right allow smoking of larger quantities of meat.

Smokehouses and Smokers

An efficient smokehouse is very simple and inexpensive to build. It may be constructed from so many different materials that one's imagination is the only limiting factor. Some smokehouses are available from retail stores and mail-order outlets; for the most part, these are too small to smoke large pieces of meat. If you want to prepare hot-smoked food in small batches for individual meals or for parties, commercially available smokers may meet your needs. Most of these products rely on hot smoking, so the food must be consumed immediately.

For cold smoking, you'll need to provide for the following when building a smokehouse: a fire pit, a smoke chamber where the meat is actually smoked, and a smoke tunnel to direct the smoke from the fire pit to the smoke chamber. With these three units in mind, it takes but little imagination to find material around the house that can be used to build a successful smokehouse.

> Meat is never cooked during cold smoking, because the smoke never becomes hot enough.

Basic Components of a Good Electric Smokehouse

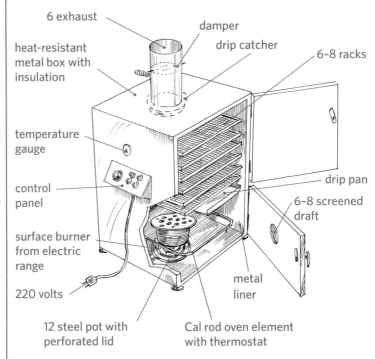

6 exhaust

heat-resistant metal box with insulation

damper

drip catcher

6–8 racks

temperature gauge

control panel

surface burner from electric range

220 volts

12 steel pot with perforated lid

drip pan

6–8 screened draft

metal liner

Cal rod oven element with thermostat

A Simple Homemade Smokehouse

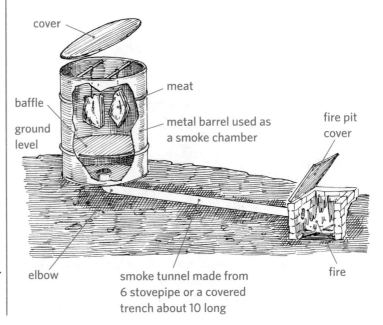

cover

meat

baffle

ground level

metal barrel used as a smoke chamber

fire pit cover

elbow

smoke tunnel made from 6 stovepipe or a covered trench about 10 long

fire

Dried Meat

Dried meat or jerky is made by cutting meat into thin strips and drying them. Often the meat is marinated before it is dried. Meat from most large game animals, such as deer, may be used. Beef and poultry jerky are also delicious. Lean meat keeps well when dried, but fat portions of meat soon turn rancid. For that reason, pork is not often made into jerky. To avoid having your jerky turn rancid, use only the leanest meat for drying, and carefully trim all possible fat before you dry.

In addition, meat to be made into jerky should be cooked by baking or simmering before being dried. Just using the oven or a dehydrator will inactivate microorganisms but will not kill them. The right conditions of heat and moisture may enable the microorganisms to become active, causing a potentially dangerous situation.

To cook the meat, steam, braise, or simmer it in a small amount of water or marinade. For beef, fish, and game, the meat must reach an internal temperature of 160°F (71°C) on a meat thermometer. For poultry, the internal temperature should be 180°F (82°C). Drain and cool the meat, then cut it with the grain into strips that are about

> When done, the strips will be dry throughout but should be pliable enough to bend without snapping.

⅛ to ¼ inch thick; slightly frozen meat is easier to slice thinly and uniformly. Jerky made from meat cut across the grain (as you would carve a roast) will be crumbly and will lack the chewiness desired in jerky. You may find it easier to cut the meat first and then cook the strips. Alternatively, you could simmer the meat in a marinade until the desired internal temperature is reached. Use a meat thermometer in the liquid to measure the temperature.

To dry the meat, preheat the oven to 170°F (77°C). Spread the meat sparingly on trays. Dry the meat in the oven for 5 to 6 hours with the oven door ajar. The meat will shrivel and turn almost black. You may also dry meat in an electric dehydrator. Set it at 140 to 170°F (60 to 77°C); follow the manufacturer's instructions.

When done, the strips will be dry throughout but should be pliable enough to bend without snapping. Cool and pat off any beads of fat. Separate the strips and store in quantities that will be used at one time. Larger quantities may become moist with repeated opening of the storage container.

Store jerky in airtight containers in a cool (38 to 40°F [3 to 4°C]), dry place. Check the jerky within 24 to 48 hours; if moisture appears on the inside of the container, repeat the drying procedure in the oven. If properly dried, jerky will last for one to two months. If too much moisture is left in the meat, it will become mouldy. You may also freeze the jerky, sealed tightly in plastic bags, for up to one year.

Marinades and seasonings — especially salt — are welcome additions to jerky. Before drying, you can brush on sauces or marinate the strips in soy or Worcestershire sauce. Be sure to marinate meat in the refrigerator. You can also brush on spices, such as seasoned salt, freshly ground pepper, and chilli powder (use 1 teaspoon of spices per 3 pounds of meat). A mixture of 1 part brown sugar to 3 parts salt can also be used.

Beef Jerky

2 pounds very lean beef (chuck or round)

¼ cup soy sauce

¼ cup Worcestershire sauce

1 tablespoon tomato sauce

1 tablespoon white vinegar

1 teaspoon salt

1 teaspoon sugar

¼ teaspoon chopped dried garlic

1. Trim all traces of fat from the meat. Freeze until firm and solid enough to slice easily. Cut with the grain into very thin (⅛-inch) slices, and then cut the slices into strips 1 inch wide.

2. Arrange the strips in rows in a shallow baking pan.

3. In a blender or shaker jar, combine the soy sauce, Worcestershire sauce, tomato sauce, vinegar, salt, sugar, and garlic. Pour over the meat, and then refrigerate overnight.

4. Preheat the oven to 325°F (163°C). Remove the meat strips from the pan and dry with a clean paper towel. Place the jerky on racks set over baking sheets. Allow the edges to touch but not overlap. Bake until the internal temperature of the meat reaches 160°F (71°C) on a meat thermometer. Alternatively, you could simmer the meat in the marinade before drying until a meat thermometer in the liquid reaches 160°F (71°C).

5. Reduce oven heat to 140°F (60°C).

6. Drain the meat strips and lay them in rows over baking sheets, being careful not to overlap them. Dry in the oven (or an electric dehydrator according to manufacturer's instructions) until strips splinter on the edges when bent in half, about 18 to 24 hours.

Homemade Cheese

Few families, even those with several milk drinkers, can keep up with the output of a good cow, and most goats will average a gallon of milk a day during the summer months. The best solution to a surplus of milk is cheese — the most delicious, nutritious method of preserving milk yet devised.

Even if you do not have a cow or goat of your own, you can probably find fresh raw milk, without chemicals, from a farm or a dairy. You can often buy milk at a lower price during the summer.

Not only is homemade cheese cheaper than supermarket cheese; it is also better tasting and better for you, because it contains no preservatives. If you are a vegetarian, you can make your own cheese with an all-vegetable rennet. Making cheese is a simple procedure that is easily adapted to the kitchen. Few ingredients are involved, and most of the necessary equipment is already on hand.

The instructions for making cheese sound complicated, but the process is really much simpler than baking a cake. For each cheese recipe, review the basic cheesemaking directions first, then read the specific recipe. With only a little practice, you can become an expert at making cheese.

As you gain confidence, you will learn the variables of cheesemaking — the degree of ripening of the milk and its effect on flavour; the length of time the curd is heated and how that affects the texture; the amount of salt, the number of bricks used in pressing, and the effect on moisture content; and how long the cheese is cured for sharpness of taste. The more you learn about it, the more fascinating cheesemaking will become.

The Three Basic Kinds of Cheese

Hard cheese is the curd of milk (the white, solid portion) separated from the whey (the watery, clear liquid). Once separated, the curd is pressed into a solid cake and aged for flavour. Most hard cheeses are better flavoured if they are aged. The longer the ageing period, the sharper the flavour. The heavier the pressing weight, the harder the texture. Hard cheese is best when made with whole milk.

Soft cheese is made the same way as hard cheese, but it is

Cheesemaking Terms

Clabber. To curdle or sour; milk that has curdled

Culture. The live bacteria used to develop or sour milk for sour cream and yogurt

Curd. The white, solid portion of milk

Rennet. A product, usually made from the stomach lining of animals, that causes milk to curdle quickly

Whey. The clear, watery, liquid component of milk

pressed just briefly. It is not coated, and it is aged a short time or not at all. Most soft cheeses can be eaten immediately and are best when eaten within a few weeks. Soft cheese can be made with whole or skimmed milk.

Cottage cheese is a soft cheese prepared from a high-moisture curd that is not allowed to cure. Commercially, it is usually made of skimmed milk, but it can also be made of whole milk.

Ingredients for Cheesemaking

- **Milk.** Raw whole milk from goats, cows, or sheep makes the richest cheese, but partially skimmed milk can also be used.

- **Starter.** Starter is necessary for good cheese flavour. You can buy buttermilk, yogurt, or a commercial powdered cheese starter, or you can make your own tart starter by holding 2 cups of fresh raw milk at room temperature for 12 to 24 hours, until it curdles. If you can't get raw milk, buy starter-culture kits (in freeze-dried packets) from a cheese supply catalogue.

- **Flake salt.** Flake salt is absorbed faster than table salt.

Yogurt Herb Cheese

Drain 3 cups of very fresh yogurt for 6 to 8 hours, or overnight, in the refrigerator. Scrape into a bowl and add 2 cloves of crushed garlic, ½ teaspoon of crushed pepper (about 20 turns on the pepper mill), 1 teaspoon each of crushed dried herbs — thyme, basil, and oregano — and ¼ cup of chopped chives or parsley. If this seems a little too tart for your taste, whip ½ cup of double cream to a thick, but not fluffy, consistency and beat it into the yogurt cheese. Refrigerate so that the flavours can blend.

Making Soft Cheese

The simplest soft cheese is fresh curds. Your great-grandmother might have made it by setting fresh warm milk in the sun until the curds separated from the whey. The most familiar soft cheese is cream cheese, which is made by draining curds for a few minutes in a cloth bag. If you gather from this that making soft cheese is not nearly as complicated as making hard cheese, you are right. Here are some of the simplest recipes.

Cream Cheese

The classic spread for bagels, cream cheese is wonderful on its own or in any number of recipes.

- Add 1 cup starter to 2 cups warm cream and let it sit for 24 hours. Add 2 quarts warm cream, and let it clabber for another 24 hours. Warm over hot water for 30 minutes, and then pour into a cloth bag to drain. Let it sit 1 hour. Salt to taste, and wrap in wax paper. It is now ready to use. Refrigerate to store.

- Another method of making cream cheese is to add 1 tablespoon salt to 1 quart thick sour cream. Pour into a drain bag and hang in a cool place for three days.

Neufchâtel Cheese

The original French cheese, Neufchâtel, is from the town of that name in the Normandy region of France. Because it's made from milk, it's lighter than cream cheese.

- To make it at home, cool 1 gallon of freshly drawn milk or heat refrigerated milk to 75°F (24°C). Add ⅓ cup of sour milk or starter. Stir for 1 minute, then add half of a rennet tablet dissolved in ¼ cup of cool water. Stir for 1 minute longer. Let it sit, undisturbed, in a warm place (about 75°F [24°C]) for 18 hours.

- At the end of that time, pour off the whey on the surface of the curd. Then put the curd into a cheesecloth bag and hang it in a cool place to drain. When the curd appears dry, place it in a bowl and add salt to taste. Mix in the salt thoroughly.

- Ladle the salted curd into a cheesecloth-lined cheese form, press it smooth with a spoon, and top with a layer of cheesecloth. Insert the wooden follower and apply pressure (six bricks).

Rolling Cheese

Soft cheeses may be rolled in finely chopped herbs, cracked peppercorns, chopped nuts, or toasted sunflower or sesame seeds. Wrap in plastic wrap after rolling, and use within a day or two.

The length of time required to press the cheese into a cake suitable for slicing varies according to the temperature, the amount of moisture, and the weight applied, but it is usually from 45 minutes to 1½ hours. When the cheese is firm enough to cut, it is ready to eat. It is best fresh but will keep a week or more in the refrigerator.

Soft Goat Cheese

This is a delicious, soft goat milk cheese. The milk is ripened for a lengthy period with goat cheese starter culture. A very small amount of rennet is also added to the milk. After 18 hours, the milk coagulates. It is placed in small goat cheese moulds to drain and in two days small and delicious 1½- to 2-ounce cheeses are ready for eating. These are firm yet spreadable cheeses that will keep under refrigeration for up to two weeks.

½ gallon whole goat milk

1 ounce mesophilic goat cheese starter culture

4 tablespoons cool water

Liquid rennet

1. **Ripening and rennet-ing.** Warm goat milk to 72°F (22°C). Stir in 1 ounce of mesophilic goat

Garlic-Herb Cheese

Make a sensational spiced cheese for bagels, sandwiches, and hors d'oeuvres. Into 8 ounces of fresh cream cheese, mash 3 cloves garlic; 1 tablespoon each dried basil, chives, caraway seeds, and dillweed; 2 teaspoons dried parsley; and freshly ground black pepper to taste. If you use minced fresh herbs, triple the quantities.

cheese starter culture. Put the water in a measuring cup. Add 1 drop of rennet and stir. Add 1 tablespoon of this diluted rennet to the milk. Stir thoroughly. Cover and allow the milk to sit at 72°F (22°C) for 18 hours, until it coagulates.

2. **Moulding and draining.** Scoop the curd into individual goat cheese moulds. These are made of food-grade plastic and measure 3¼ inches in height. When the moulds are full, they should be placed to drain in a convenient spot at 72°F (22°C).

3. **Finishing.** After two days of draining, the cheese will have sunk to about 1 inch

Drain the whey from soft cheese by hanging the curds in a cloth bag.

in height and will maintain a firm shape. The cheese can now be eaten fresh or can be wrapped in cellophane or plastic wrap and stored for up to two weeks in the refrigerator. If desired, the cheese may be lightly salted on its surface, immediately after being taken from the mould.

Yield: Almost 1 pound

30-Minute Mozzarella

Mozzarella was first made by the monks of San Lorenzo di Capua, Italy, from sheep's milk. In the sixteenth century, when water buffalo were introduced to Naples, the rich milk of those animals started to be used. The following recipe from Ricki Carroll, author of *Home Cheesemaking,* is a quick and easy way to make fresh mozzarella at home in less than 30 minutes! (Make sure the milk you use for this cheese is

not ultrapasteurized. The protein is damaged in the process and will leave you with ricotta rather than mozzarella.)

For a party treat, slice the mozzarella and arrange it alternately with ripe tomato slices. Then drizzle with fresh pesto, scatter with sun-dried tomatoes, and top with a smattering of pine nuts. Serve with crusty bread and wine.

1½ level teaspoons citric acid dissolved in 1 cup cool water

1 gallon pasteurized whole milk (see *Note* in step 1)

⅛–¼ teaspoon lipase powder (optional) (see *Note* in step 1) dissolved in ¼ cup cool water and allowed to sit for 20 minutes (for a stronger flavour

¼ teaspoon liquid rennet (or ¼ rennet tablet) diluted in ¼ cup cool, unchlorinated water

1 teaspoon cheese salt (optional)

1. Pour the milk into your pot and stir vigorously while adding the citric acid solution. (If using lipase, add it now.)

   Note: You may use skimmed milk, but the yield will be lower and the cheese drier. If you add lipase, you may have to use a bit more rennet, as lipase makes the cheese softer. Try the recipe without it first and experiment later.

2. Heat the milk to 90°F (32°C) over medium-low heat, while stirring gently.

3. Remove the pot from the burner and gently stir in the diluted rennet solution with an up-and-down motion for approximately 30 seconds.

4. Cover the pot and leave it undisturbed for 5 minutes.

5. Check the curd. It will look like custard and will have a bit of shine, with a clear separation between the curds and whey. If the curd is too soft or the whey is milky white, wait a few more minutes.

6. Cut the curd with a knife that reaches to the bottom of your pot. (See page 310.)

7. Place the pot back on the stove and heat to 105°F while slowly moving the curds around with your spoon. (*Note:* If you will be stretching the curds with the water bath method instead of the microwave (see box at right), heat the curds to 110°F in this step.)

8. Take the pot off the burner and continue stirring slowly for 2–5 minutes. (More time will make a firmer cheese.)

9. Pour off the floating whey and ladle the curds into a large microwavable bowl. Drain off as much whey as you can without pressing the curds too much.

10. Microwave the curds on high for 1 minute (see box at right). Drain off all excess whey. Gently fold the curds over and over (as in kneading bread) with your hand or a spoon. This distributes the heat evenly throughout the cheese, which will not stretch until it is almost too hot to touch (135°F [63°C] inside the curd).

11. Microwave for another 30 seconds. Drain again and stretch the curd. If it is not hot enough, microwave for another 30 seconds.

No Microwave?

If you don't have a microwave, you may want to put on heavy rubber gloves at this point. Heat the reserved whey to at least 175°F (79°C). Add ¼ cup of cheese salt to the whey. Shape the curd into one or more balls, put them in a ladle or strainer, and dip them into the hot whey for several seconds. Knead the curd with spoons between each dip and repeat this process several times, until the curd is smooth and pliable.

12. Add salt to taste after the second time (optional). Knead and stretch the cheese quickly until it is smooth and elastic. When it stretches like toffee, it is done. If the curds break instead of stretching, they are too cool and need to be reheated.

Stretch the cheese until it is the consistency of toffee

13. When the cheese is smooth and shiny, roll it into small balls and eat while warm. Or place them in a bowl of ice water for ½ hour to bring the inside temperature down rapidly; this will produce a consistent, smooth texture throughout the cheese. Although it is best eaten fresh, if you must wait, cover and store in the refrigerator.

Yield: ¾ to 1 pound

Troubleshooting: If the curds turn into the consistency of ricotta cheese and will not come together, change the brand of milk: It may have been pasteurized at the factory to too high a temperature (over 172°F).

Alternative: If all the store has is ultrapasteurized milk, a very delicious option is to use dried milk powder and cream. Reconstitute enough instant milk powder overnight to make 1 gallon of milk. When making mozzarella, use 7 pints of this mixture with 1 pint of single cream. (Because of the ratio, the cream may be ultrapasteurized.)

Making Hard Cheese

Here are general directions for making hard cheeses. You will find many variations in specific recipes, particularly for processing temperatures and pressing times.

- 2–3 gallons milk
-   2 cups cheese starter
- ½ teaspoon liquid rennet or
-    1 tablet rennet dissolved in
-    ½ cup cool water (optional)
- 1–2 tablespoons flake salt
- ½ pound cheese coating

1. **Ripen the milk.** Warm the milk to 86°F (30°C) and add the starter. Stir thoroughly for two minutes. Cover and let sit in a warm place overnight. In the morning, taste the milk and assess it. If it has a slightly acidic taste, it is ready for the next step. If you are not using rennet, skip the next step and let the milk sit 18 to 24 hours longer, until the curd has formed and the whey is separating.

2. **Add the rennet.** With the milk at room temperature, add the rennet; stir for 2 minutes to mix it in thoroughly. Cover the container and let it remain undisturbed until the milk has coagulated, 30 to 45 minutes.

3. **Cut the curd.** When the curd is firm and a small amount of whey appears on the surface, it is ready to cut. With a clean knife, slice the curd into ½-inch cubes. Stir the curd carefully with a wooden spoon; cut any cubes that do not conform to size.

4. **Heat the curd.** Place a small container into a larger one filled with warm water, double-boiler style. Heat the curds and whey slowly at the rate of 2 degrees F (1 degrees C) every 5 minutes. Heat to a temperature of 100°F (38°C) over 30 to 40 minutes, then hold this temperature until the curd has developed the desired firmness. Keep stirring gently to prevent the cubes of curd from sticking together and forming lumps. Test the curd for firmness by squeezing a small handful gently, then releasing it quickly. If it shows little tendency to stick together, it is ready. When the curd is firm, remove the container.

5. **Remove the whey.** Pour the curds and whey into a large container lined with cheesecloth. Lift the cheesecloth with the curd inside and let it drain in a

colander or large strainer. Reserve the whey for optional use. When most of the whey has drained off, remove the curd from the cheesecloth, put it into a container, and tilt it several times to remove whey. Stir the curd or work it with your hands to keep the curds separated. When it has cooled to 90°F (32°C) and has a rubbery texture, it is ready to be salted.

6. **Salt the curd.** Sprinkle the flake salt over the curd and mix well. Once the salt has dissolved and the curd has cooled to 85°F (29°C), spoon the curd into a cheese form whose sides and bottom have been lined with cheesecloth.

7. **Press the curd.** Place a circle of cheesecloth on top of the curd. Insert the wooden follower and put the cheese form into the cheese press. Start with a weight of three or four bricks for 10 minutes, remove the follower, and drain off any whey that has collected. Replace the follower and add a brick at a time until you have six to eight bricks. After an hour under this much pressure, the cheese should be ready to dress.

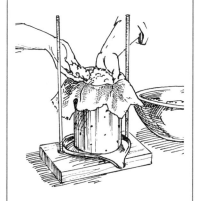

8. **Dress the cheese.** Remove the weights and the follower and turn the cheese form upside down so the cheese will drop out. Remove the cheesecloth and dip the cheese into warm water to remove fat from the surface. Smooth over any small holes with your fingers to make an even surface. Wipe dry.

Cut a piece of cheesecloth 2 inches wider than the cheese is thick and long enough to wrap around it with a slight overlap. Roll the cheese tightly, using two circles of cheesecloth to cover the ends. Replace the cheese in the cheese form, insert the follower, and press with six to eight bricks for 18 to 24 hours longer.

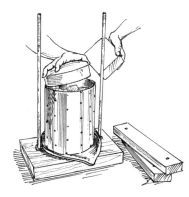

9. **Dry the cheese.** Remove the cheese, take off the cheesecloth, and wipe the cheese with a clean, dry cloth. Check for any openings or cracks. Wash the cheese in hot water or whey for a firm rind. Seal holes by dipping the cheese into warm water and smoothing with your fingers or a table knife. Put the cheese on a shelf in a

You've probably eaten sheep's cheese, even if you didn't know it. Many French and Italian cheeses, such as Roquefort, Romano, and pecorino, are generally made from sheep's milk. Sheep's milk is ideally suited for cheesemaking because it contains almost double the solids of cow milk and is high in proteins and minerals; you can produce more cheese with less milk. It also contains a higher percentage of butterfat than cow's milk.

Collecting enough sheep's milk to make cheese takes quite some time for one person with just a few sheep. You can collect, chill, and freeze the milk until you have enough to make cheese.

This recipe yields a versatile, low-fat cream cheese that makes a great dip or spread when seasoned with parsley, chopped onion, pressed garlic, pepper, or other herbs. When sweetened, it makes a delicious filling for cake.

    1 gallon pasteurized whole sheep's milk
    ¼ cup cold water
    ½ rennet tablet
    ½ cup fresh commercial buttermilk
1–1½ teaspoons salt

1. Pasteurize the sheep's milk by heating it in a large, stainless-steel pan to 155°F (68°C) and keeping it at that temperature for 30 minutes.

2. Cool the milk to 85°F (29°C).

3. Pour the water into a small bowl. Dissolve the rennet tablet in the water.

4. Add the rennet mixture and the buttermilk to the cooled sheep's milk. Stir gently for 10 minutes or longer. Stop stirring when you notice a slight thickening or setting. If you stir too long, you will get a mushy product instead of a firm curd.

5. Keep the mixture at 80 to 85°F (27 to 29°C). Don't let it get any hotter, or the rennet will be destroyed. The best way to hold this temperature is to set the cheese bucket in a large pan of warm water in which you can add hot water from time to time as it cools. Let the mixture stand until whey, the watery-looking liquid, covers the surface and the curd breaks clean from the sides of the bucket (like gelatin) when it is tipped.

6. Cut the curd into 1-inch cubes by running a long, thin knife through it in both directions, right to the bottom of the pot. Cut the strips horizontally by inserting the cheese knife and drawing it across the bucket.

7. Place a bowl underneath a clean muslin bag or fine colander lined with cheesecloth. Pour or ladle the mixture into the bag or colander. Allow it to drain until nearly all of the whey has been caught in the bowl. Use a cheese press to squeeze out the rest of the whey. If you don't have a cheese press, place a dish on top of the bag and weight it down with a jar filled with water.

8. Keep the whey in the refrigerator until the cream rises and becomes firm enough to skim off. The cream will have a butterlike consistency. Work it back into the cheese, mixing thoroughly. (Save the thin whey to use as the liquid in bread baking, or feed it back to the sheep.)

9. Once the cheese feels firm, work in the salt.

cool, dry place. Turn and wipe it daily until the surface feels dry and the rind has started to form. This takes three to five days.

10. **Coat the cheese.** Follow the package directions on the coating; coatings are available from catalogues that offer cheesemaking supplies.

11. **Cure the cheese.** Put the cheese back onto the shelf to cure. Turn it daily. Wash the shelf once a week and dry it in the sun. After about six weeks of curing at a temperature between 40 and 60°F (4 and 16°C), the cheese will have a firm body and a mild flavour. Cheese with a sharp flavour requires at least three months of curing. Curing time depends on individual taste.

Cheddar Cheese

With a little effort in the spring, you can have perfectly ripened cheddar in time for autumn.

To make cheddar cheese, follow the basic directions for hard cheese through step 5, removing the whey. Then place the cubes of heated curd in a colander and heat to 100°F (38°C) in a double-boiler arrangement or in the oven. After 20 to 30 minutes, the curd will form a solid mass. Slice it into 1-inch strips, which must be turned with a wooden spoon every 15 minutes for even drying. Bake or cook these strips at 100°F (38°C) for 1 hour. Remove from heat and continue with the basic directions, beginning at step 6. Cure the cheese for six months.

Variations

To make flavoured cheddars, you can use 1 to 3 tablespoons of fresh chopped or dried sage, ½ to 2 tablespoons of caraway seeds, or ½ to 4 tablespoons of chopped jalapeño peppers to flavour 2 pounds of cheese. The amount depends on the degree of flavour you want in the final cheese. Place the desired seasoning in ½ cup water and boil for 15 minutes, adding water as needed, so that it does not all boil away. Strain the flavoured water into

the milk to be used for cheesemaking. Follow directions for cheddar cheese. Add the sage, seeds, or peppers during the salting process.

Colby Cheese

Colby is similar to cheddar but is softer and milder, and it's ready to eat without a long curing time.

To make a small Colby cheese, add 3 tablespoons of starter to 1 gallon of lukewarm milk. Let it stand overnight to clabber, and then proceed with the basic directions for hard cheese through step 4, heating the curd.

When the curd is heated to the point where it no longer shows a tendency to stick together, remove the container from the heat and let it stand 1 hour; stir every 5 minutes.

Now continue with step 5, removing the whey. After pressing the curd for 18 hours, the cheese can be dried for a day or so and used as a soft cheese spread or ripened for 30 days.

Romano Cheese

Romano is a hard, granular Italian cheese often used for grating. In this recipe, skimmed milk can be used.

Follow the basic directions to step 4, heating the curd. At this point, heat the cut curd slowly to 118°F (48°C) and hold it at that temperature, stirring occasionally until the curd is quite firm (you can tell by touch or by tasting).

Then proceed with the basic directions to step 7, pressing the curd. Follow the directions, pressing the cheese for 18 hours. Then remove the cheese from the form and immerse the cheese in salt brine (¼ cup salt dissolved in 1 quart warm water). Let it stand 2 to 3 hours. During the first stages of the curing process, salt is rubbed onto the surface.

For a real Italian Romano appearance, colour the coating black and rub the surface of the cheese with olive oil at the end of the curing period. Romano is cured for five to eight months for slicing and one to two years for grating.

Make Your Own Cheese Press

To make a cheese press, you'll need scrap wood, a wooden broomstick, bricks, and a 2-pound coffee tin. Take a 36-inch piece of ¾-inch plywood or a 36- by 12-inch board and cut the wood to make two pieces about 11½ by 18 inches each. Drill a hole about 1 inch in diameter in the centre of one of the boards. Whey will drain through this hole.

Drill two holes in the other board, each 1 inch in diameter, 2 inches from each end of the board. The holes should be just big enough so the broomstick moves through them easily.

Cut the broomstick into three lengths: two pieces 18 inches long and one piece 15 inches long. Nail each 18-inch piece 2 inches from the ends of the bottom board, matching the holes in the top board. Nail the other length to the centre of the top board and nail round cheese follower (a circle of ½-inch plywood cut to a diameter slightly smaller than that of the coffee tin) to the broomstick at the other end. Nail two blocks of wood to the bottom or set the press on two bricks or blocks so you can slide a container under the drainage hole to catch the whey.

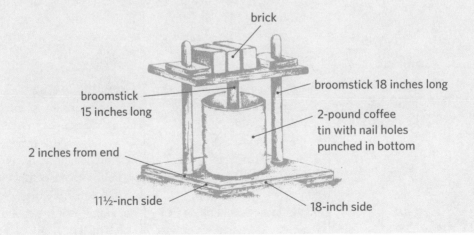

brick

broomstick 15 inches long

broomstick 18 inches long

2-pound coffee tin with nail holes punched in bottom

2 inches from end

11½-inch side

18-inch side

Making Yogurt

The process for making yogurt is essentially the same as for making cheese starter. The milk is warmed to 100 to 110°F (38 to 43°C), the culture is added, and the mixture is kept at the desired temperature for several hours. At about 100°F (38°C), you can make yogurt in 5 to 6 hours, but you can leave it 10 to 12 hours if you like a tarter flavour.

It is important to keep the mixture at the proper temperature for the necessary length of time to let the culture develop. If you have a yogurt maker, simply follow the manufacturer's directions. If you don't, use one of the ingenious methods described below.

Basic Yogurt Recipe

Homemade yogurt has a delicate, creamy body that is hard to find in the multitude of supermarket concoctions, full of additives and flavourings. Making it at home is a simple matter of adding culture to milk and keeping it warm for several hours.

- 1 quart whole milk
- ⅓ cup instant dried milk (optional; it produces a thicker texture and increases the protein content by 2 grams per cup)
- 3 rounded tablespoons plain yogurt or recommended quantity of powdered culture, also called a starter

Making Yogurt without a Yogurt Maker

With a thermos. Almost fill a thermos bottle (preferably widemouthed) with milk heated to 100°F (38°C). Add 3 tablespoons of plain yogurt and mix thoroughly. Put on the lid and wrap the thermos in two or three terry towels. Set it in a warm, draft-free place overnight.

In an oven. Pour 1 quart of milk into a casserole dish and add 3 tablespoons of plain yogurt. Stir well and cover the casserole. Place in a warm (100°F [38°C]) oven with the heat off. Let it sit overnight.

On a heating pad. Mix 1 quart of milk and 3 tablespoons of plain yogurt. Set an electric heating pad at medium temperature and place it in the bottom of a cardboard box with a lid. (A large shoebox works well.) Fill small plastic containers with the milk-yogurt mixture; put on the lids. Wrap a heating pad around the containers and then cover them with towels to fill the box. Put the cover onto the box and let it sit, undisturbed, for 5 to 6 hours.

In the sun. Pour 1 quart of warmed milk into a glass-lidded bowl or casserole dish. Add 3 tablespoons plain yogurt and cover with the glass lid or a clear-glass pie dish. Place in the sun on a warm (not too hot) summer day and let it sit for 4 to 5 hours. Watch it to

An insulated cooler is yet another way to keep yogurt mixture warm while it's incubating.

make sure it is not shaded as the sun moves.

On the back of a woodstove. Many of our grandmothers made clabber by setting a bowl of freshly drawn milk on the back of the stove after supper. Make yogurt this way by adding 1 cup starter to 2 quarts milk and letting it sit, loosely covered with a dish towel, on the back of the cooling woodstove overnight.

In a Slow Cooker. Preheat a slow cooker on low for about 15 minutes, until it feels very warm to the fingertips. Put covered containers of milk and yogurt into the slow cooker, cover it, and turn it. Let mixture sit overnight.

Flavoured Yogurt

It's fun to enhance yogurt with different flavourings, preserves, and sweeteners. Treat your family to nutritious flavoured yogurts for snacks and dessert.

- Scald 1 quart of milk and stir in ¼ to ⅓ cup of sugar, honey, maple syrup, chocolate syrup, malt, molasses, or artificial sweetener. If other flavours are desired, after dissolving the sugar or honey, stir in 1 tablespoon of extract, such as vanilla, lemon, almond, or peppermint, or instant cof-

Equipment for Making Yogurt

Not much is required for making yogurt. You can buy yogurt-making machines that will keep your yogurt at the steady warm temperature that is best for incubating, but you can easily improvise. Here are the supplies you will need:

- Candy thermometer (or yogurt spoon thermometer supplied with yogurt makers)
- 3- to 4-pint saucepan
- Measuring spoons
- Large jug or bowl (for mixing)
- Wire whisk
- Various containers with lids: glass or porcelain jars; stainless-steel, enamel, or porcelain bowls

Unless your equipment is sterilized, some undesirable bacteria may be present, which can destroy your yogurt culture. To eliminate them, run your utensils through a dishwasher cycle (if they are clean, the rinse cycle is adequate) just before you begin to heat the milk. That way, the utensils are prewarmed, and you'll know that your equipment is absolutely clean. An alternative is to immerse the utensils in a pot of boiling water for 1 minute. Various-sized glass jars with screw-on or snap-on lids make excellent yogurt containers.

fee. Another time, try adding 1 teaspoon of ground spices, such as cinnamon, nutmeg, mace, ginger, or your own special combination. Add the instant dried milk, cool the mixture to 110°F (43°C), and stir in the culture. Pour into warm containers, cover, and incubate.

- For jam, preserve, and peanut butter flavours, put 1 tablespoon of the flavouring into the bottom of 1-cup containers and pour the warm milk-yogurt mixture over. Cover and incubate as usual.

- If fresh, tinned, or dried fruit is desired, it is best to make such additions to the yogurt after it has incubated. The acid content of some fruits can curdle the milk-yogurt mixture and prevent proper fermentation.

- Whenever you are flavouring yogurt, always remember to leave 1 cup plain, so that you will have fresh starter for the next batch.

What Went Wrong?

Problem	Cause(s)
Yogurt won't thicken.	• Starter was inactive.
	• Not enough starter was used.
	• Incubating temperature was too hot or too cold.
	• Milk was too hot or too cool when starter was added.
	• Culture was stirred or moved while incubating.
	• Utensils were not clean.
Yogurt is too thin.	• Starter is too old.
Whey separates from yogurt.	• Yogurt incubated too long.
	• Culture was stirred or moved while incubating.
Yogurt is too tart.	• Yogurt incubated too long.

Making Butter

Butter can be made from sweet or sour cream. Butter made out of sweet cream is generally preferred for its mellow, bland flavour. Butter made from sour cream has a richer taste. Butter made from sweet cream takes longer to churn than sour-cream butter, especially if the cream is very fresh. Both sweet and sour cream churn more quickly if they have been aged two to three days in the refrigerator.

Butter

If you make butter weekly from cream accumulated during the week, it will give the cream time to ripen a little, which improves the taste and makes it easier to whip. Or leave the cream a day or so at room temperature, until it begins to clabber. One quart of well-separated double cream makes about 1 pound of butter and ½ quart of buttermilk.

1. Pour the cold, double cream into a chilled mixing bowl. Turn the mixer slowly up to high speed and let the cream go through the stages of whipped cream, stiff whipped cream, and finally, two separate products — butter and buttermilk. As the butter begins to separate from the buttermilk, turn the speed to low.

    To make butter in a food processor, chill the processor bowl and metal blade in the freezer for 15 minutes. Process, scraping down the sides of the bowl at least once, until the solids separate from the liquids.

2. When the separation has taken place, pour off the buttermilk and save it for making biscuits or pancakes.

3. Knead the soft butter with a wet wooden spoon or a rubber scraper to force out the milk, pouring off the milk as you knead. When it seems that all of the milk is out, refill the bowl with ice water and continue kneading to wash out any remaining milk. Any milk left in with the butter will spoil the butter. Pour off the water and repeat until the water is clear.

4. You now have sweet butter. If you want it salted, mix in a teaspoon of flake salt. If you want it bright yellow instead of white, add butter colouring.

Sour-Cream Butter

Sour-cream butter was probably invented by lucky accident when lack of refrigeration made it difficult to keep milk fresh. Souring the cream first yields a butter that churns more rapidly and has a distinctive, rich flavour.

Butter in a Jar

This very simple way to make butter at home uses just a large jam jar and a marble. Pour 1 pint of well-chilled double cream into a clean, large jam jar. Add a glass marble and close the jar. Shake the jar vigorously until the cream begins to thicken, then more gently until suddenly you have a lump of butter in the jar. (The shaking process will take 30 to 40 minutes; you can do it while you listen to music, or pass the jar around while you chat with friends!) Reserve the buttermilk for another purpose. Rinse the butter, kneading gently with a rubber spatula, in several changes of cold water. Knead in a pinch of salt, if you like.

1. Ripen cream by adding ¼ cup of starter (see page 310) for each quart of cream. Let it sit at room temperature for 24 hours, stirring occasionally. Chill the ripened cream for 2 to 3 hours before churning.

2. Pour the cream into a wooden barrel or glass-jar churn. If desired, add butter colouring at this point. Keep the cream and the churn cool and turn the mechanism with a moderately fast, uniform motion. About 30 minutes of churning will usually produce butter, but the age of the cream, the temperature, and whether the cream is from a morning or night milking will affect the length of time required.

3. When the butter forms grainy lumps, draw off the buttermilk and add very cold water. Churn slowly for 1 minute, then draw off the water.

4. Move the butter to a wooden bowl and sprinkle it with 2 tablespoons of flake salt for each pound of butter. Let it stand for a few minutes and then press it with a wooden paddle to work out any remaining buttermilk or water and to mix in the salt. Taste. If the butter is too salty, wash with cold water. If it's not salty enough, add a bit more salt. Keep the butter cold while you're working.

Making Ice Cream at Home

In England, the first recorded serving of this rare luxury was in 1672 to King Charles II. The first English cookery book to give a recipe was *Mrs Mary Eales Receipts* published in 1718. By the second half of the nineteenth century, ice cream had become a treat for ordinary people. Italy led the way and Italian immigrants to Britain brought with them a wealth of expertise.

With the widespread use of refrigeration, electricity, supermarkets, and convenience foods in the early twentieth century, homemade ice cream became a delicacy for special occasions because we came to accept commercially made ice creams and other frozen desserts as food.

Over time, what was once a simple mixture of milk, sweetener, flavouring, and possibly eggs became a frozen chemical soup of more than 60 additives with almost 50 percent more air than in homemade ice cream.

For many, making ice cream at home has a great deal of mystique. Recipe books warn that the proportion of salt and ice has to be just right for the mixture to freeze correctly. Use too much sugar and the mixture won't freeze; too little, and it will freeze as hard as a brick. Many cooks encourage the use of perfectly good ingredients such as gelatin and flour, but somehow these seem alien to such a simple delight.

Making ice cream and other frozen desserts yourself makes good sense and is a lot of fun. The flavours you can create are limitless, and the ingredients are readily available. Your ice cream will cost less than the premium brands and will be vastly superior to the cheaper brands. Most important, you can control what goes into your ice cream, making it as sinfully rich or as austerely slimming as you want, with no unnecessary ingredients.

For the best smooth texture and a minimum of ice crystals, ice cream needs to be constantly agitated throughout the freezing process; this is easily achieved with a modern ice cream maker with a freezer unit or with an old-fashioned ice cream maker, ice, and rock salt. Ice cream made with this process is called "churned" ice cream, because the dasher in the machine constantly churns the mixture to aerate it and scrapes the freezer container's sides, breaking up any ice clusters that have formed.

How to Make Fresh-Churned Ice Cream

Be sure to follow the manufacturer's directions for your particular equipment.

1. Prepare ice cream, pour into a bowl, cover, and

The Scoop on Scooping

Our favourite kind of scoop is the solid aluminum, rounded type without a lever. Running the scoop along in smooth, long lines helps get perfect scoops. Don't wet the scoop: The water will freeze to a thin layer of ice and add ice crystals to your otherwise perfectly textured ice cream.

refrigerate for several hours.

2. Wash the dasher, lid, and bowl of the ice-cream churn, then rinse and dry. Refrigerate to chill.

3. Pour the chilled mixture into the chilled bowl, making sure it is no more than two-thirds full to allow for expansion. Put on the lid.

4. Put the can into the freezer tub and attach the crank-and-gear assembly.

5. Fill the tub one-third full of ice. Sprinkle an even layer of salt, about ⅛ inch deep, on the top. Continue adding layers of ice and salt until the tub is filled to the top of the can.

6. If using ice cubes, add 1 cup of cold water to the ice and salt mixture to help the ice melt and settle. If using crushed ice, let the ice-packed tub sit for 5 minutes before beginning to churn. While churning, add more ice and salt in the same proportions, so the ice remains up to the top of the can.

7. For hand-cranked churns, crank slowly at first — slightly less than one revolution per second. When the mixture begins to pull, churn as quickly and steadily as possible for 5 minutes. Churn at a slightly slower pace for a few minutes longer, or until the mixture is reasonably hard.

8. For electrically powered churns, fill the can with the mix and plug in the unit. Allow it to churn until it stops (15 to 20 minutes). To restart if necessary, turn the can with your hands.

9. When the ice cream is ready, remove the crank-and-gear assembly. Wipe all ice and salt from the top, so that none can fall into the cream when you uncover it. Remove the lid and lift out the beater. The ice cream should be the texture of mush.

Ice Cream Ingredients

- **Dairy products.** Heavy cream, light cream, half-and-half, whole milk, low-fat milk, buttermilk, evaporated milk, sour cream

- **Sweeteners.** Granulated white sugar, brown sugar, honey, unsulfured molasses, maple syrup, light corn syrup, dark corn syrup, fructose, maltose, sorghum

- **Flavourings.** Vanilla extract, chocolate, carob, fruits, nuts, coffee, liqueurs

10. Scrape the cream from the beater. Add chopped nuts and fruit or sauce for ripple, if desired. Pack down the cream with a spoon. Cover with several layers of wax paper and replace the lid, putting a cork in the cover hole.

11. Eat the ice cream in its soft state, or ripen and harden the ice cream by placing it in a deep freezer or refrigerator freezer, or repack it in the tub with layers of ice and salt until the bowl and lid are covered. Use more salt than you previously used, making each layer about ¼ inch deep. Cover the freezer tub with a blanket and set it in a cool place until ready to serve, about 1 hour.

Basic Vanilla Ice Cream

There's nothing like rich, high-butterfat ice cream, but in this basic recipe, there's an option of making the ice cream lower in calories.

- 1 quart double or single cream or 2 cups each double and single cream
- 1 cup sugar or ½ cup honey
- 1 tablespoon pure vanilla extract

1. Scald the cream. Although the ingredients can be mixed and used as is, scalding concentrates the milk solids and improves the flavour. To scald, slowly heat cream in a saucepan until just below the boiling point. Small bubbles will begin to appear around the edges. Stir for several minutes, then remove from the heat.

2. Stir in the sugar. Pour into a bowl, cover, and chill. When completely cooled, add the vanilla.

3. When the mixture is thoroughly chilled, follow directions for churned ice cream.

Yield: 2 pints

Butterfat Content

Double cream has 36 percent butterfat and produces the richest ice cream, but with the most calories. Most kinds available in supermarkets are ultrapasteurized and contain emulsifiers and stabilizers.

Single cream contains 20 percent butterfat and makes relatively rich ice cream.

Whole milk has 3½ percent butterfat. It's the basic ingredient in most ice creams.

Low-fat milks, with 2 percent butterfat, 99 percent fat-free, and skimmed (less than ½ percent butterfat), are useful when you want to limit calories, but you will get a coarser texture in the ice cream.

Vanilla Variations

Once you've mastered basic vanilla ice cream, the variations are limited only by your ingredients. Here's a sampling:

Banana ice cream. Use the basic recipe, but add 1 tablespoon lemon juice and 1½ cups mashed banana to the cream mixture just before freezing.

Butter pecan ice cream. Use the basic recipe, but add to the mushy ice cream ⅔ cup chopped pecans that have been sautéed in 3 tablespoons butter until lightly browned.

Chocolate chip ice cream. Use the basic recipe, but add 1 cup finely chopped chocolate chips to the cream mixture just before freezing.

Chocolate ice cream. Use the basic recipe, but melt two to six (1-ounce) squares of dark chocolate in a small pan over low heat and add to the scalded milk. Increase the sugar to taste, usually doubling the standard quantity.

Coffee ice cream. Use the basic recipe, but dissolve 3 tablespoons instant coffee or espresso in 4 tablespoons hot water or a ¾ cup brewed coffee. Add to the cream mixture just before freezing.

Fruit ice cream. Use the basic recipe, but before freezing add 1½ cups fruit puree stirred with 2 teaspoons fresh lemon juice and 2 tablespoons sugar or 1 tablespoon honey. Use fresh or unsweetened frozen fruit. If you use pineapple, use tinned, not fresh. Strain fruits with seeds, such as raspberries and blackberries, after puréeing.

Ice milk. Use the basic recipe, but substitute whole, low-fat, or skimmed milk for the cream.

Mint ice cream. Use the basic recipe, but reduce vanilla extract to 1 teaspoon and add 2 teaspoons peppermint extract to the chilled cream mixture.

Pistachio ice cream. Use the basic recipe, but add 1 teaspoon almond extract with the vanilla. Add 1 cup finely chopped pistachio nuts when the ice cream is mushy. If desired, add green food colouring with the extracts.

Super-creamy vanilla ice cream. Use the basic vanilla recipe, but soften 1½ teaspoons unflavoured gelatin in ¼ cup water and add with the sugar to the scalded milk. Continue cooking over low heat until the gelatin is dissolved. Or substitute 1½ tablespoons agar for the gelatin.

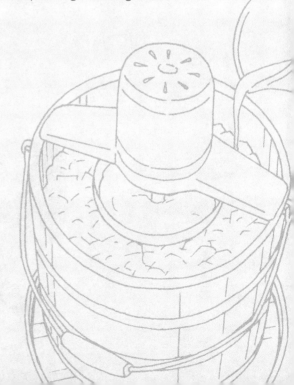

CHAPTER 7

Food from the Wild

An amazing bounty of food can be foraged from hedgerows, disused railway lines, and other common ground. On a recent walk around a post-industrial city that suffers from some neglect, I foraged a fabulous array of edibles — wild grapes, cornelian cherries (fruits of the cornelian dogwood tree, *Cornus mas*), and gumi (fruits of *Elaeagnus umbellata*). In the latter case, I consider my harvesting to also be a service to the community, as it keeps the plant from spreading farther afield. In the spring, there is wild garlic, young nettles and ostrich ferns ready for picking. In woodland areas I've found a number of mushrooms, including chanterelles, porcini, and shaggy inkcaps. In autumn, field mushrooms pop up in the meadows and blackberries fill the hedges. When you begin to understand the edibility of the plants and fungi you pass by every day, you start to see potential food sources everywhere you turn.

Although we have a tendency to think of cultivated food crops as our only source of nutrition, wild foods can be a good supplement. When you consider fishing and hunting as forms of foraging, you can envision ways to supply yourself with all four food groups from the wild. Even the fifth group — sugary treats — can be sourced from plants by keeping honeybees (this last is really more a form of livestock than a way to forage, but it does have wild origins).

There are caveats, of course. *First of all, you must know what you're eating!* That can't be stressed enough. Find an expert in your area, take a class, buy a good identification guide, and do some studying before you get started. Start with something easily identifiable, like domesticated food plants that have escaped cultivation, and move on to wild plants once you've gained some experience.

And always be sure to get permission from landowners before you set out. While they probably won't be opposed to your digging up dandelions from their front lawn, they might wonder just what you're up to if you don't take the time to introduce yourself first.

Beekeeping

The rewards of keeping bees are many: You'll have all the honey you need for cooking and table; you'll have a supply for wonderful gifts; your garden will be pollinated by your own bees, and will grow better for it; and you may eventually earn money for your honey. Best of all, you will have a fascinating hobby.

What You Need to Get Started

The location of your hives should be selected with care. Check with your local authority that beekeeping is permitted. Choose a quiet, sunny, secluded spot. Bees follow a landing and takeoff pattern in front of the hive — be sure that their flight path doesn't cross a pavement, road, or footpath. If your hive will not be near a natural source of water, provide one.

Time. Beekeeping demands little time and fits in well with other weekend chores.

Timing. In cold regions, it is important to get your bees early in the season. They must have time to build their combs and raise new bees so that the hive population will be large at the season of the main honey flow. Arrange to have the bees delivered about when fruit trees bloom in your area.

Knowledge. A little bit of knowledge will get you started, and you'll know it all. Begin by following a good manual; from there, you can explore the subject in as much depth as you want.

Bees. Bees can be obtained in many ways. You can buy them from mail-order beekeepers. You may be able to purchase an established hive from a nearby beekeeper. Or you might have a nearby beekeeper place a swarm of bees in a hive for you. If you buy an established hive, ask for a certificate of inspection signed by a Bee Diseases Officer stating that the hive is free from disease.

The most popular bees to start with are Italian bees. They are industrious, and a good queen will quickly build up a strong hive. Start with a 3-pound package of bees (about 10,000 bees).

Equipment. Bee equipment firms sell beginner's kits. If you buy one, make certain that you get all of the items in the equipment box before you begin setup.

Step by Step

Keeping bees is not complicated, but upkeep is essential, and a manual on beekeeping will be a necessary companion to teach you the tricks as you go along. Here is a rundown of

drone bee

worker bee

queen bee

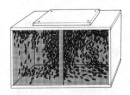
a package of bees

Beekeeping Equipment

Your basic start-up needs are listed below. The cost may vary, depending on your local supplier.

- A standard 10-frame hive with bottom board, entrance block, outside cover, inside cover, frames, and foundation

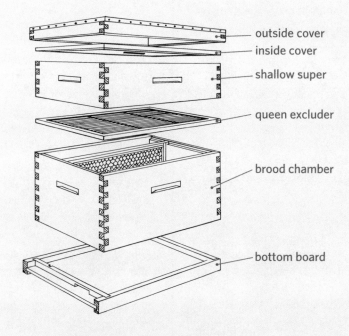

- outside cover
- inside cover
- shallow super
- queen excluder
- brood chamber
- bottom board

- A 3-pound package of bees, with queen

- A bee veil (to protect your face)

- Gloves

- A bee smoker

- A hive tool (for prying apart the hive and frames)

- A feeder (to feed the bees sugar syrup until they can support themselves with nectar)

- A bee brush

- A beginner's book on beekeeping

the basic steps that a novice beekeeper will need to learn.

Installing bees in the hive. A few general hints: Don't rush. Work calmly. Install the bees in the evening. And remember that they aren't inclined to sting you after they are fed. Follow this basic installation procedure:

Prepare the hive. Before you get your bees, the hive should be assembled, painted, and placed in its permanent location. Remove five frames to make an open chamber. Fill the entrance feeder with syrup.

Get your package of bees. As soon as you get the bees, feed them. They'll need to subsist on sugar water until they start producing honey. Install them as soon as possible; hold them no more than two or three days.

Get yourself ready. Light the smoker. Don your bee attire and net. Have a hive tool and bee brush handy.

Open the shipping cage. Pry off the cover of the cage with the hive tool. Remove the queen cage. Replace the cover.

Look at the queen cage. Get a good look at the queen, so you'll learn to recognize her. Place the queen in the hive.

Put the bees in the hive. Carefully replace the wire frames. Working gently, so that you don't pinch the bees, replace the cover.

Getting Stung!

Here's the big question: Will you get stung? Yes. You almost certainly will get stung from time to time, but after a while you'll begin to tolerate it pretty easily. Many stings can be avoided. Here are some tips:

- Work in the hive during good weather when the bees are out of the hive and gathering nectar.

- Wear protective gear and light-coloured clothing. Bees tend to crawl into dark places, so have tight wristbands on your sleeves and tuck the bottoms of your trousers into your socks.

- Use a smoker when working with bees. Watch the reaction of the bees to the smoke. You will soon learn the minimum amount that can be used to subdue them.

- When you get stung, remove the stinger quickly by scraping it with the hive tool or your fingernail. Don't try to pull it out with your fingers, as this will only force more venom into your body.

- Finally, make certain you are not allergic to bee stings. Most beekeepers eventually develop immunity to stings. If you become allergic to bee stings and the effects of the sting grow worse each time, consult an allergist. Such an allergy can become deadly.

How Bees Make Honey and Wax

The nectar that bees collect is generally one-half to three-quarters water. The bees evaporate most of the water by adding enzymes to it. These enzymes change the nectar into honey. The bees seal the honey into cells of the honeycomb.

Beeswax begins as a liquid exuded from the abdomen of worker bees. As it hardens into tiny wax scales, the worker bees use it to build honeycomb.

Beekeepers often provide their bees with honeycomb foundations made of sheets of beeswax. They fit into hive frames and become the base of the honeycomb. These foundations enable bees to speed up comb construction and provide a pattern for straight and easy-to-remove comb.

Confine the bees to the hive. Plug the hive with the entrance feeder and a handful of grass. Check several days later. Replenish the syrup, if necessary.

After about a week. Using a little smoke, remove the covers and check the queen.

Maintaining the hive. The hive should be maintained about once a week throughout the spring and summer to prevent feeding problems or preparations for swarming. The best time to work on the hive is on a sunny day. Here's what it takes:

Put on your protective clothing.

Light the smoker.

Open the hive. Pry it open, using the smoker to subdue the bees.

Check frames. Look for cell building and honey production.

Keep feeding. Replenish sugar syrup until bees have a large store of honey.

Check on the queen. Look for eggs and larvae to be sure that the queen is producing.

Add to the hive. When the hive becomes full of honey and bees, add extra stories, called "supers", to the hive.

Watch for swarming. Check the bottom edges of the hive for large queen cells, which may indicate that the hive intends to swarm (evacuate the hive body en masse).

There are several things you can do to reduce the chance

The Flavours of Honey

There are as many flavours of honey as there are flowers. The distinct aroma, flavour and colour of honey is determined by the type of flower from which the bee collects the nectar. Most honey is polyfloral which means that it comes from bees foraging on many different nectar sources. Monofloral honey is made by bees that feed primarily on a single flower type. In the British Isles honey is harvested from bees that have been at work on apple blossom, cherry blossom, hawthorn, lime blossom, dandelion, borage and heather. Honey is harvested all over the world and the range of plants that provide the nectar sources is immense and varied. Popular honeys from further afield include leatherwood, orange blossom and wild thyme.

of swarming: Provide room by adding supers before they are needed; requeen every year; and replace honeycombs in the brood chamber with empty cells for egg laying.

Harvesting the honey. The flowers have bloomed and fed the bees. The bees have painstakingly collected and stored the honey. You've placed super on super on super, and they are all filled. What next? It's time to enjoy the fruits of your bees' labours.

The honey in the frames is ready to be taken when the bees have capped it with a layer of wax. It has a finished, packaged look, and none of the honey will leak out.

Removing the super. You will take honey from the super on the top of the hive. Fit a bee escape into the inner cover and wait 24 hours, so that most of the bees will have time to find their way down into the hive. Take the super off the hive.

Brush off any lingering bees near the hive entrance. Take the super inside to work on it.

Taking the comb honey. You're now ready to package your honey in one of its most delicious and natural states. You will need the following materials:

- a wire cake rack, 12 by 18 inches
- a baking pan, 12 by 18 inches or larger
- containers for the honey
- a knife for cutting the comb
- a spatula to move the chunks to the containers

Using the knife, cut the comb from the frame and place this large chunk on the rack. Cut smaller chunks to fit your containers. Separate the chunks and let the honey drain from the sides. Then place them in the containers and seal.

Another method of packing cut comb honey is to cut

Cut comb honey can be conveniently packed in square plastic boxes, available from bee equipment suppliers.

the chunks and place them in widemouthed glass jars. Heat some honey to 150°F (66°C), let it cool, and fill a jar with it. This type of pack is commonly called chunk honey. The honey in these jars tends to crystallize quickly, even though you have heated it to prevent this.

Sharing with the bees. Remember that you should always leave enough honey in the hive to allow the bees to winter over comfortably. Requirements vary throughout the country, so precise amounts are difficult to compute. Consult the British Beekeepers' Association.

Foraging

If you love the idea of getting something for nothing, foraging for wild edibles may be a good way for you to supplement your homegrown food. Since most wild foods have such a short season, foraging is a fabulous way to stay in tune with the seasons and be more in touch with the natural world, not to mention the exercise you'll get from all that walking. And foraging isn't just about picking berries and nibbling roadside weeds — it also includes fishing and hunting for game.

There are a few caveats, however. Unlike eating vegetables from your garden, harvesting wild foods can be deadly if you're not fastidious about identifying the plants and mushrooms you've collected. Use a respected guidebook, take classes, and seek out an expert to give you a lesson on what's edible in your area. In short, do what you need to in order to become properly trained before you start picking.

If you're interested in hunting, shooting and fishing, you'll need to check what regulations apply in your particular part of the country. For example, you will need to find out when the fishing season is open and what kind of permit you'll need for coarse fishing on your local river or lake. Alternatively, you may want to try your luck fly fishing on a private stretch of chalk stream or joining the local pheasant shoot. These activities require more preparation than foraging for blackberries does. Again, do the research.

Find a Good Guide

If you are interested in learning enough about plants to harvest some wild edibles, you will need a good field guide, preferably one that addresses the plants in your particular area. Some guides have photographs, while others have drawings. Usually the drawings are in colour. The quality varies rather dramatically from guide to guide. A book with clear photographs may be your best bet, especially if the photographs show the plant you are interested in at different stages of development, since a plant may look entirely different during each part of its life cycle. A good drawing, however, is better than a poor photograph. You want to be able to clearly see leaves, stems, stalks, and flowers. The guide should also provide information about habitat, look-alike plants, possible toxicity, and methods of harvesting.

Harvesting wild foods can be deadly if you're not fastidious about identifying the plants and mushrooms you've collected.

Get Permission First

If you're considering venturing onto another person's land to forage, be sure to contact the landowner and obtain the proper permission before starting. The same holds true for public places — many national parks prohibit visitors from taking anything outside the boundaries of the park. Get permission before you harvest.

Tools

Foraging requires very few tools. The few that are helpful are probably in your kitchen or garden shed. A trowel is useful for digging up roots. A penknife or paring knife with a sheath is also necessary, as is a good pair of leather work gloves. You will need something in which to carry home your treasures. A basket or cloth bag is preferable to paper, which will fall apart when wet, or plastic, which will cause your tender greens to wilt.

Harvesting

There are two big issues to keep in mind when harvesting wild foods. The first is toxicity. Mother Nature is not always benign. Just because a berry is blue doesn't make it a blueberry. Poisonous berries abound and some are killers. Don't eat *anything* unless you are absolutely certain about its identity and edibility. Stick to the plants you know well, and try to learn about one or two new species each year. Rely on your field guide in addition to the advice of an expert forager whom you trust before you eat something new.

Even knowing that a plant is generally edible doesn't ensure that it is edible at every stage or that every part is edible. Some plants are tasty and healthful only when cooked, and a few require several changes of water. This is where a good field guide and a knowledgeable mentor are essential.

Mushrooms require special consideration, as the results of a mistake won't be just uncomfortable; they can be deadly. If you want to learn about mushrooms, join an established mushroom club and learn from experts. If you're interested in growing mushrooms, there are kits available that enable you to grow almost any variety you like. The kits are fairly foolproof if you follow the directions carefully. Mushrooms can be grown in basement areas that are not good for growing anything else.

If you come home with a bounty of greens, wash them well in clean water. Greens gathered near waterways can be infested with giardia, a nasty intestinal parasite carried by animals and passed into the water with their faeces. Soil can carry a number of germs and bacteria, not just on tubers but also on the leaves and stems of many plants. Fortunately, a good scrub with plenty of clean water will remove them.

In general, avoid collecting plants from heavily trafficked areas, along roadsides, and from other potentially polluted spots such as streams beside animal pastures.

The next issue in harvesting is protection of the plant. Don't harvest any plant on the rare or endangered list. If any plant is locally scarce (not necessarily endangered but just not abundant where you live), take small amounts from as large a group-

---

About Nettles

If you've ever come into contact with stinging nettles, you'll undoubtedly recall with dread the swift, nasty rash that they caused when they touched the skin. However, you might be very pleasantly surprised by how mellow and delicious nettles are when they are cooked. They lose their characteristic prickle and taste like a mild, tender spinach.

Wearing long sleeves and rubber kitchen or gardening gloves, pick whole nettles when they are very young, or pick just the small-leaved tops of more mature plants. Using tongs, swish the nettles in a bowl of cool water, then drop them directly into a pot of boiling water. Do *not* touch the nettles or try to chop them or work with them until they are cooked.

ing as possible. Leave behind enough of the plant that it can reproduce.

If you exercise common sense and take the time to learn about the foods in your area, foraging is a wonderful way to get closer to nature and understand more about our place in it. You probably won't ever need to rely on the woods, pastures, and streams to provide you with all you need for sustenance, but it's good to know where there is a ready supply, free for the picking.

Look for these favourite wild foods:

- Apples
- Blackberries
- Blueberries
- Cherries (wild)
- Crab apples
- Dandelions
- Damsons
- Elderberries
- Garlic (wild)
- Milkweed
- Nettles
- Ostrich ferns
- Raspberries
- Rose hips
- Sloes
- Strawberries (alpine)
- Sweet chestnuts
- Violets

Rose Hip Jam

    4 cups rose hip pulp

    5 cups sugar

    1 tablespoon lemon juice

1. For the pulp, collect ripe rose hips, preferably just after the first frost. Wash and stem the hips. In a medium-sized saucepan, cover rose hips with water; simmer until soft, about 15 minutes. Run pulp through a food mill or sieve.

2. Combine the pulp, sugar, and lemon juice. Bring to a boil; reduce heat. Simmer until the mixture reaches 220°F (104°C). Ladle into hot jars.

3. Adjust lids and process in a boiling-water-bath pan (see page 80) for 5 minutes.

Yield: 2 to 3 pints

Harvesting Dandelions

It is likely that your neighbours will be delighted if you ask to collect dandelions from their lawns (assuming their lawns haven't been sprayed). Be sure to gather from environmentally clean areas at least 50 feet away from busy roads and where no pesticides have been used. Roots will be easiest to harvest after a

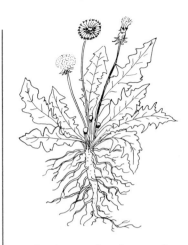

good rain or a few hours after the yard has been watered. If your neighbours don't live on a busy street and don't spray their lawns, ask permission to collect dandelions — then bring them some dandelion wine to show your gratitude.

Should you live where dandelions simply don't grow, such as in a high-rise block of flats, check your local supermarket, farmers' market, or health-food store. Nowadays many retail grocery stores carry dandelions in their fresh produce departments.

Leaves. Dandelion leaves are best collected in the spring before the plants flower. People who claim to dislike the taste of the greens have very likely collected the leaves after a plant has flowered, when the greens have turned bitter. If you wash the leaves before drying, be sure to dry them well to discourage mould. Cut the leaves at their base with a knife or snap them

About Rose Hips

In late autumn, after the leaves have dropped, snip the partially dried orange-red rose hips from your rosebushes. Trim off and discard both ends; cut the remainder into thin slices. Dry the slices according to your favourite method.

Dehydrator: Spread slices thinly over trays and dry at 110°F (43°C), stirring occasionally. Dry for 12 to 18 hours, or until crisp and hard.

Outdoors: Spread slices over trays in a thin layer and allow to dry in a well-ventilated, shady area for two or three days, until crisp and hard. Take the trays inside at night.

Oven or homemade dryer: Spread slices thinly over trays. Dry at 110°F (43°C), stirring occasionally, until crisp, about 18 to 24 hours.

Rose hips are a good winter source of vitamin C. Rose hip tea benefits from the addition of other herbs, such as lemon balm and mint. To make rose hip tea, cover ⅓ cup dried rose hips with 1 quart cold water. Cover and slowly bring to a boil. Simmer over low heat for 15 minutes. Strain liquid, mashing the hips with a fork to extract all the vitamin-rich juice. Drink hot or cold with a spoonful of lemon juice and honey or sugar.

off with your fingers. After the plant has seeded, there will be a new growth of leaves later in the summer and these also can be collected. Avoid leaves that are yellow and wilted as the flavour will be inferior.

Flowers. When collecting flowers, it is helpful to have small children with you — they'll love to help. Spread the blossoms on a large cloth to allow some of the insects to crawl and fly away before you bring them inside.

For appearance and efficacy, use the flowers the same day that they have been collected.

Roots. There is a wonderful tool called a dandelion digger (available at gardening supply shops) that you can use for digging the deep dandelion taproots. To obtain large roots, gather plants that are at least two years old. The best roots will be found in unmowed patches of land and in soil that is rich and loose. Here a root is likely to be single and juicy. (In poorer soil, the root tends to be forked and tough.) The plant is most effective in its fresh state. Roots from older plants will be leathery to eat but can still be used for medicine and in teas.

The ideal times to collect roots are in early spring before the plants flower and then again in autumn after the first frost.

Spring-harvested roots are sweeter than those taken in the autumn, as they are higher in fructose and less bitter and fibrous. But they must be collected before the flower buds are big, or all of their energy will go into producing the blossom, depleting the root. From September to February is also a good time to collect the roots, when the plants are highest in inulin, which imparts a sweet taste. Spring roots are higher in taraxacin, which stimulates bile production, and fructose, a

A dandelion digger is good for digging out any plant with a deep taproot, not just the dandelion.

simple sugar, than are autumn roots.

Autumn-harvested roots are more bitter and richer in inulin, which makes them more of a therapeutic medicine. This combination is partly because during the growing season, the fructose in the roots converts to inulin. The winter freeze then breaks down the inulin back to fructose, which sweetens the spring roots.

Dandelion Coffee

One popular beverage is a dandelion "coffee" made from the dried and roasted roots. This drink tastes rich and earthy, similar to coffee but without the caffeine. It is non-addictive and much kinder to the stomach. Dandelion roots tend to be more bitter in summer and autumn and sweeter in spring.

- **To prepare the roots:** Dig the roots (20 should give you enough for a small supply) in the autumn and wash well, using a vegetable brush to scrub them.

Slice the roots lengthwise and allow them to dry in a warm place for two weeks.

- **To roast the roots:** When dry, roast them for 4 hours in an oven heated to 200°F (93°C). An alternative is to roast the dried, sliced roots in a cast-iron skillet, stirring constantly, until they are dark brown. Cool completely before storing in a glass jar. Roasting dandelion roots releases aromatic compounds and converts the starch inulin into fructose, sweetening their taste.

- **To brew:** Simmer 1 heaping teaspoon of the root in 1 cup of water, covered, for 10 minutes, then strain. The resulting dark, rich beverage will help you feel warmer. If you want, you can also use the roasted roots as a coffee substitute by percolating or using the drip method.

- **To enjoy:** You can drink this as you would coffee with milk and either sugar or honey.

Dandelion Wine

Dandelion wine, believed to be of Celtic origin, is regarded as one of the fine country wines of Europe. In the late 1800s and early 1900s, it was not proper for ladies to drink alcohol; however, dandelion flower wine was considered so therapeutic to the kidneys and digestive system that it was deemed medicinal even for the ladies.

6 pints dandelion blossoms
1 gallon water
2 oranges, with peel
1 lemon, with peel
3 pounds sugar
1 ounce fresh yeast
1 pound raisins

1. Collect the blossoms when they are fully open on a sunny day. Remove any green parts; they will impair the fermentation.

2. In a large pot, bring the water to a boil and pour it over the flowers. Cover and let steep for three days.

3. Peel and juice the oranges and the lemon, saving the peels and reserving the liquid.

4. Add the orange and lemon peel to the flower-water mixture and bring to a boil. Remove from heat, strain out the solids, then add the sugar, stirring until it is dissolved. Allow to cool.

5. Add the orange and lemon juice, yeast, and raisins to the liquid. Put everything into a plastic bucket with a loose lid (so gas can escape) to ferment.

6. When the mixture has stopped bubbling (two days to a week), fermentation is complete. Strain the liquid through several layers of cheesecloth and transfer to sterilized bottles. Slip a deflated balloon over the top of each bottle to monitor for further fermentation. When the balloon remains deflated for 24 hours, fermentation is complete. Cork the bottles and store in a cool, dark place for at least six months before drinking.

Flower Fritters

Although nasturtiums aren't strictly wild plants, so many have escaped from gardens tumbling over walls and into roadsides, that they sort of count and they are fun to forage. Basil flower stalks and small clusters of sage leaves may also be prepared this way.

⅔ cup flour

½ teaspoon salt (or more)

½ teaspoon garlic powder

¼ teaspoon freshly ground black pepper

Pinch cayenne pepper (optional)

1 egg yolk

⅓–½ cup beer

Vegetable oil (for frying)

12 nasturtium flowers

1. Line a plate with several paper towels. In a small bowl, combine the flour, salt, garlic powder, black pepper, and cayenne. Add the egg yolk; mix until well blended.

2. Add beer, a little at a time, whisking constantly, until the mixture is the consistency of thick pancake batter.

3. Heat about 2 inches of oil in a deep skillet. Drop a little batter into the oil; when the batter starts to brown, reduce the heat to medium. Pick up a nasturtium flower by the stalk and swish it in the batter to coat the whole flower except the part you're holding.

4. Place the batter-covered stalks in the hot oil, a few at a time. Fry until brown on both sides, turning once.

5. Transfer the fritters to the paper-towel-lined plate; serve immediately.

Yield: 12 fritters

Ostrich ferns

If you know where to find them, ostrich ferns are delicious picked young and fresh. Looking like fuzzy green spirals, they are the tightly furled fronds of *Masteuccia struthopteris*. They have a flavour reminiscent of asparagus.

Preparing ostrich ferns takes a little care. Soak them in water for a few minutes, then ruffle the curled ferns with your fingers to release as much of the fuzzy brown coating as possible. It will come off in small particles and should be skimmed off the water and discarded. Blanch the cleaned ostrich ferns for 2 minutes in boiling water; immediately refresh them under cool water, then drain thoroughly. Place the ostrich ferns in a fresh pot of boiling water for 2 more minutes, then drain. Boiling the ostrich ferns in two changes of water is thought to remove a certain heat-labile toxin that can make some people sick.

Blanched ostrich ferns are delicious when sautéed with butter and garlic, cooked in an omelette, or added to pasta or soup. They may also be served with a light cream or cheese sauce.

Resources

Seed Companies

Chiltern Seeds
www.chilternseeds.co.uk

Herbal Haven
www.herbalhaven.com

Nicky's Nursery
www.nickys-nursery.co.uk

Thompson & Morgan
www.thompson-morgan.com

Preserving Supplies

Lakeland
www.lakeland.co.uk

Fruit Nurseries

Chris Bowers & Sons
www.chrisbowers.co.uk

Brewing Supplies

Brew
www.brewuk.co.uk

Craft Brewing Association
www.craftbrewing.org.uk

Hop Shop
www.hopshopuk.com

Baking Bread

Real Bread Campaign
www.sustainweb.org

Poultry Keeping

British Waterfowl Association
www.waterfowl.org.uk

The Domestic Fowl Trust
www.domesticfowltrust.co.uk

The Domestic Waterfowl Trust
www.domestic-waterfowl.co.uk

Henkeepers Association
www.henkeepersassociation.co.uk

The Poultry Club
www.poultryclub.org

Rare Poultry Society
www.rarepoultrysociety.co.uk

The Traditional British Fowl Company
www.traditionalbritishfowl.co.uk

Turkey Club UK
www.turkeyclub.co.uk

Keeping Livestock

British Goat Society
www.allgoats.com

The British Pig Association
www.britishpigs.org.uk

National Sheep Association
www.nationalsheep.org.uk

Rare Breeds Survival Trust
www.rbst.org.uk

Beekeeping

The British Beekeepers' Association
www.britishbee.org.uk

Supplies for Smallholdings and Farms

Mole Valley Farmers
www.molevalleyfarmers.com

Cheesemaking Supplies

Moorlands Cheesemakers
www.cheesemaking.co.uk

Advice and Courses

Allotment vegetable growing
www.allotment.org.uk

Garden Organic.
Britain's leading advisory body on organic gardening
www.gardenorganic.org.uk

The Wildlife Trusts.
A charity devoted to wildlife and habitat conservation
www.wildlifetrusts.org

Worldwide Opportunities on Organic Farms (WWOOF)
Network of organic farmers, gardeners and smallholders who provide food and accommodation in exchange for unpaid work
www.wwoof.org.uk

River Cottage HQ
Classes include butchery, baking and beekeeping
www.rivercottage.net

Conversion Tables

The recipes and DIY projects included in this book are based on the US measurement system. You will be able to convert these to metric and other household measuring units commonly used in the UK by making the calculations at right.

For cup quantities of dried goods, it may be helpful to use a household cup that is equivalent in volume to 16 tablespoons.

To convert area	Multiply by
Square inches to square centimetres	6.45
Square feet to square metres	0.093
Square yards to square metres	0.836
Acres to hectares	0.4
Square miles to square kilometres	2.6

To convert liquid volume	Multiply by
US tablespoon to UK tablespoon	1.040
US teaspoon to UK teaspoon	1.387
Cups to litres	0.236
Pints to litres	0.473
Quarts to litres	0.946
Gallons to litres	3.785
Bushels to litres	35.23

To convert dry weights	Multiply by
US tablespoon to UK tablespoon	1.040
US teaspoon to UK teaspoon	1.387
Cups to UK tablespoons	16.00
Ounces to grams	28.34
Pounds to kilograms	0.453

To convert length	Multiply by
Miles to kilometres	1.6
Miles to metres	1609.3
Yards to metres	0.9
Inches to centimetres	2.54
Inches to millimetres	25.4
Feet to centimetres	30.5

Credits

Illustrators

© **Michael Austin:** 3, 6–7, and decorative art

Sarah Brill: 151, 152 top, 153, 157, 158 top right, 162 right, 163 top left, 167 left, 168 top, 206–210

Bethany Caskey: 231, 232 left, 235

Beverly Duncan: 20, 24, 26, 27, 135 bottom right, 137, 143–147, 161 top, 168 bottom center, 171

Judy Eliason: 38, 40, 41, 42 left: top two, 45 left and right, 46, 67 top, 139

Brigita Fuhrmann: 36 middle and bottom, 70, 152 bottom, 154, 159 center, 162 left: top, middle, and bottom, 163 right, 164 right: top and bottom, 166 left, 168 bottom right, 237–239

Carol Jessop: 259, 264 bottom, 266, 269, 272, 274

Charles Joslin: 135 bottom left, 158 left and center, 159 left and right, 161 bottom three, 163 bottom left and center, 164 left and center, 165, 166 center and right, 167 center and right, 168 bottom left

Alison Kolesar: 19, 23, 33–35, 42 bottom three, 44, 51, 52, 54, 65, 69 bottom, 73, 79, 81 right: top, middle, bottom, 82, 95, 150, 160, 185, 214, 308, 315, 316, 318, 320–322, 326, 329, 334

Susan Berry Langsten: 39

Randy Mosher: 212

Douglas Paisley: 25, 62 left, 66 left, 68, 97–99, 333

Anne Poole: 47, 48 top: left and center; bottom, 49, 63, 67 bottom

Mary Rich: 198, 200, 202, 211, 216

Louise Riotte: 324 mushrooms, 332

© **Elayne Sears:** 13–15, 22, 28, 29, 36 top, 43, 45 center, 48 top right, 57–61, 64, 69 top, 71, 75, 76, 77, 81 left: top and bottom, 88, 89 left, 92, 93, 101–105, 110–112, 115, 116, 125, 126, 129, 130, 132, 135 top, 184, 188–191, 194, 203, 204, 225, 226, 228, 232 right, 236, 241, 244, 245, 248, 249, 251, 252, 260, 262, 263, 264 top, 273, 277, 280, 285, 288, 289, 291, 294, 296–298, 301–303, 309–311, 313

Authors

Sections of the text in this book have been excerpted from *500 Treasured Country Recipes*, by Martha Storey & Friends, *Storey's Basic Country Skills*, by John and Martha Storey, and the following books previously published by Storey Publishing:

Chapter 1
The Big Book of Preserving the Harvest, by Carol W. Costenbader
The Gardener's A–Z Guide to Growing Organic Food, by Tanya L.K. Denckla
Incredible Vegetables from Self-Watering Containers, by Edward C. Smith
Making & Using Dried Foods, by Phyllis Hobson
The Vegetable Gardener's Bible, by Edward C. Smith
The Veggie Gardener's Answer Book, by Barbara Ellis

Chapter 2
The Big Book of Preserving the Harvest, by Carol W. Costenbader
The Busy Person's Guide to Preserving Food, by Janet Chadwick
From Vines to Wines, by Jeff Cox
Fruits and Berries for the Home Garden, by Lewis Hill
Landscaping with Fruit, by Lee Reich
Making & Using Dried Foods, by Phyllis Hobson

Chapter 3
Don't Throw It, Grow It!, by Deborah Peterson and Millicent Selsam
Herbal Remedy Gardens, by Dorie Byers
Herbal Tea Gardens, by Marietta Marshall Marcin
Herbal Vinegar, by Maggie Oster

Chapter 4
Homebrew Favorites, by Karl F. Lutzen and Mark Stevens
The Homebrewer's Garden, by Joe Fisher and Dennis Fisher
The Vegetable Gardener's Bible, by Edward C. Smith

Chapter 5
A Guide to Canning, Freezing, Curing & Smoking Meat, Fish & Game, by Wilbur F. Eastman Jr.
Barnyard in Your Backyard, by Gail Damerow
Basic Butchering of Meat and Game, by John J. Mettler Jr. DVM
Storey's Guide to Raising Chickens, by Gail Damerow
Storey's Guide to Raising Turkeys, by Leonard S. Mercia
Storey's Illustrated Guide to Poultry Breeds, by Carol Ekarius

Chapter 6
A Guide to Canning, Freezing, Curing & Smoking Meat, Fish & Game, by Wilbur F. Eastman Jr.
Barnyard in Your Backyard, by Gail Damerow
Basic Butchering of Meat and Game, by John J. Mettler Jr. DVM
Home Cheese Making, by Ricki Carroll
Storey's Guide to Raising Dairy Goats, by Jerry Belanger
Storey's Guide to Raising Pigs, by Kelly Klober

Chapter 7
Just In Case, by Kathy Harrison

Index

Page references in *italics* indicate illustrations; page references in **bold** indicate charts.

A

A-frame trellis, 49, *49*
acid blend, 129
acreage plans, 13–15, *13–15*
African goose, 250–51, *251*
African Pygmy goat, 263, *263*
agrimony, *135*, **173**
ale recipes
    brown ale, 219
    dandelion bitter, 218
    fresh hop ale, 217
    pale horse pale ale, 219
almonds, 140
Alpine goat, 259, *260*
altitude adjustment for bottling, 83
Ameraucana chicken, 232
Ancona chicken, 224, *224*
Angora goat, 259
Angus cattle, 280, *281,* 284
anise, 13, **155, 173, 177**
anise hyssop, 172
apple tree, **117**. *See also* fruit trees
apples
    bottling apple purée, 114
    drying, **127**
    freezing, 95
    juicing, 136–37, *137*
    root cellar storage, 56
    storage of common varieties, **114**
apple purée, 79, 114
apricot tree, **117**. *See also* fruit trees
apricots

drying, **127**
    vinegar recipe, 139
Araucana chicken, 232
artichokes, 32
    Jerusalem, *65,* 65–66, 73
asparagus, 32, 54
    harvesting, *54,* 55
    planting, 37, **37,** 54, *54*
Australorp chicken, 224, *224*
aubergines, **21,** 29, 32–33
    combining with courgette, 57
    planting, 37, **37,** 65, *65*
    saving seeds, **53**
autumn olive, **117,** 325
Ayrshire cattle, 278, *279*

B

bachelor's button, 30
Bacillus thuringiensis (Bt), 66
bananas, drying, **127**
bantam chickens, 227
barley, 180, **193**
    growing for beer, *206,* 206–7
    malting, 209–211
    planting, **181**
basil, 26–27, 29, **155,** 157, *157*
    cooking with, **177**
    flower stalks, in fritters, 335
    pesto recipe, 157
    tea, 172, **173**
    vinegar, 169
bay leaves, **155,** 158, *158,* **173, 177**
beans, 20, **21,** 31–32
    bush, 19, *19,* 26, 29, 32
    crop rotation, **24**
    description and types, 55

dry, growing for storage, 55
    green, 18, 37, *37,* 55
    harvesting, 55–56
    inoculating, 55
    limas, 20, **37,** 55–56
    pickled, 60, 64
    saving for seed, **53,** 56
    soybeans, **53,** 56
    sprouting, 193–94, *194*
    succession plantings, 26, *26*
    threshing, 56
    trellises for growing, 47–48, *47–48*
bee balm, 172, **173**
beef
    cuts, 285
    freezing, 292–93, *293*
    jerky recipe, 304
    parts of a beef animal, 280, *280*
beef steer. *See also* cattle
    acreage needs, 15
    meat protein comparison, **291**
Beefmaster cattle, 284
beehives, 326–27, *327*
    acreage needs, 13–14
beekeeping, 326–29
    drone, worker, queen, *326*
    equipment, 327, *327*
    getting stung, 328
    harvesting the honey, 329
    installing bees in the hive, 326–27
    maintaining the hive, 328–29
    what you need, 326
beer, making, 209–19
    basic homebrew recipe, 211–15

coltsfoot, *135,* **174**
Columbia sheep, 271–72
compost, 17–18, 23, 39, 61
coneflower. *See* echinacea
container gardening, 17, 28–29
    self-watering container, 11,
      17, 28, *28,* 29
Continental (European) cattle
    breeds, 281–83, *282*
cooking with grains, 192–205
    bread, 197–202
    cornmeal, 195
    pasta, 202–5
    polenta, 196
cool season crops, 31
coriander, **174, 177**
corn, 20, **21,** 32, *62,* 180
    combining with limas, 57
    corn bread recipe, 195
    cornmeal, **193,** 195
    drying and storing, 184–85
    harvesting, 183–84
    nutritional values, **193**
    planting, 37, **37,** 62–63,
      181, 182–83
    polenta recipes, 196
    pollinating, 63
    popcorn, 32, **53,** 183
    saving seeds, **53**
    tasseling, 63
corn salad, 31
corn sugar, 211, 216
cornelian dogwood tree, 325
cornflower. *See* bachelor's
    button
Cornish chicken, 224, *224*
Corriedale sheep, 272, *273*
cornmeal pancakes recipe, 195
costmary, 159, *159*
country chicken sausages recipe,
    300
courgette, 18, **21,** 32
    combining with aubergine,
      57
    on a small plot, 19, *19*
cow, 257, 277. *See also* cattle
crab apple tree, **117**

cream cheese, 306
crop rotation, 20, 22
    successful practices, **24**
    sun-blocker rotation, 20, *20*
Crossbreed swine, 287–88, *288*
cucumbers, 18, 20, **21,** 26,
    32–33, 44
    cages and trellises, 48–49,
      49, 63
    combining with onions, 57
    crop rotation, **24**
    making pickles, 64
    on a small plot, 19, *19*
    planting, 37, **37,** 63, *63,* 65
    plastic cloches for, 34
    saving seeds, **53**
culture, 305
cumin, **155**
curd(s), 305–11
    hanging curds to drain the
      whey, *308*
currant shrub or hedge, *116,*
    118

D

dairy breeds
    cattle, 278, *279*
    goats, 259–62
dandelions, *332*
    bitter ale recipe, 218
    coffee, 334
    digger, *334*
    flowers, 333
    growing for tea, **174**
    harvesting, 332–34
    leaves, 332–33
    roots, 333–34
    wine, 129, 135, 334–35
Darwin, Charles, 222
daylilies, 332, 335
decoction, herbal, 171–72
dehydrator, 79, 128, 153–54,
    184, 333
    hours needed to dry fruits,
      127
Delaware chicken, 226

Dexter cattle, 280
dianthus, 30
dill, 26, **155,** 159, *159,* **174, 177**
Dominique chicken, *226,* 227
Dorset sheep, 272, *273*
double-dig your garden, how to,
    39, *39*
drying
    fruits, **127,** 127–28, *128*
    vegetables, 79, *79*
ducks
    about, 246
    average mature weight, **250**
    breeds for eggs, 248, *248*
    breeds for meat, 248–50,
      249–50
    butchering, 253–54
    egg profile, **249**
    feathers, using, 253
    feed conversion, 252
    freezing the meat, 292–93,
      293
    raising for meat, 252–53
    roasting the meat, 255
    storing the meat, 254–55
Duroc swine, 287–88, *288*
dwarf fruit trees, 108

E

echinacea, 152, 159–60, *160*
    growing for tea, **174**
    tincture, 160
edible flowers, 30, 158
edible landscaping, 115–26
egg production, 227–34
    collecting and storing eggs,
      230
    determining freshness,
      231–32
    ducks, **249**
    estimating harvest, 15
    gauging egg quality, *231*
    geese, **251**
    good laying hens,
      characteristics, *228,*
      228–29

lazy layers, 228–29
nutritional value, 230
preserving and storing eggs,
  233
replacing pullets, *229*
shell colour, 232
eggs, cooking with fresh
  beating egg whites, 234
  hard-boiled eggs, 232, 234
  how many eggs to use, **234**
Egyptian goose, 250
elderberries, 332
Embden goose, 251, *252*
endive, **21**, 31, 69
Epsom salts, 72
erosion, reducing, 23

F

feathers, duck and goose, 253
feeder pigs, 286–87
feijoa, 116, 125
fence trellis, 48, *48*
fennel, 31, **155**, 161, *161,* **174,**
  177
fermentation, 60, 64
fertilizer and fertilizing, 22, 28
  10-10-10, 54–55
  5-10-10, 63, 65, 67, 69,
    71, 77, 78
  blueberries, 98
  grapes, 100
  seedlings, 41
feverfew, 161, *161,* **174**
fig tree, 126
figs
  drying, **127**
  freezing, 95
filberts, 140–41, 145
fish emulsion, 75, 78
fish, freezing, 292–93, **293**
fleece, 33–34
Florida White rabbit, 291, *291*
flour mill, selecting a, 191, *191*
flower fritters, 335
fluorescent lights for seedlings,
  41, *41*

foam insulation in a cold frame,
  36
foraging, 325, 330–35
  harvesting, 331–32
  permission, 325, 330
  rose hips, 332–33
  tools, 331
  wild food favourites, 332
freezing
  corn, 185, *185*
  eggs, **233**
  fruit, 56–57, 95, *95*
  herbs, 156
  meat, 292–93, **293**
  sausages, **293**, 298
  vegetables, 56–57, 78–79
frost
  planting dates in relation
    to, 37
  protection, 33–37, 90
  resistant plants, 50
fruit trees, 107–114
  diameters of full-grown
    trees, **108**
  drying fruit, **127**, 127–28,
    128
  dwarf fruit trees, 108
  estimating harvest, 15
  harvesting the fruit, 112–13
  planning an orchard, 107–8
  planting in three simple
    steps, 110, *110*
  pollination requirements,
    107, 109, 113
  pruning, 111–12, *111–12*
  recommended varieties,
    108–9
  subtropical fruits, 125–26
  thinning out early fruit, 114
fruit vinegar, 139
fruiting glossary, 86
fruits and nuts
  acreage plans, 13–15
  back garden history, 85

G

Galloway cattle, 280
garden fork, 39
garden journal, 18
garden planning, 10–15, 20–21.
  See also vegetable garden
    chart, **21**
  designing on a grid, 20
  saving your plan, 57
  seasonal plans, 26–27,
    26–27
garlic, 11, 18, 20, 27, 32, **155,**
  161, *161*
  cold and flu garden, 152
  cooking with, **177**
  growing for tea, **174**
  herbal broth for colds, 156
  in soft cheese, 306–7
  plaiting, 162, *162*
geese
  average mature weight, **251**
  breeds, 250–52, *251–52*
  butchering, 253–54
  egg production, **251**
  feathers, using, 253
  feed conversion rate, 252
  freezing the meat, 292–93,
    293
  getting along with, 246–47
  raising for meat, 252–53
  roasting the meat, 255
  storing the meat, 254–55
Gelbvieh cattle, 282, *282*
geraniums, scented, 166, *166,*
  172
germinating seeds
  indoors, 41
  outdoors, 43–44
ginger
  growing for tea, **174**
  how to grow, 151, *151*
goat's cheese, making, 307–8
goat's milk, 264–70
  contents of, 264
  goat's vs. cow's milk, 270

Further Reading
from Storey Publishing
and Timber Press

A Short History of the Honey Bee, by Ilona and E. Readicker-Henderson

Follow the journey from flower to hive to honey with this engaging text
and gorgeous photography.
164 pages. Hardback. Timber Press. ISBN 978-0-88192-942-3

Growing Citrus, by Martin Page

Everything the gardener needs to know to successfully grow citrus trees in temperate climates.
192 pages. Hardback. Timber Press. ISBN 978-1-88192-906-5.

Home Cheese Making, by Ricki Carroll

From equipment to starter cultures this has everything you need to know
to make small batches of homemade cheeses.
288 pages. Paperback. Storey Publishing. ISBN 978-1-58017-464-0.

Made from Scratch, by Jenna Woginrich

A memoir written by a part-time smallholder, who shares the honest satisfaction
of learning forgotten skills and always finds humour along the way.
192 pages. Hardback. Storey Publishing. ISBN 978-1-60342-086-0.

**_The Complete Chilli Pepper Book,_ by David DeWitt
and Paul W. Bosland**

All the information that anyone with an interest in chilli peppers could ever hope to find.
336 pages. Hardback. Timber Press. ISBN 978-0-88192-920-1.

These and other Storey and Timber Press books are available
from all good bookshops or by calling (01476) 541080.
Timber Press books are also available from _www.timberpress.co.uk._